A *TimeTraveller's* Guide

Exploring
the Fur Trade Routes
of North America

DISCOVER THE HIGHWAYS THAT OPENED A CONTINENT

Barbara Huck et al.

Heartland
Winnipeg, Canada

Printed in Manitoba, Canada

National Library of Canadian Cataloguing in Publication Data

Huck, Barbara
Exploring the Fur Trade Routes of North America

ISBN 1-896150-04-7

1. Fur trade—Canada—History.
2. Fur trade—Snowbelt States—History.
3. Waterways—Canada—Guidebooks.
4. Waterways—Snowbelt States—Guidebooks.
5. Canada—Guidebooks.
6. Snowbelt States—Guidebooks.

I. Title.
HD9944.N672 H83 2002   971   C2002-910394-0

Heartland Associates Inc.
PO Box 103, RPO Corydon
Winnipeg, Manitoba, Canada R3M 3S7
hrtland@mts.net
hrtlandbooks.com

5 4 3 2

Pukaskwa National Park, Ontario
MIKE GRANDMAISON

Credits

Contributing authors

Sally Gibson, Site Manager, Fort St. Joseph National Historic Site,
Sault Ste. Marie, ON

Doug Whiteway, Associate Editor, the *Beaver*: Canada's History Magazine,
Winnipeg, MB

Peter St. John, the Earl of Orkney, Professor of Political Studies,
Winnipeg, MB

Michael Payne, Head, Research and Publications, Government of Alberta,
Edmonton, AB

Ken McGoogan, Author and Journalist,
Calgary, AB

Ken Favrholdt, Curator and Manager, Secwepemc Museum
Kamloops, B.C.

Jerry Kautz, Kautz Photographer and Graphic Designer,
Nanton, AB

Doug Taylor, Exhibit Technician and Writer,
Livelong area, SK

Robin and Arlene Karpan, Writers and Photographers,
Saskatoon, SK

John Woodworth, C. M., Executive Secretary,
Alexander Mackenzie Voyageur Route Association,
Kelowna, BC

Robert Pruden, Great great great grandson of John Peter Pruden,
Winnipeg, MB

Editorial assistance

Scott Stephen, Sally Gibson, Doug Whiteway, Gail and Michael Evans-Hatch

Research assistance

Jane Huck, Jerry and Violet Kautz, Mary Anne Nylen, Paul Vermette and Dennis Fast

Design and maps
Dawn Huck

Prepress
Image Color 2000, Winnipeg, MB

Printing
Printcrafters, Winnipeg, MB

Cover photographs
Dennis Fast

Back cover photograph
Black beaver pelt, by Scott Robertson
Courtesy Robertson's Trading Post

Acknowledgements

North America is vast and diverse and the fur trade covered much of it. Gathering material for each of the two editions of this book was greatly aided by experts and enthusiasts across the continent. We are grateful to all of them.

The fur trade crossed many boundaries as it moved from east to west and we will do the same here. In Quebec, Stan Georges, provincial biologist, and Marie-Michäle Parent, with the Parcs des Grands-Jardins et de la Jacques-Cartier, assisted with information and images; Joseph Agnew, executive director of the Canadian Recreational Rivers Association in Ottawa, helped with up-to-date information on Canada's heritage rivers and Jean Matheson at the National Archives in Ottawa sped through the reshooting of many of the archives' rarely used images. The staff and volunteers at the Canadian Canoe Museum in Peterborough, Ontario, reviewed information, while Molly Perry, director of the Marquette Mission Park and the Museum of Ojibwa Culture in St. Ignace, Michigan, shared both information and artwork.

Frances Robb, Parks Canada historian, shared some of her recent research on Fort St. Joseph; Carol Maass and Mary Graves with Minnesota's Voyageurs National Park spent time reviewing and correcting our site information; Pam Hawley, curator of the museum in Fort Frances, Ontario, provided current information and Ed Oerichbauer, director of the Koochiching Museum, did the same for International Falls, Minnesota, across the Rainy River.

David and Rosemary Malaher of Winnipeg provided maps and information about past and present conditions of Lake of the Woods, as well as a fascinating description of David Thompson's surveys. Roger Turrenne of Winnipeg and Alan Smith of Kenora allowed us to use their photographs. Peter Walker, with Manitoba Culture, Heritage & Tourism, provided us with interpretive drawings of the fur trade in Manitoba; Gaileen Irwin, site supervisor at Rocky Mountain House, Alberta proofed copy and assisted with information, while the Provincial Museum of Alberta allowed us to use their images. Gail DeBuse Potter, director of the Museum of the Fur Trade in Chadron, Nebraska, provided information and contacts and the people at both Fort Union National Historic Site in North Dakota and Fort Nisqually in Washington provided images. Alex and Scott Robertson showed us what the life of modern fur traders is like and Wilf and Wanda Tolboom, who spent 50 years in the fur trade, shared their experiences of the past.

In England, Rachel Allard, head teacher at Grey Coat Hospital in London provided information on the school and its students and in Orkney, Bryce Wilson, Jim Troup, Helen Manson and George Esson all assisted with information, proofing and images.

For the second edition, we were assisted by a number of knowledgeable historians across North America, including some who had found errors in our first edition and others who felt we had missed sites of crucial importance. We are grateful to Laird Rankin, publisher of *The Beaver* and author of a book on the HBC replica of the *Nonsuch*, for additional information on the routes the little ship took in 1970, and to Ken Favrholdt, curator of the Secwepemc Museum in Kamloops, B.C., who set us straight over the routes of the Brigade Trails. In the U.S., we had generous assistance with information and/or images from Valerie Naylor and Dean Knudsen at Scotts Bluff National Monument in Nebraska; Mildred Pape at the Museum of the Mountain Man in Pinedale, Wyoming; the staff at the Idaho State Historical Society in Boise, Susan Seyl at the Oregon Historical Society in Portland, and Earline Wasser and Gary Honald at The Dalles Mural Society on the Columbia River. Special thanks to consulting historians Gail and Michael Evans-Hatch of Astoria, Oregon for their meticulous review of both the Lewis and Clark and Oregon Trail sections. The input of all has significantly enhanced this new edition.

Talbot Lake, Jasper National Park, near the site of Jasper House JERRY KAUTZ

Exploring the Fur Trade Routes

This is not so much a guidebook as a window on the past. In pursuit of furs, Europeans penetrated the rivers, the plains and the mountains of North America. Between 1530 and 1860, moving ever westward along some of the world's most spectacular waterways, they changed a continent, its people and its wildlife forever.

In pursuit of this fascinating history, my husband Peter St. John and I followed in their wake, though by car not canoe. Over more than a decade, we discovered that in hundreds of places and in many ways, the fur trade is with us still. A growing interest in the period has resulted in dozens of superb fur trade reconstructions in the past two decades, and thanks to recent research, our view of this long and complicated past has undergone a much-needed refurbishing as well. Historians are increasingly clear-eyed about the fur trade, with all its repercussions, and their work is allowing us to understand, perhaps for the first time, what really happened in North America during the past 500 years.

Fort Nisqually Historic Site, Washington COURTESY OF FORT NISQUAL

Exploring the Fur Trade Routes of North America follows that story, moving from east to west along the main trade routes. But it's not necessary to traverse the continent by canoe (as Alexander Mackenzie did) to find this guide useful. Because this is a route-oriented, site-specific driving guide, it can be used almost anywhere, to visit a single site or spend a month exploring. Time travellers can create their own itineraries, combining sites from several routes.

Though this is not a canoeing guide, several sections have been written by avid canoeists and others beckon even novice paddlers. Hikers too will find sections to make their feet itch. From the 8½-mile Grand Portage on Lake Superior's northwestern shore to the granddaddy of fur trade trails – the 350-kilometre Alexander Mackenzie Heritage Trail in west-central British Columbia, there is something here for everyone. Many sites also have walking trails for those with less lofty pedestrian dreams.

We found ourselves drawn into this fascinating past, and discovered we are not alone. Dozens of people, from Quebec to California, even from Britain, wrote to us after the first edition was published, many with wonderful stories or observations. Their input is an indication of the tremendous interest in our shared North American history and, on the cusp of the bicentennial of the journey of Lewis and Clark, we believe that interest is about to grow. More important, perhaps, in both Canada and the United States, we are taking steps to understand better what the fur trade meant to the people who were crucial to its operation, and who paid the ultimate price for its success – the original populations of North America.

Barbara Huck
April 2002

Note: Throughout the book, metric measurements are used for sites in Canada and imperial measurements for those in the United States. A hybrid Canadian spelling is used throughout.

Table of Contents

Bandolier National Monument, New Mexico   PETER ST. JOHN

The North Americans

From the snowy forests of the Canadian Shield and the grasslands of the western plains to the misty shores of the Pacific, North Americans were perfectly at home in the continent's endlessly diverse environments. Europeans adopted a number of North American technologies, such as snowshoes, below, toboggans, birchbark canoes and pemmican, but largely misunderstood the continent's cultures.

Today, on the cusp of a new millennium, North Americans have more tools than ever before for travelling though time. Thanks to new technologies and new perspectives, we are well equipped to imagine life five thousand or five million years ago. We can contemplate doing blood tests on the body of an ancient trader found high on an Alpine pass or cloning a woolly mammoth in China. Yet for the most part, an appreciation of life here just 500 years ago eludes us.

Imagine then, a land where people lived in towns and large villages, tilled the fertile soil and grew a remarkable array of crops – corn, squash, melons, beans and tobacco. Not far away, the lakes and rivers were full of fish and the forests abounded with game. The women of this land did much of the fishing and farming; the men, for the most part, had other interests. While their wives and sisters and mothers planted and tilled and cared for the children, the men travelled far from home, trading north and south, hunting and, as often as not, fighting. Theirs was a powerful nation, with many allies and intentions of expanding across a great river at the edge of their land.

Across the great river were low mountains and thick forests, bisected by rushing rivers. Here, the people were mainly hunters. Small, mobile groups spent the winters in the forests and gathered in the summers in large camps along the shores of one of the many lakes or rivers, fishing and gathering the bountiful fruits and nuts that grew everywhere.

And who were these people? They might have been Europeans of the Middle Ages, the people of the Rhine Valley perhaps, eyeing the territory across the water, or the English under Richard I, with dreams of an empire based on the cross and the sword.

They might have been, but they weren't, for this was another world. The farmers were Iroquoian – the Seneca, Cayuga, Onondaga, Oneida and Mohawk – who by 1500 occupied a large territory south of the St. Lawrence River and would soon unite to become the Five Nations Iroquois. To the north were the Innu and their Algonquian-speaking allies, from the Mi'kmaq of the Atlantic shores to the Anishinabe of the upper Great Lakes.

These cultures differed from one another as much as Scots differ from Spaniards today, or Finns from French. Some North American societies were settled and agrarian, others were seasonally mobile; some turned to the sea for their livelihood, others lived off the bounty of the inland plains.

As in Europe today, the societies of 15th and 16th century North America spoke dozens of different languages. And like their modern counterparts,

C.W. JEFFREYS / NATIONAL ARCHIVES OF CANADA / C-069758

ALFRED J. MILLER / NATIONAL ARCHIVES OF CANADA / C-408

most of these languages could be traced to a handful of common language groups.

Contrary to popular belief, at the time of contact there were people everywhere in the western hemisphere. Parts of North and Central America were among the most densely populated places on Earth. Some anthropologists have estimated the total population of the continent 500 years ago, including Mexico and Central America, at between 112 and 140 million. Mexico, the spectacular Aztec capital, was one of the three largest cities in the world when the Spaniards first laid eyes on it.

Much of Canada and the United States was considerably less populated than that – estimates put the total population of both at between nine and 12 million – but North America was not,

as some have imagined it, *terra nullius*, a land without a people. And many societies, such as the Iroquoians, were healthier, more prosperous and less class-bound than their European counterparts of the same period.

Just as the citizens of today's Western world share ideas and technologies – a global view and the microchip – the cultures of 15th-century North America had in common many fundamental values, despite differences in lifestyle. But the Americas were literally a world apart and North American values and beliefs were very different – in some ways almost directly contrary – to the perspectives of the strangers who began to arrive on their shores in the early 1500s, the beginning of the contact period.

THOMAS WESLEY MCLEAN / NATIONAL ARCHIVES OF CANADA / C-069781

Exploring the Fur Trade Routes of North America

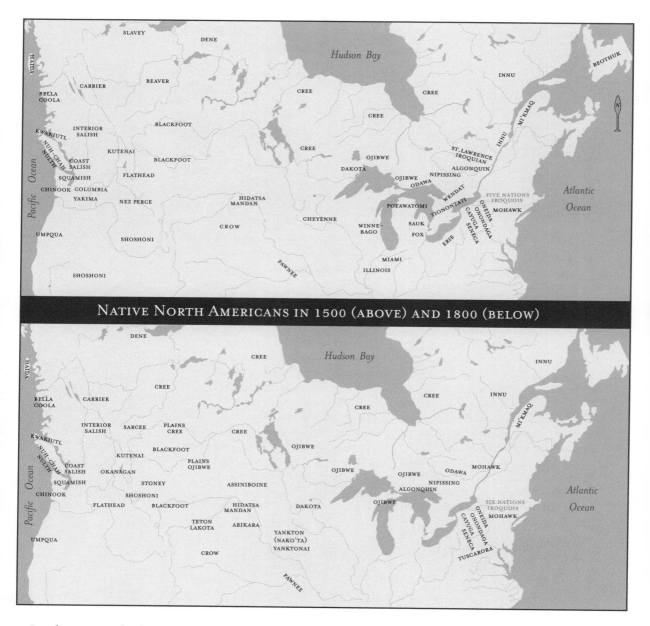

NATIVE NORTH AMERICANS IN 1500 (ABOVE) AND 1800 (BELOW)

Involvement in the fur trade and displacement from settlers vastly changed the map of North America for the continent's many cultures between 1550 and 1850. Some peoples, such as the Beotuk of Newfoundland, disappeared completely, while others, including the Dakota, were pushed from their homelands far to the west. (Included on these maps are groups mentioned in the text.)

Indeed, it's hard to imagine two more conflicting world views. Whether farmers or hunters, the vast majority of the people of what are now Canada and the United States lived communally, in groups of various sizes. The territories they inhabited were not owned, as we recognize land ownership, but rather commonly acknowledged to be theirs to use. They governed by consensus, valued generosity and self-reliance, and loathed acquisitiveness and coercion. Stinginess and miserly behavior were strongly condemned. Almost everywhere it was considered immoral to allow anyone to go hungry if food was available.

Though decision-making was by consensus, most North American cultures put great stock in individual independence and lauded effort on behalf of the community. Status was achieved not by owning property but by giving it away. Religion permeated every aspect of their lives and was based on respect for the Earth and all living things.

Among some groups, conflict was common and wars were generally fought to settle blood feuds. Murders were avenged with the death of the suspected killer or his family, and the violence often escalated.

The newcomers from Europe had a very different world view. Theirs was a class society, governed in an authoritarian way by men who viewed land and its resources as objects to be exploited. They greatly admired the accumulation of personal wealth and assigned positions of power to those who were particularly successful at amassing goods and money. Generosity was viewed as philanthropy, an act of charity not necessity.

Their primary allegiance was to the concept of nation-state and national identity was strongly tied to language, religion and race. They believed implicity in European superiority and felt compelled to try to persuade other cultures to embrace their world view. Yet with few exceptions, Europeans proved woefully unprepared for survival in North America. The first 250 years of European contact were fraught with disorientation, disaster and privation. Native North Americans provided guiding services, information, interpretation, clothing, medicine and food, as well as wives and extended families. All this was in addition to the furs that were the primary objects of early French and later British interest. And time after time they rescued the newcomers from starvation. Yet the Europeans never did comprehend that this spontaneous, culturally entrenched generosity required reciprocity. Instead, native North Americans in need were termed beggars.

This climate of misunderstanding colored the fur trade and the progress of Europeans across the continent. From the 16th-century St. Lawrence Valley to the Pacific coast 300 years later, the pattern was repeated again and again. Recognizing it is fundamental to appreciating the profound changes that took place in North America between 1550 and 1860, and perhaps just as important in understanding today's attempts to rectify some of the mistakes of the past.

DENNIS FAST

This beautifully quilled birchbark basket from the collection of the Kenora Museum in Northwestern Ontario illustrates – albeit with a modern theme – the artistry demonstrated in thousands of different ways across North America.

BARK INTO BOATS: A TRIUMPH OF INGENUITY

The birchbark canoe is among humankind's cleverest inventions and, like many great ideas, it was sparked by a confluence of necessity and convenience. North America's vast expanse of Precambrian Shield is a place of rock and trees and rivers. Travel is nearly impossible except along the many waterways. However the shield, particularly in its eastern half, is (or was, before Europeans arrived) also prime habitat for giant white birch, white cedar and spruce trees.

Birchbark canoes cleverly combined these available materials – birchbark for the skin of the craft, cedar for its ribs and sheathing, and spruce roots and gum for the sturdy lashing and caulking that united the component parts – to create a light, lissome, remarkably strong boat that could be produced, paddled and portaged by one person. No one really knows when the first birchbark canoe was produced or where, though archaeological excavations on Morrison Island in the Ottawa River (where large birch, cedar and spruce were all readily available) revealed copper awls believed to be 5,000 years old. While awls of this type are essential to the construction of birchbark canoes, they are also used for other purposes, so their discovery in such an ancient context does not prove that birchbark canoes were being made this early, it simply makes it a possibility. Morrison Island also revealed 5,000-year-old beaver teeth that had been ground to create a curved knife, similar to the "crooked knives" of slate or steel later used to carve canoe ribs.

Dugout canoes undoubtedly predate those of birchbark and while the latter may have evolved independently in North America, they may also have come from Asia. The Ainu, aboriginal people who once inhabited present-day Japan, built a crude birchbark canoe, and ancient Siberians made sturgeon-nosed canoes similar to those used by British Columbia's Kutenai.

Champlain was the first European to realize the potential of birchbark canoes after encountering Algonquin traders near present-day Quebec City in 1603. He was impressed by the speed and capacity of Algonquin canoes, which ranged in length from tiny personal craft of 2.5 metres to transport canoes five metres long. Within a decade, the Algonquin and Ojibwe were making canoes to order for the fur trade (see Canoes of the Montreal Trade on page 67).

Though birchbark canoes, all of slightly different design, were made by many North American nations, the fur trade spread their use far beyond the ideal environment for constructing them. Fur brigades therefore often carried large rolls of birchbark and *watap* or spruce root with them for mending or producing canoes.

The art of birchbark canoe building came close to dying during the 20th century, but today is enjoying a revival of sorts. The Canadian Canoe Museum in Peterborough not only has examples of dozens of types of canoes, but offers a range of programs about their history and construction, alongside excellent installations.

The Algonquin canoe, above, was the design with which the French were most familiar, but birchbark canoes came in many shapes and sizes across the continent, including the sturgeon-nosed Kutenai model, at the bottom of the page.

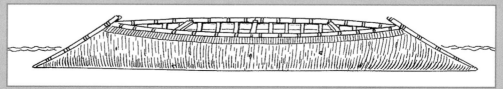

The Europeans

The French

The French were relative late-comers to northern North America. Greenlanders had attempted to settle on the north shore of what is now Newfoundland almost 1,000 years

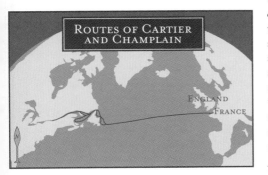

ago and three brothers from the Portugese Azores – Gaspar, Miquel and Vasqueanes Corte-Real – are believed to have made voyages to Labrador and Newfoundland sometime in the late 1490s.

In 1497, Genoese-born John Cabot sailed from the English port of Bristol to Newfoundland. Cabot's reports of codfish so thick they could be taken by lowering baskets from the side of a ship soon had English, Spanish and Portuguese fishermen flocking to the Grand Banks off Newfoundland's south coast.

The French were not far behind. Initially, most of their enormous catches were salted on board, but soon some fishermen – many from Normandy and Brittany on the north coast of France – were setting up shore stations to make

"dry fish". Lightly salted and sun cured, dried cod proved easy to keep, simple to ship and soon became Canada's first major export to the world.

These coastal fishing stations undoubtedly provided the first extended contact with North Americans, and trade between the local people and the strangers from afar must have occurred soon after. It's easy to imagine: an approach by a Beothuk or Mi'kmaq seeking one of the knives the fishermen were using to clean and filet the cod, an offer of fox or beaver pelts in return, and the deal was done. But it's clear from the writings of Breton sea captain Jacques Cartier, who believed that the Iroquois he met along the shore of the Gaspé Peninsula in 1534 "had not anything above the value of five sous, their canoes and fishing nets excepted", that early Europeans had little understanding of the potential worth of the furs they thus obtained.

It's more likely that France funded successive voyages to America for other reasons, including curiosity, a desire to know what was beyond the mouth of the great river and a very real hope that the river might lead to the Pacific and China; acquisitiveness, a belief that the region might be rich in gold, silver or other precious metals, and religious zealotry. Europeans had a remarkable

Salt cod, below, still favored by several southern European countries today, was Canada's first major export to the world. Beginning in the first decades of the 16th century, cod drew fishermen west across the Atlantic to the once overwhelmingly bountiful Grand Banks of Newfoundland. But some, including Jacques Cartier and Samuel de Champlain, were fishing for things other than cod.

PETER ST. JOHN

THOMAS WESLEY McLEAN / NATIONAL ARCHIVES OF CANADA / C-69709

In the late 15th and early 16th centuries, ornate ships such as these were a common sight off the coast of Cape Breton and in the mouth of the St. Lawrence.

intolerance for other religions and a deep conviction that their particular brand of Christianity was the only true faith. Add to this the avid desire of individual Europeans for status and recognition (in French, *la gloire*) and the reasons for returning to North America, despite the hardships that climate and their own ignorance imposed, are clear.

By 1545, the difficult climate and the hatred of the Iroquois (prompted by barbarous treatment of the very people who had more than once saved French lives), convinced the French to end – for a time at least – their first foray into the "new world".

They would be back. When they returned, at the beginning of the 17th century, they were driven by many of the same motives – a search for glory, souls and gold – but the gold was now recognized to lie not in glittering metal but in soft, lustrous fur. By 1600 the trade in fur, particularly beaver fur for felting, by seasonal fishermen was so lucrative that many visited the coastal shores to fish for fur rather than cod and a succession of nobles were petitioning the French crown for the right to participate – or better yet, monopolize – the trade in North America.

Having heard the old tales of the fearsome winters along the St. Lawrence, none of these royal suitors really believed that colonizing what was now being called New France was a reasonable prospect. But the profits to be made in furs justified signing agreements that demanded the establishment of settlements. And over the next 150 years, those two unsuitable partners – fur trade and settlement – would create a pattern of penetration of North America that can still be seen today, in the people who still dominate the region that gave its name to Canada, in French place names as far west as Oregon and in French spoken as far south as the Gulf of Mexico.

Unlike the Anglo-American occupation pattern of what is now the United States, which began with settlements on the Atlantic Coast and moved steadily from east to west in an irregular frontier of cleared land and almost continuous conflict with the original inhabitants, the French penetrated North America – both north and south of the 49th parallel – in a pattern that resembled the branches of a tree. Following the rivers and lakes, their forays inland began with the construction of a major post on a main river leading to the interior and continued with a series of smaller outposts on rivers that stretched far into the centre of the continent. Using Montréal on the St. Lawrence and New Orleans on the Mississippi, the French developed a network of trading posts that extended

16

as far west as the plains of North and South Dakota and as far north as central Saskatchewan.

In the main, the French were not interested in colonization. They recognized early that settlement and the fur business were diametrically opposed. Clear the land for agriculture and the animals disappear along with the forests. The French also realized that North Americans knew how to live and travel in their own lands and, more rapidly than their British counterparts, they adopted the birchbark canoe, the moccasins and snowshoes, that a large proportion of their young men were instead adopting the ways of the people they called the *Huron* and *Montagnais*, or later, the Cree and Ojibwe. For a time, the missionaries tried to keep their charges apart, but this quickly failed, for native North Americans were absolutely crucial to the trade in furs and everywhere the Récollets and later Jesuits established their missions, the traders built a fur post.

Until the Treaty of Paris brought their occupation of North America to an end in 1763, the French dominated the fur trade, penetrating the continent

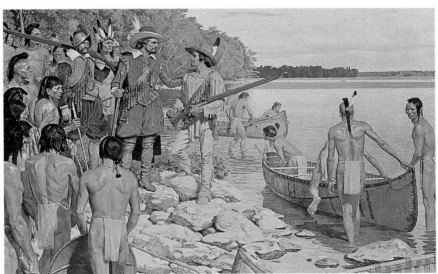

REX WOODS / COURTESY ROGERS COMMUNICATIONS INC.

Samuel de Champlain and Etienne Brûlé, pictured on the shores of Lake Simcoe in September 1615, joined the Wendat of Huronia in a series of ultimately costly attacks on the Five Nations Iroquois.

the tobaggan (from the Mi'kmaq word *tab'agan*) and the travelling rations of dried corn and dried buffalo meat or pemmican that North Americans had been manufacturing for millennia. They were also quick to learn new languages and marry into local tribes.

Initially, this tendency caused concern both in France and Québec. Rather than converting North Americans to what they firmly believed was a superior culture and religion, the French found more deeply than any other European nation. And even after France turned its territories over to England (in the east) and Spain (in the west), the imprint of 150 years of trade and acculturation remained. Francophone Canadians were the lifeblood of both the Montreal and Missouri fur trades and their descendents can be found today from the Atlantic to the Pacific and from New Mexico and California to Canada's Northwest Territories.

The British

Just five years after Christopher Columbus's first voyage, the English began the search for the Northwest Passage, which many were certain would lead to the riches of "Cathaia". In 1497, John Cabot reached the "New Found Land", his son Sebastian may have sailed into Hudson Strait in 1508 and John Rut, sailing from Bristol, ran into heavy sea ice near Greenland in 1527.

These early voyages proved one thing without a shred of doubt – it was cold up there, much colder then than it is today. It was also much colder than it had been centuries before when, it now seems, Nordic Greenlanders or other, even earlier voyagers, had penetrated North America's great inland sea – Hudson Bay. But more on that later. After the attempts of the early 16th century, the English lost interest in explorations for a time. But England was on the verge of a "golden age of culture and enterprise", as Robert McGhee put it in *Canada Rediscovered*. The reign of Elizabeth I [1558-1603] saw an explosion of ideas and the rise of English nationalism. The queen was interested in the arts, the sciences and in building a nation with a truly global reach. To fund these pursuits, she was interested in enterprises that paid well. When, in the 1570s, veteran seadog Martin Frobisher proposed renewing the search for the elusive passage in order to snatch the lucrative Oriental trade from the Portuguese and Spanish, the queen approved the idea, prompting London merchants to finance the venture.

Frobisher sailed in June 1576 with a small fleet of small ships. The smallest of the three sank west of Shetland and the largest turned back off Greenland, leaving only Frobisher's own tiny ship, *Gabriel*, to go on alone into what he originally believed might be the passage he was seeking. It turned out to be Frobisher Bay on Baffin Island's southern tip, but the captain was apparently unaware of this. Encountering Inuit hunters in kayaks (which he thought at first were "Porposes or Ceales"), the English engaged in trade. Then, when a small boat with five crew members left the ship for shore and failed to return, Frobisher responded as other Europeans had, abducting one of the locals, kayak and all, and hightailing home.

This obvious evidence of inhabited northern lands and the possibility that Frobisher had located the passage to the Orient might have been enough to excite the expedition's backers, but these inducements were overshadowed by the possibility of mineral wealth when, by a strange series of circumstances, a rock given to the expedition by the Inuit was appraised to contain gold.

The following year, Queen Elizabeth added £1,000 of her own money to funds for a second expedition, which included a large naval ship

Early English adventurers sailed the unpredictable north Atlantic in surprisingly small ships, including the narrow-sterned pink, below, which took its name from the Dutch pincke.

COURTESY *THE BEAVER*

and 120 men, most of them miners. Again, after an initially congenial encounter with an Inuit party, the English tried to take two additional hostages, which led to skirmishes, Inuit deaths and more kidnappings.

Frobisher hoped to trade his captives for the five Englishmen who had gone missing the previous year, but they were never seen again. In late August, with his ships full of rock, Frobisher sailed home.

Still after gold, he returned in 1578 with an enormous fleet – 15 ships and 400 men, even now the largest Arctic expedition ever mounted. The miners attacked a small island – Kodlunarn or "White Man's" Island, the Inuit afterward called it – at the mouth of Frobisher Bay, excavating two enormous trenches that can be seen in aerial photographs today. But plans of colonizing these northern reaches were thwarted when the ship carrying the building materials sank. On Frobisher's return to London, the real results were in on the "ore" he had mined; it was worthless.

Despite this dismal failure, the quest for the Northwest Passage and the mineral riches of northern North America continued, resulting over the next three centuries in the death of both men and dreams. In fact, only in the 21st century do these twin nemeses of polar adventurers appear to be yielding. The first, the passage, was pieced together by a long series of Arctic travellers, with the last bits of the puzzle determined by an Orcadian who was one of the world's finest Arctic travellers, but who has never received due credit for his work – Dr. John Rae (see page 64).

Rae did much of his investigating on land; the relentless ice claimed many others who tried to pass by water and it was only in 1903 that a Norwegian herring boat made it through the passage intact. Still, the trip was so treacherous that the channel has never been used with anything approaching regularity. That may be changing, however, thanks to sophisticated marine technology and global warming. The latter has caused such rapid thinning of the vast Arctic ice sheets in the past decade that scientists believe the prospect of a truly navigable passage may be realized as early as 2010 or 2015. By contrast, Frobisher and those who followed him were seeking a way through the ice-bound passage at perhaps the worst possible time in the last 10,000 years – the depths of the Little Ice Age, a period of dramatic global cooling between 1350 and 1850.

The mineral wealth of the vast northland has also yielded to modern technology. As the second millennium opened, reserves of gold said to rival those of South Africa were being mined in the Northwest Territories. Elizabethan adventurers and their successors were not only out of step with their age, they were also lacking fundamental information about the Earth. They were unaware of global climate change or plate tectonics or continental drift, which have altered and rearranged the Earth's continents since the beginning of time. They had no concept of ice ages or glaciations, and certainly knew nothing

The Elizabethan age in England saw great improvements in navigational aids. The astrolabe, above, and nocturnal, below, were used by mariners to fix their positions by observing heavenly bodies and were instruments of considerable accuracy, a great improvement over the suspended lodestones of earlier eras.

Exploring the Fur Trade Routes of North America

of isostatic rebound, the inexorable springing back of the Earth's crust once a great weight of ice is removed. But, it appears, they did know of Hudson Bay, long before Henry Hudson ever sailed there.

For centuries, historians have assumed that Hudson, too, was looking for the Northwest Passage when he set sail from London in April 1610. But recent interpretations have quite a different take on his intentions, based on the route he took and the description of his activities once in the bay. Passing through the fog-bound strait that today bears his name, he sailed into the east side of Hudson Bay. Instead of bearing west, however, as one searching for an outlet to Asia would predictably do, he turned the *Discovery* abruptly south and traced the east shore of Hudson Bay south to James Bay. For the balance of the brief summer and fall, using a sounding line, he zigzagged up and down the length of the lower bay at intervals of approximately 22 kilometres, carefully surveying it. But for what?

Carl Schuster, a New York writer of Arctic history, believes it was almost certainly not the Northwest Passage, which is deep and blue and tidal. Hudson was a veteran mariner, a man who had captained several trans-Atlantic voyages, a sailor who knew how to read the sea. Even those with much less experience can tell that James Bay is not an ocean. It is shallow, laden with sediment and barely tidal. Landlocked and fed by many large rivers, it has only a fraction of the salinity of ocean water. It doesn't even smell like the sea. Yet Hudson patiently tacked up and down, measuring

With its ancient blue granite and ragged spruce, right, the shoreline of Hudson Bay was stark, beautiful and, particularly in the early years, often deadly for Europeans. Yet these early adventurers kept coming, and over time discovered places – such as Wintering Creek on the Hayes River, above – where they could survive the long, bitter months of cold.

and mapping, trying to avoid the huge glacial erratics that hid beneath the water nearer shore.

Schuster and others believe that rather than charting new territory, Hudson was following ancient maps, representations of the bay based on information that was hundreds of years old. And those maps showed a coastline very different from the one Hudson encountered. Several surviving early 17th-century European maps show some of these features – islands, ridges and deep bays not found today, or in the early 17th century. Because of iso-static uplift, which

is still raising the land around Churchill at a rate of 60 centimetres a century, the Sutton Ridges, once offshore islands, are now 250 kilometres inland.

Clearly, though Hudson has long been credited as the first European to sail into these waters, others – Norse seamen perhaps? – had preceded him and returned to chart their findings. Did information about a wealth of minerals accompany these ancient maps? Was Henry Hudson, on behalf of a group of wealthy, titled backers, seeking gold or silver, as Frobisher had?

Whatever his motives, they were as unclear to his crew as they are to us today. When, after a miserable winter on the southeast shore of the bay, Hudson continued the search in the spring rather than heading home, they mutinied. He,

his young son and seven crew members were set adrift in a shallop and never seen again. However the following winter, far to the south along the Ottawa River, word of an English ship that was wrecked in the northern sea was received by the Tessouat and his Algonquin people, who in turn passed it along to Samuel de Champlain.

Hudson's men returned to London where, after many delays, they were tried and acquitted. Despite this dismal failure, others quickly followed in his wake, including Jens Munk of Denmark, who spent a deadly winter on the Churchill River in 1619. Arriving with two ships and 63 men in the fall of that year, the Danes established a winter camp near the mouth of the river, but his men soon began dying of scurvy. By spring, only Munk and two others were still alive and some-how these three sailed one of the ships all the way home to Copenhagen.

By mid-century, the English had concluded that if the Northwest Passage existed, it did not flow from Hudson Bay. Some took rather longer to dismiss the idea of mineral wealth around the bay (see Churchill on page 54), but more than one noticed that wealth of another sort abounded in this cold, northern region. And it was this "gold" that would draw the English back to the frozen bay 30 years later.

George Back's 19th-century painting, An Iceberg, a Ship and some Walrus, *portrays in almost Gothic overtones the haunting menace of Hudson Strait and Hudson Bay. The man for whom both are named is remembered in the Henry Hudson Memorial Window, below, in the Church of St. Ethelburga the Virgin in Bishopsgate, London.*

Exploring the Fur Trade Routes of North America

The Beaver
by Doug Whiteway

Early adventurers braved the Atlantic in search of Cathay gold, but the treasure of the northern "new world" was not precious metal, exotic spices or fine silks, but something far more ordinary – a peculiar sort of large rat with a flat, paddle-shaped tail, huge teeth and a single-minded talent for engineering. A rodent, to be precise, but a rodent with one very desirable characteristic – a fur coat ideal for the manufacture of felt hats that between the 17th and 19th centuries were as much a part of a European gentleman's wardrobe as a shirt and tie is today.

The beaver is the largest rodent in North America and, save the capybara of South America, the largest in the world. When mastodons and mammoths walked the continent, North America had giant beavers three metres long and weighing more than a horse. The modern beaver is much smaller, averaging a metre long and weighing up to 35 kilograms, but large enough to be of considerable worth. A Paris hatter could turn the pelt of one large *castor canadensis* into as many as 18 *chapeaux* and luckily, beaver were abundant in North America. They once ranged from the Arctic Ocean to the Gulf of Mexico, wherever streams and deciduous trees were to be found.

Thickset creatures with dark brown fur consisting of long guard hairs over dense, soft underfur, beavers unwittingly signalled their presence with a fondness for building things. Using long, sharp incisors, they can fell trees of all sizes; with dextrous handlike front paws, they can perform complex construction tasks.

A dam is a beaver's first order of business. Constructing them from logs, sticks and mud, they create a pond deep enough to stay unfrozen at the bottom during winter. The ponds, in turn, protect lodges – on average five metres in diameter and two metres high – with entrances above and below water.

Dam building is usually done in August, lodge building a month later and October is reserved for storing a winter's supply of food. Beavers don't hibernate. They remain active under the ice, plucking branches from their underwater pantry and feeding on the succulent bark. Rare among mammals, beavers mate for life and usually produce a litter of three or four well-furred, large-toothed kits each June.

Otters are important predators and wolves or wolverines may dispatch an occasional drifter on land, but man has been the beaver's greatest foe. By the middle of the 19th century, the beaver was trapped almost to extinction when the fickleness of fashion saved it. The beaver hat suddenly went out of style and silk hats became the rage. It was the worm's turn.

BRIAN WOLITSKI

*The animal kingdom's master builder, the beaver (*Castor canadensis*) signals its whereabouts in its remarkable constructions, including large lodges, below. With entrances above and below right, beavers are safe from almost every predator – except man.*

PETER ST. JOHN

THE BEAVER HAT by Doug Whiteway

That North America teemed with beaver was a godsend to the hatters of Europe. The beaver hat originated in 14th-century Russia, but stepped onto the world stage with Sweden's successes during the Thirty Years War (1618-1648). Swedish soldiers wore wide-brimmed hats with such romantic appeal that everyone had to have one.

The hats were of beaver, not the thick, glossy pelt but the underfur, turned into a tight, supple felt that would hold its shape through rough wear and wet weather. Beaver felt was why Swedish soldiers had such glorious headgear and for two centuries, Europeans evolved a series of imposing hats, from the cascading cavalier's hat to the cocked tricorne and the decorous top hat. You were no gentlemen unless you owned a "beaver", and as the bourgeois classes expanded in Europe, every man aimed to be a gentleman. Alas, by the early 17th century, Europe's beavers were trapped out.

Enter North America. If Europeans had been satisfied with cloth caps, who knows what turns North American history might have taken? But Europeans wanted beaver hats and North America had beavers aplenty. And so a continent was invaded to serve a purpose we might consider frivolous – fashion.

Turning beaver into felt, which included separating the beaver "wool" from the pelt and guard hairs, required a sophisticated process that involved boiling the fur in a mix of water and nitric acid, then applying heat and pressure to "felt" the result. The new material was then blocked, dyed, stiffened, waterproofed, ironed, trimmed and turned into the latest fashion.

Other furs, notably rabbit, could be felted, but the result was hats of lesser quality. Then in the mid-18th century, an innovation in felting signalled the beginning of the end for the North American fur trade. It was found that salts of mercury added to the nitric acid greatly improved the felting qualities of rabbit, which was cheap and available. The effect of mercury on hatters was debilitating; it led to shakes and addled speech (hence Lewis Carroll's Mad Hatter in *Alice in Wonderland*), but for the trade, mercury was a boon. By the early 19th century a quality chapeau needed only a few ounces of beaver for the outside veneer. Only an aficionado could tell the difference.

But the demise of the fur trade was due to the fickleness of fashion. Someone in Paris devised a hat of silk that was light, glamorous and cheaper than the beaver version. By the 1840s, beaver-felt hats were old-fashioned. Gentlemen now wore top hats made of a lustrous fibre produced by, of all the ignoble creatures, worms.

HUDSON'S BAY COMPANY ARCHIVES / C-308

The style of a "beaver" often announced its wearer's calling, political sympathies or station in life and some styles had names of their own.

Clockwise from top right: the hat worn by 18th-century clerics; a "Navy" cocked hat of 1800; the Wellington (1812); the Regent (1825) and the "Continental" cocked hat of 1776.

The French Fur Trade (1534-1763)

Canada takes its name from Kanata, *an Iroquoian term for the region around Quebec City. As they returned with Jacques Cartier after a year in France in 1535, two young Iroquioans from the region scanned the shoreline from the deck of the ship. Recognizing familiar territory, the brothers shouted, "Kanata! Kanata!" which Cartier translated as "Homeland". And so it has become for millions from around the world, though native North Americans have often been treated like outcasts in their own land.*

Though French fishermen had been trolling the Grand Banks of Newfoundland and the Gulf of St. Lawrence since before 1510, it was not until a quarter-century later that France began to take an official interest in North America. French reluctance was due in part to a papal bull that had divided the vast New World, sight largely unseen and unimagined, between Spain and Portugal. When, in 1533, Pope Clement VII (a relative by marriage of the French king, François I) limited this edict to lands "already discovered" by Europeans, it opened the door to France. The following year, Jacques Cartier, a veteran mariner from Saint-Malo, was outfitted by the Crown and sent to see whether North America's northern reaches might possess the same riches Spain had found in Mexico, or even better, a shortcut to China.

Cartier found neither on his first voyage, but he did sail to the western tip of Anticosti Island, which sits like a popped cork in the mouth of the St. Lawrence River, far enough west to meet a large party of Iroquoians. Led by a man named Donnacona, they were far from home, a village named Stadacona in Kanata, a region well upstream. Today, old Quebec City sits on the land Stadacona once occupied and Kanata has

given its name to Canada, one of the world's most privileged nations.

Until recently, the assumption has been that Donnacona's party – nearly 300 men, women and children in 40 canoes – had travelled east to fish or to launch an attack against their neighbors, the Mi'kmaq. But the presence of so many women and children make it unlikely that the group was either fishing or itching for war. Instead, they probably intended precisely what transpired – to meet Europeans who might want to trade.

Anthropologists call Donnacona's people St. Lawrence Iroquoians. Living at the northern edge of Iroquoian territory, they combined the agrarian talents of their southern neighbors, who would soon unite to become the Five Nations Iroquois, with the hunting skills of the Algonquian-speaking peoples to the north. They gave Cartier and his men a warm welcome, though only after hiding their young women in the forest, a telling indication they'd met Europeans before. And they clearly understood Cartier's intent, if not his words, when he erected a large wooden cross bearing the inscription *Vive le Roy de France.* Donnacona reacted with anger, and Cartier responded by backtracking and dissembling. The cross, he indicated, was simply a navigational device to enable him to find the place again.

AMANDA DOW

24

It's easy to believe, in the absence of a common language, that Cartier might have been equally oblique when he set sail for home with two of Donnacona's teenaged sons on board. His journal claims that Donnacona approved the trip, though surely the Iroquoian had no better idea of the world beyond the sea than Cartier did of the land beyond the great river. Did Donnacona believe a trade relationship was important enough to volunteer his sons to a fate he surely could not imagine? Or was this a kidnapping, with Cartier intent on bringing back proof of his travels and training a pair of interpreters for future adventures?

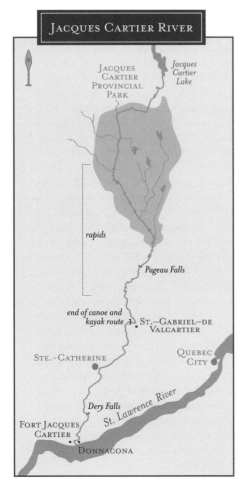

JACQUES CARTIER RIVER

JACQUES
CARTIER
PROVINCIAL
PARK

Jacques
Cartier
Lake

rapids

Pageau Falls

end of canoe and
kayak route

ST.-GABRIEL-DE
VALCARTIER

STE.-CATHERINE

QUEBEC
CITY

Dery Falls

St. Lawrence River

FORT JACQUES
CARTIER

DONNACONA

As it turned out, the two boys – Domogaya and Taignoagny – proved to be adaptable, clever young men. Not only did they survive the sea voyage and the winter in northern France, but they quickly learned to speak French. What they told Cartier and his sponsors, including the king, was apparently enough to convince them to launch a larger expedition the following spring.

Cartier's voyage of 1535-36 carried him farther along the St. Lawrence than he or any other European had ever been, but in many ways it was less successful than his first trip, for by the time he sailed home he had largely alienated his North American contacts.

Initially however, Donnacona was delighted to see his two globe-trotting sons, alive and well and full of information about the French when Cartier arrived at Stadacona in early September, 1535. This initial pleasure soon gave way to suspicion as Cartier made clear his intention to travel farther west. Upriver, Donnacona knew, was Hochelaga, a region larger and more powerful than his own. Should Cartier establish relations there, Donnacona might easily be pushed aside from the role he planned for himself, that of liaison with the French and middleman in a lucrative trade.

To dissuade Cartier he tried a number of tactics, including a performance by his shamans. He embellished

The encounters between Donnacona and Cartier took place more than 450 years ago, but echoes of these crucial meetings of two cultures can still be found in many place names around Quebec City. Only 40 minutes north is Jacques Cartier Provincial Park, where the Jacques Cartier River, left, winds through a wooded valley in a series of dramatic falls and rapids. Continuing south through several communities, it joins the St. Lawrence at the town of Donnacona. The river was nominated as a Canadian Heritage River in 1987 for its scenic beauty, natural and historic importance and superb recreation value.

The Grande Hermine, *above, was Cartier's largest ship at 126 tons.*

the stories Cartier clearly liked to hear about the Saguenay, a fabulous land of riches peopled by white-skinned men like the French. He offered several small children as gifts, but refused to allow his sons, who had steered well clear of the French since setting foot on home turf, to accompany the strangers upriver. And quite truthfully he warned Cartier that his men might well perish during the looming winter if they shunned the protection of Stadacona.

But Cartier was determined and, like a long line of Europeans to follow, not about to let the wisdom of the locals alter his plans, however untenable. Leaving most of his men to build a winter post near Stadacona, he headed upstream with a small party.

It took him nearly two weeks to reach Hochelaga and its main town, Tutonaguy, a community of more than 2,000. Located at the foot of a low mountain on a large island in the St. Lawrence, the town occupied a site near the heart of today's Montreal (see McGill University on page 71). Landing on the shore of the island, very near the present location of the bridge that bears his name, Cartier and his men – less than three dozen of them – found themselves facing a crowd estimated at more than 1,000 people.

His journal states that he was greeted like a god and conducted like royalty down the long road into town. In fact, the reception the Hochelagans gave Cartier was, according to many subsequent accounts, apparently typical of Iroquoian hospitality, undoubtedly enhanced by natural human curiosity. Cartier and his men must have seemed very strange, with hair growing upon their pale faces and odd clothing covering their entire bodies, though summer was barely over. And everyone was aware of their coming, for the French boats had passed several small villages as they struggled upriver.

Despite the bravado expressed in his journal, Cartier was likely disappointed with his trip. Far from being another Mexico, a vast city of wealth and power, Tutonaguy turned out to be a farming town. Worse, from the summit of the mountain – which he named Monte Real in the spirit of being king for a day – he could see that the great river below was blocked by rapids. And alas, to the west and north and south lay endless stretches of land. This was not, as he had hoped, his shortcut to China. Hugely outnumbered and feeling vulnerable, he beat a hasty retreat downstream to Stadacona.

The winter was long and cold. Even today, Quebec City experiences months of frosty weather and lots of snow. But winters in the mid-1500s were very likely longer and colder than they are today. This was, after all, the middle of what we now know as the Little Ice Age, a period of global cooling that began about 1350 and lasted for 500 years. The French, used to the cool maritime climate of northern France, were woefully unprepared for the conditions. They were unaccustomed to hunting in deep snow and by Christmas many were suffering from scurvy, a mysterious disease that soon killed 25 men. Moreover, relations with Donnacona and his people continued to deteriorate. In mid-winter, Stadacona was suddenly hit by a deadly scourge that killed 50 members of the community. Cartier believed they too were suffering from scurvy, but this is highly unlikely since it was Domogaya who saved the remaining French by showing them how to prepare an infusion of cedar leaves and bark. Instead, the Iroquoian deaths were probably the result of the first of a deadly series of European diseases that would strike defenceless North Americans across the continent and ultimately reduce their numbers by more than 75 per cent.

26

There was still the dream of the Saguenay, however. Deaths and disappointments might be overcome if Cartier could bring home the possibility of a land of riches. So as spring approached, he planned yet another abduction. On May 3, he lured Donnacona, his two bilingual sons and two other village leaders aboard and held them prisoner. When they sailed the next day, the departure was accompanied by great wails of grief and followed by a string of canoes carrying Stadaconans bearing beaver and seal pelts, copper knives and shell ornaments, gifts of ransom for the captives.

None of the Iroquoians ever returned to Kanata; all but one, a small child Cartier had earlier been given, died in France within the next year or two. And when Cartier finally came back to Canada in 1541, intending to establish a settlement (though without permission and on land that was clearly not his), he was met by suspicion and scarcely veiled hostility. This attempt and that of French nobleman Jean François de la Roque, the Sieur de Roberval, the following year quickly ended in failure, with the chastened survivors returning to France, the dream of colonizing Canada snuffed out for more than 60 years.

In any event, the focus of the French court for the last half of the 16th century was on other matters, including civil strife and wars with Spain. The trade in furs, however, did not stop. Every year French ships crossed the Atlantic to fish and many travelled on down the St. Lawrence looking for furs. Every summer at Tadoussac, where the Saguenay River pours down from the northern shield, the Innu (the French called them *Montagnais* or "mountain dwellers"), Algonquin and, in the early years, the St. Lawrence Iroquoians were waiting, laden with pelts trapped in

their own territories or traded from their neighbors to the west and north.

Over time, this trade changed the balance of power along the river. The Mohawk, residents of a landlocked region of upper New York State, began a series of raids aimed at obtaining a piece of the river and its trade. Attacking Kanata and Hochelaga, they drove the St. Lawrence Iroquoians out of the St. Lawrence Valley and far southwest to Huronia. But the Mohawk could do little to change the French preference for dealing with the Algonquian peoples, for the thick furs obtained from the cold northern territories were demonstrably better in quality than the thin pelts the Mohawk trapped in warmer regions.

In 1603, an experienced Breton trader, François de Pontgravé sailed for Tadoussac with a young observer, Samuel de Champlain, on board. Skilled as a seaman from boyhood, tempered by war as a youth and, it seems, experienced as an intelligence officer against the Spanish during two years in the West Indies, the 33-year-old Champlain was not satisfied to simply exchange French goods for Canadian furs at Tadoussac. But like Cartier before him, he was blocked from going north on the Saguenay River by Innu and Algonquin traders, loathe to lose their status as middlemen by allowing French penetration into the hinterlands, and farther upstream by the impassable rapids at the place we now know as Lachine.

Returning to France, Champlain was not ready to give up. The trade could be greatly increased, he reported, if the French could find a way to deal directly with northern trappers. And who was to say a way could not still be found to China? In 1604 Henri IV responded by granting a powerful Huguenot, Pierre du Gua, the Sieur de Monts, a 10-year

PETER ST .JOHN

An infusion of cedar leaves, above, and bark (or north of its range, spruce), rich in Vitamin C, was used by many North American nations to prevent scurvy. Rose hips, left, served the same purpose out on the plains. Both were available through the winter.

DENNIS FAST

FRENCH FURS: THE DEATH KNELL OF A NATION

Among the earliest allies of the French fur trade, the inhabitants of Huronia were a people apart long before Europeans arrived. Descended from two closely related agrarian cultures that inhabited southern Ontario at least 1,000 years ago, by 1600 the Wendat controlled the fertile territory that stretched south of Ontario's Lake Muskoka from the shore of Georgian Bay east to encompass Lake Simcoe. They spoke an Iroquoian language and farmed extensively like their relatives south of the Great Lakes, but were mortal enemies of the Five Nations Iroquois. Instead, they were linked by treaties and friendship to the Algonquian-speaking tribes of the northern shield, a relationship the Five Nations deemed treasonous.

The "three sisters" of North American agriculture, corn (above), beans (opposite) and squash together provided the staff of life for the Wendat and many other agrarian cultures.

At the time of European contact, the Wendat (the name means "Islanders" or "Dwellers on a Peninsula") encompassed five groups or tribes totalling nearly 30,000. The French dubbed them *Huron*, which came from an old term meaning "boar's head", likely a reference to the bristly Iroquoian hairstyle some wore.

PETER ST. JOHN

Their land, "Huronia", with its rolling hills, hardwood forests and shallow rivers and streams, was densely settled. The people lived in villages, often located for security on hilltops. The trails between them were packed hard from continuous use. Reminiscent of medieval European strongholds, the main villages were surrounded by tall palisades topped by galleries, where defenders could repel an invasion with boulders, bows and arrows and water to douse fires set along the walls.

Inside were dozens of longhouses, each home to several related families. Outside in large fields, the women cultivated corn, squash, beans, pumpkins and tobacco. The fruits of their harvests provided a complete diet and the Wendat and their near neighbors to the south, the Tionontati or "People of the Hills" (the French called them *Petun*, a word describing the tobacco they grew), appear to have been largely vegetarian, though they augmented their meals with fish and some game. The harvest surplus was stored in warehouses, providing security against lean years ahead.

A powerful and canny people, the Wendat were keenly alert to possible advantage. When the Innu (or *Montagnais* as the French knew them) began trading at the new French post at Québec in 1608, they soon knew of it. Samuel de Champlain and his small group, with their outdated but thunderous arquebuses and their desire for furs, were perfect potential allies. The following year, a war party of more than 60 Wendat and Algonquin met Champlain and his ragtag band of survivors to solicit aid for an attack on the Iroquois. To enlarge his all-important fur highway, Champlain agreed.

The ensuing skirmish pitted the small party, with its three Frenchmen armed with heavy rifles, against more than 200 Mohawk. A few years later, this would have been unlikely odds, but in 1609 the Iroquois did not yet have English firearms and the unexpected impact of the cumbersome French rifles, not to mention the noise, sent them fleeing in disarray.

The Wendat were delighted. They could not have known the victory marked the first nail in a coffin that would soon swallow their nation. Within 30 years, nearly half would die from disease, their conversion to Christianity never the blessing they'd been promised. Many of the rest fell before repeated waves of Iroquois invaders during a series of raids on Huronia between 1646 and 1648 or died of starvation when their stores were burned in the wake of the attacks. The remainder fled Huronia to be assimilated by other Iroquoian tribes or sought refuge with the Jesuits that had lived in their midst, first on what is now Christian Island in Georgian Bay and later near Québec City, where the only remaining Canadian Wendat – the Huronne Wendat of Lorette – live today. As they left, they burned their villages to the ground to prevent them from falling into Iroquois hands.

A small number, joined by displaced Tionontati, migrated southwest. In exile, they joined forces and emerged as the Wyandot. Though remarkably resilient – as soon as peace was negotiated, they were back trading furs in the St. Lawrence Valley in 1654 – they were essentially a displaced people. They attempted to settle near Detroit in the 18th century, but 100 years later American settlement forced them to move yet again, this time west of the Mississippi, where remnants of this ancient people still remain in modern Kansas and Oklahoma.

By 1650, Huronia was no more. Only piles of ashes marked the sites of once-thriving villages and clearings in the forest, the fields where corn and squash had once grown. However, the final flowering of Wendat life can be glimpsed today at Huronia Heritage, a reconstructed village and Jesuit mission at Midland, Ontario, in the heart of the land that was theirs for so long. And a reconstructed longhouse at St. Ignace, Michigan (see page 104), recalls the wanderings of Wendat refugees.

Though not as long as many were in Huronia, this reconstructed Wendat longhouse at the Marquette Mission Park and the Museum of Ojibwa Culture in St. Ignace, Michigan, where Wendat refugees settled for a time in the late 1600s, demonstrates the unique construction of these communal houses.

MIKE GRANDMAISON

In 1615, accompanying the Wendat to their home territory in what is now Ontario's Lakelands, Samuel de Champlain paddled the aquamarine waters of Georgian Bay, seen here at Bruce Peninsula National Park. Three decades later, this close alliance with the French proved disastrous for the Wendat.

monopoly to trade in a huge area of what was now being called New France, on condition that he establish a colony and embark on missionary work.

Despite the royal imprimatur and his own dreams, Champlain spent little time on the St. Lawrence for the next three years. Instead, he and Pontgravé charted the Atlantic coast for several summers, looking for another way into the continent. Returning to the St. Lawrence in 1608, they were stymied by Basque traders at Tadoussac. Pontgravé continued upstream and where the river narrowed, at the site of the former village of Stadacona (today's Quebec City), Champlain built a small post in the fall of 1608.

If anything, he and his men fared worse than Cartier's company had nearly 75 years before. With the Stadaconans gone, there was no one to show them the secret of the cedar bark tea and before spring 20 of the 28 men were dead of scurvy or dysentery. But Champlain was nothing if not determined and instead of heading home, he and the remnants of his bedraggled band set off upstream. Within days they met a war party in search of European allies for an attack on the League of the Iroquois

Sensing his opportunity to break out of the St. Lawrence to the north and west, Champlain agreed. The price was a skirmish that left him wounded and a

conflict with the Iroquois that involved the French for nearly a century, but the advantages were also both immediate and long lasting. Following victories in 1609 and 1610 over the Iroquois, who did not yet have access to European firepower, he was all but adopted by the Wendat. They happily agreed to take one of his young men, Etienne Brûlé, home to learn their Iroquoian language and entice others to bring furs down to trade. In exchange, Champlain took a young Wendat, whom he called Savignon, with him to France. This exchange worked so well for all parties that a year later, Champlain sent Nicolas de Vignau to winter with the Algonquin at Lac des Allumettes, up the river we now call the Ottawa.

Vignau returned in the spring with word that he had travelled with the Algonquin to a northern sea where an English ship had been wrecked (see The British on page 18). This, as it turned out, was an exaggeration, for Vignau himself had not set eyes on the "northern sea" and the English "ship" must have been the lifeboat in which Henry Hudson and his supporters were cast adrift, but the episode speaks volumes about how quickly news travelled over vast distances and terrain that is difficult even today. For Champlain, it confirmed what he had always believed that a North Sea, accessible from Europe, lay beyond the northern lands – and he determined to see it for himself.

His trip up the Algonquin River, as it was then known, in May of 1613, involved a small party of just four Frenchmen in two canoes, led by an Algonquin guide. Though Champlain had recognized early that birchbark canoes and netted snowshoes – both Canadian inventions – held the keys to summer and winter travel in North America, he and his men were anything but adept at using them and the trip turned out to be one long lesson. They learned about the rivers of the Canadian Shield, with their innumerable rapids and impassable falls, and they learned about canoeing, but not before Champlain nearly drowned. Circumventing the roaring Chaudière Falls, they learned to depend on local knowledge and, bypassing the Calumet and Allumette Rapids, they learned about the importance of packing properly.

Here, crossing to the tiny Muskrat River not far from today's Renfrew, Ontario, Champlain lost his astrolabe (see The Cheneaux on page 82). Without it, determining location was nearly impossible and the journey, which had already proven to be considerably more onerous than Vignau had promised, began to seem insurmountable. At the Algonquin camp, Champlain discovered that Vignau had in fact not travelled to the northern sea. Such a trip was long and dangerous, if possible at all. And so Champlain began to learn about the immensity of North America.

In succeeding years Récollet priests filled with missionary zeal, and growing numbers of traders lusting after fur travelled far beyond Lac des Allumettes, to the Mattawa River and Lake Nipissing, down the French River into Georgian Bay and eventually on through the North Channel of Lake Huron to the vast freshwater ocean of Lake Superior. This was a route that had been travelled for thousands of years by North Americans and would, in time, be the North West Company's mainline to the west.

Champlain himself travelled only as far west as Huronia, but his impact on Canada was permanent. And his cumulative travel of a lifetime is breathtaking, even today. He crossed the Atlantic 23 times and spent 13 winters in Canada, including his last, in 1635. Champlain understood that the keys to both the fur trade and the continent's geography were held by North Americans. His "young men", skilled in various North American languages and acculturated through winters spent in camps in the *pays d'en haut*, expanded on these ideas.

In 1623, Etienne Brûlé travelled from Huronia to the great rapids that separated Lake Huron from its much larger neighbor to the northwest, Lake Superior. Fifteen years later, Jean Nicolet, who had spent 10 years with the Algonquin, followed in his footsteps but turned south at what was soon to be called Sault Ste. Marie. Following the Upper Michigan peninsula, he reached Mackinac Island and the Straits of Mackinac. Continuing on into Lac des Illinois (now Lake Michigan), he traced its northern shore to Green Bay and, from the bay's western side, followed the Fox River to its upper reaches. From here, it was just a short distance to the Wisconsin River, a tributary of the Mississippi. Though he went no farther, Nicolet heard stories about the mighty river and the South Sea into which it flowed.

In the footsteps of these disciples of Champlain came the *coureurs de bois*, a breed of independent traders that arose

A statue of Chaplain and his soon-to-be-missing astrolabe towers over the Ottawa River in Canada's national capital. Led by Algonquin, Wendat, Ojibwe and Cree guides, the French penetrated much of eastern North America before 1730 and were pushing west across the Great Plains.

PETER ST. JOHN

after 1640, at least partly in response to the northward thrust of the Iroquois. Backed by the Dutch and English, supplied with arms they once lacked, the Iroquois launched a war against the Wendat and their allies, including the French, that within 10 years had drawn a cordon around the St. Lawrence. The Wendat were all but obliterated; the Nipissing and Algonquin were driven north and the French were forced to spend great time and effort on self-defence. Yet France, embroiled in its own wars, offered little assistance, though it was clear that the war with the Iroquois would inevitably lead to war with the English in North America.

If the fledgling French colonies were to survive, the French court said, the funds had to come from the fur trade. But the only people who could succeed in the trade in conditions that amounted to a blockade were those who knew the land intimately, who spoke native languages fluently and who could live like a North American, for months or even years at a time. Increasingly, these were French-Canadians, young men of Breton or Norman stock, born in North America and at home in its untamed vastness. They were not, on the whole, the kind of men to whom New France granted its trading licences. And so an illicit trade grew up.

Some of these budding *coureurs de bois* continued to farm during the summer, leaving in the fall to spend the winters inland, travelling to Algonquin or Nipissing or Ojibwe camps to purchase furs; this practice would later be known as trading *en dérouine*. The furs were then spirited through the Iroquois cordon and down to Québec.

The coureurs de bois were known as "wood-runners" by the English and "bush-lopers" by the Albany Dutch.

Others made trading their lives. Following ancient river routes that had been used for millennia by North American traders, learning their languages and their lore, the *coureurs* began to develop a reliable knowledge of the geography north to James Bay, west beyond the Great Lakes and south into the Ohio country.

A few also began to develop ideas of their own about how the trade – and by extension the economy of New France – ought to be run. One of these was Médard Chouart des Groseilliers, who arrived in Canada about 1641 at the age of 23. He found work with the Jesuits at the mission of Sainte-Marie in Huronia and learned to speak the Iroquoian language of the Wendat. Driven from the Georgian Bay area by the Iroquois War (1648-53), he retreated to Québec.

A negotiated peace in 1653 allowed a party of refugees from Huronia, who had fled west of Lake Michigan, a chance to travel and trade after six years of war. They arrived on the St. Lawrence the following spring and des Groseilliers immediately saw the opportunity for what it was. That August, when the Wendat refugees headed west again, des Groseilliers went with them. Over the next two years, he ranged widely over what is now Michigan and Wisconsin, trading and reconnoitering. When he returned in the summer of 1656, he was accompanied by 50 canoes and a fortune in furs.

The French authorities were not impressed. Independent trading was a threat to colonial revenues; when des Groseilliers tried to purchase a *congé* or trading licence in 1659, the governor of Trois-Rivières demanded half the profits. Des Groseilliers refused and was forbidden to leave the colony. So in August, accompanied by his young brother-in-law Pierre-Esprit Radisson, he slipped past the authorities and paddled west again. Trading around the margins of Lake Superior, the brothers-in-law heard stories of "a great store of beaver" to be found along the shores of a "bay of the North Sea". Even better, they were told that the bay was just a

turned back. Frustrated, the two French-men sailed to London. Following a series of adventures, they found a ready ear (see The English on the Bay, page 48) and a successful trading venture to

HOWARD SIVERTSON / FROM *THE ILLUSTRATED VOYAGEUR*

The idea of trading en dérouine, *in the winter camps of North American peoples, rather than waiting for furs to be brought in to the fur posts, made sense to the French. Many English traders resisted the idea for a time, but eventually realized the results justified the increased effort.*

week's journey by river from Lake Superior's east shore (see Michipicoten on page 116).

With their heads full of plans for the future, they sped home to Trois-Rivières accompanied by 60 canoes and another fortune in furs. But instead of becoming wealthy, they were arrested and charged with illegal trading, all their furs confiscated.

After an unsuccessful attempt to seek justice in France, des Groseilliers and Radisson turned their backs on New France and in 1662 travelled south to Boston to solicit English help in establishing a trade into Hudson Bay. An expedition by sea the following year got as far as the mouth of Hudson Strait but

James Bay in 1668 led to the founding of the "Governor and Company of Adventurers tradeing into Hudson's Bay" – better known as the Hudson's Bay Company – on May 2nd, 1670.

The brothers-in-law were eventually enticed back to New France (though the mercurial Radisson switched sides yet again and finally retired to Westminster), but the damage was done. Though the initial years of English presence on Hudson and James Bays were precarious and the company's methods anything but assertive, particularly in its first century, slowly the transplant took. Over 150 years, the Hudson's Bay Company established its presence and eventually its dominance across northern

A MODEL OF AMERICAN UNITY

Numerous and largely agrarian, Iroquoian-speaking people lived for hundreds of years around the Lower Great Lakes. They were accomplished agriculturalists, depending on their crops of corn, beans and squash (the "three sisters" of North American agriculture) for more than three-quarters of the food they consumed. Their villages of communal longhouses, typically housing 1,500 or 2,000 people, lined the shores of Onhatariyo ("Handsome Lake" in Iroquois – a word the English shortened to Ontario). Here and farther south, the women farmed the deep alluvial soil and raised their families. The men, meanwhile, spent the summers away from the clan settlements hunting, fishing, trading and, quite regularly, making war.

An Iroquois sachem *or leader holds up a wampum belt in this artist's conception of a meeting of the Five Nations Confederacy in the mid-1500s. The Iroquois were known for their diplomatic and oratorial skills, as well as for their innovative and successful federation.*

As their numbers grew (some estimates place the precontact Iroquoian population, before the great pandemic of 1520, at more than a half-million), conflict between the various tribes increased during the 15th and 16th centuries. For some, this friction led eventually to war, but for others, it was a prelude to one of the world's longest-lasting alliances.

In the 1500s, while English and Scots were butchering one another over religion in Britain, a pair of visionary Iroquoian leaders, Deganawida and Hiawatha (no relation to Longfellow's romantic invention), convinced the five tribes who occupied the land from Lake Erie to what is now eastern New York State – the Seneca, Cayuga, Onondaga, Oneida and Mohawk – to form a military and political alliance. Drawing on their geographical locations and the symbolic form of the longhouse, the League of the Iroquois was established with the Seneca and the Mohawk as the respective keepers of the western and eastern doors, and the Onondaga as the keepers of the fire, with responsibility for calling and hosting meetings of the confederacy.

The union, which allowed each member nation considerable autonomy, provided crucial alliances for war. And 150 years later, when the handful of English colonies on North America's Atlantic coast were contemplating independence and unity, the Iroquois confederacy provided a model. In the summer of 1744, Canasatego, an Onondaga *sachem* or leader, told a gathering of commissioners (including the young Benjamin Franklin) from Pennsylvania, Maryland and Virginia,

> "We heartily recommend union and a good agreement between you …Our wise forefathers established union and amity between the Five Nations; this has made us formidable; this has given us great weight and authority with our neighboring nations."

CHARLES WALTER SIMPSON / NATIONAL ARCHIVES OF CANADA / C-13949

When Samuel de Champlain and a few armed French joined the Wendat and their Algonquian allies in campaigns against the Mohawk in 1609 and 1610 and against the Onondaga in 1615, it served as a war cry for all Five Nations Iroquois.

The call to arms was reinforced by terrible population losses over the next three decades and enabled by trade alliances with the Dutch and English, who provided firearms. The arrival of Europeans brought with it a scourge of deadly diseases against which the Iroquois, like the original inhabitants of the Americas everywhere, had no defence. By 1646, a desire for retribution and the need to repopulate with enemy captives spurred the war against the Wendat and their allies. Five years later, the Iroquois controlled all the land west to Lake Huron and north to the French and Mattawa Rivers. And a generation after that, the Jesuits wrote that some tribes of the Iroquois confederacy consisted largely of ex-captives. The Oneida, they wrote, "were two-thirds Huron and Algonquian".

Despite their 17th-century territorial control, the Five Nations (which became Six Nations in 1722 when the Tuscarora from North Carolina sought admittance to the confederacy) were eventually pressed on the east and the south by increasing numbers of British settlers. Using diplomacy and negotiation – skills they possessed in abundance – they tried to hold their borders against the incoming horde.

The Mohawk, most exposed by their eastern position to European settlement and vices, had long been staunch British allies. But from the outset some were critical of the trust the confederacy put in British promises. As early as the 1670s, a substantial number headed north to settle among the French on ancient Iroquoian territory at Kahnawake (which means "At the Rapids"), opposite Lachine, and at Oka on Lake of Two Mountains north of Montréal. Many of these people involved themselves in the fur trade and substantial numbers eventually settled in Alberta and eastern British Columbia, where they married Cree or Shuswap women.

The rest backed the English during the Seven Years War (1754–1763), assisting in the final defeat of the French. Spurred by British promises and the persuasive eloquence of a brilliant young Mohawk named Thayendanegea (known as Joseph Brant to both British and Canadians), the Mohawk were drawn, much against their will, into the Revolutionary War that gave birth to the American nation. As British allies, they were forced from their land when the war ended. Some fled west to Wisconsin and many moved north to settle in Canada, where land was made available to them along the Grand River, near today's Brantford.

JOHN VERELST / NATIONAL ARCHIVES OF CANADA / C-92420

Iroquois leader Etow Oh Koam, called Nicholas by the British, was one of four Mohawks who went to England in 1710. Young and handsome, "the four kings", as the papers called them, caused a sensation in London and all were painted in a neoclassical style by portraitist John Verelst. In this portrait, Etow Oh Koam is holding a ballhead war club or o-ji-kwa.

North America – a vast commercial concern that in many places inaugurated the contact period and foreshadowed European settlement in the west, with all its repercussions.

In New France, meanwhile, there were growing concerns that the fur trade was bleeding off the flower of Canada's youth. By 1670, the problem had attracted notice even in France. In 1672, the new governor of New France – the imperious Louis de Buade, Comte de Frontenac – was instructed to focus on establishing defensible colonies, strengthening maritime links with France and developing colonial agriculture and industry. Typically, he took an opposite tack. The following summer, he forced the habitants of Montréal to provide labor and materials to construct a fort at the eastern end of Lake Ontario, a move that not only annoyed the laborers, but angered the Iroquois, who regarded the region as their hunting territory.

Over the next 15 years Frontenac vastly expanded the network of fur trading posts on the Great Lakes and along the tributaries of the Mississippi. And despite vocal opposition from both the clergy and colonial officials, he introduced brandy as a stock trading item.

Encouraged by Frontenac, Louis Joliet and Father Jacques Marquette undertook an epic two-year journey to the Mississippi in 1672. Travelling down the huge river almost to its confluence with the Arkansas, they determined that this was the river Hernando de Soto had written about more than a

century before and that it flowed to the Gulf of Mexico, not the Atlantic or Pacific. But here, they told Frontenac on their return in 1674, was a fur route to a port that could be used year-round.

Another in the governor's coterie was René-Robert Cavelier (later Sieur de La Salle), a restless young man who had been dismissed from a Jesuit seminary in Paris in 1667. Seeking adventure, obsessed by the idea of a passage to China, the 24-year-old set off for Canada, where his brother Jean was a Sulpician priest in Montréal.

Within a year, the Sulpicians had granted him a seigneury, which he wryly called La Chine, near the rapids of the St. Lawrence; the name stuck and eventually was applied to the entire area.

Robert Cavelier was not cut out for farming however, and his expansionist ideas attracted the attention of Governor Frontenac, who sent him to take charge of the new post at Cataraqui (now Kingston). The original fort was of wood, with palisades and log buildings, but the new seigneur had grander ideas. Renaming the place Fort Frontenac, he had the wooden walls and buildings replaced with stone and embarked on an expensive ship-building program. Though ostensibly built to protect Montréal, in reality the fort was meant to secure the fur trade with the Seneca and expand it into the Ohio Valley.

Over the next few years, the newly created Sieur de La Salle and his friend and ally, Louis Hennepin, a Récollet friar, ventured farther and farther south, establishing a chain of posts on Lake Michigan and on the Illinois and Mississippi Rivers. Though La Salle was often ill with bouts of fever, his lust for the unknown burned with even greater intensity. In 1680, he constructed Fort Crèvecoeur on the Illinois and then Fort St. Louis and Fort Prudhomme on the

The Sulpician Seminary, home of Montréal's first administrators, was among the first buildings to be constructed. It still stands today (see page 69) and its clock, shown here in a 19th-century drawing, is the oldest public timepiece in North America.

WALTER BAKER / NATIONAL ARCHIVES OF CANADA / C–106728

Mississippi, below its junction with the Ohio. During the same years, he sent men north to establish trade with the Odawa and Assiniboine, despite strict orders not to interfere with trappers who normally sent their furs to Montréal.

Finally in 1682, led by North American guides and accompanied by Hennepin and a small party of Frenchmen, he followed the Mississippi to its mouth. Arriving at the Gulf of Mexico in early April, he named the region Louisiana, claiming it for Louis XIV. If he could establish a post here, he reasoned, he could bypass New France, with all its restrictions, and deal directly with merchants in Europe.

Returning to France, La Salle found his agents, a pair of ambitious priests with royal connections, plotting even grander plans. What if France could use Louisiana as a base to conquer the silver mines of New Spain? The problem, of course, was proximity. Louisiana and the Mississippi were perhaps too far east to make the plan plausible. To sell the idea to the king, a few details of geography would need to be changed. So La Salle redrew his maps, moving the Mississippi far to the west, and claimed that the river (which was nearly impassable at the mouth for large craft) would support ships for a great distance from the Gulf.

Whether La Salle himself was confused by these falsifications is not clear, but when he sailed from France with four ships and 300 colonists in 1684, he overshot the mouth of the Mississippi by 600 kilometres. One of his ships ran aground on a sandbar near Matagorda Island on the Gulf Coast of Texas and sank with much of the expedition's food, tools and weapons. The would-be colonists struggled ashore and built a small post, named Fort St. Louis, but disease and alligators, as well as disputes with the local Karankawa people soon disposed of most of them.

Despite the hardships, La Salle continued his search for the evasive Mississippi. When his ship, *La Belle*, was grounded and abandoned in 1686, he set off overland. But even this failed. Ill and despondent, he returned to the fort. In the spring of 1687 he was apparently murdered by one of his own men. He was just 43.

Only six people, including La Salle's brother Jean Cavelier, eventually made it back to France via Canada. La Salle's body was never found, but in 1995, after a 17-year search, *La Belle* was discovered off the Texas coast, the oldest shipwreck in the Americas. In 1997, the site was walled off by a cofferdam and archaeologists began an excavation that has unearthed a treasure trove. Along with the timbers of the ship's hull, they found bronze cannons, pewter plates, glass beads, pottery and a human skeleton. The bones have undergone DNA testing and may provide yet another link between North America and the people of France.

La Salle's bold disregard of colonial trading regulations caused concern among the merchants and free traders of New France, but it also sparked imitators and soon others were establishing tiny far-flung outposts around the Great Lakes and beyond. The strategic importance of both the St. Marys River, which separates Lake Huron and Lake Superior (see Sault Ste. Marie on page 96), and the Straits of Mackinac between Lake Huron and Lake Michigan had been understood for decades. In 1670, Father Claude Dablon had travelled south from his Ojibwe mission at Sault Ste. Marie to the Straits of Mackinac. Impressed by the crossroads location, the safety

BARBARA ENDRES

Snowshoes were manufactured in many shapes and sizes by North Americans, to suit the many different snow conditions across the continent. These broad, snub-nosed "swallowtail" snowshoes were used for travel through soft, deep snow in wooded areas.

The colonial nations of Europe began carving up huge swaths of North America in the 17th century. By 1700 they had laid at least theoretical claim to vast stretches of the continent. This map would change dramatically over the next century as France ceded its territories to Britain and Spain and the Thirteen Colonies became the United States of America.

offered by Mackinac Island and the bounty of the region, Dablon contacted Father Marquette, who was seeking a safe haven for the Wendat driven out of Huronia more than 20 years before. They had briefly settled at the western end of Lake Superior, but that was Dakota territory and conflict loomed. The Straits of Mackinac, inhabited for centuries by Ojibwe and Odawa, traditional allies of the Wendat, was much safer.

Just one summer convinced the Wendat that the soil on Mackinac Island was too thin for agriculture, so the village was moved to the north side of the straits in 1671. Here, Marquette established two missions, St. Ignatius Loyola (today St. Ignace, Michigan) for the Wendat, and St. Francis Borgia among the Odawa, before leaving with Joliet for the Mississippi.

A fur trade community, with warehouses and a small post, quickly grew up beside the Mackinac missions and for the next century and a half, the Straits of Mackinac played a crucial role in the North American fur trade (see The Fur Trade in Old Michigan on page 102). A depot of this nature greatly increased the number of small traders. In 1672, the number of *coureurs de bois* was estimated at between 300 and 400; eight years later, there were at least 800 and perhaps many more for, as one official in New France wrote, "I have been unable to ascertain the exact number because everyone associated with them covers up for them."

At Mackinac, French soldiers and sailors were not far behind the missionaries and traders. In the 1680s, they built the first military post, Fort DuBuade, at St. Ignace. Constructed mainly to block English expansion into the western Great Lakes, the soldiers also attempted to restrict the fur trade to licenced operators. A glut of furs in Europe in the late 1690s caused the fort to be closed and shortly after, the Odawa moved across the Straits of Mackinac to the south shore, where new land could be broken. When French soldiers returned to the area in 1714, they too settled on the south shore and built Fort Michilimackinac (see page 106).

But the fur trade never faltered. The departure of French troops from St. Ignace in 1697 only made life easier for the *coureurs de bois* and over the next century, as the forts and posts changed hands from French to British to American, the straits continued as a centre of free trade.

Because they were adept at circumventing regulations, the attributes and talents of the independent traders were largely unappreciated by officialdom in New France, but these talents were crucial to the fur trade. Of prime

NORTH AMERICA 1700

Pacific
Ocean

AREAS CLAIMED BY SPAIN
AREAS CLAIMED BY FRANCE
AREAS CLAIMED BY BRITISH
AREAS CLAIMED BY BRITISH & FRENCH

Hudson
Bay

RUPERT'S LAND

NEW FRANCE

New-
foundland

Nova
Scotia

VICE-ROYALTY
OF
NEW SPAIN

LOUISIANA

THIRTEEN COLONIES

Atlantic
Ocean

Gulf of
Mexico

A MAN FOR TWO WORLDS

Because most could neither read nor write, the stories of French and Metis free traders have largely gone untold. Joseph La France's tale is an exception, thanks to a journey he took to England in 1742, where he was interviewed by Sir Arthur Dobbs, an Irishman opposed to the Hudson's Bay Company.

COURTESY THE HUDSON'S BAY COMPANY MUSEUM COLLECTION

La France's story reveals that the *coureurs de bois* lived in two worlds, combining the skills of both. He was born about 1707, likely at St. Ignace, Michigan, to a French father and an Ojibwe mother who died when he was young. At five or six, Joseph made his first journey from the Straits of Mackinac to Québec and repeated this long trip many times until his father's death when he was 15 or 16. The following year he travelled alone to Montréal to sell the family's furs.

La France spent the next decade with his mother's people near Michipicoten, learning their ways and travelling every spring to the Straits of Mackinac. By 1734, he was ready to expand his horizons and his timing could hardly have been better. A French military onslaught against the Fox nation west of Lake Michigan had largely emptied the countryside between Green Bay and the Mississippi. La France was among the first *coureurs de bois* to penetrate this war-torn territory. The following year, responding to limits on trading privileges at Michilimackinac, he turned east and smuggled furs to the English at New York.

Then, hoping to legitimize his business, he returned to Québec, his canoes loaded with furs, to apply for a trading licence. To enhance his chances, he paid the governor-general 1,000 crowns and gave him a valuable pack of marten skins. But the licence was not forthcoming; instead, he was charged with trading in brandy and threatened with arrest.

The setback seems typical. Returning to Michilimackinac, La France found few trading there. Superior goods and returns from the English, as well as a boycott by native trappers disgusted by the greed of colonial officials had turned the free traders against New France. Yet still he hoped for a licence. En route once more to the St. Lawrence in 1738, he was arrested on the French River, his supplies and furs confiscated. Facing prison, he fled in the night.

A year later, La France decided to try to reach York Fort on Hudson Bay. Trekking west of Lake Superior, he spent 1740 and '41 trapping and trading in what is now western Manitoba, likely relying on goods from the La Vérendryes' posts. In the spring of 1742 he joined the flotilla to Hudson Bay and travelled to London in the fall.

Dobbs hoped to use him on one of his expeditions to Hudson Bay, but before plans could be made, La France died of fever at the age of 36.

Many French and Metis trappers and traders, particularly those with talented country wives, lived remarkably well in some of North America's wild places. This beautifully made, exquisitely embroidered buckskin coat is indicative of the abilities of North American women.

importance was their excellent rapport with native North Americans. This began with language proficiency; the *coureurs de bois* were always bilingual and often spoke three or even more languages. They also had remarkable wilderness skills and an appreciation of North American cultures and lifestyles. Many, though born in New France, were almost as much at home among the Odawa, Ojibwe, Cree or Assiniboine. This sense of familiarity quite naturally led to relationships with North American women, and to off- spring that combined two very different cultures.

DENNIS FAST

Guns, metal weapons and implements and alcohol were among the most sought-after trade items, but early trade guns were noto- riously unreliable. Perhaps affected by the cold northern win- ters, they often back- fired, maiming and sometimes even killing their owners. As a result, many native North Americans con- tinued to prefer their own reliable weapons long into the fur trade era. By the early 1800s, when these rifles at Minnesota's North West Company Fur Post were manu- factured, trade guns were much improved.

Particularly prior to 1760, most of these men left little or no record of their lives. Like the large majority in Canada itself, most could not write. But one man, Joseph la France, left his story through an unusual series of cir- cumstances and it may have been fairly typical of the period.

Shortly after 1700, the intensive trapping prompted by the presence of so many traders began to take a notice- able toll on the fur-bearing animals south of the Great Lakes and the French began to look farther afield for pelts. The Fox people, who lived along the Wisconsin River and who, like the Wendat and Odawa before them, served as middle- men in the trade, resented these attempts to move west and deal directly with other nations. In the first two decades of the 18th century, they created what

amounted to a trade barrier; anyone dealing with the French was punished with stinging attacks. North and west, the Dakota, a large and powerful nation of the upper Mississippi region, deeply resented French – or any other – incursion into their territory.

These factors made explorations northward, through Lake Superior and northwest to Lake Winnipeg, seem an ob- vious alternative. And New France had never given up its search for a route to the Western Sea. In 1731, officials awarded Pierre Gaultier de Varennes et de La Vérendrye a trading lease for the area west of Lake Superior, on condition that he under- take expeditions to try to find a route to the *Mer de l'Ouest*.

For the next 12 years, La Vérendrye (see page 204), his four sons and a nephew covered enormous dis- tances through the western plains and parklands, establishing a string of posts as far north as the Saskatchewan River and travelling as far southwest as the Big Horn Mountains of Wyoming. These expeditions extended the reach of the French fur trade over a vast area and did much to end speculation about an easy route to the Western Sea, but they also caused trouble with the Dakota.

In addition to furs, the La Véren- dryes were apparently also involved in trading slaves. Pawnee or Dakota cap- tives seized in raids on western villages and encampments by the Ojibwe and Assiniboine were traded to the French and then shipped to Montréal, where they were obliged to work as servants. Though undoubtedly an exaggeration, it was said of La Vérendrye that while he commanded the western posts, he shipped more slaves to Montréal than bales of fur. The family's involvement in this unsavory business may have been among the factors that eventually led to the death of La Vérendrye's eldest son (see Fort St. Charles on page 151).

Meanwhile, along the Mississippi and its major tributaries, French posts were slowly turning into tiny settlements, connected by the river to the port community at New Orleans. Cahokia, founded in 1698 near an ancient community, was the earliest of these riverbank communities that still exist today. Others followed, and many of the inhabitants spent at least part of the year trading or trapping furs. But diminishing returns from the Ohio territory (in which the English were increasingly interested – though for settlement, not furs) affected these men as well. By the middle of the century, enterprising traders were working farther afield, west up the Arkansas and lower Missouri Rivers and their tributaries.

As they expanded their tenuous routes ever more distant from New France, the traders' interest in colonial matters and imperial ambitions generally dwindled, except when there were direct consequences on the trade itself. The Seven Years War, which in North America pitted expansionist English colonialism and settlement against the French fur trade, was harder to ignore, for it spelled the end of French involvement in North America.

The French hold on Lakes Ontario and Erie, as well as the Ohio Valley, ended with the fall of Fort Frontenac in 1758 and Fort Niagara a year later. But the canoe brigades still left Montréal, taking the northern route to the Upper Great Lakes, and the Louisiana trade continued.

The autumn of 1759 was disastrous for New France, however. Québec fell in mid-September and Montréal surrendered the following spring. Though the official transfer of imperial sovereignty would wait until the Treaty of Paris in 1763, the French era in North America was effectively over.

About 1,600 people, mostly French officials and about half the army sent to Canada to fight, departed almost immediately for France. But tens of thousands who had made their lives on the land and the waterways and in the forests of North America stayed. Determined to make the best of the new situation, they continued to leave their mark on the changing continent.

The La Vérendrye family, charged with finding a route to the Western Sea and dependent on fur revenues to finance these travels, pushed far out onto the western plains during the 1730s and '40s. Travelling by water to the Saskatchewan River and overland to the foot of the Bighorn Mountains, they proved conclusively that there was no easy overland route to the Pacific.

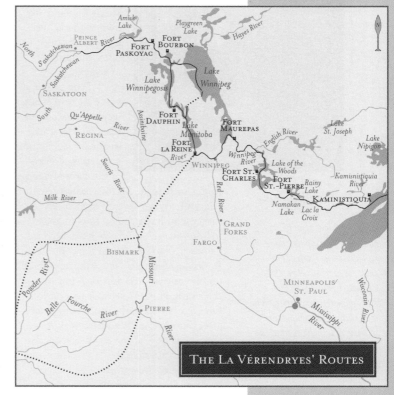

THE LA VÉRENDRYES' ROUTES

London:
The Epicentre

by Peter St. John

Like so many international endeavors of the time, the Hudson's Bay Company grew out of developments in the international balance of power in 17th-century Europe. A flood of French Huguenot refugees had brought the art of hat-making to England, and as a result beaver hats were the rage in Stuart England. To own a fine beaver hat was proof of one's standing in society.

The problem was that British hats were dependent on Russian furs and treatment techniques and Dutch control of the transportation routes to Russia. All this changed with a fateful voyage by two French adventurers who had decided to change sides. In 1666 two *coureurs de bois*, Médard Chouart des Grosseilliers and Pierre Radisson, deserted New France with all its bureaucratic restrictions and made their rather circuitous way to London. On October 25th, they met with a very attentive Charles II and from that encounter flowed the royal prerogative that made possible the "Governor and Company of Adventurers of England tradeing into Hudson's Bay" – much better known as the Hudson's Bay Company. A remarkable confluence of commercial and royal interests followed. The king placed his cousin Prince Rupert of the Rhine, the Duke of Cumberland, in charge of the commercial initiative and soon Rupert, Radisson and des Grosseillers were plotting to wrest the lucrative fur trade from the French by developing the rich fur resources of Hudson Bay.

An initial voyage in 1688 by the ships *Eaglet* and *Nonsuch* revealed the potential for rich returns, even though the *Eaglet* was forced to turn back. With the considerable assistance of his secretary, Sir James Hayes, Prince Rupert – Bohemian prince, founding fellow of the Royal Society and Governor of Windsor Castle – set up the Hudson's Bay Company, which would soon operate much like a kingdom itself.

Suddenly mercantile concerns became national interests in England and Crown and City of London money combined to revitalize a spirit of commercial innovation and adventure not seen since the days of Martin Frobisher.

A governor, deputy governor and seven committeemen ran this burgeoning enterprise from the City's financial district. As Canadian author Peter Newman points out, they were ultimate absentee landlords. For more than two centuries none of them travelled to North America to see the beaver that "became the breathing equivalent of gold", though its pelt was transported in huge numbers to

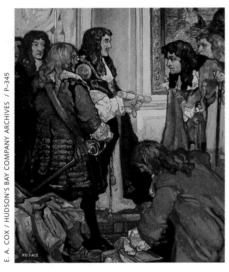

Charles II undoubtedly had no idea of the size or scope of the territory he was granting his cousin Rupert with the royal charter that created the Hudson's Bay Company, but this act was the first step along a long road that led to the creation of Canada.

London where it was auctioned and distributed to a voracious European market.

Six of the original HBC investors were on the King's Privy Council and eight members of the company were founding members of the Royal Society. To all intents and purposes, the HBC was an instrument of foreign trade policy in England. The king wanted money, and thus moved to issue a Royal Charter to the company in 1670. Four weeks later, a second pair of ships, the *Prince Rupert* and the *Wivenhoe*, set sail for Hudson Bay. They took care to leave the British Isles from the nearest point to Hudson's Bay, Stromness in Orkney. Meanwhile the seven committeemen met once a week in Rupert's lodgings in London and soon that city began to challenge Amsterdam, Paris and Vienna as the preeminent European fur centre.

At the outset, the sale of furs was split into two auctions "by candle". Each bundle of furs was auctioned for a set length of time, determined by a short length of candle. When the candle sputtered out, the person bidding at the time would receive the furs. The first auction was held at Thomas Garraway's Coffee House at No. 3 Exchange Alley, off Cornhill near the Royal Exchange, on January 24, 1672.

Soon a class of middlemen and fur brokers grew up in London. One of these was the Worshipful Company of Skinners of London, which bought skins in large lots and converted the fur into hat makers' "wool" to sell to hatters. Independent fur auction businesses began to appear in London and of these the longest-lasting and most celebrated was Samuel Robinson's, founded in 1730. During the Seven Years War,

Robinson auctioned the cargoes of captured French vessels from the fur trade; one of them, the *Sauvage*, with as many as 13,000 beaver skins aboard, later sold for £30,000.

By 1762, the action had moved over to the Pennsylvannia and Carolina Coffee House in Birchin Lane, run by an American, Edward Clarke. Clarke's coffee house lasted well into the next century though it changed names many times reflecting its owner's weather eye for new fur sources. It became the New York and Nova Scotia Coffee House, then the New York, Rhode Island and Nova Scotia Coffee House, but situated always in Sweeting's Alley by the Royal Exchange and "being one of the largest and most commodious of the coffee houses in London".

For 200 years spectacular fur auctions were managed by Robinson at rented space at the Steel Yard or Dyer's Hall or at No. 7 Sweeting's Alley. The coffee house was also used as a *poste restante* for merchants visiting from Canada and it became the first Canada Club in London, a clearing house for news, friendships and business.

The timing of the fur sale was crucial to success, both in attracting buyers and servicing the continent. Furs arrived from Canada with the fall fleet from Montreal and Hudson Bay, usually in early December or sometimes January. Three major sales occurred – in January, at the end of February and on the last Thursday in March. The second sale was timed to allow furs to be shipped to the Leipzig Easter Fair. Between 1760 and 1792, furs – not only beaver,

Prince Rupert was a young man when Anthony Van Dyck created this engraving, but already he had a range of interests that would later serve the fledgling Company of Adventurers well.

Familiar names from the days of the fur auctions abound in today's London, among them Exchange Alley, where the very first HBC auction was held at Garraway's Coffee House in 1672, and Birchin Lane, where Edward Clarke's popular establishment (with its revolving series of names) was the hot spot for fur buyers a century later.

STUART CLARKE

STUART CLARKE

but deerskins, marten, muskrat, raccoon and many other types of pelts – worth almost £6 million were sold between 1760 and 1792. Robinson (or his son and namesake) charged a brokerage fee of one per cent. By 1851, some have estimated that total HBC profits were in excess of £20 million.

After 1763 it was no longer possible for the HBC to crouch on the shores of Hudson Bay. Intense challenges from English, Scots and French free traders and, after 1779, the North West Company called for inland competition, which in turn demanded inland forts on inland waterways. Canadian author Peter Newman has pointed out that within 20 years of banding together the Nor' Westers controlled 78 per cent of Canadian fur sales and in retrospect it's hard to understand how the HBC survived and why in 1821 the Nor'Westers did not take over the combined companies in its own name instead of the reverse. The answer probably lies in the power of London's financial district to implement its own will, even half a world away.

Another possible reason for HBC staying power was the emergence, first as deputy governor and then as governor in London, of a remarkable businessman, lawyer and man of letters – Samuel Wegg. His father George Wegg became a Hudson's Bay stockholder in 1697 and the shares passed to Samuel on his father's death in 1748. Samuel thus was a stockholder from 1748-1799, a member of the committee from 1760 onward and finally deputy governor and, after 1774, governor for 17 years. His intellectual curiosity led him to

Samuel Wegg had been governor of the Hudson's Bay Company for more than a decade when this silhouette on glass was done.

become a member of the Royal Society, which actively cooperated with the HBC under his leadership. Later he joined a famous dining club called the Royal Philosophers or Thursday Club, which brought him into frequent social contact with many leading visitors to and citizens of London including Benjamin Franklin, Alexander Dalrymple and Captain Cook.

It is significant, writes Professor Richard Ruggles of Queen's University, that the four decades of Samuel Wegg's career as an executive member of the HBC exactly coincided with huge changes in the latter's trading practices. They included an increased awareness of the commercial value of an enhanced geographical knowledge of its trading area through exploration, survey and mapping, along with greater acceptance of a role in transmitting scientific information to the public.

In March 1795, while Wegg was governor, the company moved to a freehold property at Nos. 3 & 4 Fenchurch Street, where auctions were held through much of the next century. Before this move, the company's first official residence, from about 1682, was at Scrivener's Hall in Aldersgate, followed by a move in 1782 to Culver Court, Fenchurch Street. This latter address was across from the Elephant Inn, where the famous painter William Hogarth had earlier created a painting of London porters, who moved the bales of furs into the auction houses, going to dinner.

The building of inland posts in Canada necessitated a huge change of outlook by the company that was mirrored in London by Samuel Wegg and on the Hudson Bay by the appointment as governor of William Tomison, a reliable, intelligent Orkneyman who had risen from the lowest ranks of the company.

To learn more about the vast territory it had been bequeathed by charter, the London Committee hired Philip Turnor, a trained surveyor, in 1778. For the next 17 years, he extensively mapped the waterways along the coast and inland from Hudson Bay and trained others to do the same. To provide Turnor with at least minimally trained assistants, the company increased its intake of young apprentices from the London charity schools and provided its employees with a stock of surveying instruments with which to measure direction and distance and assist with drawing maps and plans. Finally, the HBC paid for extra services and for promoting its policies. One of the largest of these bonus payments was the £200 paid to Samuel Hearne in 1773 for the epic journey he undertook to the Coppermine River three years earlier.

Under Wegg's stewardship the company abandoned its policies of

secrecy and afforded certain explorers and scientists access to its state-of-the-art information and data. It is also probable that Wegg was influential in encouraging the collection of animal and bird specimens of the Hudson Bay area undertaken by Andrew Graham. One thing is certain: in Samuel Wegg the HBC benefited greatly from the services and leadership of an unusual and farsighted man, the type we might today call a Renaissance man, in a signal period of its illustrious history.

One wonders whether Prince Rupert and his fellow investors ever dreamed that their company would become a kingdom unto itself. Its enormous territory, Rupert's Land, which included the entire Hudson Bay drainage system, covered 43 per cent of what was later to be the total territory of Canada. Prince Rupert was governor from 1670 to 1682 and after two bumpy years under the king's brother James, Duke of York, the company had another effective governor in John, Lord Churchill, later Duke of Marlborough, who presided between 1685 and 1692.

This watercolored pen and ink drawing of the Hudson's Bay Company's armorial bearings was created in 1921; other, earlier versions were even more ornate.

In 1782, the London committee moved to Fenchurch Street, where this watercolor of Hudson's Bay House was painted in 1845.

CITY OF LONDON

FENCHURCH STREET EC3

← 13 - 90   1 - 12 →

STUART CLARKE

Since 1670, 35 governors have presided over the Hudson's Bay Company operations. Recent incumbents are Canadian, but it was 264 years before the first London governor, Lord Amory, actually visited Rupert's Land in 1934.

In addition to Samuel Wegg, other strong governors emerged at crucial junctures. After the great rivalry between the North West Company and

Beaver House, in Great Trinity Lane over the Mansion House Station on Garlick Hill in the City. On the company's 255th birthday, in 1925, the new building was opened with much fanfare by Governor Sir Robert Kindersley. Over the main doorway the HBC coat of arms was carved in bas relief, with the centre window containing a maple leaf for Canada and an oak leaf for

The only headquarters building actually constructed by the HBC, Beaver House in Great Trinity Lane, was demolished after being transferred to the Government of Canada. Today, the Bank of Canada, right, sits on the same site.

STUART CLARKE

the HBC came to a head in 1821, Sir John Pelly was governor from 1822 to 1852, while George Simpson ruled with an iron hand in Canada. In the last year but one of his governorship, Sir John Pelly presided over a Hudson's Bay Company of 152 posts, 45 chief factors, five surgeons, 154 clerks and postmasters, 1,200 post employees or "servants" and the crews of the inland canoes, the York boats and the sea-going supply ships. This vast fur empire was directed from London, yet there is little left to commorate this era of power and prestige in the City of London today.

During the 1920s the company decided to erect its first real headquarters,

England. The building was used as the company headquarters until it was transfered to Canada in 1970 after which, sadly, Beaver House was torn down.

Today, little remains in London of the great fur empire of the bay, though the interested visitor can visit Prince Rupert's grave in Westminster Abbey, and Grey Coat Hospital, now a state school for girls but otherwise largely unchanged over the centuries. One can also tour the City of London, taking in the Royal Exchange and noticing the huge silhouette of Sir Christopher Wren's St. Paul's Cathedral. The rest of fur trade London must be left to the imagination of informed time travellers.

LONDON STATE SCHOOLS CONNECT WITH CANADA

In the 18th century, charity schools – called "hospitals" – were championed by the English middle class in order to "prevent irreligion and pauperism" in London, and to create opportunities for apprenticeship for boys and girls so that they could live "good, industrious lives".

Early in the history of the HBC, the decision was made to train some of its servants by the apprenticeship system and by 1684 there were 10 apprentices on the rolls. Two institutions were of particular benefit to the company: the prestigious Christ's Hospital, the Blue Coat school near St. Paul's Cathedral in the City and the Grey Coat Hospital of the Royal Foundation of Queen Anne Street, Westminister. The former was an old establishment, begun in 1553. Its mathematical school, endowed by Charles II in 1673, drew some of the brightest students – the King's Boys – and provided eight well-schooled apprentices to the Hudson's Bay Company between 1680 and 1717. Christ's Hospital numbered among its early governors such luminaries as Samuel Pepys, Sir Issac Newton and Sir Christopher Wren.

The Grey Coat Hospital was younger, established in 1698, and more modest. However it sent more apprentices to the HBC – a total of 11 in its first century – and it continues today as a school that still provides a focus on maths and science. Since 1874, the students have all been female.

David Thompson was undoubtedly the best known HBC graduate of the Grey Coat Hospital, as today's students are well aware. In 1998, a number of senior students celebrated their school's achievements, its most illustrious graduate and connection to Canada by travelling to British Columbia and canoeing part of the Thompson River.

STUART CLARKE

The entrance of the Grey Coat Hospital is graced by two figures that accurately represent the school's 300-year history in instructing first boys and then girls. There should, perhaps, be a small maple leaf somewhere, to recognize the impact graduates of the school have had on Canada. But even without a Canadian symbol, Grey Coat students are aware of the school's history, as was made evident in 1998 when a group of them paddled the Thompson River, below, to honor alumnus David Thompson.

PETER ST. JOHN

The English on the Bay

The interest and support of Prince Rupert, cousin to Charles II, were key to the involvement of the English on Hudson Bay. And from his first meeting with Médard Chouart des Groseilliers and Pierre-Esprit Radisson late in 1666, Rupert was interested and supportive. The picture the brothers-in-law painted fascinated this man of ideas and imagination. A syndicate to finance an exploratory venture into the bay was quickly organized and two ships were acquired. A two-masted ketch, the *Eaglet*, was leased from the king and a smaller ketch, the *Nonsuch*, was purchased for less than £300. Both were outfitted and made ready to sail in the spring of 1668.

The plan was for the larger ship to winter over on the bay and the smaller to return home with the furs traded during the summer, but it didn't quite work out that way. The *Eaglet*, though larger, was low amidship and was nearly swamped in a storm off Iceland. The sturdy little *Nonsuch*, captained by Zachariah Gillam, sailed on alone through Hudson Strait. Following the path Henry Hudson had taken nearly 60 years before, she traced the eastern shore of Hudson and James Bays to the

DENNIS FAST

Polar bears (Ursus maritinus), *among the world's largest carnivors, are synonymous with Hudson Bay. Though they can appear playful as they wait for the bay to freeze, the bear the Cree call* Wapusk *and the Inuit know as* Nanuk *is lightning fast, enormously strong and completely unpredictable.*

mouth of the Rupert River at the southeastern corner. With most of the supplies for the winter aboard the *Eaglet*, the venture might have turned sour as had so many other European attempts to winter in this unforgiving land. But aboard the *Nonsuch* was des Groseilliers, perhaps the most experienced and successful independent fur trader then alive. In short order the crew had constructed a small wintering house, dug a cellar below the frost line to store food and beer and purchased geese and fish from the local Mistassini Cree. Des Groseilliers knew that native North Americans held the key to success on the continent and, like John Rae nearly 200 years later, he emulated and befriended them wherever he went.

Not long before, Europeans had died in droves of scurvy during the long North American winters, but des Groseilliers made the men drink his evil-tasting concoction of spruce beer, a trick he'd learned from the Cree. That and fresh meat obtained by hunting caribou, ptarmigan, rabbits and moose saw them through until spring. In May the Mistassini people came back down the river with canoes full of pelts and by October the ship was home to appraise Rupert and the syndicate that, as promised, a land of gold – thick, lustrous gold – lay within England's reach.

King Charles responded by presenting Rupert and his friends with the largest land grant the world had known in the royal charter that created the

"Governor and Company of Adventurers of England trading into Hudson's Bay". The award encompassed Hudson Bay and all the land that drained into it – nearly half of today's Canada as well as a large portion of North Dakota and Minnesota, though no one at the time had any idea of the extent of the land involved.

That the king and the Privy Council had neither the right nor the authority to award such territory, and that thousands of people living on the lands thus carelessly transferred were never contemplated, let alone consulted, seem to have entirely escaped everyone involved. Steeped in a culture of European dominance and entitlement, they likely never even considered the

Without question commerce and the notion of containing the French on the St. Lawrence were the primary motivations behind the charter, but there were also several clauses concerning the establishment of "Plantacions or Colonyes in America called Rupert's Land". Six of the 18 "Adventurers" had earlier been involved in establishing the colony of Carolina, where business and plantations went hand in glove.

In the first few years, the fledgling company did well under its newly-annointed governor on the bay, a Quaker named Charles Bayley with a singular past. In the early years, des Groseilliers and Radisson aided the establishment of posts – Charles Fort (soon renamed Rupert's House and now

BARBARA ENDRES

question. But the ramifications of this and other Eurocentric decisions over the next 250 years continue to haunt Canada today.

known as Waskaganish) on the Rupert River, and Moose Fort, on an island in the Moose River (see page 120), but in 1674, frustrated by English reluctance

(see page 120)

The Nonsuch

A replica of the Nonsuch was built for the HBC's 300th anniversary in 1970.

Transported to Canada by cargo ship, the replica was refitted on the St. Lawrence in Quebec. She spent the next three years sailing the Great Lakes, before being converted in Superior, Wisconsin, into a flatbed trailer. Turned on her side, with wheels added, the little ship was towed across the United States to Seattle. There she spent a summer on the Pacific coasts of Washington and British Columbia, before being brought overland once more to Winnipeg, where a wing of the Manitoba Museum of Man and Nature was built around her.

What must the Mistassini Cree have thought as the Nonsuch sailed up the Rupert River in the fall of 1668, and a small party of Englishmen began building a log tent on the shore? The Cree knew better than to spend the long, cold winter at the edge of the bay and as they packed to move inland, they must have wondered about the wisdom of the newcomers.

The willow ptarmigan, caught in the act of changing its seasonal plumage, lives by the bay year-round, wintering along the coast in willow thickets or windswept tundra. For nearly 100 years, the range of the Hudson's Bay Company was much the same. Establishing a series of posts on the major rivers along the coast, the company was content to wait for convoys of Cree and Ojibwe trappers and traders to make their way down from the hinterlands, their canoes loaded with furs.

to move inland to trade directly with Cree and Ojibwe trappers, the two Frenchmen allowed themselves to be wooed back to New France.

There, they assisted in the establishment of La Compagnie du Nord and in 1682 sailed to Hudson Bay to establish the company's first post on the Nelson River. Arriving on the bay, they managed to intimidate both a party of New England traders and the English at the newly constructed York Fort, confiscate their furs and sail away to the St. Lawrence. Yet once again the brothers-in-law had their property confiscated and their furs heavily taxed. Des Groseilliers retired in disgust, while Radisson changed his stripes one last time.

On the bay, meanwhile, such French outlawry was decried, but life went on. The committee in London was happy with returns and in 1683 sent out not only a new bayside gover-

nor, Henry Sargent, but his wife and young son, her female companion, a chaplain and several male servants. As it had for nearly a decade, the company also sent seeds along with the trade goods, with instructions for each post to "apply your selfe to trey in all places were we ar settled what the earth will bring forth". Though the efforts at gardening had varying degrees of success over the next 200 years, the Sargent family comprised the only real English attempt at settlement in Rupert's Land for more than a century.

The Sargents and their entourage wintered at Moose Fort and then made their way to Fort Albany, newly constructed on the south side of the Albany River. There, for two years, they tried to create a speck of English domesticity on the western James Bay shore. Then, in the spring of 1686, Chevalier Pierre de Troyes and a small army of French and Algonquian warriors suddenly appeared on the Moose River one morning in late June, having come overland all the way from Montréal. They took the English at Moose Fort completely by surprise.

In quick succession, Charles Fort and the supply ship *Craven* were captured; fitting the ship with a cannon from the fort, de Troyes sailed on to Albany, arriving in mid-July. Governor Sargent, apparently unaware of what had transpired, welcomed the familiar ship by firing guns of greeting and then, despite musket fire from the ship, apparently gathered his family for dinner. As a servant poured the wine, a cannon ball passed under his arm. Another sailed past Mrs. Sargent's face, causing her to faint. Sargent quickly surrendered Moose and Charles Forts on the Bottom of the Bay; these the French held until 1713 when

EARLY
HUDSON BAY FORTS

Hudson Strait

Hudson Bay

PRINCE OF WALES' FORT

Churchill River

YORK FORT

YORK FACTORY

NEW SEVERN HOUSE

James Bay

Charlton Island

FORT ALBANY

Lake Winnipeg

MOOSE FORT

CHARLES FORT

DENNIS FAST

DENNIS FAST

all French possessions were returned as part of the terms of the Treaty of Utrecht.

The following winter was difficult, to say the least. The English were taken to Charlton Island, a desolate chunk of land in eastern James Bay, to await the English supply ship, while De Troyes set off overland for Québec, leaving Pierre le Moyne d'Iberville in charge. The supply ship failed to reach the bottom of the bay, however, and supplies were short in the extreme. With little food and only 40 French soldiers to watch 52 prisoners, d'Iberville put Sargent and 30 men on an HBC yacht and sent them off to winter at posts still in English hands. They sailed to York Fort, then on the Nelson River, but the influx was too much for the little post to manage, so a handful of men were sent south along the bay to an even smaller outpost – New Severn on the Severn River.

The remaining 21 Englishmen were left on Charlton Island to fend for themselves. Loath to spend the winter there, they cobbled together a raft and sailed to Moose Fort, where d'Iberville was less than delighted to see them.

Giving them guns and nets, he turned them out to hunt for themselves and persuaded the local Cree to take a dozen or so in for the winter.

Somehow, this hardy band of refugees all survived and the following summer was sent overland to Québec. At York Fort, meanwhile, 20 of Sargent's 30 men died before spring.

For the next decade, the English hung on to York Fort, continuing to trade with the Cree in a large territory in what is now Manitoba and even, in 1690, sending young Henry Kelsey inland with some homeward-bound Assiniboine. Though he was less than precise about where he went, it is widely believed that he travelled west at least as far as the lower Saskatchewan River, where he saw great herds of bison.

But the French, and particularly d'Iberville, were not finished on the bay. Named commander-in-chief of Hudson Bay before he was 30, d'Iberville found the English presence at the mouth of the Nelson River a continuing irritant. Finally in 1697, he was authorized to end the English occupation. Sailing to the bay,

Exploring the Fur Trade Routes of North America

his ships were icebound for three weeks in Hudson Strait. Finally, aboard the 44-gun *Pélican*, d'Iberville struggled free and reached York Fort in early September. Having left the rest of his fleet behind in the ice, he reconnoitred the fort while waiting for the other ships to join him. Spotting sails on the horizon, he raised anchor to meet them. But when they came near, he saw they were English, not French ships – two armed freighters and a Royal Navy frigate.

Outgunned more than two to one and hugely outmanned, d'Iberville fought with savage fury. When the four-hour battle was over, the *Pélican* had somehow overcome the impossible odds. The English frigate had been sunk, one freighter had fled and the other had surrendered. With the exception of Fort Albany, where an English presence continued, the French controlled trade on Hudson Bay for 16 years.

At war's end, the British found little to save around the bay. The small post at Churchill had been burned and York Fort was little more than a collection of hovels. In the fall of 1714, James

Knight was sent by the HBC to begin work on a new post on the Hayes River, which provided a more accessible route to the interior. He also began to cast about for a way to increase trade with the Dene to the north, whose fear of the well-armed Cree kept them from travelling to York to trade.

Looking for a liaison, Knight recruited a young Dene woman who had been captured by the Cree. Her success at establishing peace between the Cree and the Dene in the spring of 1715 did much to ensure a productive trade at the post he established the following year at the mouth of the Churchill River.

Within two decades, all the old posts had been renewed and fortified and for more than a half-century, the English were largely content to wait by the bay for the annual fleets of Cree and Ojibwe to descend the rivers, their canoes loaded with furs. Only the posts at the Bottom of the Bay made an effort to meet the native traders part way, and then because French *coureurs de bois* were siphoning off the furry bounty at an alarming rate.

At Albany in the spring of 1743, post master Joseph Isbister wrote, "these french fellows is not above 60 mile up this river." Without consultation with London, which would have taken at least a year, he decided to build an outpost, more showroom than trading establishment, at the junction of the Albany and Kenogami Rivers.

Because the Albany was broad and shallow and the post was located a considerable distance upstream, it was difficult to service and supply the new outpost, Henley House, with small Algonquian canoes. To remedy the problem Isbister, an Orcadian with long experience around small boats, designed a craft suitable for the job – the Henley barge. The first flat-bottomed boat was

Though outmanned and outgunned, the French warship Pélican *managed to sink the English frigate* Hampshire *in the Battle of the Bay in 1697.*

NORMAN WILKINSON / HUDSON'S BAY COMPANY ARCHIVES / P–401

produced in the fall of 1745, long predating the York boats, which were also inspired by Orkney vessels, that eventually carried most of the freight for the Hudson's Bay Company.

Encroaching thus on territory the French considered to be theirs, Henley House was an isolated target and was twice attacked and destroyed in the 1750s. Despite these setbacks, the Hudson's Bay Company policy of trading on the bay was slowly changing. By the early 1750s the company was feeling the effects of increased French trade even west of the bay in Manitoba. James Isham, post master at York at the time, wrote to the London Committee to suggest that a post be created far inland, at Cumberland Lake perhaps, to take the trade away from the French. The committee demurred, but agreed with Isham's other suggestion, to send "a proper person" inland with inducements to draw the Cree and nations farther west down to trade.

Isham chose Anthony Henday, an English netmaker (and one-time smuggler) who had proven to be an adept traveller, largely it appears because Henday volunteered. Escorted by Cree and Blackfoot guides, Henday's journey in 1754 and 1755 took him right across the plains to the foot of the Rockies in what is today western Alberta. But the Blackfoot were not on the whole interested in making the long and tedious trip to the bay. Though Henday never felt that his efforts were properly appreciated, his travels did begin a new phase in company policy. In succeeding years, a half-dozen others, including Joseph Smith, Joseph Waggoner, Matthew Cocking and William Tomison (see page 167) were sent inland to trade and try to coax trappers down to the bay.

The company's real move inland didn't occur until its livelihood was seriously threatened, however. Perhaps because it was directed by men who had never visited North America and whose most intimate contact with the trade was the fur auctions in London, the Hudson's Bay Company was strangely unresponsive to the changes in the "Nor'Wast", as the increasingly Orcadian employee base called it. Though licensed French traders left the country after 1763, by mid-decade they were replaced by even more ambitious French-Canadian, English, Scots and New England free traders. Finally, faced with "the pedlars swarming" upcountry and "overrunning Rupert's Land", the HBC made its first, tentative step toward what was eventually to be a continent-wide network of posts with the construction in 1774 of Cumberland House (see page 165) on Cumberland Lake in what is now northern Saskatchewan.

Their tents stretching almost to the horizon, the Kainai welcomed the Hudson's Bay Company's Anthony Henday to their central Alberta homeland in 1755, as portrayed here in the First Contact Diorama at the Provincial Museum of Alberta.

Superb bison hunters with roots deep in the western plains, the Kainai and other members of the Blackfoot Confederacy had little use for the fur trade for nearly a half-century. Eventually, when posts were established on the fringes of their territory, they did a brisk trade in buffalo hides and pemmican for the European goods they desired.

Churchill

by Michael Payne

DENNIS FAST

Prince of Wales' Fort, above, seems an impregnable stronghold, but it was immediately surrendered the only time it was ever challenged.

Every spring white beluga whale mothers and their gray calves gather in the river estuaries along the bay. Protected today, they were hunted in the 19th century.

The archaeological sites at Seahorse Gully and other locations near Churchill offer clear evidence why the Hudson's Bay Company established a post here. Aboriginal people, including the Cree, Dene and Inuit, have used the area for thousands of years. Churchill's location at the mouth of the Churchill River on Hudson Bay, at the transition between tundra and boreal forest, meant that it offered access to a remarkable variety of resources from caribou and arctic fox to beluga whales and char. These resources attracted aboriginal groups to the coast as part of their seasonal round, and in turn these potential trading partners drew the Hudson's Bay Company to Churchill.

The first attempt to establish a post at Churchill in 1689 was a dismal failure; the post burned while still under construction. By the early 18th century, however, the HBC was ready to try again. James Knight, who was sent to reestablish York Fort in 1714, was particularly interested in expanding trade with "Northern Indians" or Dene. Unfortunately, the Dene were reluctant to visit York because of the hostility of the "Southern Indians" or Cree. A post at Churchill would help solve this problem, as well as offer prospects for trade with the Inuit and perhaps a whaling operation. Knight was also fascinated by stories of rich mineral deposits in the north and thought a post at Churchill would serve as a base for exploration. Indeed, he would

later die on Marble Island north of Churchill in a vain search for those gold and copper mines.

In 1715-16 Knight sent William Stuart and a Dene woman, Thanadelthur, north with a group of Cree to arrange a peace with the Dene. Thanks in large measure to Thanadelthur's efforts, the expedition was a success, and a post was built at the mouth of the Churchill River in 1717. The new post was officially named Prince of Wales' Fort in 1719. Although trade was never as great as Knight had hoped, the fort averaged returns of well over 10,000 Made Beaver per year up to 1782.

In 1730, the company's London Committee decided to construct a large stone fortress at Churchill. No one knows why this decision was taken, though some historians have speculated that the HBC planned to use Churchill and its excellent harbor as a defensible place of refuge in the event of another war with France. According to this view, under threat of attack the HBC could abandon its other posts on Hudson Bay and move its employees and goods to Churchill. So long as the HBC retained at least one post on the bay, it would be able to demand some recompense at any peace treaty, as had happened in the Treaty of Utrecht in 1713.

In truth, however, building a stone fortress at Churchill was an expensive and rather dubious plan. Company officials later calculated that they had spent between £30,000 and £40,000 on the fort, a staggering sum at a time when the entire company was only capitalized at just over £100,000. The extreme weather conditions at Churchill meant that the walls needed regular repair and

DENNIS FAST

construction lagged. As a result, work began on the new fort in 1731 and continued until at least 1771. In addition, the fortress had design flaws. There was no interior well, meaning it could not have withstood much of a siege, and the walls were initially much too narrow.

Still, Prince of Wales' Fort seemed imposing. A square fortress with walls about 90 metres long and 3 metres high, it boasted corner bastions and 42 cannon. A battery to house additional cannon was also built across the river at Cape Merry. Properly manned with trained troops, the fort and battery would have made it very difficult for any enemy to enter the mouth of the Churchill River. Unfortunately the men who served at Prince of Wales' Fort were not trained artillerymen, and most had little desire to risk their lives in battle defending furs and trade goods. When a French naval squadron did attack in 1782, the officer in charge at Churchill, Samuel Hearne, surrendered without firing a shot. With just 39 men at the post, Hearne, who had seen active service with the Royal Navy and knew just how overwhelming the French force was, realized that the situation was hopeless. The French destroyed the fort and took Hearne and his men prisoner before sailing on to York Fort, which was also captured. The fort at Churchill remained a ruin until the 1930s when the Government of Canada began restoration work on it. It was declared a national historic park in 1941 and is now open to the public. The destruction of Prince of Wales'

Fort did not end the Hudson's Bay Company's interest in Churchill, however. In 1783 Hearne returned to reopen the post. He eventually selected a new site about four kilometres upriver. This new post was renamed Fort Churchill and it served as the base for HBC operations in the area until about 1930, when the arrival of the railway led to the moving of Churchill townsite to its current location across the river. The new Fort Churchill never achieved the trade success of Prince of Wales' Fort largely because the HBC was expanding its network of posts inland after 1774. With posts much closer to home, the Dene had little interest in making the long trip overland to Churchill. Instead the new post served a smaller local population of Cree, along with some Dene and Inuit who remained in the area. George Simpson estimated in the mid-19th century that about 400 people regularly traded at Churchill.

By 1879, George Simpson McTavish noted that the name Fort Churchill was "very imposing", but that the reality was a "dilapidated hamlet .... Wooden pickets or stockades [surround] the few houses" and enclose "less than two acres of ground". Despite this, McTavish also described a lively community of mixed Cree, Inuit, Dene, Orkney and Scots background that survived well into the 20th century, based on an economy of furs and whaling.

When Prince of Wales' Fort, left, was first built, the rampart inside the outer wall was only about 7.5 metres wide. When a cannon was test fired on the rampart it recoiled so far that it fell into the courtyard. The interior wall had to be rebuilt and the ramparts widened to more than 12 metres across.

Samuel Hearne was among those who carved their names in the granite at Sloop Cove, where the company once moored its small sailing boats or sloops. Because of isostatic uplift, the cove, just upstream from the fort, is now a meadow.

Exploring the Fur Trade Routes of North America

CHURCHILL'S DENE DIPLOMAT

Women played an enormous, but largely ignored, role in both the European penetration of North America and the fur trade that propelled it. Because they were not paid employees of the fur trade companies, they were mentioned in the journals only when their activities were truly heroic. Thanadelthur was one of these outstanding women, though in 1715, when she proved herself one of the outstanding diplomats in fur trade history, she was hardly more than a girl.

When the Treaty of Utrecht (1713) temporarily ended hostilities between the English and French, the Hudson's Bay Company returned to the bay eager to extend its trading territory north into country inhabited by the Dene, an Athapaskan-speaking people that the English called *Chipewyan*. But, fearful of the well-armed and hostile Cree on their southern border, the Dene showed no inclination to make the trip to the bayside fur posts. Arriving at York Fort in 1714, James Knight determined to somehow end hostilities between the two nations and draw the Dene in to trade. In November, while he was mulling over the means to do this, some of his goose hunters arrived at the post with a woman called Thanadelthur, who was "Allmost Starved".

In her seminal book on women in the fur trade, *Many Tender Ties*, University of Toronto history professor Sylvia Van Kirk told the remarkable story of Thanadelthur, whom many called "the Slave Woman". She had been captured by the Cree in a raid on her family's Dene camp in 1713 and kept as a slave for more than a year.

Late in 1714, she and another woman escaped their Cree captors and headed north to find their people. With only the clothes they were wearing and small snares to catch game, they were soon in desperate straights. When the other woman died, Thanadelthur turned back in despair, hoping to encounter the English with whom the Cree traded. Crossing the Nelson and Hayes Rivers, she stumbled, barely alive, into a goose hunting camp on Ten Shilling Creek.

Despite her condition, Knight was immediately struck by Thanadelthur's "extraordinary vivacity" and keen intelligence and, as soon as she had recovered, he decided to send her with one of his men, William Stuart, and as many Cree as could be persuaded to go, on a peace mission to the Dene.

Accordingly, in late June, Thanadelthur and Stuart set out with a delegation of about 150. The party spent most of a year on the tundra, covering hundreds of kilometres and the long trek took its toll. Food was in short supply and several expedition

A number of willow species grow in the region around Churchill and were widely used by the Dene for purposes as diverse as children's toys and topical coagulents. Tubes of willow bark were made into children's whistles, or straws for drinking water from a stream, while willow leaves, chewed to a paste were found to stop bleeding or reduce the swelling of insect bites. Young leaves and buds are rich in Vitamin C and were eaten raw or boiled.

LINDA FAIRFIELD

56

members fell sick. To survive, the large party broke up and over the months many turned back. In the end, the party was reduced to Thanadelthur and Stuart, along with the Cree leader and about 12 of his people. Then, nearing their destination, they came across the bodies of nine Dene, apparently killed by marauding Cree. Terrified that they might be blamed for the deaths, the men refused to go any farther.

When attempts to persuade them to continue failed, Thanadelthur extracted one last concession; if they would make camp and wait for 10 days, she would find her people and bring them back to make peace. Then, alone, she struck out over the barrens and within a few days came upon several hundred Dene.

AMANDA DOW

Convincing them to return with her was not easy; Stuart later reported that she made herself hoarse "with perpetuall talking", until more than a hundred finally agreed to accompany her. In true epic fashion, she and two emissaries sighted the Cree camp on the 10th day.

Negotiating between the parties, she "made them all Stand in fear of her she Scolded at Some and pushing of others and forced them to ye peace," Stuart reported. Then, heading a delegation of 10 Dene, including her brother, she led them back to York Fort in May 1716.

At the post, she quickly became one of Knight's chief advisors. Seeking her thoughts on a variety of plans, he found her to be one of the most remarkable people he had ever encountered. And when she fell ill early in 1717, he was nearly frantic. She, on the other hand, responded in characteristic fashion. Realizing she was dying, she spent hours teaching one of the young HBC men to speak Dene, so that he could take her place.

When she died in early February, Knight was nearly inconsolable. "She was," he wrote, "one of a Very high Spirit and of the Firmest Resolution that ever I see any Body in my Days and of great Courage & forecast."

" *Indeed She has a Devillish Spirit and I believe that if thare were but 50 of her Country Men of the same Carriage and Resolution they would drive all the [Cree] in America out of there Country.*"

William Stuart.

Orkney

by The Earl of Orkney

As Isaac Cowie wrote in *The Company of Adventurers* in 1913, "Orkney has a romantic history

PETER ST. JOHN

Archaeologists are not certain who the inhabitants of Skara Brae, above, were, but their level of sophistication is clear even now, 5,500 years after the first inhabitants lived here. The village has recently been declared a World Heritage Site.

of great antiquity". Others claim that Orkney's 74 islands have the greatest concentration of Neolithic remains in Europe. Among the finest is the village of Skara Brae, discovered almost whole following a storm in 1850 and thereby establishing settlement on Orkney to at least 5,500 years ago. These sophisticated early residents – the village houses are complete with shelving units, wall nooks and are connected by covered passages – also constructed enormous stone rings, which still stand today on Orkney's main island – The Mainland. More than 1,000 years ago, the then Pictish community was invaded by the Norse.

Norse rule created a population apart from the rest of the British Isles and a link with Norway that continues even today. Orkney also has binding connections to France; the earls of Orkney and dukes of Norway were descended from the Norse earl Rolf Rognvaldson of Möre. In fact, in the first centuries of Norse rule, Orkney wielded more power through its *yarls* or earls than the king of Scotland.

This singular history has produced a rational, independent citizenry that is egalitarian in outlook and perfectly at home abroad. These qualities, along with Orkney's geographic location off Scotland's north coast, almost directly east of Greenland's southern tip, made the islands an obvious watering and provisioning point for voyagers heading west and – after 1702 – for fur traders in search of recruits.

In the late 16th century Martin Frobisher stopped at Orkney on his voyages of exploration. During the English-French wars of the 17th and 18th centuries, the need to avoid travel into the Altantic via the English Channel enhanced Orkney's strategic location. Ships sailing up Britain's eastern seaboard could slip into Scapa Flow, Orkney's great natural harbor, which afforded fine anchorage off the port of Stromness. Perched on Hamnavoe or "Haven Bay", Stromness has long served as a gateway to the west. From there, generations of Hudson's Bay ships would make for the southern tip of

Greenland and Davis Strait en route to the posts on Hudson Bay. In time of war, merchantmen assembled in Stromness harbor waiting to be escorted by ships of the Royal Navy. Whalers and sealers set out from here for Greenland, as did Arctic adventurers intent on the search for the Northwest Passage. The British ships *Erebus* and *Terror*, bearing Sir John Franklin on his ill-fated last voyage, left from Stromness after watering at Login's Well.

In 1702, an HBC ship bound for the bay stopped, as usual, for water and fresh provisions and engaged a few likely looking lads. Orcadians were hardy men ashore, good fishermen, splendid boatmen, strong, hardy and obedient to authority. The qualities that eventually made them excellent lighthouse keepers were equally appropriate in a cramped inland fur trading post on the bay. Even better, they were more sober and tractable that the Irish and would engage for lower wages than either the English or the Scots: £6 per annum in the 1790s. By 1730, recruitment was a regular feature

of the stop at Stromness. And for nearly 200 years, until the eve of the First World War, Orcadians joined the company ranks in large numbers.

Other organizations also noticed the stellar qualities of Orcadians. During the Napoleonic Wars (1796-1815), the British Navy often visited Orkney to pressgang local sailors into service. Mothers resorted to hiding their children in caves to avoid the Royal Navy's predations. So devastating was the drain on Orkney manpower that 14-year-olds would end up "thankfully" on the bay. But at least many could read and write, where often the Scots and English boys could not, so they made good keepers of post journals and meticulous employees.

Between 1772 and 1800, writes Orkney historian James Troup, the HBC labor force grew from 181, mainly on the bay, to 592 spread across the country to the Rocky Mountains. Of the larger number fully three-quarters were Orcadian. Philip Turnor, an Englishman and the first HBC surveyor, observed that "Orcadians are a set of the best men I ever saw together, as they are obliging, hardy, good canoe men." They were also esteemed by the Cree and Dene, whose languages they learned with relative ease and with whom they freely intermarried.

The Ring of Brogar, below, which dates to approximately the same period as the village of Skara Brae, is a marvel of engineering. Originally comprised of 60 massive stones in a huge circle, the monument was encircled by burial grounds. Visitors today often say they can feel these ancient spirits, but for Orcadians such antiquity is commonplace.

PETER ST .JOHN

Though a thoroughly modern community today, Stromness is in many ways unchanged from the height of the fur trade, when so many young men from the islands left for the "Ould Nor'Wast". When their service was over, many stayed in Canada, which now has an Orcadian population many times larger than Orkney's 20,500 inhabitants.

PETER ST. JOHN

Sir John Franklin expressed wonderment at how the Orcadians, often wet to the skin, could manoeuvre and paddle company boats with good humor, hour after hour, day after day. The only other comparable group was French-Canadian voyageurs.

In Volume I of his *Company of Adventurers*, Peter Newman quoted Bernard de Voto's evocative description of Orcadians as "constituting a legion of brave and hardy men who pulled the wilderness round them like a cloak, and wore its beauty like a crest."

As the fur trade stretched along the rivers and across the lakes of what is now Canada, canoes gave way to York boats to carry growing loads of goods. York boats were designed on the basis of the contemporary Orkney yole, which in turn was descended from Norse inshore craft.

The strategic use of Stromness as a provisioning point for the bay was bound to impact the town itself. For 200 years Login's Well, situated on the main street opposite Login's Inn, supplied water to the ships of the HBC, as well as Captain Cook's ships *Resolution* and *Discovery*. The well was sealed in 1931, but attractively enough that it is much photographed by fur trade *aficionados*.

Farther down the main street on Stanger's Brae is a cannon reported to be from the American privateer *Liberty*, which was captured in 1813. Brought back to Orkney and installed above the harbor, it was used to signal the arrival of the Hudson's Bay Company ships.

In 1702, Captain Grimmington of the HBC was authorized to secure in Stromness 10 or 12 "stout, able young men" to help on the bay. Two years later, 24 more men were needed, as well as two tailors. By the Act of Union between England and Scotland in 1707 (Orkney has been rather reluctantly part of Scotland since 1468), the floodgates to Orkney employment opened. In 1791, David Geddes was appointed agent for the HBC in Stromness; he continued in the post until 1812, doing £2,000 to £3,000 worth of business annually,

ORKNEY

Papa Westray
North Ronaldsay
Westray
Sanday
Eda
Rousay
Stronsay
SKARA BRAE
Mainland
RING OF BRODGAR
Shapinsay
John Rae's Grave
STROMNESS
KIRKWALL
Stromness Museum
Scapa Flow
Hoy
Barray
Flotta
South Ronaldsay
Tomison Centre
SCOTLAND

according to James Troup, at a time when only £2,000 pounds worth of goods were being shipped from Stromness.

Keeping the position in the family, George Geddes succeeded as HBC agent between 1812 and 1819, when John Rae, father of Dr. John Rae, the Arctic explorer, took over as agent in charge until 1836. Each in turn owned the premises called The Haven on the Stromness waterfront. Later, in 1851, Lady Franklin lived here during Rae's search for the Franklin expedition.

Dr. John Rae was born near Orphir in a beautiful home called the Hall of Clestrain that is still standing today, but badly in need of repair and restoration. His truly remarkable career as post master of various HBC posts, medical doctor, and famous northern adventurer and mapper has not until very recently been appreciated or even understood.

Research done by Canadian author Ken McGoogan has shown that Rae not only discovered the fate of the Franklin expedition, but also established beyond doubt which waterway (Rae Strait) completed the Northwest Passage.

An unusual marble memorial in ancient St. Magnus Cathedral in Kirkwall, Orkney's capital, has Dr. Rae stretched out on the ground with his gun beside him, as he might have slept in the "Nor'Wast".

John Rae, Sr. was instructed by the HBC to start recruiting early in the year, before the whaling ships arrived with their voracious appetites for men. Sometimes 700 men in one year were recruited by the whalers until the collapse of whaling after the 1830s.

As the years passed, growing numbers of Orcadian men opted to remain in Canada, but a substantial number returned to Orkney when their term of employment was finished. As James Troup has written, "the return of the HBC men was anxiously anticipated as they were generally men for purchasing and men of money". Unable to spend their money on the bay, Orcadians would frequently come home with several years' wages, with which they would buy or rent a farm or start a business. Isaac Cowie, for instance, recalls a large colony of Orcadians known as the peerie ("small")

This plaque next to Login's Well lists just a few of the many ships that stopped at Stromness for water over the centuries.

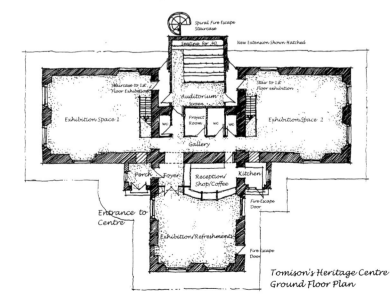

Tomison's Heritage Centre Ground Floor Plan

Tomison's Heritage Centre (the ground floor plan is shown at left), in Tomison's Academy will celebrate the life of Governor William Tomison (see page 167) and the strong ties between Orkney and Canada.

Exploring the Fur Trade Routes of North America

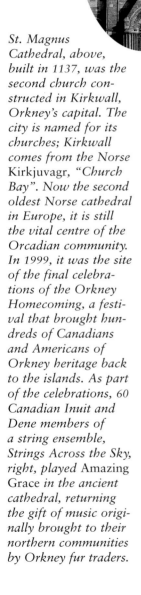

St. Magnus Cathedral, above, built in 1137, was the second church constructed in Kirkwall, Orkney's capital. The city is named for its churches; Kirkwall comes from the Norse Kirkjuvagr, "Church Bay". Now the second oldest Norse cathedral in Europe, it is still the vital centre of the Orcadian community. In 1999, it was the site of the final celebrations of the Orkney Homecoming, a festival that brought hundreds of Canadians and Americans of Orkney heritage back to the islands. As part of the celebrations, 60 Canadian Inuit and Dene members of a string ensemble, Strings Across the Sky, right, played Amazing Grace in the ancient cathedral, returning the gift of music originally brought to their northern communities by Orkney fur traders.

lairds of Harray, whose opulence encouraged further HBC recruitment. There is no doubt that for more than 150 years the fur trade substantially contributed to the growth in wealth and population of Stromness. In fact in 1821, Stromness was larger than it is today. The parish then had a population of 2,944, whereas today it is only about 2,300.

During the fur trade era, the annual arrival and departure of ships highlighted the Stromness social calendar and some ships' captains developed the habit of entertaining parents and relatives of young Hudson's Bay recruits on board before sailing to the Nor'Wast.

At the end of the 18th century probably 80 per cent of the Hudson's Bay Company workforce was Orcadian. William Tomison, who rose from the laboring ranks to be the only Orcadian governor of the company in Canada, stands out. For 51 years, he laboured faithfully and effectively, before returning to South Ronaldsay, the southernmost island in the archipelago, to endow a school in perpetuity. Tomison's Academy was initially established in a small building (still locally known as "The Old Schoolhouse", but now a private home) in 1790, but a much grander building was constructed on

the top of a hill overlooking the Pentland Firth and northern Scotland in 1851. Tomison Academy served the people of South Ronaldsay's South Parish continuously until the 1960s, when it was closed in favor of bussing students to school in St. Margaret's Hope. Today, the beautiful building is being renovated by a local trust to serve as an interpretive centre celebrating the ties between Orkney and Canada and the remarkable man who had a substantial impact on both.

Other Orcadians became HBC factors, traders and post masters, including Joseph Isbister, who as master at Albany established the first inland post in 1743, Alexander Kennedy, who became a chief factor after the union with the rival North West Company in 1821, as well as John Ballenden, Edward Clouston and James Sutherland.

Hudson's Bay Company employment also gave the people of Orkney choices. It offered an escape from the authoritarian control of laird and kirk and opened an alternative way of life beyond the reach of customary social mores. Despite the numbers of men involved and the annual contact between Orkney and Hudson Bay, there was surprisingly little long-term communication between the two countries. When Orkneymen came home, they were usually alone. For more than a century, the Hudson's Bay Company frowned on liaisons with North American women, though it often signed on virile 18-year-olds for terms of up to seven years. In part this policy was a result of the systemic racism that was an accepted part of the English (and by extension Scottish and Orcadian) world view, but it was also a matter of practicalities. The company did not want to be responsible for fur trade families or bothered with the problem of where they might settle when the men retired. In practice, of course, this proved to be a completely unworkable policy. Native North American women were enormously skilled in all the techniques needed for survival and success in the fur trade – they served as interpreters, guides and negotiators; they gathered and cooked food, tanned skins, sewed clothing, made moccasins, built and often paddled canoes and were generally indispensible in a hundred or more ways. Their children, bridging two cultures, were just as vital to the company as the years passed. Moreover, the men largely refused to be without them and many, when their term of service was over, had no desire to go home to Orkney. Some simply preferred the freedom of life in North America; others realized their families would have difficulty fitting into European society – even a society as comparatively egalitarian as Orkney was in 19th-century Britain.

Despite this, some men did send their children back to be educated and a few returned with wives. In Orkney such unusual relations were usually absorbed by the extended family and schooled in the usual way and there are in Orkney today families that can trace their ancestry to ancient North American roots. But these are only a fraction of the enormous number of Canadian families that can claim Orkney roots.

All across Canada, Orkney names record the impact this small archipelago had on the creation of a nation. There are towns called Orkney and Kirkwall in Ontario; Binscarth and Westray in Manitoba, Birsay and Orkney in Saskatchewan, Scapa in Alberta and Stromness Bay on Victoria Island in the Western Arctic. In the Cree community of Nelson House in northern Manitoba, nearly half the population of 2,500 people bears the names Spence or Linklater.

The Stromness Museum, founded in 1837 by the Orkney Natural History Society, has an excellent collection of fur trade artifacts to impress and enlighten visitors from abroad. Like an acorn growing into a massive oak, so has the small population of Orkney (historically about the same as it is today – 20,500) impacted the second-largest country in the world.

The recently refurbished displays at the Stromness Museum include this diorama, below, of John Rae crossing an Arctic river in an inflatable boat. When he was ready to depart, Rae discovered that its paddles had been left behind. Ever inventive, he used two tin dinner plates to power the boat. Behind the diorama hangs the flag that flew over the HBC agent's office when the company was recruiting.

KEITH ALLARDYCE / STROMNESS MUSEUM

BRYCE S. WILSON / THE ORKNEY MUSEUM

Though Sir John Franklin and the crew of his last voyage were lost, a number of articles belonging to the expedition were found, including this powder horn.

ORKNEY'S UNSUNG HERO by Ken McGoogan

In 1833, having sailed with the Hudson's Bay Company as a ship's surgeon, 20-year-old John Rae spent his first winter in Rupert's Land. Forced by impassable pack-ice to winter over on Charlton Island in James Bay, Rae discovered he adored this "wild sort of life". The following spring, he signed on to serve two years as a doctor at Moose Factory and so sealed his destiny: Rae would become the greatest Arctic explorer of the 19th century, and arguably of all time.

Born and raised in Orkney, Rae spent his boyhood climbing, fishing, hunting and sailing small boats around Stromness, the final port of call for ships crossing the Atlantic. He studied at Edinburgh medical school and sailed on graduation. Serving as an HBC doctor at Moose Factory, Rae learned the fur trade and also indigenous techniques of hunting, trapping and survival.

Physically almost superhuman, Rae became legendary as a snowshoe walker; once, returning from a house call, he covered 166 kilometres in two days. In 1844, HBC Governor George Simpson appointed Rae to complete the geographical survey of the Arctic coast of North America – part of the centuries-old quest for the Northwest Passage.

That winter, to learn surveying techniques, Rae snowshoed from Red River (Winnipeg) to Sault Ste. Marie, covering nearly 2,000 kilometres in two months. The following year, after wintering at York Factory, he led a dozen men north in two small sailboats. At Repulse Bay, while serving as the expedition's chief hunter, Rae became the first European to winter in the High Arctic without relying mainly on imported provisions or native hunters.

In the spring of 1847, with five men and two dogsleds, Rae travelled northwest Inuit-style, building snowhuts as he went. After reaching Lord Mayor's Bay, which had been attained from the north, he returned to Repulse Bay. With four men, he trekked up the west coast of Melville Peninsula, battling fierce winds, drifting snow and hummocky ice to come within a few kilometres of Fury and Hecla Strait – another known location. Rae had not only charted 655 miles of new land and coastline, but demonstrated that "Boothia Felix" was a peninsula, and that no channel or passage led west out of Hudson Bay.

In 1848, Rae served with Sir John Richardson as second-in-command of an overland search expedition for Sir John Franklin, who had disappeared into the Arctic with two ships and 128 men. Rae and Richardson travelled down the Mackenzie River and searched the coast eastward to the mouth of the Coppermine River. After wintering at Fort Confidence, Rae tried repeatedly to approach Victoria Island by boat but was prevented by fast-flowing ice.

In 1851, resuming the search for Franklin, Rae – now a chief factor – attained the island by trekking across a frozen strait. He traced the coastline of Wollaston Peninsula north almost to Prince Albert Sound, and then returned to the mainland, a journey of 1,728 kilometres. Rae caught the spring thaw and, using two boats he'd designed, sailed east along the Victoria Island coast to a point north of Albert Edward Bay. Halted

Guide Louie Kamookak, who accompanied author McGoogan on his pilgrimage in John Rae's footsteps, kneels by the remains of a cairn built by Rae in 1854.

KEN McGOOGAN

by ice, he hiked farther north through jagged debris, "and before the day's journey was half done every step I took was marked with blood".

Back in the boats, Rae tried three times to cross Victoria Strait to King William Island 65 kilometres away, where the truth of the Franklin expedition lay waiting. Impenetrable pack-ice blocked his path. Sailing home, completing his voyage of 2,225 kilometres, Rae found the first relics of that lost expedition – two pieces of wood from one of the ships. That winter, returning to England, Rae travelled from Athabasca to St. Paul, Minn. on snowshoes – 2,770 kilometres, the last 720 (aided by dogs) in 10 days. The Royal Geographical Society awarded him a gold medal.

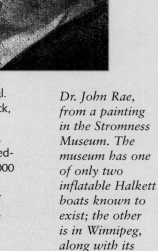

KEITH ALLARDYCE / STROMNESS MUSEUM

In 1853, Rae again sailed to Repulse Bay. After wintering there, he led a sledge party 500 miles northwest through blowing snow, gale-force winds and bitter cold. On the west coast of Boothia Peninsula, he slogged north with his two best men, a Cree and an Inuit, and discovered that a narrow channel separated Boothia from King William Island. This waterway, now called Rae Strait, would prove to be the final link in the Northwest Passage – the only such channel navigable by ships of that time. When Roald Amundsen became the first to navigate the Passage 50 years later, he sailed through Rae Strait.

Returning to Repulse Bay in 1854, Rae encountered Inuit who revealed that the Franklin expedition had ended in disaster; some of the last survivors had resorted to cannibalism. Rae purchased a variety of identifiable relics, among them a silver spoon, a fork and a medal. Back in London, when he delivered the news, Victorian England reacted with shock, outrage and denial.

Lady Jane Franklin, Sir John's widow, led a fierce campaign to discredit Rae. Novelist Charles Dickens castigated him for accepting the "Eskimo savages" as credible witnesses. Despite this opposition, Rae and his men received the posted £10,000 reward for having ascertained the fate of the Franklin expedition.

Unrepentant, Lady Franklin glorified her dead husband as "the discoverer of the Northwest Passage" and celebrated Francis Leopold McClintock, who led a later expedition that found bodies and a note, for having ascertained his fate. Yet McClintock and others only elaborated and clarified Rae's findings.

John Rae revolutionized Arctic travel. He was the first European to fully adopt such Inuit techniques as icing sledge runners and living primarily in igloos. The chief hunter of every expedition he led, Rae by his own estimate travelled 10,500 kilometres on foot and 10,700 kilometres in boats, surveying more than 2,800 kilometres of uncharted territory. He solved the two great mysteries of 19th-century Arctic exploration, discovering both the fate of the Franklin expedition and the final link in the Northwest Passage.

Yet Rae was the only major British explorer never to receive a knighthood. He died in London in 1893 and was buried in his beloved Orkney.

Dr. John Rae, from a painting in the Stromness Museum. The museum has one of only two inflatable Halkett boats known to exist; the other is in Winnipeg, along with its box, which is addressed to Sir George Simpson.

Montreal to Sault Ste. Marie

LINDA FAIRFIELD

With emerald leaves that turn gold in fall, the white (or canoe) birch (Betula papyrifera), is beautiful as well as functional. In addition to canoes, baskets and tipi covers, the tree was also used for dozens of other purposes: the bark's white powder for infant diaper rash, the sap for syrup and sugar, and the wood for snowshoe frames, toboggans, canoe thwarts and paddles.

Ancient rock and clear blue water make Georgian Bay, right, seen from Ontario's Killarney Provincial Park, a favored place for canoeists.

This is the fur trade's "old road". For 250 years, from 1613, when Champlain's small party paddled up the Ottawa River to Tessouat's Algonquin village, until 1870, when the Hudson's Bay Company sold its territorial rights to Rupert's Land and began the move from furs to fashion, brigades left Lachine almost every spring, bound for Sault Ste. Marie and beyond.

Departing as soon as the ice was off the lakes in early May, the voyageurs established a tempo they would sustain for most of the summer. Paddling 40 to 50 strokes a minute through rain and cold or blistering heat, staggering with huge loads over the portages through clouds of mosquitos and black flies, they averaged seven to nine kilometres an hour for up to 18 hours a day. It was a remarkable pace, given the rugged terrain, the turbulent rivers and the huge, hazardous lakes. And express canoes, with 12 to 14 paddlers, four passengers and a light load, made even better time.

The brigades usually comprised four to 10 canoes and employed experienced guides. Each canoe was manned by an *avant* or bowsman, who carried a large paddle for manoeuvring in fast water, a *gouvernail* who steered at the rear, and five to 10 paddlers, the voyageurs.

From Lachine they ascended the Ottawa River to its junction with the Mattawa, climbed the Mattawa to Lake Nipissing and shot down the French River to Georgian Bay. Following Lake Huron's North Channel, they reached Sault Ste. Marie on the St. Marys River, a fur trade crossroads for centuries.

Though Canada has greatly changed since the fur trade era, time travellers will find much to explore. The Trans-Canada Highway's Voyageur Route shadows its waterways, allowing easy access to reconstructed fur trade sites and parks that preserve scenic sections of the waterway. Cosmopolitan Montreal boasts several souvenirs of its 17th- and 18th-century fur trade past, including The Fur Trade at Lachine National Park, while the National Capital Region (Ottawa-Hull) celebrates the era in the Museum of Civilization, the National Archives, the National Gallery and a number of parks and sites.

MIKE GRANDMAISON

Those seeking a more authentic voyageur connection will find magnificent rivers and Lake Huron's north shore, among Canada's most spectacular places to canoe.

EXPANDING ON NORTH AMERICAN INGENUITY

From the first time the French ventured inland, their main mode of transport was the one that had served North Americans for millennia – the birch-bark canoe. These light, manoeuvrable craft were ideal for the fur trade – perfect for navigating wild northern rivers, easily portaged and quick to repair with local materials. Even better, for 150 years they were supplied by native North Americans.

By 1750, however, the Algonquin and Ojibwe were no longer able to meet the expanding demand, and a factory was established at Trois-Rivières. Here, the canoes began to grow. To carry ever larger loads ever greater distances with ever increasing numbers of men, they stretched from four or five metres (a canoe that might carry four people, but could be paddled by one), to eight and finally nearly 12 metres in length.

By 1785, two types of canoes were being built – the enormous *canot du maître* and the smaller *canot du nord*. The former, the "master" or Montreal canoe, averaged 10 to 12 metres in length and was nearly two metres wide. It carried a crew of eight to 12 men, their provisions and more than four tonnes of cargo. For nearly 40 years, these huge canoes plied the route between Montreal and the company's inland headquarters on northwestern Lake Superior. Between the two were 2,000 kilometres of rivers, dozens of portages and the unpredictable waters of the world's largest lake.

The Montreal canoes went no farther west than Grand Portage (or, after 1803, Fort William), for the diminishing size of the rivers, not to mention the punishing number and length of the portages, demanded craft of a more manageable size, the *canots du nord*. Usually seven or eight metres long with a carrying capacity of one-and-a-half tonnes, north canoes could be paddled by four to six men and portaged by two.

Born of North American ingenuity in the great northern forests, these marvellous craft opened the continent's waterways to Europeans.

DENNIS FAST

Crafted of light-weight, seemingly delicate birchbark, above, Montreal canoes could carry an astounding complement of cargo, as illustrated here, as well as between seven and 12 men with their provisions and gear.

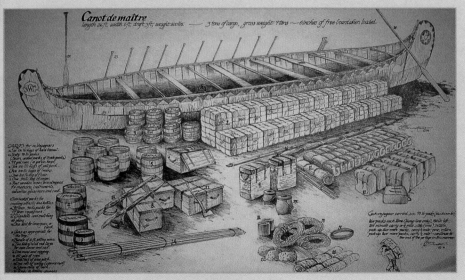

NEIL BROADFOOT

The North West Company

Simon McTavish, seen at right in a painting in Old Fort William's Great Hall, was canny and stubborn, with a genius for business. Arriving almost penniless in America at the age of 13 in 1764, he built a commercial empire that stretched from Quebec to the Rockies by the time of his death 40 years later. McTavish and his Highland Scots kin also had a flair for fine living that is reflected in the company's ornate armorial bearings.

To the rival Hudson's Bay Company, they were the "pedlars from Quebec" and Washington Irving called the North West Company a feudal clan, but at least one historian has anointed Simon McTavish, the undoubted head of the company, a grandfather of Confederation. The truth is likely somewhere in between.

The Montreal traders who revolutionized the fur trade between 1779 and 1821 were members of a Scottish mafia of sorts (by 1800, most of the senior partners of the NWC were Highland Scots and related in some way), but they were also among the first truly North American entrepreneurs.

The North West Company grew out of the fur trade free-for-all that followed the fall of New France in 1763. Though French-Canadians continued to be involved in the trade, it was mainly newly arrived English, Scots and American colonials who formed the Montreal-based partnerships that soon dominated the trade. Competition between these small independent companies was fierce, but it was war that brought them together in the fall of 1779.

In the midst of the American Revolution, Governor Sir Frederick Haldimand was reluctant to hand out trading licences, fearing the goods would wind up in enemy hands.

Believing that Haldimand might respond more positively to a united approach, eight partnerships (including that of McTavish and Patrick Small) combined to form the first North West Company. This common front convinced the governor to award the necessary licences.

The new company reinvented itself at least twice in the first four years and by 1787, McTavish and his partners – Joseph Frobisher in Montreal and Small and Nicholas Montour in the fur country – held 11 of the 20 shares. McTavish, a Highlander who'd been apprenticed in New England before coming to Montreal in 1774, was 37 at the time. By the time he turned 50, both the North West Company and his adopted city had grown substantially, and he had become Montreal's wealthiest man – all a result of the company's unprecedented assault on the fur trade. Further, a number of his relatives – among them his cousin Simon Fraser and his nephews William and Duncan McGillivray – had been drawn into the trade.

NWC men had descended the Mackenzie River to the Arctic Ocean, crossed the western mountains to the Pacific and brought the mighty Hudson's Bay Company almost to its knees. All this, despite enormous challenges of geography and communication, as well as war in Europe, where the bulk of the furs were sold.

McTavish died suddenly in 1804, thus missing both the final flowering and abrupt decline of his company, which merged with its main rival under the HBC banner, in 1821.

DENNIS FAST

DENNIS FAST

Montreal

The history and early growth of the city of Montreal are inextricably linked to the fur trade, but religion prompted the first successful attempt at settlement on the island.

Jacques Cartier was looking for inland access (and a route to China) when he arrived at Île de Montréal in 1535. But the great rapids at Lachine, and the desperate winter that he and his compatriots spent on the St. Lawrence put a damper on his dreams. Seventy-five years later, Samuel de Champlain had furs in mind when he established a fortified post and called it Place Royal, but war against the Iroquois made the isolated post a dangerous place to be.

Paul de Chomedey de Maisonneuve saw opportunity, not peril, when he arrived with 53 French colonists in May 1642. Fired with evangelistic zeal, Maisonneuve was undeterred by the growing danger from the Five Nations Iroquois, who deeply resented France's alliance with their enemies, the Wendat and Algonquin.

For 60 years, life was tenuous in the settlement, but the colonists were determined. A hospital was founded in 1644 and a seminary was built for the Sulpicians, the island's first administrators. Continually improving the village fortifications, the first citizens of Montréal (never more than 1,000 of them) stubbornly held out until peace was negotiated with the Iroquois in 1701.

In the early years, Maisonneuve and the Sulpicians had established homes for themselves around a square they called Place d'Armes on the fortified riverfront. In 1706, echoing the new reality, the square became a public market and was renamed Place du Marché. It became the practical heart of the community. Here, people could peddle furs, purchase food, sell handicrafts, fight duels, watch someone be pilloried or attend a hanging.

The fur trade was Montréal's main industry, an engine of commerce that soon made the community the business capital of New France. But

ERIN HUCK

One of Montreal's original buildings, the Old Sulpician Seminary features a clock and a gateway that are virtually unchanged in hundreds of years.

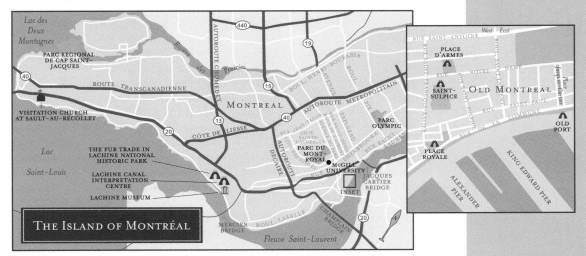

Today, viewed from Mount Royal, Montreal stretches into the distance as far as the eye can see. The little city was very different in 1812, when Thomas Davies painted it from the slopes of the mountain, far right. Then, though more than 150 years old and growing fast, Montreal was still a fur trade community largely dependent on the river. Davies' picturesque view was painted in the last year of his life.

this was also the gateway to the rest of North America and, as the years passed and the village became a town, Montréalers scouted the better part of a continent in pursuit of fur.

The French colonial era came to an end in 1763, with the Treaty of Paris that concluded the Seven Years War. The new British administrators dropped the accent from the town's name and Scots and English flooded in, but Montreal remained essentially French.

The fur trade, meanwhile, was undergoing its most dramatic transformation. Under the auspices of France, its undeniably important commercial character (François de La Vérendrye and Charles de Langlade had been accompanied by 1,200 Ojibwe and Assiniboine trappers and traders and a canoe armada when they came down to Montréal in 1759) had been controlled by agents of a European power. Now, the Montreal fur trade had come home. Tentatively at first, then more decisively, a handful of independent trading companies gained experience and economic clout between 1764 and 1778. Finally, rather than compete, they agreed to cooperate. The result, in 1779, was the first incarnation of the North West Company. The fur trade had become big business.

By 1786, the company's tactics had forced its major competitor, the Hudson's Bay Company, to also embark on a period of aggressive expansion. Before this competition ended with the merger of the two companies in 1821, it had pushed Europeans right across the continent.

The zenith of the fur trade coincided with rapid growth in Montreal. When Britain lost its American colonies to the fledgling United States in 1783, the city was suddenly the main outpost of British colonial power in North America. Within three decades it tripled in size, to 15,000.

Today, though it has expanded by 200 times since the heyday of the NWC, reminders of the fur trade can still be seen. Montreal retains much of its French character and two of its main bridges bear the names of its earliest traders. McGill, a prestigious university founded with fur trade money, lies in the heart of the city, and the sights and smells of the era can be recaptured at The Fur Trade in Lachine National Historic Park. Oh yes, and The Beaver Club, once a roving fortnightly feast for a privileged few, is now an elegant restaurant located in the comfortable confines of the Queen Elizabeth Hotel.

McGill University

Situated in old Montreal, at the foot of Mount Royal, McGill University occupies land that resonates with fur trade history. When Jacques Cartier first set eyes on the island in 1535, it was known as Hochelaga. Though many equate the name with the large Iroquoian town at the base of the mountain, anthropologists now believe "Hochelaga" actually described the region. The farming community of about 2,000 was probably called Tutonaguy. Archaeological excavations on the university grounds have pinpointed its location and a sign on Sherbrooke Street locates the site for visitors.

By the time Samuel de Champlain arrived on the island nearly 75 years later, the Iroquoian longhouses, pallisades and fields of corn and beans had long been abandoned, but the significance of the island – strategically located at the western end of navigable water in the St. Lawrence – as a centre of the fur trade was only beginning.

Because the trade depended on the waterways, the first settlers located their homes near the river. The community grew slowly and it was more than a century before farms again began to climb the lower slopes of the mountain. About 1790, James McGill, a Glaswegian immigrant who had made a small fortune in the fur trade, began to purchase the land the Iroquoians had once settled. McGill collected land as some people collect antique cars or fine paintings, beginning with bits and pieces that captured his fancy. By 1801 he was buying large tracts – 10,000 acres here and 32,000 acres there. The land on which the university now stands was among his favorite places; he called it Burnside and made it his summer home.

Though today the view south is impeded by apartment buildings, shops and restaurants, when McGill's family spent the summers here the vista was across sloping farmland to the burgeoning riverside community. The town was in transition, expanding from a population of about 5,500 in 1790 to a small city of 15,000 by the time of his death in 1813 and he must have felt a certain satisfaction in knowing that he'd had a hand in the changes he could see unfolding.

Like his contemporary William Tomison of the Hudson's Bay Company one thing concerned McGill greatly, however. Schooled in 18th-century Scotland, he put large stock in education and even as a relatively young man was involved in efforts to develop educational facilities in Montreal. In 1787, he created a petition and sent it to London. It read in part, "We hardly know of a single school in the district for teaching boys. Only one boy in five can read or write."

This plaque, mounted on a rock on the grounds of McGill University, recalls the large Iroquoian village that once occupied the site. Dozens of longhouses sheltered a community of perhaps 2,000, who farmed extensive fields of corn and beans beyond the palisade that enclosed the town.

THOMAS DAVIES / NATIONAL GALLERY OF CANADA, / NO. 6286

A FAIR TRADE: FURS FOR EDUCATION

Born in Glasgow and therefore a Lowland, rather than Highland Scot, James McGill was nonetheless part of the exodus from Scotland in the decades after the Battle of Culloden in 1745. When he was in his mid-teens, he and his younger brother John sailed to the Carolinas in search of opportunity, but by the spring of 1766, at the age of 21, he had joined a growing trickle of Scots drawn to Montreal by the promise of the fur trade.

ERIN HUCK

In May of that year, with a canoe weighed down with trade goods, he left with the brigades for Michilimackinac. By fall he was on the shores of Green Bay in today's Wisconsin. Like many French-speaking *coureurs de bois*, McGill realized early that trading *en dérouine*, directly with native trappers, was the way to maximize profits. Young, resourceful and smart, McGill learned the ropes quickly. Within six years, he was leading 12 canoes and 75 men west. In 1773, one of those men was Peter Pond, an impulsive American who left an indelible stain on the early fur trade.

In 1773, McGill and Isaac Todd went inland together, beginning a friendship that would last for 40 years. Todd was a bluff, friendly man with strong connections to the Americans. McGill, though generous and public spirited, was more retiring. When he was only 30, the pair put voyaging behind them and became merchants in the trade. Four years later in 1779, Todd, McGill Company threw its lot in with an innovative fur cooperative – the North West Company.

Despite his efforts, the situation was little improved nearly a quarter-century later when, in 1811, he sat down to make his will. The community needed to be prodded to action and McGill had just the stick. He bequeathed the city £10,000 and his Burnside estate for the creation of a university or college, but only if it could be established within 10 years of his death.

The deadline was crucial. Legal wrangling with one of McGill's heirs and bureaucratic delays stalled proceedings for years and only the looming deadline prompted the creation of a charter in 1821. Though instruction at the institution did not begin until 1843, McGill is Quebec's oldest university, an institution that owes its existence largely to the Canadian fur trade.

McGill University, shown left, is located in the heart of Montreal, on the north side of Sherbrooke Street, west of University.

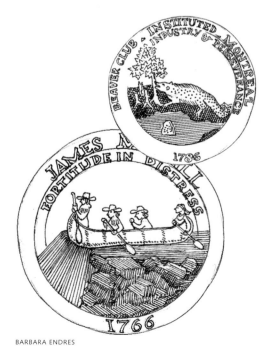

BARBARA ENDRES

The Fur Trade in Lachine

For more than 150 years, Lachine was synonymous with the North American fur trade, for it sat at the upper end of the great rapids of the St. Lawrence River, an obvious launch point for travellers heading north or west. The name – *La Chine* or "China" – was a touch of irony, bestowed in the late 1660s by a twentysomething adventurer named René-Robert Cavelier (but better known by his latter-day title, Sieur de La Salle).

Seventeenth-century life in Lachine was not for the faint-hearted. Periodic war between the Iroquois and French made settlement anywhere in New France precarious and Lachine lacked the natural geographic defences of Québec or the stone fortifications of Montréal. The little settlement on the western shore of the island was an easy target during an uneasy time.

Real growth did not begin until peace was negotiated in 1701, but within a few years, this was one of the busiest places on the continent, particularly in the spring and fall. Over the next century and a half, many, perhaps most of the major figures of the fur trade passed this way. Today, their echoes can be heard at The Fur Trade in Lachine National Historic Park.

Much of the site's authenticity comes from the building – the Old Stone Shed – and its remarkably undeveloped surroundings. Built in 1803 by Alexander Gordon, a merchant who had served as a clerk for the Hudson's Bay Company, the "shed" is in fact a large, well-constructed edifice that was built as a warehouse for the fur trade.

Like others of the same sort on the West Island, this was where trade goods and furs were stored, the former to be shipped out with the canoe brigades in the spring for places as far-flung as Lake Athabasca, the latter bound for Montreal and London.

When the building was constructed, the old Lachine Canal (which now runs right past it) had not yet been

excavated. The old launching place was just upstream, across from the imposing Convent of Sainte-Anne. Every May, hundreds of huge canoes laden with the myriad goods of the trade – pots, axe heads, rifles and ammunition, tea, cloth, brandy, blankets and dozens of other items – set forth on a journey that

The departure of the first of the spring brigades from Lachine was a festive event, drawing more than the usual cadre of fur traders. Franklin Arbuckle captured this celebratory spirit in his illustration of the Old Stone Shed for the Hudson's Bay Company's 1948 calendar.

FRANKLIN ARBUCKLE / HUDSON'S BAY COMPANY ARCHIVES / P–412

would carry some of the wares more than halfway across the continent. Until 1821, the vast majority of the canoes and goods belonged to the North West Company, which dominated the trade in North America.

After 1821, when the NWC and the rival Hudson's Bay Company merged, the majority of furs were shipped to London by the shorter route from Hudson Bay. But Lachine was not forgotten, in part because it was a favored place of the new governor of the expanded HBC, George Simpson (see page 243).

(see page 243).

The company established its headquarters in Lachine, the first canal was built by 1824, easing transportation difficulties between Lachine and Montreal, and the Old Stone Shed continued to serve Hudson's Bay Company posts on the Great Lakes and Ottawa River for decades. In the 1840s, Simpson built a home right across the street, allowing him to keep a gimlet eye on proceedings on the rare occasions when he was home. The house was torn down in 1888 to make room for a new wing of the convent.

When the Montreal fur trade finally ended in 1861, the Old Stone Shed was purchased by the Sisters of Sainte-Anne and added to the convent grounds. Over the next 115 years, it served as a classroom, dormitory,

The "new wing" of the Convent of Sainte-Anne was built more than a century ago on land once occupied by Sir George Simpson's home. Across the street, the Old Stone Shed, below, now a national historic site, looks very much as it must have when the governor was in residence.

PETER ST. JOHN

laundry and finally, as apartments for convent employees.

Today, the building looks much as it must have in the early years of the 19th century, the golden age of the Montreal fur trade. Be still for a moment and you can almost hear the shouts of the fall brigades as they near the landing place; breathe deeply and you can almost smell the pungent odor of raw pelts as they are unloaded for transport into Montreal.

The Fur Trade in Lachine National Historic Park is located on Montreal's West Island. Take Highway 20 East or West; exit at the National Park signs and follow 32nd Avenue west to Remembrance. Travel south on Remembrance to 15th Avenue, which skirts the northern edge of Parc La Salle, then turn west on 15th to Boulevard Saint-Joseph and the Lachine Canal.

PETER ST. JOHN

The Ottawa River

Today's Ottawa River – with its dozen dams and reservoirs – is a docile, domesticated descendant of the wild waterway the fur traders knew. Then, particularly between Mattawa and Montreal, the river was a punishing and often deadly series of cataracts. But for fur traders en route to the Great Lakes, it was also nearly 500 kilometres shorter than the alternative route down the St. Lawrence and through Lakes Ontario and Erie.

Distance was time and money, for summer was but a fleeting respite between long months of snow. So each May for more than 200 years, fur brigades loaded with trade goods left Lachine on an arduous journey that began with 15 kilometres of rapids known as the Long Sault. A stretch of calm followed, but the difficulties had hardly begun. North 100 kilometres, where Hull and Ottawa sit today, was the first major challenge – the torrent of Chaudière Falls.

Upstream, the Ottawa was a giant staircase of wild rapids and torrential falls. In quick succession, the Little Chaudière and Deschênes Rapids forced voyageurs ashore, a line of lovely falls was portaged at Chats Falls, and the Chenaux, a stretch of fast water through the islands at the upper end of Lake Chats, was poled or lined near the Quebec shore.

Struggling past the Allumette Rapids, portaging going up and running them on the way down, the brigades reached a long spit of sand that stretched into the river from the western shore. Point au Baptême was a perfect place for initiation ceremonies.

Now the pine-clad granite cliffs of the shield closed in. From the confluence of the Mattawa River, the Ottawa stretches north through Lake Timiskaming, but the brigades turned west instead and struggled up the Mattawa en route to the Great Lakes.

Rising 250 kilometres north of Canada's national capital, the Ottawa River follows a circuitous course for more than 1,100 kilometres to its confluence with the St. Lawrence. For nearly half that distance, it goes west through a ribbon of interconnected lakes before dropping southeast in a sinuous curve through Lake Timiskaming. Over its length, it falls 360 metres from the Canadian Shield to the St. Lawrence Lowlands.

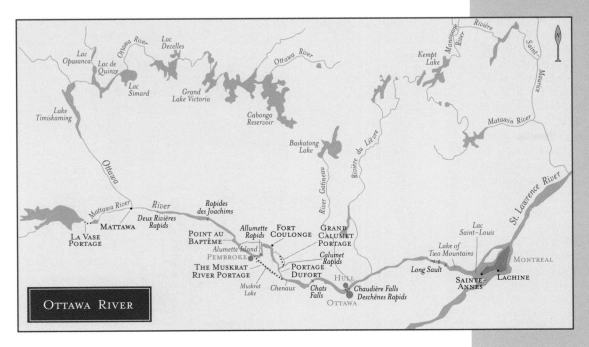

OTTAWA RIVER

THE ANISHINABE TRADERS

Like the Ojibwe to the west, the Odawa are members of the Anishinabe Nation, a large linguistic and cultural group that now extends from the Ottawa Valley on Ontario's eastern boundary to the Assiniboine Valley in western Manitoba.

At the beginning of the 17th century, the Odawa, (literally "the traders") occupied much of the north shore of Georgian Bay, as well as Manitoulin Island in Lake Huron and the Bruce Peninsula to the south. There, they were neighbors and allies of the Iroquoian-speaking Wendat of Huronia and two related Algonquian-speaking peoples – the Nipissing, who lived to the east around the lake of the same name, and the Algonquin, who occupied what is now called the Ottawa Valley.

Their proximity to the Wendat encouraged a more diversified lifestyle than many related Anishinabeg. They cultivated corn, beans and squash, but also excelled at fishing and varied their diets with such locally available commodities as wild rice and maple sugar.

Like their neighbors to the east, the Odawa were allied with the French; they were participants in the early fur trade and the focus of French missionary work. And like the Wendat, Nipissing and Algonquin, the Odawa were driven from their homeland by the Iroquois War of the late 1640s and early 1650s. Forced far to the west, some settled around Jesuit missions along the Straits of Mackinac in what is now Michigan. Despite continued unrest, others stayed involved in the fur trade and soon replaced the decimated Wendat as middlemen. When peace was negotiated with the Iroquois at the beginning of the 18th century, many Odawa occupied the river valley that led north and west from the St. Lawrence. Quite sensibly – given its size and its rapids and cataracts – they called this waterway *Kitchi Sipi*, Great River, but the French soon gave it another name: Rivière des Outauais, the Ottawa River.

Today, Odawa heritage is celebrated at a cultural centre in Ottawa, Ontario.

Wild rice was not just harvested, but managed by the Odawa. The women seeded the rice in suitable lakes and were responsible for substantially extending the natural area of wild rice growth. Governed by natural conditions, the harvest was successful about two years of three, but when it was, a small lake could produce enough rice to feed a family for a winter, sometimes with a surplus that, by the early 1800s, was traded west to the fur posts. Today, the Anishinabeg harvest wild rice for commercial purposes.

EAR OF WILD RICE

HARVESTING

Wild rice was an important cereal food among the Indians of the Great Lakes region.

DRYING

HULLING

WINNOWING

The Long Sault

In early May, as soon as the ice was off the larger lakes, the North West Company *canots du maître* left Lachine, departing shortly after dawn from the launch place at the head of the rapids. Setting their usual pace, the brigades crossed Lac Saint-Louis to Sainte-Annes, where they were partially unloaded and paddled *demi-chargé* up the mild rapids. There, in a little church that today is part of a convent, the voyageurs left their mite and received the priest's blessing.

This custom likely reflects an earlier practice of the Algonquin, who once controlled the valley. Before journeying upriver, they often stopped to leave offerings and sing prayers.

Upstream the Lake of Two Mountains loomed; with luck and good weather, they would camp at its upper end. If surviving this first day was celebrated – as it often was – with "a wee dram", the next morning was more of a trial than it might have been. Ahead lay the Carillon Rapids, the beginning of the Long Sault, 15 kilometres of rapids in three sets that marked the place where the river tumbled off the Precambrian Shield into the St. Lawrence Lowlands. This was both a physical and a psychological ordeal, for everyone knew it was here in 1660 that Adam Dollard des Ormeaux and his small party of French, Algonquin and Wendat were ambushed by Iroquois warriors as they were about to portage. Moreover, at the foot of almost every rapid small crosses could be seen, testament to the paddlers who did not survive.

Trying to ignore these warnings, the voyageurs dragged their canoes up the rapids. Champlain wrote: "In tracking my canoe, I nearly lost my life. The canoe turned broadside into a whirlpool and had I not luckily fallen between two rocks, the canoe would have dragged me in."

Though the rapids and portage trails are drowned today beneath the water of the Carillon Dam, reminders of them can be found in Voyageur Provincial Park, south of Chute-à-Blondeau (named for the middle set of rapids). The cataracts have been replaced by riverside marshes and shimmering bays, but the Laurentian Mountains provide a familiar backdrop to the east, and early morning visitors may see a busy beaver along the 3.2-kilometre Coureur de Bois nature trail.

Voyageur Park is east of Ontario Highway 417 (Exit 5), one hour east of Ottawa on the Quebec border. It includes a full-service campground, an interpretive centre and bilingual staff. Canoes, boats and horses can be rented during the summer months. Cross-country ski trails are groomed in winter.

White-tailed deer (Odocoileus viginianus) abound along the Ottawa River, just as they did during the fur trade era. With an almost uncanny ability to hide in even densely populated woodlands, explosive speed when discovered and a relatively high birth rate (most births are twins) white-tails have withstood heavy predation for millennia and extended their territory far to the west.

The dappled fawns are born with an instinctive ability to hide, withholding feces and urine until their mother appears to ingest what the fawn passes, thus ridding the area of tell-tale scents.

Ottawa

PETER ST. JOHN

Perched high above the Ottawa River just west of the Rideau Canal, the Parliament Buildings were begun in 1859, less than two years after the town was chosen by Queen Victoria as Canada's national capital, and were in use by 1866.

Ottawa – Canada's national capital – is a suitably picturesque city that boasts many treasures for history buffs. But the history of the city itself is relatively short. Despite its place at the crossroads of a river that has been travelled for so many centuries by Europeans, it was not until Queen Victoria bestowed federal status on it in 1857 that Ottawa began a significant growth spurt. In the space of less than 150 years it has made up for that relatively late start and today it's an excellent place to explore the history of the nation, as well as the regional echoes of the fur trade.

The Canadian Museum of Civilization, featuring magnificent interpretive displays that span thousands of years nationwide, is located on the Quebec side of the river in Hull; the National Gallery, and the National Archives and Library are on the river on the Ontario side.

Other points of interest include the Canadian Parliament, the Canadian War Museum and the Astrolabe Outdoor Theatre, located on a rise above the river immediately below a towering statue of Samuel de Champlain holding aloft his astrolabe which went missing a little farther up the river.

Rideau Falls, which were bypassed by the Rideau Canal in the 19th century, join the Ottawa River just below Chaudière Falls. As they have for millennia, they fall in a veil of water over a limestone shelf from the Rideau Valley, a hanging valley in geological terms. In the mid-1600s, Algonquin warriors – canoes and all – sometimes hid behind the falls from their more powerful Iroquois enemies.

For the fur traders, the most significant feature in the area was Chaudière Falls. *Chaudière*, a "boiler" or "kettle", was a name favored by the French to describe turbulent waterfalls and a

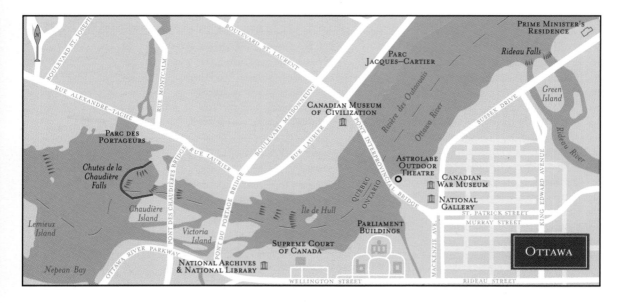

number of imposing cataracts along the fur trade routes bore the same name, but few deserved it as did the cataract between Ottawa and Hull.

Now greatly diminished by the head-pond of the Carillon Dam 100 kilometres downstream, the main channel of Chaudière Falls once resembled a cauldron; over time the pounding water had hollowed out a great basin in the limestone bed of the river. Had early French traders missed this fact, they were aided in recognizing it by their Algonquin guides, who called the falls *Asticou* or "boiler".

Portaging was the only way around the torrent, but the season determined where the canoes were portaged. In the spring, paddling anywhere near the foot of the falls was impossible. So the portage began downstream, where a long, narrow gorge in the limestone created a pool of quiet water on the north shore. Here, the brigades heading inland could unload their canoes and, with great effort, drag them to the top of the cliff. There they followed a path that was so close to the edge that, depending on the wind, the voyageurs were often drenched with spray.

Homeward bound in September, their canoes laden with furs, the river was much lower and the brigades were able to cut the portage short and use the "summer landing", a small bay at the foot of the falls, just below today's Chaudière Bridge.

Heading upstream in the spring, one portage was barely over when another, the trail around the Little Chaudière

Falls, beckoned. Those tracing the route today will have no trouble finding this historic trail, for the city of Hull has created a park – Parc des Portageurs – complete with biking and hiking trails, to commemorate it. One section of the original trail, which lies just below Brébeuf Park, is particularly interesting. Here, a set of low stone steps – built by the voyageurs according to canoe historian Eric Morse – can clearly be seen mounting a bank from a submerged stone shelf at the water's edge.

From the head of this portage, the voyageurs paddled across a small bay to begin tracking and poling up the Deschênes Rapids, the final obstacle in this triathlon of fast water.

Beyond, Lac des Chênes (or today, Deschênes) – "Lake of the Oaks", named for the great trees that once graced its shores – stretched west for 50 kilometres.

For the Nor'Westers, the thundering torrent at Chaudière Falls meant unloading several tonnes of goods and hefting them and the enormous canoes up and around the cascade. The trail passed so close to the falls that an on-shore wind could drench the men with spray.

Below: A set of crude stone steps at the edge of the river can still be found between Parc des Portageurs and Brébeuf Park in Val Tetreau. Here, the voyageurs circumvented the Little Chaudière Falls just below the Champlain Bridge.

AMANDA DOW

PETER ST. JOHN

Chats Falls

Named for the raccoons – *les chats sauvages* – that were once abundant in the area, the Sault des Chats Sauvage, or Chats Falls, at the lower end of Lake Chats (pronounced "Shah") created the next barrier in the upstream journey of Lake Superior-bound voyageurs.

The Ottawa River at this point is nearly three kilometres wide, and the falls spilled over and around a series of granite outcroppings and small islands in 15 or 16 beautiful falls. Even weary travellers were captivated by the sight, particularly in the spring; one wrote that they were "second only to the incomparable Niagara".

Rather than go around on either shore, the falls were portaged across one of the main islands midstream, from a bend in the river known as Big Bay. A free trader, Joseph Mondion,

operated a small post on the point of land across Big Bay. The view must have been delightful, but diminishing returns or perhaps competition induced him to sell the place in 1800 and it soon passed to the North West Company (and after 1821 to the Hudson's Bay Company). Under both, it operated as an outpost, trading for furs and sometimes providing supplies to the fledgling logging operations that began in the area about 1810.

Later in the 19th century, the falls became a major tourist attraction, drawing visitors aboard the riverboat *Lady Colborne* to see the spectacle. All this came to an end in 1929, with the construction of the dam and generating station at Chats Falls, but the rocks and rapids can still be seen from Fitzroy Provincial Park on the river's southern shore, just below the dam.

Before the dam was built, Chats Falls tumbled over a granite ridge (unlike the limestone found downstream at Ottawa) in a line of beautiful falls that was more than 1.5 kilometres wide.

CHARLES RAMUS FORREST / NATIONAL GALLERY OF CANADA / C–16653

Though the area was extensively logged in the mid-19th century, the intervening 150 years have allowed the habitat to reestablish itself, dominated by magnificent stands of white pine, Ontario's provincial tree. Some of the trees are stately giants more than 30 metres tall, which provide crucial habitat for osprey and bald eagles.

During the fur trade era, the river immediately above the falls was also a challenge, for five kilometres of rapids had to be traversed before the brigades arrived at the bottom end of Lake Chats, which – then as now – offered smooth sailing.

Today, the dam has rendered this stretch of the river deeper and calmer, but the beauty of the area can still be enjoyed at the Morris Island Conservation Area near the community of Fitzroy Harbour. The 47-hectare site includes a series of small islands, linked by bridges and a causeway, along the south (or Ontario) side of the river.

This is an excellent place to see the geological bones of the upper Ottawa Valley, for unlike the region around Ottawa to the east, where the

bedrock is mainly limestone, the predominant rocks here are granite and quartz. Outcroppings of marble are also common and can be easily viewed while walking along the causeway.

BRIAN WOLITSKI

Studies have shown that even where giant white pines comprise only one per cent of a forest, they harbor more than 80 per cent of bald eagle and 75 per cent of osprey nests.

Though the soil is shallow, the islands are covered with a dense mixed forest, much as they were during the fur trade. And wildlife – including white-tailed deer, porcupines and beaver, as well as raccoons – inhabit the area. Wolves have been sighted during the winter and the island woodlands draw a variety of birds, including pileated woodpeckers.

Both Morris Island Conservation Area and Fitzroy Provincial Park are located north of the Trans-Canada Highway (No. 17) east of Arnprior. Turn northeast onto Highway 22 and follow it through Galetta and across the Mississippi River. To access Morris Island, turn northwest onto Logger's Way and follow the signs. For Fitzroy Park, continue on Highway 22 and follow the Ontario Parks signs.

The Chenaux

Sporting an antique patina of its own, an Historic Sites and Monuments Board of Canada sign tells of the remarkable recovery in 1867 of Champlain's astrolabe, lost 254 years before as he portaged along the Muskrat River, right.

At the upper end of Lake Chats, the Ottawa River was again bridged by islands. Travellers heading upstream faced a section of fast water – the Chenaux – and then a stretch of rapids and falls as the river split and flowed around Calumet and Allumette Islands.

For much of human history, this tedious section was bypassed, at least going up, with a series of carries through a chain of 12 small lakes to the Muskrat River, which winds through the countryside to debouch into the Ottawa at modern Pembroke. With 25 kilometres of canoeing and 12 of portaging, this route – suitable for small Algonquin canoes – was the one along which Champlain and his little band were led in 1613.

Somewhere on the trail, Champlain, laden with arquebuses, paddles, food and clothing, lost his astrolabe, a kind of sextant used for surveying. He was probably hours farther along before he noticed it missing and he never recovered it. In fact, though Algonquin and later Odawa trappers must have tramped the trail for decades afterward on their journeys inland, the missing astrolabe did not turn up for more than 250 years. In August of 1867, a teenager, Edward George Lee, finally found it in a field. He may not have known what it was, but there was no doubting its antiquity; when it was cleaned and polished, it clearly bore the date 1603 – the year of its manufacture in France.

 The Chenaux, with its quartet of rapids – the Décharge du Derigé, the Mountain Portage, the Décharge du Sable and Portage du Fort – are drowned now beneath Lac du Rocher-Fendu ("Lake Split Rock"), created by the Chenaux Dam. The portage Champlain took began about three kilometres below the dam on the west side of Lake Chats and followed a stream coming down from Town Lake. Today the Trans-Canada Highway (No. 17) crosses the portage route and an historic marker on the highway notes Edward Lee's recovery of the astrolabe, which is on display at the Museum of Civilization in Hull. Pembroke celebrates Champlain's journey with a mural on one of its downtown buildings. Nearby, the Muskrat River flows into the Ottawa beneath a series of bridges and through a charming riverside park.

FANNING A SPARK OF RESISTANCE

Fifty years of conflict with the Iroquois and their English allies, and the inexorable westward movement of settlers below the Great Lakes, had bred in the Odawa a deep hatred of the British. When the French marched against Fort Duquesne (which was being constructed by the British at present-day Pittsburgh) in 1754, there were many Odawa in their ranks. Odawa warriors were also part of the force that soundly defeated Major-General Edward Braddock and his well-armed troops when the British tried to take back the fort the following year.

Among those who fought at Fort Duquesne was a 35-year-old Odawa warrior named Pontiac. The resounding victory may have ignited in him a spark of resistance that soon blazed across the countryside.

Even before 1763, when the Treaty of Paris ended the French regime in North America, the charismatic Pontiac was gathering allies for a movement against the British. In a series of secret meetings, he won the support of the Seneca of the Six Nations Iroquois, as well as most of the Odawa's traditional allies – the Ojibwe, Wendat and Potawatomi. In the end, a total of 18 North American nations were united in a last desperate attempt to hold the land that had been theirs for so long.

The rebellion began in the spring of 1763, with the siege of Fort Detroit and the capture of nearly 50 English soldiers at Point Pelee. The uprising quickly spread as Michilimackinac (see page 106) and other newly British strongholds fell to the widening alliance. But distances were large and communications difficult and Pontiac, based near Detroit, could not hold the diverse groups together as winter approached.

By 1764 the uprising was over. The following year Pontiac was among a number of signatories to a series of peace treaties, an act those still hostile to the British saw as nothing short of treason. Even his own people turned against him. Forced into exile, he wandered west. In the spring of 1769, he was killed by an assassin in the ancient town of Cahokia on the Mississippi River.

Pontiac's Rebellion spread as far west as Fort Michilimackinac. There, a large party of Odawa and Ojibwe lulled English suspicions by engaging in a game of lacrosse on the field just outside the landward gate. Moving closer and closer to the open gate, they suddenly snatched a cache of weapons concealed by their blanketed women, below, and poured into the fort. Alexander Henry was among the few to escape; the rest were killed or captured.

BARBARA ENDRES

Calumet & Allumette Islands

Above the Chenaux, the Ottawa River splits to circumvent Île du Grand Calumet – Calumet Island. The name comes from the dense white limestone – like alabaster in color and consistency – found there. This stone was, as Alexander Henry noted, "soft enough to be whittled into pipes or calumets", first by North Americans and later by the French.

The eastern channel was the one generally taken by the canoe brigades, for most of the drop in the river could be picked up in the Grand Calumet Portage, at just over two kilometres the longest between Montreal and Grand Portage. The long, uphill portage trail circumvented two steep ravines. Today the rapids have largely disappeared beneath the Calumet Dam and the portage trail has begotten two island roads.

Above Calumet Island, the river broadens into Lac Coulonge. Nicolas d'Ailleboust, the Sieur de Coulonge, founded a French fur post – Fort Coulonge – here about 1635. It begot a town of the same name just east of the lake, from which one can follow Promenade de Parc des Chutes to Coulonge Falls, with its network of walking paths, chasm bridges and lookout points.

At the top of Lac Coulonge, the Ottawa splits again around Île aux Allumettes – Allumette Island – named for the placid stretch of the river on its west side – Allumette Lake. Here, reeds and cattails grow; they once provided torches – *allumettes* in French – for the valley's Algonquin.

To get to the lake, the fur traders had to circumvent another set of rapids around what is now called Morrison Island. Inhabited for at least 5,000 years, it was controlled for decades by a series of 17th-century Algonquin leaders named Tessouat, who regulated all commerce on the main river with a toll operation. Today's downstream paddlers won't find any tolls, and the curling white water of the Allumette Rapids is still exciting, even with higher water levels.

Allumette Lake is long and narrow, stretching northwest to the ancient Laurentian Mountains. Native-born voyageurs, whether North American or French-Canadian and Highland Scots felt at home in this landscape of rugged cliffs and tenacious trees. But early French traders and later Orcadians, used to rolling green countryside, often found the terrain forbidding. It would remain so – if often stunningly beautiful – for nearly 2,000 kilometres west.

Highway 51 from Pembroke to Petawawa parallels Allumette Lake. Just south of Pembroke, Highway 148 crosses the lake to Allumette Island on the Quebec side of the river, then curves down through Fort Coulonge.

William Henry Bartlette's Lac des Allumettes, *painted in 1842, has about it a quality of foreboding that many English and French traders apparently felt as they entered the Canadian Shield.*

WILLIAM HENRY BARTLETT / NATIONAL ARCHIVES OF CANADA / C–002360

The Upper Ottawa

Upstream of Pointe au Baptême, the voyageurs encountered the Precambrian or Canadian Shield, an enormous swath of ancient rock and trees and water that extends from Labrador in the east to Yukon in the west. For many, this landscape is synonymous with Canada; for the fur traders, this was the *pays d'en haut*.

Traversing this primeval landscape, the Ottawa River was forced into existing cleavages in the rock. Near the town of Deep River, it flows along a giant fault in the bedrock, a cleft very likely caused in the same cataclysmic period that formed the Laurentian Uplands on the eastern shore. Even today, there are minor tremors along this fault line.

During the fur trade era, the stretch between Deep River and Mattawa was strewn with obstacles, the worst of them at Des Joachims (pronounced in the valley as "Da Swisha"), where a double portage was needed to circumvent the rapids at the bend of the river.

Today, these are gone beneath the hydro dam. The dam's headpond – Lake Holden – has also drowned the rapids upstream – Roche Capitane, Deux Rivières, the Trou and l'Eveiller – but this wider, calmer river allows not just canoeists, but boaters generally to enjoy the river.

Visitors can admire this ancient landscape at Driftwood Provincial Park, on a quiet bay on the river's west side. The bay, which traps large quantities of driftwood, was formed by higher water levels resulting from the dam, but the park landscape is much older, encompassing a series of sand and gravel ridges left by the retreating glaciers 10,000 years ago. The park is on the east side of the Trans-Canada Highway (No. 17) between Stonecliffe and Rolphton.

MIKE GRANDMAISON

Pointe au Baptême

Where the Ottawa River narrows as it meets the encroaching shield, a long sandy point juts far out into the waterway.

PETER ST. JOHN

For brigades heading upstream, this was an obvious campsite that took on a special significance. Here, the veteran voyageurs "baptized" any novices in the crew, and these greenhorns were required to stand drinks – a régal – all round. For paddlers today, the point, which emerges from the pines on the Ontario shore and extends halfway across the river, is virtually unchanged and easily recognized. For landlubbers, however, it is out of bounds, for it sits on property that belongs to Atomic Energy of Canada.

The Mattawa River

The view of the Mattawa from the Red Pine Trail in Samuel de Champlain Provincial Park is worth the short climb to the overlook.

PETER ST. JOHN

Connecting Lake Nipissing to the Ottawa Valley, the eastward-flowing Mattawa River follows an ancient fault line in the Precambrian bedrock. Though strewn with rapids and falls, for more than 6,000 years it was the main highway from the Great Lakes to the St. Lawrence. Appropriately, Mattawa means "meeting of the waters".

The cataclysmic fracturing of the Earth's crust that produced the valley, with its soaring walls and visible thrust lines, occurred about 600 million years ago. Even now there are tremors along the fault line, which may explain the ancient stories of spirits in the cliffs.

There was more cataclysm about 11,000 years ago, at the end of the last glaciation, as meltwater from the receding ice sheets roared down the fault into the Ottawa Valley. The raging ancestral Mattawa carried great boulders with it; between Pine Lake and McCool Bay, these huge cobblestones pave an area that today is more than 15 metres above the river.

The modern Mattawa is tame by comparison, a 65-kilometre swath of spectacular scenery that echoes ancient native traditions and the stories of the fur trade. For early North Americans, this was more than a highway; it was also the path to a very important mine. Below Paresseux (or "Lazy") Falls – named for a pair of voyageurs who, while awaiting the arrival of a new canoe, took an unauthorized vacation at the foot of the picturesque five-pronged falls – they had discovered a place of power. Three metres above the river, a cave in the canyon wall yields blood-red ochre. This mineral oxide of iron was used right across the continent for dozens of ritual purposes; ochre adorned soaring cliff walls in rock paintings and tiny artifacts in burial places. The Mattawa River mine, with its wet, red walls and womblike contours, was a particularly important ochre quarry.

Etienne Brûlé, one of Samuel de Champlain's "young men", was the first European to set foot in this land, in 1610. Over the next 250 years, thousands of others – Frenchmen, Scots, Englishmen and Americans – paddled, poled and portaged the same route. In brigades sometimes surpassing 100 canoes, they lugged vast quantities of trade goods inland to waiting trappers and bore the resulting wealth of furs out to Montreal.

For all these reasons, 33 kilometres of the river east of the eastern end of Trout Lake was named Ontario's first Provincial Waterway Park in 1970 and a Canadian Heritage River in 1988. At the eastern end of the designated section, Samuel de Champlain Provincial Park (with its excellent, hands-on interpretive centre) protects an additional 2,500 hectares of land on both sides of the river.

The Canadian Heritage portion of the river includes Paresseux Falls and Talon Chutes, two of the most attractive sites on the river. It also includes

Talon Portage, only 275 paces long by the fur traders' estimate, but according to Alexander Mackenzie (who had seen most of them), for its length, the most difficult, most dangerous portage on the continent.

Most of the rest of the sections of white water are considered tame by experienced paddlers, although the rapids at La Cave and La Prairie (Petit Paresseux) are rated difficult in high water, and high winds can render some of the larger lakes dangerous.

For voyageurs heading west to the rendezvous on Lake Superior, one of the highlights of the trip was Anse des Perches, just above Talon Chutes. This was the last section of white water that required the use of setting poles (or *perches*) for poling up the rapids. At its upper end, the heavy poles could be thrown away; from here to Lake Superior's western shore, all obstacles could either be run in the canoes or circumvented by portaging.

The Mattawa River begins in Trout Lake. For west bound Montreal brigades, this marked the end of the upstream portion of their journey. Once over a small height of land – La Vase Portage – they reached Lake Nipissing and the French River, which flowed west to Georgian Bay and Lake Huron.

TONI HARTING

The Trans-Canada Highway (No. 17) parallels the Mattawa River and there are no less than 12 canoe launches between the Ottawa River and Trout Lake. One of the most popular access points is the East Ferris Township Park on MacPherson Drive at the east end of Trout Lake. Many paddlers also access the river at the Campion Rapids in Samuel de Champlain Park, 50 kilometres east of North Bay. The park's interpretive centre provides an excellent fur trade overview and the 2.5-kilometre Red Pine Trail (one of many in the park) leads hikers to two panoramic overlooks over the river.

Modern paddlers, like the lazy pair for whom Paresseux Falls are named, can not resist dallying a bit at the foot of the tumbling water.

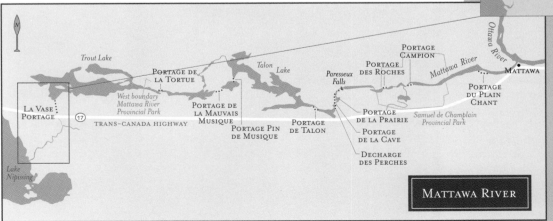

La Vase Portage

BRIAN WOLITSKI

Moose and wolves are both found around the shores of Lake Nipissing.

From Trout Lake, at the head of the Mattawa River, a small divide separates the watershed of the upper Ottawa River from Lake Nipissing and the Upper Great Lakes. This series of granite ridges and intervening bogs was one of the canoe brigades' least favorite stretches. La Vase has been translated as "Mud" Portage, but some have suggested that "Slime" or "Sludge" might be closer to the truth.

The traverse to Lake Nipissing is a total of 11 kilometres, of which eight could be paddled thanks to the dam-building efforts of industrious beavers. When the beavers were removed from the area by the very people who depended on their efforts, the voyageurs were forced to assume maintenance of the water control structures.

La Vase Portage was in use long before the fur trade era, of course. In fact, the trail is believed to be one of the oldest-known trade routes in Ontario. It began with a 1.5-kilometre portage over a height of land south of Dugas Bay at Trout Lake's southwestern corner.

The trail led to a beaver pond at the end of a small creek running into the La Vase River. From there – except for two short carrying places – the route was by water through a succession of creeks and ponds, though the North West Company's huge *canots du maître* were sometimes brushed by branches as they squeezed through. Lake Nipissing, like Lake Winnipeg far to the west, is shallow and dangerously choppy in a high wind. The brigades traversed it on the south shore, where a chain of small islands offered some protection. From the south-west arm of the lake at Dokis, the canoes were portaged over the Chaudière des François and into the French River.

The Trans-Canada Highway (No. 17) crosses La Vase Portage just east of North Bay; an Ontario historic plaque marks the site. Those who have traversed it in recent years confirm that though the mud is as slimy as ever, the beavers are back, helpfully making ponds in just the right places.

La Vase Portage still lives up to its name, at least it does here, where the Trans-Canada Highway crosses it just east of Nipissing. A plaque identifying the portage route is located on the south side of the highway.

PETER ST. JOHN

The French River

With ice-sculpted rocks along its length, white water beckoning paddlers, a network of riverside marshes and an extensive delta of polished granite, the French

PETER ST. JOHN

River is one of Canada's loveliest canoe routes. It is also habitat for several rare plants and the rare Eastern Massasauga rattlesnake.

The river served North American traders for millennia and they, in turn, led missionaries and traders along its 110-kilometre length. This early French and fur trade history is echoed in the names along the river, including Récollet Falls and the Voyageurs' and Old Fort Channels. These natural and heritage attributes earned the French River Ontario's first designation as a Canadian Heritage River, in 1986.

For westward-bound fur brigades, the French was a pleasant one-day, downstream run, a welcome change after slogging against the current all the

way from Lachine. In May, when the water was high, canoes filled with trade goods were usually slowed by only two portages – at Récollet Falls (where a wooden walkway has replaced the original portage path) and the Petite Faucille (or "Little Sickle"), close to Lake Huron.

The rest – about a dozen rapids along the main or southern channel – were generally run with a full load. Not every transit was successful, however, as divers at several rapids have discovered in recent decades. Where turbulent surface water combined with a moderate stream flow and a creviced river bottom, the divers sometimes found a stunning array of pots, kettles, muskets, flints, fire steels and traps. Some were dated from the late 18th century and had rested in niches on the rocky floor of the river for nearly 200 years.

During the height of the fur trade, many of these rapids were also festooned with crosses. As they passed, the voyageurs who had been lucky enough to escape the swirling water would tug their caps off and say a small prayer. Nor'Wester Daniel Harmon wrote, "Those who are in the habit of voyaging this way are thus obliged to say their prayers more frequently than at home. For almost every rapid we have passed since leaving Montreal, we have seen a number of crosses erected. At one I counted no less than thirty."

The brigades needed an experienced guide to find the best outlet into Georgian Bay, for the French River has four outlets. Express canoes might chose the Western Outlet and the Voyageurs' Channel, for these waterways offered

A fine fall day is a good time to enjoy a little serenity on the French River, which can be crowded during the summer months.

During periods of high water, paddlers following in the wake of the fur traders can run the Devil's Door in the Western Outlet.

the greatest protection against the open waters of Lake Huron. The majority of canoes, however, must have used the larger Main Outlet.

Near the mouth of the Voyageurs' Channel, the brigades sometimes camped at La Praire des Français, a grassy meadow large enough to accommodate the crews of several canoes. In a landscape of sculpted rock, the meadow offered a place where canoes could be repaired for the traverse of the Great Lakes.

Late May and June (as well as September) are still some of the best times to canoe the French River; in July and August it is often almost overwhelmingly popular. Canoe access is possible at several points; the most common is from the community of French River, where lodge accommodation can also be found. Highway travellers can access the river from a rest place on the west side of Highway 69, which crosses the river just south of Bigwood.

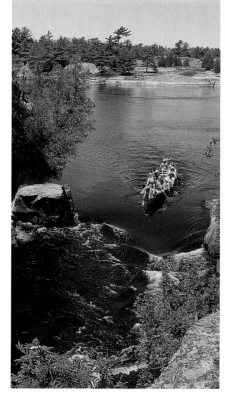

TONI HARTING

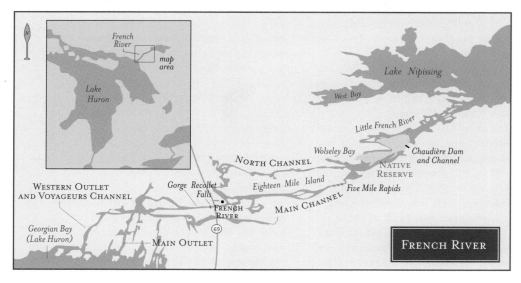

Lake Huron

Travelled for centuries by the Odawa and Wendat peoples who lived about its shores and on its islands, Lake Huron was the first of the Great Lakes experienced by the French. They were amazed by its size and depth and frigid waters. Though all these attributes were greatly exceeded by Lake Superior to the northwest, they had reason to be impressed. Almost half of France, after all, could be floated in the combined area of the five Great Lakes.

As coastal people raised largely on fish, the early French traders also found the size of the creatures pulled

Later voyageurs had little time to stop and admire the view, or the fish. Their job was to cross the top of the lake with all possible speed and in that they preferred Lake Huron to Superior, for Lake Huron's North Channel is buffered on the south by a series of islands, including Manitoulin – the world's largest freshwater island.

Emerging from the mouth of the French River, the brigades were forced around Grondine ("Moaning") Point, named for the sound of the surging waves. Then they pointed their canoes west and headed past Killarney, once a Georgian Bay fur post, toward a narrow

A piece of history much older than the fur trade can be found just west of the town of Desbarats (named for a Montrealer

PETER ST. JOHN

after ore, not furs, in the 1840s) along the Trans-Canada Highway. Just east of the turnoff for St. Joseph's Island, the highway passes through a roadcut on which ancient ripple marks can clearly be seen. These marks, caused by waves lapping on the shore of a primeval sea, are estimated to be two billion years old.

PETER ST. JOHN

from the waters of the lake to be cause for wonderment. In 1613, Samuel de Champlain, who had not yet actually seen the lake, wrote: "It abounds ... in trout ... of a monstrous size; I have seen some that are as much as four and a half feet long."

channel between Great Cloche and Little Cloche Islands. The name Cloche (or "Bell"), which has been attached to many other landforms in the region – La Cloche Creek and Lake, as well as the Cloche and South La Cloche Mountains – comes from a remarkable glacial erratic

Sculpted granite, flaming trees and deep blue water, left, combine for spectacular autumn scenery on Lake Huron.

PETER ST. JOHN

The channel the Montrealers used – the Swift (not Little) Current passage just south of the town of Birch Island – passes beneath a small bridge on Highway 6, the road to the Georgian Bay ferry. Just large enough for a canot du maître, *the channel, above, is today a favorite place for fishing; huge whitefish still cruise the crystalline waters.*

that sits on a private beach near the route the voyageurs took. Someone discovered that the dark basaltic mass rang with a low, clear tone when struck. Other, smaller "bells" lay nearby.

In the 19th century, the Hudson's Bay Company operated a post at Little Current, on the northeastern tip of Manitoulin. Lake Huron's North Channel, with its clear water, hundreds of rocky islets and beautiful mixed forests, is edged by a range of white-topped quartz hills. The combination creates some of the most spectacular canoe country in Canada. Even veteran voyageurs must have been moved by the beauty of the place.

Several north shore communities owe their names to the fur trade. Some say the town of Spanish was named for a Spaniard who fled justice along the lower Mississippi River. Travelling far to the north, he joined some French free traders on Lake Huron. And Blind River, where the Odawa gathered every summer to pick and dry blueberries, was almost impossible to see until the voyageurs were right on top of it.

Paddling, sailing and cruising are still the best ways to enjoy the spectacular scenery of Lake Huron's North Channel. A variety of lodges on Manitoulin Island, as well as in communities along Highway 6 and the Trans-Canada Highway, offer accommodation, boats and canoes for rent. Killarney Provincial Park, located on the north shore of Georgian Bay on Highways 69 and 637, offers camping facilities and superb canoeing at the foot of the La Cloche Mountains.

Spectacular scenery such as this at Whitefish Falls characterizes Lake Huron's north shore.

PETER ST. JOHN

Fort St. Joseph

If today Fort St. Joseph National Historic Site seems off the beaten track, it was not always so. When construction began in 1796 at the southwestern tip of St. Joseph Island in the St. Marys River, the fort was at the heart of international relations, both military and commercial.

Then, transportation was by water, not land or air, and the site, at the junction of canoe and shipping routes between the vast Northwest, the Mississippi River and the Lower Great Lakes, was

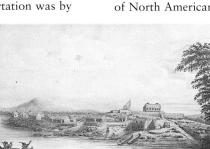

LIEUTENANT EDWARD WALSH / CLEMENTS LIBRARY, UNIVERSITY OF MICHIGAN

deemed by the English to be vitally important. The previous three decades had brought great changes to the region, not all of them favorable for Britain.

The Treaty of Paris in 1763, which ended the Seven Years War, ceded a vast swath of territory, previously claimed by France, to the British. When French officials packed up and went home, Scots and English entrepreneurs quickly stepped in to expand the fur trade. By 1780, they had established posts north to Athabasca and west to the Great Plains.

But all was not peace and harmony in British North America. First the native nations and then the New England colonies waged war against England and in 1783, Britain ceded its territory south of the Great Lakes and east of the Mississippi to the new American republic.

As part of that agreement, Fort Michilimackinac (see page 106), which for nearly a century had supplied the fur

trade in the upper Midwest and along the Mississippi, passed to the Americans – at least on paper. The British procrastinated. Not only was a huge trading territory at stake, but they believed that turning the fort on Mackinac Island over to the Americans would greatly damage their hard-won alliances with a number of North American nations. By 1785, American settlers were pouring into the Ohio Valley, displacing the native tribes who lived there.

At last, Jay's Treaty forced the British to relinquish Fort Michilimackinac and construction began in 1796 on Fort St. Joseph, across the newly drawn American border. Many of the fur traders and some of the merchants at Mackinac Island also pulled up stakes and moved to St. Joseph Island and by 1804 a thriving community was growing around the fort. While never destined to be a centre of commerce (one soldier called it "the military Siberia of Upper Canada"), Fort St. Joseph was at times a hive of activity, particularly when the canoe brigades arrived and native trappers came in with huge bales of furs.

Aware that American settlement was creating growing antipathy among native North Americans, U.S. Governor General Hull invited all the important First Nations leaders to Fort Mackinac in 1809, to win their allegiance or at least induce them to remain neutral in the coming war with Britain. At this

In 1804, Lieutenant Edward Walsh painted one of the few watercolors of Fort St. Joseph. Though the fort was only seven or eight years old, a community had already grown up outside its walls.

Grand Council, though Hull gave the native leaders many gifts, they told him that they had pledged their allegiance to Britain at Fort St. Joseph.

Angered, Hull told the gathering "to ignore the post at St. Joseph, because we Americans will seize it before the end of the summer." Listening to this was the brother of John Askins Jr., Superintendent of the British Indian Department. He relayed the message to Askins, who in turn forwarded it to his superiors.

When the tale was told, Captain Charles Roberts, the commanding officer at Fort St. Joseph, recognized immediately how vulnerable he was. His only hope of victory was to strike first, so over succeeding months he recruited the local *coureurs de bois* and at least 400 Ojibwe, Odawa, Menominee, Winnebago and plains Dakota warriors to join forces with him. When war was declared the combined force attacked Michilimackinac and later Prairie du Chien to take control of the Upper Mississippi and Western Great Lakes for the balance of the war.

Roberts then abandoned Fort St. Joseph and led his people back to Mackinac Island. The Americans retaliated by burning Fort St. Joseph to the ground and tried to retake Michilimackinac in 1814, but failed. The British finally returned the fort when the war ended a year later, but decided not to rebuild Fort St. Joseph. For a time, they operated out of a post on Drummond Island, just south of St. Joseph, but were forced to leave in 1828 when the Boundary Commission granted the island to the Americans.

This chimney, which dominates the ruins of the fort, is believed to have been part of one of two kitchens built in 1804 and 1805, following a fire that destroyed the original kitchen in 1802.

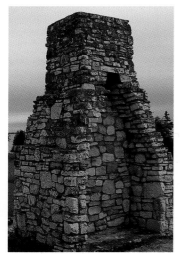

PETER ST. JOHN

Today, among the stabilized ruins of Fort St. Joseph and at an excellent interpretive centre, visitors can relive this vivid period when fur traders and

ST. JOSEPH ISLAND

native North Americans held Canada's southern boundaries against American expansionism.

St. Joseph Island is 90 kilometres south of Sault Ste. Marie and is accessed by a bridge off the Trans-Canada Highway (No. 17) just west of Desbarats. Whether you take the 51-kilometre scenic route to the fort around either side of the island on Highway 548, or cut through the centre on 10th and 5th Side Roads like the locals do (reducing the distance to 35 kilometres), St. Joseph Island, with its rolling farmland and waterside resorts, is worth a visit. The fort is open between the last weekend in May and early October, from 10 a.m. to 5 p.m. daily. Trails wind through the surrounding maple forest and white-tailed deer, moose and beaver are often seen. An admission fee is charged.

ADAPTABLE ANISHINABEG MOVED WEST WITH THE TRADE

The name Ojibwe (also Ojibwa, Ojibway and Chippewa) originated with an Algonquian-speaking people north of today's Sault Ste. Marie. Over time the designation was adopted by other linguistically and culturally similar groups and now applies to people occupying a broad swath of territory from Lake Huron west to Saskatchewan and south from Michigan to Montana. Many today prefer the designation Anishinabe, or the plural Anishinabeg (pronounced Ah-nish-in-*aah*- bay, meaning "first man" or "first people").

Like the related Odawa to the east and Potawatomi to the south, Ojibwe life of the early 17th century was a seasonal round of winter hunting and spring and summer fishing, augmented with plant foods in spring, summer and fall. Superb hunters like the neighboring Cree to the north, many made a smooth transition to trapping and hunting for the fur trade.

Large numbers of Ojibwe gathered annually to spear huge sturgeon and net whitefish near rapids and falls in many places on the Great Lakes. Finding them thus engaged at Sault Ste. Marie, the French gave them the name *Saulteurs*, "the People of the Rapids", which became "Saulteaux" (pronounced *So*-to), a name still used in Manitoba, Saskatchewan and Montana.

In addition to meat and fish, the Ojibwe relied heavily on wild rice, a nutritious cereal grass that grows in shallow water at the edge of many southern shield lakes, maple syrup, collected from maples and box elder in early spring and turned into maple sugar, and many types of berries.

As friends and allies of both the Wendat and Algonquin, the Ojibwe became involved in the fur trade in the 17th century and by the early 18th were pushing into territory west of Lake Superior. This was Dakota country (see page 144) and Ojibwe and French incursions caused war between the two nations beginning in 1736. Until 1750, when the Dakota finally abandoned the region and moved west, the beautiful pine-clad, island-studded region was a battlefield, remembered today in such place names as Warroad, Massacre Island and Sioux Narrows.

Always adaptable, the Ojibwe continued west with the trade. Expanding out onto the plains, they established villages along the Red and Assiniboine Rivers (see Peguis on page 197), intermarried with their close cousins, the Cree, to create an Oji-Cree society in eastern Manitoba, and adopted many Dakota ways to become bison hunters on the plains.

An Ojibwe Legend

An Ojibwe legend tells of an early 17th century prophet who foretold the coming of Europeans through a dream. In this vision, huge canoes with white wings like a bird appeared from the east, carrying strangers with skin like snow, whose faces were covered with hair. The people, anxious to discover whether the dream was true, sent a fleet of canoes along Great Lakes to the Great River until they came upon the strange intruders.

The Ojibwe used birchbark, widely available throughout the Upper Great Lakes, for both domed and conical lodges.

THOMAS WESLEY McLEAN / NATIONAL ARCHIVES OF CANADA, OTTAWA / C–069768

Sault Ste. Marie

by Sally Gibson

S ault Ste. Marie has long been a stopping place for travellers. Once a seamless zone of trade, the area

The St. Marys River Rapids have drawn fishermen for millennia. When William Armstrong painted his Fishing at Sault Ste. Marie, Ontario, *above, in 1869, the fishers were likely after whitefish. Today, this indigenous species is joined by salmon, which were seeded in Lake Huron and draw sport fishermen, right, in the fall.*

Modern paddlers can enjoy this historic waterway on the St. Marys River Heritage Water Trail, complete with 15 checkpoints, that has been established between Sault Ste. Marie and Fort St. Joseph. For information, contact Parks Canada or the Friends of the St. Marys River.

is now separated by the Canadian-American border and has cities named Sault Ste. Marie on either side of the St. Marys River Rapids. The rapids drop almost seven metres over less than three kilometres, draining Lake Superior. Travellers today can enjoy the natural beauty of the area and find remnants of the fur trade that stimulated early European settlement.

Drawn by abundant whitefish, ancestors of the Ojibwe settled next to the rapids more than 2,000 years ago. These *Bawatig*, "People of the Rapids", were called *Saulteur* by the French, the first Europeans to arrive. They named the area the *Saut*, meaning a "leap" or a "fall", and established a Jesuit mission on the shore in 1655. The territory was claimed for France by Sieur de Saint Lusson in an elaborate ceremony in 1671.

Strategically located, Sault Ste. Marie was central to the western fur trade. Canoes and bateaux travelling from the St. Lawrence River were funnelled through the St. Marys River corridor via a portage on the south shore.

Recognizing the importance of the location, New France granted a seigneury on the St. Marys River to

Chevalier de Repentigny in 1751. Sieur de Repentigny fortified and farmed the property, but departed five years later at the outbreak of the Seven Years War, leaving the post in the care of a free trader, Jean-Baptiste Cadotte. With the fall of New France, the British took over the post and introduced a military presence, but the small garrison withdrew to Michilimackinac, 80 kilometres south, after the post burned.

In 1765, English trader Alexander Henry was granted exclusive rights to the Lake Superior area, but others challenged Henry's monopoly and moved into the region. Rivalry of this type, here and elsewhere, led to the creation of the North West Company. One of the partners, Simon McTavish, already owned the largest post at the Sault. Managed by Jean-Baptiste Nolin, it became known as "the Palace of the North West".

Other early traders in the area included Lyman and Truman Warren, John

Sayer, John Johnson and George Ermatinger. George's younger brother, Charles Oakes Ermatinger, arrived later and built a grand house on the north shore.

After the American Revolution new boundaries were drawn, with British territory on the north side of the St. Marys

River, but English traders at the Sault continued working on the American side until 1794 when Jay's Treaty demanded that the British move to the north shore. The North West Company selected a site at the foot of the rapids and built a complex that included a canal and lock with a pathway for hauling up loaded canoes and bateaux.

Conflict between Britain and America broke out again in 1812. British traders from the Sault joined with Colonel Roberts' garrison at Fort St. Joseph and hundreds of native allies to capture Fort Michilimackinac on Mackinac Island. In 1814, the Americans retaliated, first burning the abandoned Fort St. Joseph and then John Johnson's place on the American side. The NWC holdings at the Sault were razed, though possibly by the company agent to prevent the post from falling into enemy hands. Gabriel Franchère, on his way to Montreal, arrived four days after the attack. In *Relations du voyage*, he states that he found the ruins of the buildings still smoking and the company's schooner driven down the rapids and burned.

The post was rebuilt at war's end and the fur trade, with its fierce rivalry with the Hudson's Bay Company, resumed. After the companies amalgamated in 1821, the HBC post at the Sault contin-

ued to furnish supplies for voyages to and from the Great Lakes.

Today, the Canadian Sault has a population of 80,000; its American neighbor is much smaller, but shares the rapids, which have been harnessed for hydro-electric power. The once-commercial waterfront of Sault Ste. Marie, Canada, has been transformed into a pleasant boardwalk for pedestrians and cyclists, anchored at the east end by Ermatinger/Clergue Heritage Site, a national historic site.

A reconstruction of the original canoe lock, also a national historic site, is located west of the downtown boardwalk. Continuing on the boardwalk and across the Francis Clergue Generating Station is the Sault Ste. Marie Canal National Historic Site. Here visitors can cross the lock gates and follow the Attikamek Trail to the St. Marys River Rapids.

On the American side, Portage Avenue, where once voyageurs portaged their bateaus and cargo, parallels the river. The River of History Museum tells the story of fur trade activity in the area. John Johnson's house, moved a short distance from its original location and opened on a limited basis to the public, is a memorial to independent traders who settled in this hinterland.

PETER ST. JOHN

The Ermatinger/ Clergue Heritage Centre

by Sally Gibson

The stone house that independent trader Charles Ermatinger built on the shore of the St. Marys River is no ordinary structure.

PETER ST. JOHN

The fieldstone base of the Clergue Blockhouse, below, was part of the original North West Company post at Sault Ste. Marie.

Constructed in a classic Georgian style, with grounds sloping to the water, it was an imposing sight for early 19th century travellers on the waterway. Today, completely restored and refurnished, it continues to draw thousands of visitors.

The two-storey, hip-roofed structure has a front porch with slender pillars supporting a pediment. It was constructed with typical Quebec masonry methods and is immensely strong. Underpinned in the basement by cedar logs at least 38 centimetres in diameter, the house has stone walls almost a metre thick. Ermatinger also cleared the land and constructed a flour mill.

In this gracious environment, the Ermatingers offered hospitality to both area residents and weary travellers.

Henry Rowe Schoolcraft, an American Indian Agent who was married to the daughter of British trader John Johnson on the American side of the river, often remarked on the social gatherings at the Ermatinger home. Invitations to the annual caribou dinner were eagerly sought. The Ermatingers lived in the house until 1828, when they returned to Montreal.

The house changed hands many times after the Ermatingers left Sault Ste. Marie. Finally, in the 1960s it was commemorated as a national historic site and authentically restored. The summer kitchen, which had burned, was reconstructed in 1983-84 and the grounds were enhanced in 1998-99. Elegantly furnished in early 19th-century style, the house is operated by the City of Sault Ste. Marie and is open to the public from April to the end of September and by appointment in October and November. The Clergue Blockhouse was moved from its original site on the riverbank to the Ermatinger property in the 1990s.

Follow the signs for the downtown waterfront from the Trans-Canada Highway (No. 17) or after crossing the International Bridge. Ermatinger House is located at 831 Queen Street and can be reached by travelling to the eastern end of Bay Street and turning left into the parking lot.

FUR TRADE FREE AGENT by Sally Gibson

Charles Oakes Ermatinger was the son of a prominent Montreal family of Swiss descent. His father, Lorenz, worked for Forrest Oakes, a fur trade merchant, and married his sister Jemima Oakes. Lorenz was an original member of the North West Company, first organized in 1779.

Charles became engaged in fur trade activities with the North West Company at the headwaters of the Mississippi, west of Fond du Lac in what is now Minnesota. It was here that he met and married Mananowe (Charlotte), the daughter of the prominent Ojibwe policy maker, Katawabeda.

In 1808 Charles parted ways with the North West Com-pany and moved to the north shore of the St. Marys River. He settled with his wife and their growing family in a log house while constructing a large house of stone. They had 13 children; seven lived to adulthood.

During his stay at Sault Ste. Marie, Charles Oakes Ermatinger operated as an independent trader involved with various fur companies, including the American Fur Company on Mackinac Island, and continued to trade south of Lake Superior in American territory.

At the outbreak of war in 1812, Ermatinger joined the British forces at Fort St. Joseph to capture Fort Michilimackinac on Mackinac Island. However in 1814, when the Americans arrived after burning Fort St. Joseph, Ermatinger was captured and questioned, but released. His house was not touched, though the North West Company post was burned, as was John Johnson's home on the American side.

After the war, Ermatinger served as an agent for the Hudson's Bay Company from 1816 to 1820. During this time he was visited by Lord Selkirk and the two travelled together to Britain.

PETER ST. JOHN

Ermatinger House has been a landmark on the north shore of the St. Marys River for nearly 200 years. Today, fully restored and surrounded by period gardens, the house easily draws visitors back to the 1820s, when an invitation to dine was eagerly sought.

The North West Company Lock

by Sally Gibson

The first lock at Sault Ste. Marie was constructed in 1797, soon after the North West Company was forced to relocate to British territory on the north shore of the St. Marys River. A lock and canal would efficiently transport goods around the St. Marys River Rapids. In 1799, Alexander Mackenzie, still a NWC partner, reported that the lock was nearing completion. The following year, George Heriot wrote in *Travels Throughout the Canadas* that there was a good canal with a lock, as well as a road by which carriages might bypass the rapids.

In 1799, the NWC partners reached an impasse and Mackenzie formed a splinter group, the XY Company. A bitter dispute over the use of the canal followed. The following description of the lock comes from an 1802 report by Royal Engineer Captain Bruyàres, who had been directed to examine the situation at the Sault:

"The landing is in a bay immediately at the bottom of the fall on the nearest channel to the land of the north shore. A good wharf for boats is built at the landing, on which a store house, 60 feet long, 20 feet wide is erected. The wharf is planked all around it. Close to the store a lock is constructed for boats and canoes, being 38 feet long, 8 feet 9 inches wide. The lower gate lets down by a windlass; the upper has two folding gates with a sluice. The water rises 9 feet in the lock. A leading trough of timber, framed and planked, 300 feet in length, 8 feet 9 inches wide, 6 feet high supported and levelled on beams of cedar through the swamp is constructed to conduct the water from the canal to the lock. A road raised and planked 12 feet wide for cattle extends the whole length of the trough. The canal begins at the head of it which is a channel cleared of rocks and the projecting points excavated to admit the passage of canoes and boats. This canal is about 2,580 feet in length, with a raised bridge or pathway of round logs at the side of it 12 feet wide for oxen to track the boats. About 170 feet from the upper part of the canal a storehouse is built 36 feet long, 23 feet wide. An excellent saw mill for two saws is constructed ..."

The XY Company finally constructed a second portage road north of the canal and in 1804, on the death of Simon McTavish, controlling partner of the NWC, the companies amalgamated. By this time the company had small sailing vessels on the Upper Great Lakes and goods were loaded and unloaded at wharfs at either end of the portage road. Later references indicate that goods may well have been carted on the road originally used to track the boats.

The reconstructed lock is located just north of the office building of the St. Marys Paper Company on Huron Street. Follow the signs for the downtown waterfront from Highway 17 to Huron Street or continue on Huron Street after crossing the International Bridge. Now a national historic site, the lock is marked with a Historic Sites and Monuments Board plaque.

PETER ST. JOHN

France H. Clergue, an American entrepreneur, purchased the lands of the former post in 1894. Learning of the existence of the lock, he followed the watercourse, discovered it covered by silt and debris and reconstructed it with permanent stone walls. This portion of the HBC lock in its original location is the last vestige of a fur trade post that was once a significant presence on the St. Marys River corridor.

TRADING GOODS FOR TROOPS by Sally Gibson

Transportation has always been treacherous on the Great Lakes and not only for canoes. La Salle's ill-fated *Griffin*, the first ship on the Great Lakes, disappeared on its maiden voyage in 1679. Despite this, the number of ships gradually increased during the French colonial period, particularly between Niagara and Detroit. The latter became a major ship-building centre. For a long time, the falls at Niagara and the rapids at the Sault impeded shipping as a means of facilitating the fur trade, but eventually the Great Lakes route was more widely used than the northern canoe route.

Superior was the most daunting of the lakes. The Sieur de la Ronde, a knight of the order of St. Louis, built the first ship on Superior in 1734. After the French era, Alexander Henry took over the post at the Sault and in 1770, established a ship-building centre and air furnace for assaying ore at Point aux Pins on Lake Superior, just west of the Sault.

In 1784, the North West Company was granted permission to build a ship to be used on Lake Superior. The 45-ton *Beaver*, unable to get up the rapids to Superior, was allowed to sail on Lake Huron. A few years later the sleek and speedy *Nancy*, with a figurehead maiden on her prow, was making regular trips for the company. Along with cargos of fish and furs, she often carried maple sugar from the Sault and St. Joseph Island. In 1793, the 75-ton *Otter* was built, but she and the *Discovery* were both lost in an attempt to bring them down the St. Marys River Rapids. The *Athabasca*, however, was successfully floated down the falls.

Both the *Beaver* and the *Athabasca* were used in the War of 1812, which took a heavy toll on ships of the upper Great Lakes. The *Caledonia*, used in the capture of Fort Mackinac in 1812, was lost later that year. The *Nancy*, which had harrassed American ships, was finally burned and sank in the mouth of the Nottawasaga River in 1814 and the *Mink* was captured on Lake Huron. When the NWC post was burned at the Sault, the *Perseverance* was also burned.

Mineral wealth, settlement and eventually western grain drove the need for large ships and easy passage on the lakes. The St. Marys Falls Ship Canal opened on the American side in 1855 and in 1895 the Sault Ship Canal opened in Canada. Today, huge lakers 300 metres long edge their way through the locks, but a canoe can still be locked through the Canadian canal. A plaque at Point aux Pins, 11 kilometres west of Sault Ste. Marie, Canada, commemorates ship building on Lake Superior. And the charred hull of the *Nancy* is in a museum at Wasaga Beach.

Determined to keep the last of the North West Company's ships out of American hands, Captain Robert McCargo sailed the Recovery, *below, to Isle Royale and anchored her out of sight at the end of a long bay now called McCargo Bay. Her masts were taken down, she was covered with trees and branches and left to freeze into the ice, hiding from marauding American ships. The ruse worked and in 1815 she was retrieved and put back to work, carrying fur trade supplies between Fort William and Sault Ste. Marie.*

HOWARD SIVERSTON / FROM *THE ILLUSTRATED VOYAGEUR*

The Fur Trade in Old Michigan

LINDA FAIRFIELD

The wild red currant has tasty berries similar to its cultivated cousins. Rich in Vitamin C, currants can be eaten fresh or dried. The Anishinabeg have harvested these and other berries for centuries.

Sleek and silky, beautifully tanned black beaver pelts, such as this one, right, established the standard against which all other trade items, both furs and goods, were measured. Each company set its own rates, which varied according to location and competition.

The Straits of Mackinac (pronounced *Mack*-in-aw), between the two vast bodies of water we know today as Lake Huron and Lake Michigan, has always had a special significance. Not only is this a bountiful place, teeming with fish and wildlife, it also provides access from the Precambrian Shield and the Eastern Woodlands to the Mississippi Valley and the Great Plains beyond.

North Americans have passed this way for thousands of years. Beginning at least 1,000 years ago, the *Natamissing Bemadisidjig Michinimakinang* – the "First People of Michilimackinac" occupied summer fishing villages on the shores of the strait and on the islands that strategically occupy its mouth.

The Anishinabe descendants of these early Woodland People – the Odawa of northern Lake Huron and Manitoulin Island, the Ojibwe of the Algoma region north of Sault Ste. Marie and the Potawatomi of lower Lake Michigan – were still living around the lakes when French adventurers first arrived in the 1630s. By 1670, the Ojibwa and Odawa were heavily involved in the French fur trade and, with the displaced Wendat of Huronia, had admitted Jesuit missionaries into their midst.

A decade later, traders had established fur posts and French soldiers had built the region's first fort beside the Jesuit missions at St. Ignace, and adventurers had pushed much farther afield (see the French Fur Trade on page 24).

Over the next 150 years, the fur trade dominated life at the Straits of Mackinac and a thriving community grew up on both sides of the straits. After 1763, British traders and soldiers joined the mix. Though they got a decidedly cool welcome at first, changes in British policy toward native North Americans and the growing realization that there would be no French "rescue" of the formerly French colonies, as well as a mutual dependence necessitated by the fur trade slowly created strong alliances between the British military and the Ojibwe, Odawa, French-Canadian and mixed-blood or Metis peoples of the region. Though the battles of the Revolutionary War were never actually fought in the region, threats of attack in the late 1770s prompted the British to move their fort and its surrounding community from Michilimackinac on the south shore of the straits northeast to Mackinac Island, where the island's limestone cliffs provided greater protection. The threatened strikes never came, but the fort was lost at the negotiating table as the Straits of Mackinac passed to the newly created United States of America with the treaty of 1783.

Loath to abandon their unfinished bluff-top fort on Mackinac Island

SCOTT ROBERTSON / COURTESY ROBERTSON'S TRADING POST

The clear, blue water of Lake Huron and its bountiful surrounding forests had long supported a diversified lifestyle for the Anishinabeg and their ancestors.

and the lucrative trade it protected, the British procrastinated about leaving for more than a decade. Finally, in 1796, they turned the region over and moved north (see Fort St. Joseph on page 93), taking their hard-won native allies and many French-Canadian fur traders with them.

Tension simmered in the region for 15 years as American settlers poured across the Ohio River and finally exploded with the declaration of war in 1812. Before word had reached the young American commander on Mackinac Island, the British, bolstered by hundreds of North American, French-Canadian and Metis allies, had landed and were positioned to take Fort Mackinac. It was surrendered without a fight and held by the British until war's end in 1815.

The peace that followed quickly brought a return of fur trade prosperity to the Straits of Mackinac. John Jacob Astor reopened the office of the American Fur Company he'd established on Mackinac Island just before the war, and quickly built a trade that from the early 1820s to the mid-1830s was truly global in scope. Then changes in fashion in Europe and depleted fur resources in North America combined to spell the beginning of the end of a very long era.

Today, the history of the region is celebrated in a rich variety of interpretive centres, museums and heritage reconstructions at St. Ignace, at Colonial Michilimackinac, the reconstructed fort at Mackinaw City, and on Mackinac Island, where time seems to stand still.

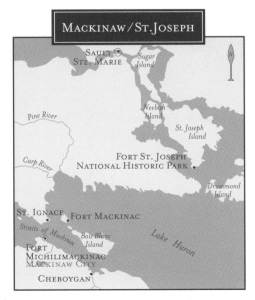

MACKINAW / ST. JOSEPH

SAULT STE. MARIE
Sugar Island
Pine River
Neebish Island
St. Joseph Island
Carp River
FORT ST. JOSEPH NATIONAL HISTORIC PARK
Drummond Island
ST. IGNACE FORT MACKINAC
Straits of Mackinac
Bois Blanc Island
Lake Huron
FORT MICHILIMACKINAC
MACKINAW CITY
CHEBOYGAN

The derivation "Mackinaw" – either in pronunciation or spelling (as in Mackinaw City) likely comes from a misreading of old French manuscripts, where the letter "c" often resembled a "t". Mackinac therefore became Mackinat, and "at" was pronounced "aw" in Old French.

St. Ignace

Iroquoian longhouses were multifamily dwellings that housed up to six or eight families. Each house stood about 20 feet high and was 20 feet wide and anywhere from 40 to 120 feet long. This construction style travelled with the Wendat of Huronia when, as refugees, they arrived on the north side of the Straits of Mackinac in 1671.

More than 1,000 years ago, people of the Woodland Culture established a large summer fishing village on the north side of the Straits of Mackinac at what is now St. Ignace. The settlement was one of a series of camps that echoed the circular progression of the seasons. In the fall and winter, families lived in scattered groups on the Upper Michigan Peninsula, where they hunted deer, elk and moose, as well as bear and beaver. As the days lengthened they moved to their sugar camps, where they tapped the region's huge maple trees and boiled the syrupy sap down to make sugar. When the ice on the lakes melted, they gathered in large communities on both shores of the straits, as well as on the nearby islands, to spend the summer fishing.

The waters here so abounded with fish – trout, pike, sturgeon, herring and whitefish – that the people believed the straits to be "the home of the fish". Archaeological excavations at nearby Michilimackinac indicate they were not far wrong. Digs on both sides of the strait, as well as on nearby Mackinac and Bois Blanc Islands in Lake Huron, have also revealed bone fishhooks, barbed spearheads and clay pottery shards; all attest to centuries of use of the region's rich resources.

The Ojibwe descendants of the Woodland Culture were still living on Michigan's Upper Peninsula when Father Jacques Marquette and a group of Wendat refugees arrived in the area in 1670. Allies and friends of the Ojibwe, the Wendat had been driven from their homeland in Huronia by the Iroquois

Wars two decades before. After a summer on Mackinac Island, they moved to more fertile land on the north shore of the strait. Here, before leaving with Louis Joliet for the Mississippi, Marquette established two missions: St. Ignatius Loyola (which gave its name to St. Ignace) for the Wendat, and St. Francis Borgia among a group of similarly displaced Odawa, an Anishinabe group closely related to the Ojibwe.

By 1680, the mission village at St. Ignace had grown to include fur trade posts and French soldiers had begun construction on Fort DuBuade, named for the Governor of New France, Louis de Buade, the Comte de Frontenac.

The fur trade grew by leaps and bounds until 1697, when a glut of furs in Europe prompted the colonial French government to try a number of measures to curtail the trade. Fort DuBuade and other posts were closed, the soldiers recalled and trade licences revoked. But none of these moves had much impact on an industry in which so many had found employment, freedom and adventure. The community at the straits continued to thrive and quickly became a haven for unlicensed *coureurs de bois*.

Shortly after 1700, the Wendat were lured back east to settle (at least for a time) near a new French fort at Detroit, but the Odawa stayed in the region, moving with the Jesuits across the strait in the first decade of the 18th century, when their land around St. Ignace was exhausted. In 1714, the French soldiers returned and also moved across the straits, where they constructed Fort Michilimackinac.

Today, St. Ignace celebrates its long, rich Anishinabe heritage in the Museum of Ojibwa Culture, housed in the old mission church, and a reconstructed Iroquoian longhouse in Marquette Mission Park helps to interpret the lives of the Wendat refugees who came to the area with Marquette. The nearby

DENNIS FAST

grave of the Jesuit priest and adventurer has been designated a national historic landmark.

St. Ignace is located on the south shore of Michigan's Upper Peninsula, 52 miles south of Sault Ste. Marie on Interstate 75. The museum is on North State, at the north end of the boardwalk, next to the Chamber of Commerce in downtown St. Ignace. Regular hydroplane service to Mackinac Island is provided from May through October from the town's natural harbor, while "Mighty Mac", the famous, five-mile-long Mackinac Bridge, arches over the Straits of Mackinac from the south edge of town. The surrounding region of Michigan's Upper Peninsula is remarkably unchanged. Forests of maple, oak and pine can still be found in the area; deer and moose abound, along with smaller mammals and birds.

Lush furs such as these, left, as well as strategic access to Lake Michigan made the Straits of Mackinac one of the most important places on the continent for 250 years from the mid-1600s.

The Path of Paddlers

A drive west of St. Ignace along the northern shore of Lake Michigan on Highway 2 is particularly scenic, with secluded bays and panoramic overlooks. The highway shadows the route of the early French traders and an interpretive centre at Pointe Aux Chênes ("Oak Point") provides information about the area, as well as Hiawatha National Forest, celebrated in Longfellow's epic poem of Ojibwe life, The Song of Hiawatha.

Colonial Michilimackinac

The south shore of the Straits of Mackinac has been inhabited for millennia. The abundant fish they sought have been here much longer. Among millions of artifacts unearthed at Fort Michilimackinac, which boasts the longest continuous archaeological excavation in the United States, is an almost perfect fossil of a whitefish. Little wonder early Anishinabeg called these straits "the home of the fish".

European settlement here, where Lake Michigan pours into Lake Huron, is much more recent. Fort Michilimackinac, which took its name from the island that guards the straits to the northeast, was begun in 1714 when French troops returned to the area after a 17-year absence. Abandoning their earlier fort on the north side of the straits, they followed the community of Odawa, Jesuits and free traders to the south shore. At the edge of the beach they built a fortified community, combining a strategic military post with a fur trade depot.

Bolstered by Odawa and Ojibwe warriors, the French launched attacks on the Fox and Chickasaw people to the west and south, who were blocking the fur routes to the Mississippi, and later on the British to the east, who were threatening territory claimed by France. Meanwhile, the *coureurs de bois* pushed far west and north, heralding an era of tremendous change.

For a half-century, Michilimackinac flourished. Living at a crossroads of humanity, the people of the straits were at home with diversity, unfazed by racial, linguistic or religious differences. A multilingual, multiracial community evolved as French traders married local Odawa and Ojibwe women. Prefacing the Metis community that would grow up around the Forks of the Red and Assiniboine Rivers in Manitoba a century later (see page 196), their mixed-blood children soon became the dominant population of the straits.

But the long French fur trade era was coming to an end. In Europe and in eastern North America, France and Britain were immersed in war and in 1761, British soldiers took control of Fort Michilimackinac. New England traders were right behind them.

In the main, the resident French and Metis *coureurs de bois* accepted the new reality, and for the most part retained ownership of the property inside the stockade. Pragmatic and independent, their main goal was unfettered trade.

The Odawa and Ojibwe viewed things differently. Though they had fought with the French against the British for more than a century, they

Colonial Michilimackinac boasts the longest ongoing archaeological excavation in the United States and the digging is put to practical use. Each building in the fort is constructed in its original place in the manner of original construction. This vertical construction dates from the fort's early French period.

PETER ST. JOHN

did not believe that the defeat of colonial New France meant that they too had been defeated. Moreover, they expected that the established traditions of trade, including gift-giving and trading *en dérouine*, would be continued. They were angry when the British ignored these customs and many believed the French would return to rescue them.

But 1761 passed and another year followed. In the east, their old allies and even some of their old enemies spoke of rising against the English; secretly, the Ojibwe agreed to join them (see Pontiac on page 83). In 1763, under the guise of gathering for a day of sport, they overwhelmed the unsuspecting British and captured Michilimackinac, killing 21 soldiers and taking many more prisoners, along with a number of English traders.

The defeat of Michilimackinac was echoed in many places, but the widespread uprising could not be sustained. By 1764, Pontiac's Rebellion was over and the British, somewhat chastened, returned.

Michilimackinac began another growth spurt, expanding beyond the walls along the shore of the straits, but peace was short-lived. In 1775 the New England colonies rebelled and the British turned to their new-found native allies. Weighing the situation, the Odawa, Ojibwe, Winnebago, Sauk, Fox, Menominee and Sioux decided that as rigid and obtuse as the British might be, they were not bent on clearing and settling the land, as the American rebels were.

Yet Michilimackinac was almost indefensible. After several towns on the Mississippi fell to the rebels in 1778, the decision was made to move the whole community across the water to Mackinac Island, where the towering bluffs overlooking the southern harbor seemed to provide an ideal situation for a fort above and a village below.

Today, visitors to Colonial Michilimackinac have a superb opportunity to undertake what amounts to

PETER ST. JOHN

a walk through time. Each building in the reconstructed post has been painstakingly excavated, researched, rebuilt in its original location and constructed in the original manner. The archaeological excavation, which began in the 1950s and has unearthed more than two million artifacts, continues today. But Colonial Michilimackinac is anything but staid; its newest exhibits feature state-of-the-art, hands-on, interactive interpretation, drawing children of all ages into its fascinating past.

Fort Michilimackinac is located in Mackinaw City, just west of the Mackinac Bridge. Heading south over the bridge from St. Ignace, you have a brief but excellent view of the huge fort on your right. Follow the signs off Interstate 75. Fast, frequent ferries to and from Mackinac Island (and connecting to St. Ignace), make it possible to visit all the major sites in the area with ease. The ferries leave from the Mackinaw City docks off Huron Avenue.

The British took over from the French after the fall of New France in 1763, and ran Fort Michilimackinac here for more than 30 years. Today, this period is recalled in many of the interpretive programs the fort operates, from museum-quality exhibits such as this one to interactive displays and hands-on activities.

Mackinac Island

This print of Mackinac Island, below, done from a sketch drawn on nearby Round Island, was produced in 1812. The relocated Fort Michilimackinac (or Fort Mackinac, as it's known today) can be clearly seen perched on the cliff above the bay. The British moved it there from the south shore of the straits, but were well aware that the fort was vulnerable from the hill that can be seen above it. Though they lost the fort at the negotiating table, their gamble paid off in the opening days of the War of 1812. From their new fort on St. Joseph Island to the north, they sailed to Mackinac Island's northern end and took the fort without firing a shot.

According to an ancient legend, Mackinac Island earned its name from its appearance when approached by water. Hump-backed and oval, it resembles a turtle rising from the lake.

Quite sensibly the people called it *Michi Mikinack* or "Great Turtle", a term that can also be interpreted to represent the Great Spirit – *Michie* or *Gitche Manitou*. In one version of the ancient flood legend that all the world seems to share, Mackinac Island was the first land to appear above the waters after the inundation.

By the time Father Claude Dablon, who had a Jesuit mission among the Ojibwe at Sault Ste. Marie, arrived on its shores in 1670, "Missilimackinac", as he called it, was known far and wide. "[It] is an island famous in these regions," he wrote. "... situated exactly in the strait connecting the Lake of the Hurons and that of the Illinois, and forms the key and the door, so to speak, for all the peoples of the south ..."

Yet for more than 100 years, that strategic location was not utilized by Europeans. Though the fur trade grew and the traffic in the waters around the island increased, the focus of trade was not the island itself, but rather the shores of the straits – first on the north shore at St. Ignace and after 1714, on the south side at Michilimackinac.

Mackinac Island continued to sleep – largely uninhabited – during the winter months and awakened in late spring to the return of Ojibwe fishermen and their families to the summer village along the crescent bay on the south shore.

At nearby Fort Michilimackinac, French troops had been replaced by English soldiers in 1761 and over the next two decades, first Ojibwe and Odawa warriors and then American revolutionaries threatened Britain's rather tenuous hold on the region. By 1779, the inherent difficulties in defending the fort were causing real concern.

That year the new British commander, Patrick Sinclair, stopped at the Ojibwe village on Mackinac Island en route to Fort Michilimackinac. Gazing up at the limestone heights, he envisioned a much more defensible fort, but the array of Ojibwe lodges along the beach made it clear that negotiations would have to be conducted on both ends of such a move.

Talks to purchase the island began immediately and though the details of the transaction were not completed until the spring of 1781, permission to begin the move was quickly given. Times had changed dramatically over the previous two decades. In 1763, England was an old colonial enemy; by 1779, she represented a lesser evil than the American settlers who were pouring west, clearing the land and displacing the original inhabitants as they went.

NATIONAL ARCHIVES OF CANADA / C–15127

At Fort Michilimakinac, Sinclair hastened the decision to move by ordering the Roman Catholic church dismantled and dragged across the winter ice to the new village. The population quickly followed and as Fort Mackinac (sometimes called Fort Michilimackinac) rose on the edge of the bluff, a new village

French and British traders combined to put pressure on Britain to hang on to Mackinac Island. So for 13 years, as the unfinished fort deteriorated, the British army continued to promote the fur trade and strengthen its native alliances. Safe from attack, the community on the island grew.

PETER ST. JOHN

grew around the harbor. From the beginning, the British realized the new fort was dominated by an even higher hill in the centre of the island, but Sinclair felt it was too far from the fortified village. It was a calculated risk that would eventually pay off for the British themselves.

Over the next three years, many buildings at Michilmackinac were dismantled, moved to the island and reconstructed. Huge stone walls and bastions were built and an officer's quarters was begun. In 1781 Old Michilimackinac was razed.

But in May 1783, while construction was still underway, the new commander at Fort Mackinac received the unwelcome news that his fort had suddenly become United States property under the terms of the treaty of 1783. Appalled, native North Americans and

At last, Britain could procrastinate no longer; in 1796 the army left for St. Joseph Island across the new American border. The Americans moved in and began the massive task of rebuilding, changing the configuration of the walls and finishing the huge officers' quarters.

In the village below, however, British companies continued to dominate the fur trade; in 1811, John Jacob Astor merged his American Fur Company with the Montreal Michilimackinac Company in order to establish a foothold on Mackinac Island. But the struggle between the United States and Britain was not over. In July of 1812, British soldiers and hundreds of fur trade allies surprised Fort Mackinac from the hill above the fort – the Turtle's Back – and forced the Americans, less than 60 in

Fort Mackinac, above the harbor, still looks and sounds much as it did in the heyday of the Michilimackinac fur era, though today it looks down on tourists, rather than traders. The 500 permanent residents summarize the island's history with five words: furs, forts, fish, fun and fudge.

A statue of Father Jacques Marquette stands just below the fort, near a reconstructed bark chapel.

PETER ST. JOHN

As soon as war was declared, the British and an army of native North American and Metis allies sailed from St. Joseph Island to the north end of Mackinac Island. There, they quickly gained the hill known as the Turtle's Back and forced the surrender of the fort.

total, to surrender. An American attempt to recapture the island in 1814 failed. But again, Fort Mackinac was turned over to the United States at the negotiating table, this time for good. Though the fur trade in the region had suffered, for a brief time after 1815 it soared in a renewal led by Astor, administered by his partner Ramsay Crooks and run by resident manager Robert Stuart. From Stuart House, the stately home built by Astor for his valued employee, the fur business boomed. Every summer furs arrived from the vast area below the Upper Great Lakes to be sorted and repacked in the huge warehouse next door to Stuart's home, From there, Astor's ships and supply lines took them to New York City and then around the world – to England,

Paris, Germany, even China. Mackinac Island had indeed become "the key and the door to all the peoples".

This heyday of the trade could last only as long as native North Americans were able to supply a virtually unlimited supply of furs, and European hatters continued to want beaver fur for felting. By 1832, Astor, ever the astute businessman, could see that American settlement and changing fashion would bring an end to a long era; he sold the company in 1834.

The era of fur and forts on Mackinac Island was followed by fishing and, in recent years, fun and fudge, with a boom in heritage tourism. Today, the echoes of the past are easy to hear, for motorized traffic is forbidden on the island. Instead, the clip-clop of horses hooves and the whish of bicycles can be heard along the immaculately tended streets. Fort Mackinac is open to the public, as are Stuart House and several other historic buildings; the warehouse serves as a community hall.

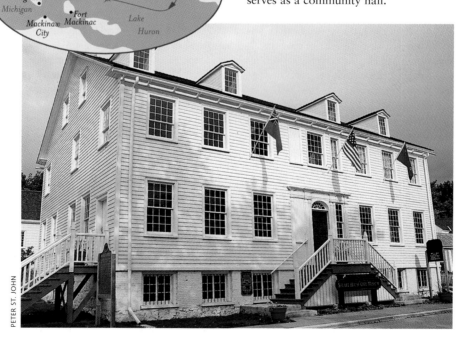

Stuart House, built by John Jacob Astor for Robert Stuart, the resident manager of his American Fur Company office, gleams in the autumn sunshine. If the size of the place makes Astor look like a spendthrift, consider this: in 1822, Stuart shipped three million dollars worth of furs, making Astor America's first millionaire and the richest man in the nation.

PETER ST. JOHN

BUILDING A GLOBAL EMPIRE

Though born in Germany, and apprenticed in London, by the age of 35 John Jacob Astor was the leading fur merchant in the fledgling United States. A global outlook and a remarkable ability to assess international markets, combined with a patient, long-term approach, allowed him to absorb the vagaries of an intensely competitive business in a tumultuous era.

Astor got into the fur business almost by accident. After four years working in London for an elder brother who manufactured and sold musical instruments, the 20-year-old Astor decided to try his luck in the United States. With his fortune tied up in a small stock of instruments, he sailed for Baltimore in November 1783. At the mouth of the Chesapeake River, his ship was marooned in ice. Delayed for weeks, he was befriended by a fur dealer. Go to New York, he was told, and invest the proceeds of your instruments in furs.

BARBARA ENDRES

It was excellent advice. With the furs, he returned to London and by the end of 1784 was back in New York, bent on a life as a fur trader. Astor spent much of the next 15 years in Montreal. Though forced to cede its political authority over the United States, Britain had largely retained its trading rights and Montreal was the trade's uncontested centre.

The Louisiana Purchase of 1803 opened a vast new American territory that the Lewis and Clark expedition soon found to be rich in furs. Astor, among others, coveted these resources, but his view went farther. Though the Pacific coast was not part of the purchase, he believed that the U.S. could make a case for ownership, giving it a gateway to the Orient. In 1808, he established the American Fur Company to take advantage of these new developments.

Early in 1810, after a failed merger attempt with the North West Company, Astor's company merged with the Montreal Michilimackinac Company, creating the Pacific Fur Company and obtaining a foothold in the strategic Straits of Mackinac.

Astor's approach to the Pacific was two-pronged – by land and by sea. The overland party, led by Wilson Price Hunt, left Montreal in June for Mackinac Island and St. Louis. From there, with winter looming, they set out up the Missouri in October, heading for the Rocky Mountains and the mouth of the Columbia. Almost everything imaginable went wrong, and it was only due to repeated help from North American peoples that only a handful of the overlanders died.

Meanwhile, in September, 1810, Astor's ship the *Tonquin* had left New York under the unfortunate command of Jonathan Thorn. Thorn had an excellent reputation as a military officer, but his rigid temperment was unsuited to captaining a commercial vessel manned with a civilian crew of Canadians and carrying several of Astor's junior partners. The *Tonquin* reached the mouth of the Columbia River in March, but soon sailed on to disaster (see page 242).

These setbacks were compounded by the War of 1812 and intense British competition over "the Columbia Department". Ever persistent, Astor reinvested in his business on to Mackinac Island as soon as hostilities ended and by the mid-'20s was shipping furs all over the world. He became America's first millionaire, and died in 1848.

John Jacob Astor was surprisingly cautious. Though when his mind was made up he often committed large sums of money toward an enterprise, he weighed his options carefully and often read the signs of economic change long before his contemporaries.

A good year before the European market for furs began to sour in the mid-1830s, he had sold his holdings in the American Fur Company to his partners. And though he was a remarkable traveller, sailing often to Europe, he never visited many of the places where his company did business, including Mackinac Island.

North of Superior

Labrador tea (Ledum decumbens), *a low shrub with clusters of white flowers, was widely used during the fur trade as a substitute for or addition to imported tea. It grows on sunny ledges, in peaty soil and amid moss and lichen.*

Lake Superior is a sea, beautiful, vast and violent. Five hundred and sixty-three kilometres long, 257 kilometres wide and more than 400 metres deep in places, it is not only the largest of the Great Lakes, but the largest lake in the world.

The history of time is written in its rocks. Minerals – iron, silver, copper and gold – are mined in many places; in Lake Superior Provincial Park, ancient volcanoes created the raw material for one of the finest pebble beaches in the world, and stromatolites, fossils nearly two billion years old, have been found in the rocks near Schreiber, on the lake's northern shore. Superior's shoreline rocks also bear the scars of repeated glaciations, which scoured its depths and eroded its ancient mountains, particularly along the north and east.

Fed by nearly 200 rivers, including many of the waterways of the fur trade – the Pigeon, Kaministiquia, Nipigon, Pic and Michipicoten – Lake Superior drains through the tumultuous St. Mary's River at Sault Ste. Marie. Like the lake itself, the river and its resources are shared by Canada and the United States.

Its great size and enormous depths give Superior a climate of its own, for its water never really gets warm. Its average temperature is 4°C. In June, the month when the west-bound voyageurs were most often crossing en route to Grand Portage or Fort William, the difference between the warm air and the cold lake frequently created dense fogs. These could be lethal for the thin-skinned birchbark canoes and brigades were sometimes fogbound for days. In July and August, large expanses of hot, bare rock along the shores of the cold lake can create sudden air currents and violent, unforeseen squalls. Then, as now, these made the lake unsafe for small craft by early afternoon. In the fall, northwesterly winds sweep across the lake, creating waves that rival those of the Atlantic Ocean.

Countering these dangers, the fur traders often paddled at night and regularly were on the water by three or four o'clock in the morning. Except where deep bays cut into the shoreline, or shallow, submerged ledges extended into the lake, they stayed close to shore, using the screen of offshore islands where they could.

For all its unpredictable, often deadly behavior, Lake Superior is hauntingly, wildly beautiful, particularly along its north and east shores. The east end of the lake is a spectacular land of contrasts. Travelling north from Sault Ste. Marie, both the

PETER ST. JOHN

lake and the Trans-Canada Highway that follows its shore trace the western edge of the Algoma Highlands. This rugged region of ancient mountains clad with mature mixed forests is famous for its autumn colors. Among the best places to see these fiery displays is Lake Superior Provincial Park.

North of the park, the Michipicoten River provides a link between the Great Lakes and James Bay. Following this ancient route, French fur traders first paddled the Michipicoten River in 1662, portaging to the Missinaibi, which took them down to the Moose River and the bay. Today's paddlers will find the Missinaibi largely unchanged, one of Ontario's last unspoiled wilderness rivers.

Farther north and west, the fur route circumvents Pukaskwa National Park, a wilderness enclave where wolves, black bears, moose and woodland caribou live, then follows the northern shore all the way to Thunder Bay.

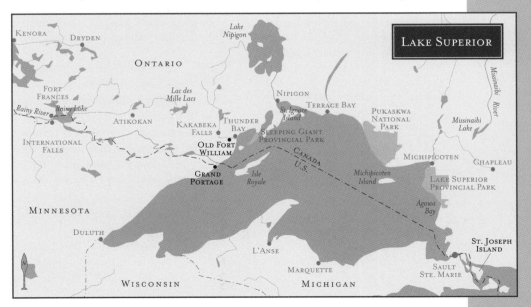

LAKE SUPERIOR

Agawa Bay

On the shores of a lake known for its size, might and dramatic shoreline cliffs, Agawa Bay on Superior's east end was a place of respite during the fur trade era. Here, a long crescent of sand provided a haven for storm-tossed brigades, giving them a place to collect themselves for their next assault on the frigid inland sea.

Agawa Bay's beaches were created by sediment carried by meltwater that poured down from the diminishing ice cap at the end of the last glaciation. Just northeast, the glacial Agawa River carved a magnificent gorge in the Canadian Shield. Today, the canyon is accessed by a special train from Sault Ste. Marie; in autumn it draws hundreds of visitors to view the waterfalls and spectacular fall colors.

Agawa Bay was known to French *coureurs de bois* from the 1660s. On advice from the Ojibwe north of the great lake, Pierre Radisson and Médard Chouart des Groseilliers followed Superior's eastern shoreline north to Michipicoten, then paddled down the Michipicoten, Missinaibi and Moose Rivers to James Bay – the "northern sea" the French had been seeking since the time of Champlain a half-century before (see The French Fur Trade on page 24). By 1717, French canoes were passing this way with regularity, carrying the trade west and north to a series of posts established under New France's *Postes du Nord* policy.

The French era ended in 1763, but British free traders were at work in the region within five years. However, a trading post was not built on the bay itself until the 1830s, when the Hudson's Bay Company opened an outpost to serve the regional headquarters at Michipicoten.

The fortunes of the little post, variously referred to as "Ahguawah", "Ogayon" and "Agawang", varied with the numbers of fur-bearers in the Algoma hills to the east, and a small community grew up near the bay between 1850 and 1915.

Today, the old post is gone, but a campground just south of Agawa River allows visitors to stroll the long swath of sand and paddle Superior's cold, clear waters. Agawa River is frequented by anglers; a famous trout pond – Burnt Rock Pool – is just upstream.

In September, the summer crowds leave and fall storms turn the great lake to gunmetal gray. It's easy then to imagine that homeward-bound brigades might be rounding Agawa Rock at the northern tip of the bay, looking for a safe campsite.

Agawa Bay edges much of the southern half of Lake Superior Provincial Park's 115 kilometres of spectacular shoreline. The campground, which is generally open from the third week of May until the end of September, lies along the lakeshore, just west of the Trans-Canada Highway, 138 kilometres north of Sault Ste. Marie. Agawa Rock Day Use Area, with its soaring cliffs and dramatic trails, is at the north end of Agawa Bay. Access is from the highway.

PETER ST. JOHN

For voyageurs facing a menacing gunmetal gray lake on their way home to Montreal, Agawa Bay was a place of refuge.

A GRAND CANVAS FOR INSPIRATION

Rising in a sheer wall from a narrow ledge on Lake Superior's east shore, Agawa Rock provided a grand canvas for the ancestral Anishinabeg to record their dreams, or perhaps their warnings for then, as now, the world's largest lake was not to be trifled with.

Using ochre – was it from the sacred mine on the Mattawa River? - mixed with grease, they painted spirit figures that can be seen even today. The work must have been done during the summer months, when warm weather and light winds temper the lake's fury. Then, the aquamarine water laps quietly at the ledge, and an artist, with the rock rising before him and the sun warming his back, could let his imagination soar.

Summer is also the best time to visit this remarkable gallery. Though the dramatic 400-metre trail to the rock, with its narrow defiles and soaring cliffs, is less crowded in the spring and fall, high winds are common in these seasons and can make it impossible to view the largest collection of figures. A total of 117 pictographs have thus far been discovered

at Agawa Rock, but others may yet be found.

Both the pictograph site, which is well signed, and the beautiful trail to the rock are located just west of the Trans-Canada Highway in Lake Superior Provincial Park.

Henry Schoolcraft, the early 19th-century geographer, said the Ojibwe created two types of pictographs, Kekeewin, things well known by the people, and Kekeenowin, sacred things, the teachings of the medas or priests. In such a dramatic site as this one, it's not hard to imagine that the latter might predominate.

PETER ST. JOHN

Michipicoten

In Anishinabe, Michipicoten means "a place of bold promontories", which aptly describes the steep sand cliffs along the lower reaches of the river. Though today the community of Michipicoten River, located two kilometres southwest of Wawa, is a quiet village, this northeastern corner of Lake Superior was a hub of activity for hundreds of years.

The ancestral Ojibwe and neighboring Cree to the north were trading back and forth long before the first Europeans hove into view in the 17th century. They discovered early that a small portage from the Michipicoten River into Lake Missinaibi would lead them to the Missinaibi River and, following that turbulent waterway for its entire length, to the Moose River and the western shore of James Bay. Both nations used this river corridor to hunt, trade and camp and the Cree often travelled down to the great lake in the spring and summer to fish.

It may have been a Cree trading party that in 1660 told Pierre Radisson and Médard Chouart des Groseilliers about this link between Lake Superior and the "North Sea". Radisson later told the English that he and his brother-in-law had actually made the trip themselves, but historians who have tracked his rather erratic career believe this boast was untrue, and simply meant to add credibility to his story.

Anyone who had actually made the journey would not have underestimated the distance between the Great Lakes and James Bay, as the two Frenchmen did. Des Groseilliers told authorities in New France that the trip could be accomplished in about a week, but the Missinaibi alone has more than 75 sets of rapids and falls, including spectacular Thunderhouse Falls. Today's wilderness canoeists find the trip from Missinaibi Lake to the bay takes nearly three weeks.

Nevertheless, over the ensuing centuries, both the French (and later Nor' Westers) on the lake and the English on the bay made use of the river highway. By 1725, the French had a post at the mouth of the Michipicoten River and for nearly 200 years a succession of French and British companies kept at least one productive post operating. In 1767, New Englander Alexander Henry – who'd been granted a licence for the entire region north of Lake Superior – built a post here and reported the existence of "a French establishment" nearby. By 1783, the North West Company, of

PETER ST. JOHN

Seen here from one of its "bold promontories", the Michipicoten River provided a haven from the great lake and a route to James Bay.

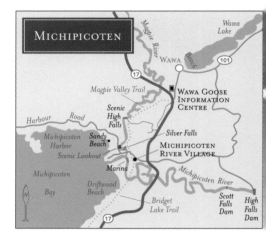

which Henry was a founding member, had extended the old post and was running it as a subsidiary to its larger operation at Sault Ste. Marie.

Michipicoten came into its own again after 1814, when the North West Company's depot at the Sault was destroyed during the War of 1812. From then on, and even more so after the NWC amalgamated with the Hudson's Bay Company in 1821, Michipicoten was the most important post on Lake Superior's east coast. By 1850, it served as the headquarters for the Agawa Bay and Batchawana outposts as well as the Missinaibi hinterland, and a new provisioning outlet – more general store than fur trade post – was built in 1876.

This solidly constructed building, with its hand-hewn beams and dovetail joints, served first the HBC and later a local mill operation for more than a century. In part, the building's longevity was due to the tin cladding that the mill owners added in 1952. This served to preserve the logs, which were rediscovered when at last the building was dismantled in 1991.

The local community wanted to save the building, but could not muster the necessary funds so an ingenious compromise was suggested. The timbers, wide plank floors and trading counter were shipped 900 kilometres southeast to Peterborough. There, festooned with a selection of trade goods and tanned pelts, they embrace a fur trade display at the Canadian Canoe Museum, which houses the world's largest collection of canoes and kayaks.

The west-flowing Michipicoten River joins the south-flowing Magpie about two kilometres southwest of Wawa ("Wild Goose" in Anishinabe). One of the main posts of the fur era was located at the rivers, on the south side, across from the marina. The area is called Michipicoten Post Park and there are plans to mark the site with signage. The village of Michipicoten River, also at the junction of the rivers, can be reached via the Michipicoten River Village Road, west off the Trans-

Canada Highway (No.17). The Michipicoten River itself can be seen from several scenic viewpoints along the Trans-Canada, which crosses the river south of the village road. Wawa caters to tourists with accommodation, nearby campgrounds and stores that carry local crafts and regional information.

The Michipicoten Trading Post, as it might have looked about 1800, has been moved – lock, stock and trading barrel – to the Canadian Canoe Museum far to the southeast in Peterborough, Ontario. There, though far from its lakeside origins, it must feel right at home among dozens of wonderful canoes.

Missinaibi River

Flowing north and east from the Great Lakes watershed to the Moose River and James Bay, the Missinaibi River served for centuries as a thoroughfare for Ojibwe and Cree peoples and their ancestors. Today, many canoeists believe the Missinaibi is one

Fairy Point, pictographs of species not seen in the region for decades.

The fur trade was simply a variation on an ancient theme. Between the late 17th and early 20th centuries, goods and furs moved along the river corridor to and from Moose Fort, which was

The canyon below the final cascade in the Thunderhouse Falls complex is for accomplished paddlers. Less experienced canoeists will find suitable sections of the river above this stretch.

TONI HARTING

of Canada's finest wilderness rivers, a silver ribbon of turbulent water, spectacular landscapes and varying habitat that is almost untouched along its 426-kilometre length. For all these reasons the Missinaibi was designated a Canadian Heritage River in 1985.

Rising five kilometres north of the watershed divide at Missinaibi Lake, the river is a short portage from Dog Lake and the upper reaches of the Michipicoten, which flows west to Lake Superior. This access to the Great Lakes created a trading corridor that was used for millennia. Archaeological excavations along the route have revealed portages that have been in continual use for 2,000 years, Iroquoian ceramics from the Lower Great Lakes, a 15th-century fishing camp, a traditional Ojibwe canoe building site and, at

established on James Bay by the Hudson's Bay Company in 1672-73, or other posts along the river over the next 140 years.

Most fur posts were on the larger lakes and many were short-lived. The exception was Brunswick House (later New Brunswick and eventually Old Brunswick House), established by the HBC on the west side of Brunswick Lake in 1789. A centre of the trade for nearly a century, it grew in the first half of the 19th century to include a farm operation with livestock and several buildings.

The Missinaibi was never an easy highway to travel, particularly upstream. From its source, the river drops almost 330 metres as it crosses the Canadian Shield to the James Bay Lowlands, flowing into the Moose River just above the village of Moose River Crossing and continuing to its broad estuary on James

Bay. Along the route are more than 75 sets of rapids and falls, including the spectacular and aptly-named Thunderhouse Falls, downstream from Mattice. Little wonder the HBC built its first short-lived post, Wapiscogamy House, well downstream of the falls.

Today's paddlers, who can access the river by both rail and road, are invariably headed downstream. Many begin at Missinaibi on Dog Lake; others take the 93-kilometre gravel road into the provincial park campground on Missinaibi Lake, thus avoiding several wet portages and the possibility of being marooned by bad weather on the large lake, but also missing most of the lake's spectacular sheer granite cliffs and the best pictograph site on the route – Fairy Point. This is the place that most believe gave the river its name, for Missinaibi is close to the Anishinabe word meaning "pictured waters".

Here, painted with ochre on the sheer granite walls, are the stone canoes of the *Memegwaysiwuk* (pronounced May-may-*gway*-shi-wuk), the mischievous, hairy-faced people who live in the crevices of the cliffs, as well as long-departed caribou and the great water lynx, spines rippling along its back, that waits in the rapids for careless paddlers. Dating pictographs is nearly impossible, but these must be at least 225 years old, for the name was in use when English traders first arrived at the lake in 1777; some believe they are much older.

Wildlife abounds here. Bald eagles and elk, part of an introduced population, live around the junction of the Hay River, while downstream otters and beaver can often be seen at Peterbell Marsh, north of the railway crossing.

Coastal caribou, sandhill cranes and semi-palmated plovers inhabit the James Bay Lowlands. Unlike the coastal reaches of Hudson Bay to the north, this region is well treed, though the spruces and poplars diminish in size as the river nears the coast.

July to September, when spring floods have receded and the mosquitos have abated, are the best months to canoe the Missinaibi. The most popular access points are the village of Missinaibi, reached by rail or Highway 651, and Missinaibi Provincial Park, accessed via the gravel road from Chapleau. From either point, intermediate paddlers will have little difficulty with the stretch north to the Peterbell crossing. Whitewater enthusiasts might want to put in at Peterbell, for the 146-kilometre stretch to Mattice, accessed by both Highway 11 and the railway, is both demanding and beautiful. Downstream of Mattice, the river is for experienced paddlers only, with challenging rapids and Thunderhouse Falls. Many canoeists leave the river at Moose River Crossing, but fur trade buffs will want to continue by river or rail to Moosonee and Moose Factory.

BRIAN WOLITSKI

The upper Missinaibi passes through the Chapleau Crown Game Preserve, a wonderful place to see wildlife, particularly moose, which are abundant and quite tame.

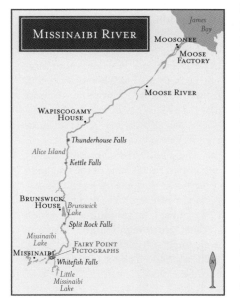

MISSINAIBI RIVER

James Bay
MOOSONEE
MOOSE FACTORY
MOOSE RIVER
WAPISCOGAMY HOUSE
Thunderhouse Falls
Alice Island
Kettle Falls
BRUNSWICK HOUSE
Brunswick Lake
Split Rock Falls
Missinaibi Lake
FAIRY POINT PICTOGRAPHS
MISSINAIBI
Whitefish Falls
Little Missinaibi Lake
N

Moose Factory

Moose Factory has always been more than just a trading post where the Hudson's Bay Company dispensed trade rifles and other articles of European manufacture. It has also been, at various times, a lumber mill that produced masts, spars and battens for the London market, a goose and duck feather factory, a market garden and a mixed farm. Today, it is a Cree community with a thriving tourism industry.

Originally called Moose Fort, this was the second post built by the Hudson's Bay Company on the shores of North America's great inland sea. Under the direction of Charles Bayley, who was named overseas governor after being imprisoned for Quaker activities in the Tower of London for seven years, the fort was constructed in 1672-73.

The English knew, thanks to Radisson and des Groseilliers, that the Moose River provided a connection with the Upper Great Lakes; they knew, too, that the route to Lake Superior passed through more than 500 kilometres of prime beaver country. Moreover, they believed the river's position on the western shore of James Bay, farther from both French interference and possible attack, was a safer place than Charles Fort (soon renamed Rupert House and now called Waskaganish) on the southeastern coast. With the French in mind, Moose Fort was situated on a large island in the centre of the river, about 15 kilometres from the mouth of James Bay.

The first dozen years of trading made the long winters on the bay seem well worthwhile as company ships returned to London each autumn with great loads of furs. But concerns about the French proved to be valid. Though headquartered hundreds of kilometres south along the St. Lawrence River, New France almost immediately felt the pinch of successful English trading on the bay in markedly diminished returns. So in

DENNIS FAST

1686, Chevalier Pierre de Troyes and a small army of 100 French and Algonquian warriors undertook an epic journey from Montreal to Moose Fort via the Ottawa River, Lakes

WILLIAM RICHARDS / HUDSON'S BAY COMPANY ARCHIVES / P-117

Timiskaming and Abitibi and the Abitibi and Moose Rivers. When de Troyes' force descended the Moose on June 20th, the English garrison, caught completely by surprise, succumbed.

In quick succession, Charles Fort and Fort Albany also fell to the French, along with the English ship *Craven*; it would be 17 years before the Treaty of Utrecht returned these and other bayside posts to the English and another 17 before trading was restored at the post that the French called Fort St. Louis.

When the British returned, however, it was for good. For the next century and a half, Moose Factory was a hub of HBC trade. One of the buildings constructed during this second British period, a blacksmith's shop built in 1740, can still be seen today, the oldest wooden structure in Ontario. Inside, a stone forge, originally built in the latter 1600s and moved about 150 years later, is one of the oldest "structures" in Ontario.

The fear of another attack lasted through much of the 18th century, however. A warehouse building erected soon after the British returned was built with crenellated embattlements along its large flat roof and mounted with brass cannons. The embellishments were an indication that the company half expected another French army to appear on the Moose River one fine spring morning. And well into the 19th century all manner of arms – sabres, flintlock muskets fitted with bayonets, cannon wheels and hundreds of cannon balls – were stored in Moose Factory's upper storeys, along with the trade goods.

Some of the HBC's earliest surveying was carried out from Moose Factory. Mapmaker Philip Turnor spent several winters based here, mapping the James Bay coast in both directions, as well as the Missinaibi and Michipicoten Rivers.

Today, Moose Factory is a Cree community of about 1,500, well equipped to provide a window on the past. Year-round at the new Cree Village Ecotourism Centre visitors can book nature excursions in one of the most unspoiled regions in Ontario. At the Centennial Park Museum, they can absorb fur trade history and learn about the ancient forge from an "apprentice smithy" at the Moose Fort

Black Smith Shop. Nearby are the cemetery, with its 300-year-old tombstones, a large fur press, and the Hudson's Bay Staff House, built by shipwrights more than 150 years ago. At St. Thomas Anglican Church, built in 1860, the altar cloth and vestments are made of beautifully beaded moosehide.

Visitors can also circumvent the northeast end of the island on a perimeter nature trail for a closer look at Ontario's only tidal river or book wildlife, nature and heritage tours to James Bay and Fossil Island.

The Ontario Northland Railway operates summer excursion and year-round regular service from Cochrane (on the northern route of the Trans-Canada Highway – No. 11) to Moosonee on the north shore of the Moose River. From Moosonee (founded by the Révillon Frères Trading Company in 1903), freighter canoes carry you to Moose Factory Island. En route is Charles Island, where Tidewater Provincial Park and its campground are located. Moosonee has lodge accommodation and restaurants, as well as the Révillon Frères Museum, while Moose Factory offers restaurants, gift and craft shops and a new lodge.

DENNIS FAST

At the southern edge of its breeding range, the semi-palmated plover is common in summer on the beaches and mud-flats around the mouth of the Moose River.

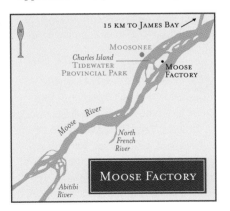

15 KM TO JAMES BAY

MOOSONEE
Charles Island
TIDEWATER
PROVINCIAL PARK
MOOSE FACTORY

Moose River

North French River

MOOSE FACTORY

Abitibi River

The North Shore

For today's travellers tracing the north shore by highway, the fur trade method of navigating Lake Superior sounds simple enough. The brigades simply shadowed the shoreline, yet even this could be hazardous for cliffs rise sheer from the water in a number

MIKE GRANDMAISON

Reverend George Munro Grant wrote, "Superior is a sea. It breeds storms and rain and fog like a sea." Breeding mist and fog, the lake laps at a volcanic beach at Old Woman Bay in Lake Superior Provincial Park.

of places, at times to heights of more than 150 metres. Skirting these walls of granite, the men had only to look up to see the power of the lake; in many places the cliffs were bare of any living thing for 10 metres above the water line.

To avoid the winds that daytime heating could bring, the fur brigades usually set off before dawn, stuck to the beautiful, deadly shore and aimed for the next safe landing site. Not surprisingly, posts grew up at a number of these safe havens, particularly at river mouths: Alexander Shaw was trading at the mouth of the silty Pic River (likely a derivation of the Anishinabe word *peek*, meaning "dark" or "muddy") in 1778 and a post was soon established.

Farther west, Nipigon lies in a deep bay framed by islands at the mouth of the Nipigon River. Its name has been variously translated as "deep clear water" or "water without end". Like

many places along the north shore, Nipigon has a history that extends almost to the retreat of the glaciers. Though it was the site of one of the earliest trading posts on Lake Superior, established in 1678, French fur traders were only among the most recent of a very long line of traders here.

Until 1803, fur brigades from Montreal headed for Grand Portage, just south of the mouth of the Pigeon River. The confirmation of the Canada-U.S. boundary put this post out of reach for Canadian-based trading operations; the North West Company responded by moving north to Thunder Bay and constructing a new inland headquarters at the mouth of the Kaministiquia River.

Paddlers still confront Lake Superior today, and still face the same beautiful, deadly shore. Thousands of years after humans first braved the waters of the great lake, it remains, as one chronicler wrote, "a place where man is and forever will be only a visitor."

Visiting is easier than it once was, even in places where nature rules such as Pukaskwa National Park. Elsewhere, communities welcome visitors and several lookout points – including Hydro Hill just west of the town of Terrace Bay – offer spectacular views out over Lake Superior.

The Trans-Canada Highway (No. 17, the Voyageur Route) traces the shoreline from Sault Ste. Marie to Thunder Bay, dipping inland to cicumvent Pukaskwa National Park. Four provincial parks – Neys, Rainbow Falls at Rossport, Sleeping Giant and Pigeon River provide a range of campground facilities on or near Superior.

Pukaskwa National Park

One of the best places to experience the timeless Lake Superior wilderness the early fur traders knew is Pukaskwa (pronounced *puck*-a-saw) National Park. This 1,878-square-kilometre preserve occupies the lakeshore's northeastern corner between the mouths of the White and Pukaskwa Rivers, an ancient, rocky landscape cut by wild rivers and cloaked in boreal forest.

There's only one road into Pukaskwa and it leads to the only serviced campground at the northwestern tip of the park. All other travel is on foot or by canoe or kayak. The Coastal Hiking Trail, a 60-kilometre, five-to seven-day, one-way journey (which depends on arrangements having been made to be delivered to or picked up from the trail's end) compares to British Columbia's West Coast Trail. The park has provided bridges over the major rivers and backcountry campgrounds at intervals, but the rest is up to each trekker.

Those who make the trip, or canoe the park's rivers or challenging lakeshore, may encounter wildlife that is rare elsewhere. About 40 woodland caribou inhabit the park; this is their most southerly Canadian range. Once abundant along Superior's northern shore and on many of its larger islands, these seldom-seen creatures are threatened here as in many other places in North America.

Moose, wolves and bears also inhabit the forests, there are coastal heron rookeries along the shore and the rivers are full of speckled and, in the fall, rainbow trout, as well as yellow pickerel and pike.

The park is located about 15 kilometres south of the Trans-Canada Highway (No. 17) on Highway 627. As well as modern services, the Hattie Cove campground has a visitor centre where backcountry guides to the rivers, trails and shores of the park can be purchased. Outfitters in nearby communities rent or sell canoes and kayaks, or provide boat or vehicle shuttles, allowing groups to canoe the coastal waters and hike back to the main campground along the coastal trail.

BRIAN WOLITSKI

Human poaching, along with logging, which destroys the fragile lichens on which caribou depend, and competition from white-tailed deer, all contribute to dwindling numbers of woodland caribou.

The name Pukaskwa, which Anishinabe linguists say should properly be written Pukasu, likely comes from the act of cooking bones to bake the marrow. The Anishinabeg have many stories about the region and the name long predates the creation of the park. The region is known in Anishinabe as Bagwaji-Gaamiing the "Wildshore", a name these huge logs, piled like pick-up-sticks on the beach, endorse.

MIKE GRANDMAISON

Nipigon

This region of Lake Superior's north shore was a focus of industry and trade long before Europeans ever dreamed of the Americas. Beginning nearly 7,000 years ago, people were surface mining copper here – the first known operation of its type in the hemisphere. For thousands of years, copper tools and art objects were produced locally by the Algonquian ancestors of the Cree and Ojibwe people, and traded over a vast area.

The French arrived in the late 1650s and travelled from Lake Superior 38 kilometres up the Nipigon River to Lake Nipigon, the largest lake entirely within Ontario's borders. The name Nipigon may be derived from the

Lookout points at several places along the Trans-Canada Highway treat visitors who take the time to stop to breathtaking views like this one.

PETER ST. JOHN

Anishinabe word *Animi-bee-gong* – "deep, clear" or "continuous water".

Daniel Greysolon, Sieur Dulhut or DuLuth, a French *coureurs de bois*

who had travelled to the headwaters of the Mississippi west of Lake Superior in 1678 and established trade relations with the Dakota there, was commissioned five years later by the colonial government of New France to do the same with the Algonquian peoples on the great lake's northern shore.

The first of Dulhut's posts was Fort La Tourette, constructed at the northeast corner of Lake Nipigon. For the next three years, until he returned to Québec to fight in the Iroquois Wars, he travelled and traded between here and another post on the Kaministiquia River at Thunder Bay.

Fifty years later, in 1727, Pierre Gaultier de La Vérendrye built a post at the mouth of the Nipigon River, near where the town's pleasant marina sits today. Later, both the North West and Hudson's Bay Companies maintained posts on Lake Nipigon.

Today the lake, with its unspoiled shores and red pillar-like cliffs, and the picturesque town on the shore of Superior are popular with people for much the same reasons the ancestral Algonquian chose this special place – superb fishing, magnificent scenery and abundant wildlife.

Nipigon sits at top of the northernmost bay of Lake Superior, where the Trans-Canada Highway splits to trace two routes through northeastern Ontario (Nos. 17 and 11). Seventeen kilometres east of town, the Kama Lookout picnic site allows a wide panorama of Lake Superior, which is particularly spectacular in the autumn.

Sleeping Giant

Stretching southwest in a curved promontory, Sibley Peninsula looms above Lake Superior like a reclining colossus. For the fur trade's Montreal-based voyageurs, the 240-metre cliffs created a welcome landmark that could be seen at a great distance. As they swept past the towering cliffs en route to Grand Portage, or after 1803, rounded the peninsula to Thunder Bay and Fort William, the end of 2,000 kilometres of paddling was at last in sight.

Geologists tell us that the landform is a series of sedimentary mesas, topped with a caprock of very hard diabase, but the Ojibwe have another explanation. They say that Nanabosho, the giant who rescued the Anishinabeg from their Dakota enemies, was sitting one day beside the lake. Scratching at the rocks, he discovered silver.

The treasure sent chills down his back; if white men heard of such riches, he knew they would destroy his people. So he made the Ojibwe bury the silver on a tiny islet at the end of the peninsula and swore them to secrecy. But one warrior could not keep the secret; he made himself weapons of silver and when he was killed in a battle with the Dakota, his killer set out to find the source of the shining metal. Nanabosho saw him coming, accompanied by two white men. To save his people, he raised a sudden storm that swamped the canoe and killed all aboard.

This wanton behavior angered the Great Spirit and to punish the giant, he turned him to stone. Today, Nanabosho can still be seen, stretched where he fell along the peninsula. The legend is remembered in Sleeping Giant Provincial Park.

The Ojibwe were not the peninsula's first inhabitants. A group of hunter-gatherers arrived here 9,000 years ago, in the wake of the receding glaciers. Anthropologists believe these Aqua-Plano people came from the western plains to hunt caribou as the climate warmed.

In a sheltered spot near the lake, protected by a wall of rock, excavations

DENNIS FAST

revealed a workshop area where distinctive spear points were crafted of a locally available stone. Today, the site is marked by a plaque along the highway.

The peninsula and park are accessed by Highway 587, south off the Trans-Canada Highway (No. 11/17), 42 kilometres east of Thunder Bay. Picnic sites, hiking trails and lookout points are located throughout the park; the full-service campground is at Marie Louise Lake, near the end of the peninsula. The park is open year round, but campground facilities operate between mid-May and mid-October.

Mining Silver

In the mid-1800s, one of the richest silver deposits in the world was found on Silver Islet, but quarrying the vein, which lay mainly under the lake, proved too dangerous and the mine was eventually closed.

Thunder Bay

Though not as famous for its fall foliage as the Algoma region at the other end of the lake, the hills and even the footpaths around Thunder Bay also put on a spectacular autumn show.

Before the city, which is today the world's largest grain-handling centre, was formed in 1970 by the amalgamation of Fort William and Port Arthur, Thunder Bay was a protected cove in the northwest corner of Lake Superior. And before the cove was named, the largest river that runs into it – the Kaministiquia – was a water highway to the west, travelled for thousands of years by North Americans.

It's not surprising then, that in 1678 Ojibwe traders advised Sieur Dulhut to put the next of his string of Lake Superior fur posts at the mouth of the Kaministiquia. From here, furs could come down the Kaministiquia from the west, while two other smaller rivers (today's Neebing and McIntyre) could be used to bring furs from the northern highlands. Ten years later,

trader Jacques de Noyon ventured upriver, following the deep gorge the ancestral Kaministiquia had cut through layers of Precambrian rock to the spectacular Kakabeka Falls.

Though by 1720 the voyageurs were aware of a shorter route – the Grand Portage – to the south, they maintained a post on the rugged Kaministiquia River for another two decades. Then the river was largely forgotten by Europeans and in the early 1780s, the North West Company constructed a large supply depot at the "Great Carrying Place", about 65 kilometres south near the mouth of the Pigeon River. This inland headquarters served the company well for two decades, but by the mid-1790s the Nor'Westers were aware the international boundary between Canada and the United States would likely fall just north of Grand Portage, compelling them to pay unwelcome duties and taxes. Looking north for an alternative site, Roderick McKenzie sought the help of the Ojibwe, who led him down the old Kaministiquia River route in 1798.

The construction of Fort Kaministiquia began three years later, in 1801, on the north shore of the river's mouth. Here, deep water extended to the shore and the company ships could sail right

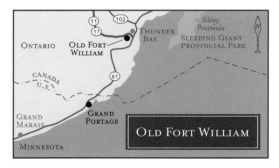

Map showing Ontario, Old Fort William, Thunder Bay, Sleeping Giant Provincial Park, Sibley Peninsula, Canada/U.S., Grand Marais, Grand Portage, Minnesota. Highways 11, 17, 102, 61. **OLD FORT WILLIAM**

DENNIS FAST

to the huge docks. A great deal of planning went into the facility, for the Nor'Westers intended it to be a showpiece, a demonstration of the company's power, as well as the capital of a commercial empire that now stretched from the Atlantic to the Pacific.

For the next two decades, the great post – named Fort William after 1807 – served its purpose well, impressing visitors from far and wide, particularly during its month-long annual "parliament" each summer. But the merger (or perhaps hostile takeover) of the North West Company by its bitter rival, the Hudson's Bay Company, in 1821 spelled the beginning of the end for Fort William.

Though it continued as a trading post for more than 50 years, without a small army of maintenance workers the vast *entrepôt* of the fur era began to molder and decay. In his 1836 history of another fur depot, *Astoria*, Washington Irving wrote a fitting epitaph: "The feudal state of Fort William is at an end; its council chamber is silent and deserted;

its banquet hall no longer echoes to the burst of loyalty, or the 'auld world' ditty; the lords of the lakes and forests have passed away."

When John McIntyre, who had been post master since 1855, retired in 1878, the post was closed and five years later all but the stone powder magazine was levelled to make way for the new era of the west – the Canadian Pacific Railway.

The CPR used the "Stone Store" until 1902, then for almost seven decades nothing remained of the grand depot of the NWC but a cairn, erected in 1916, and the names of many streets in the old part of the city, which read like a roll call of company partners.

But the people had not forgotten and in 1971 the Ontario government decided to reconstruct this fascinating period of history, not on the original site, which was covered with railyards and houses, but 14 kilometres up the Kaministiquia River, at Pointe de Meuron. Today, Old Fort William, as it's been named, bills itself as "the world's largest fur trade post" and is indeed impressive. A visit to the site, which is open daily from mid-May through mid-October, is like stepping into a time capsule, for life here exists in 1815, the heyday of the North West Company.

PETER ST. JOHN

The main gate of reconstructed Old Fort William welcomes crowds of visitors during the summer months, just as it did during its heyday, but spring and fall can allow you to wander through a quieter post that seems much like it must have been before the brigades arrived or after they left.

The fort's location on the Kaministiquia River is upstream of its original site, which was occupied in the interim by a railway yard and a housing development.

Exploring the Fur Trade Routes of North America

Old Fort William

In the beginning it was not, of course, Old Fort William at all. When construction began on a new inland headquarters for the North West Company in 1801, the plans were little short of revolutionary. The entire complex was carefully conceived, rather like today's planned communities, to combine all the necessaries of the fur trade – warehouses and storerooms, a canoe shed, shipyard and smithy – with quarters for an annual gathering of men who had crossed half a continent, and to do it with style. More than style, in fact. To do it, to paraphrase Washington Irving, with the same "gorgeous prodigality" that marked many of the dealings and actions of the company's senior partners.

Building Fort Kaministiquia – that was its original name, a sensible choice since it sat on the north shore of the Kaministiquia River – took three full years. At one time, it was said, nearly 1,000 workmen were employed in its

construction. By the summer of 1803, however, it was usable and the partners – both the wintering partners and those from Montreal – gathered for the first time in the Great Hall, the enormous dining room.

This was the inner sanctum, a space built and furnished to impress. Nearly 20 metres long and half as wide, it was hung with full-size paintings of some of the great figures and events of the age, as well as portraits of the leading partners.

Along one long wall in front of the fireplace, an enormous cherry wood dining table was laid for up to 20. Occupying the other side of the room, ranks of trestle tables were used by the agents, clerks, interpreters and guides. As many as 200 could dine comfortably.

Though the walls were of wood and not stone, a number of visitors thought the atmosphere was remarkably reminiscent of Scottish clan meetings of yore. Given the very close clan and kinship ties that bound most of the senior partners, the assessment was close to the mark.

The annual rendezvous that brought all these men together, along with hundreds of voyageurs, occupied most of a month each summer until 1821, as goods, supplies and mail from Montreal were exchanged for the bounty of the continental interior. By

Sharpened spikes, below, adorned the palisade walls all the way around the fort, warning unwelcome callers away. But those who gained entrance found a veritable village, complete with all the necessaries, including a cooper's shop, right.

DENNIS FAST

1803, the Nor'Westers knew the breadth of the continent and were well established as far north as Lake Athabasca.

The enormous operation, including a farm and housing for permanent staff, as well as an apothecary, a doctor and a variety of manufacturing facilities, was renamed Fort William in honor of William McGillivray in 1807.

The original fort did not, as indicated on the previous pages, survive the century, but the remarkable reconstruction that opened in 1981 is, if anything, better than the original. Both buildings and surroundings have been faithfully reproduced. The Great Hall, for example, is a nearly perfect duplicate of its antecedent and features several of the original paintings that graced the walls two centuries ago. Even the cows and sheep in the farm yard are heritage breeds that would have grazed there 200 years ago.

But today's version, which is located farther up the river than its ancestor, is complete with modern conveniences, interpretive staff, on-site displays and even a library of literature on the fur trade. Moreover, this Fort William welcomes outsiders, as the original undoubtedly did not (even the voyageurs slept outside the palisade). The fort has an ever-changing schedule of special events, before, during and after its regular season, which extends from mid-May to the Canadian Thanksgiving weekend in mid-October.

Old Fort William is located at the end of King Road on the north shore of the Kaministiquia River, south of the Trans-Canada Highway (No. 11/17) and west of Highway 61. From the Trans-Canada, go south on Princess Street (Hwy. 61) to Broadway Avenue and west on Broadway to King Road. There is plenty of parking next to the Visitor Centre, which has a cafe and large gift shop. The centre is open from 8:30 a.m. to 5:30 p.m. and 90-minute guided tours leave approximately every 45 minutes. The fort is a short distance from the centre; visitors can walk along a trail or take a shuttle bus to the perimeter of the fort. Canoe rides are available during July and August. Admission is charged.

DENNIS FAST

Today's visitors are welcomed by this impressive centre.

Clan Revels

"Grave and weighty councils were alternated by huge feasts and revels, like some of the old feasts described in Highland castles. The tables in the great banqueting room groaned under the weight of game of all kinds; of venison from the woods, and fish from the lakes, with hunters' delicacies, such as buffaloes' tongues and beavers' tails; and various luxuries from Montreal, all served up by experienced cooks brought for the purpose. There was no stint of generous wine, for it was a hard-drinking period, a time of loyal toasts, and bacchanalian songs, and brimming bumpers."
Washington Irving

The Voyageur

If the fur trade was North America's early engine of commerce, French-Canadian voyageurs were the fuel for that engine. Beginning

FRANCES ANNE HOPKINS / NATIONAL ARCHIVES OF CANADA / C-002771

Not all voyageurs were created equal. The hivernants or "winterers" – the men who spent years in the pays d'en haut, considered themselves above the Montreal-based mangeurs de lard or "pork eaters". At the rendezvous at Fort William, the hivernants set up camp on the west side of the fort, while the men from Montreal camped on the east. Though each camp averaged between 300 and 400 men, the western camp was observed to be a bastion of order, while the eastern encampment was a place of squalor. Was pride responsible for the difference?

in the French period and climaxing between 1763 and 1840, the voyageurs (literally "travellers") emerged as a unique class of workers with its own traditions, dialect, dress and legendary exploits.

Typically, these *engagés* or employees of the trade (as distinct from *coureurs de bois* or independent free traders) were wiry and short, on average five-foot-six in height; taller, heavier men risked going through the bottom of the fragile birchbark canoes. Despite their size, they were enormously strong and apparently inexhaustible. Dining on rations of dried peas or cornmeal and pork grease or bacon in the east and pemmican and dried fish in the west, everywhere augmented with tea and tobacco, they could paddle and carry for 15, even 18 hours a day, every day for months on end, with songs on their lips.

The pace they set was breathtaking. Paddles flashing at 40, even 50 strokes a minute, they tore upstream or battled the wind across one lake after another, averaging about 95 kilometres (and occasionally covering more than 125 kilometres) a day. At the innumer-

able portages, they stacked two or even three enormous 90-pound (or 40-kilogram) packs on leather tumplines that circled their foreheads and ran over their shoulders to support the load. Then, at a dogtrot, they traversed the rough, often treacherous portage trails, moving enormous loads from one end of an impassable rapid or fall to the other. The canoes were waded through half-full or *demi-chargé*, tracked up on ropes or carried around the obstacle.

When portages were long, the transfer was accomplished in stages, or *posés*, of about a half-kilometre each. Goods were ferried to the end of a *posé*, deposited, and the voyageur returned for another load. The longest portages on the Montrealers' mainline from Montreal to Lake Athabasca, were the 13.6-kilometre Grand Portage just south of Fort William, and Methye Portage (see page 173), a monster 20 kilometres long.

Wearing a brightly woven sash, deerskin leggings and moccasins, the whole topped by a knitted cap and, on cold days, a *capote* or blanket coat, the voyageur was instantly recognizable. His approach to life also set him apart. He lived for the day, even if the day brought danger or death. This outlook made him invaluable far and wide. John Jacob Astor, prince of American fur traders, once said he would rather have one Canadian voyageur than three American canoemen.

The life was gruelling and many endured an early and impoverished old age, but few seemed to regret it. Across from Fort William, a community of retired voyageurs grew up during the early 19th century where men spent their days smoking and telling tales, reliving the glory days of the fur trade.

Kakabeka Falls

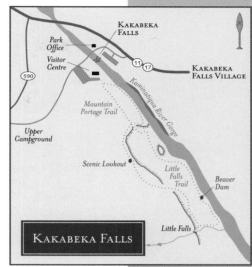

Though the Kaministiquia River has been harnessed just upstream, Kakabeka Falls still lives up to its Ojibwe name – "Thundering Water". Watching the torrent pour over the cliff into the gorge it has carved, one can begin to imagine the power of the river's glacial ancestor.

The region's geological history, written in the walls of the gorge, was revealed after the last glaciation by water cutting through the layers of rock. Young rocks – mere millions of years old – are near the surface; deeper down, the layers tell of ancient volcanoes and warm inland seas.

Near the bottom of the gorge, geologists have found stromatolites, the fossilized remains of great colonies of blue-green algae – some of Earth's oldest life forms - that lived here in the warm, clear, mineral-rich water of ancient hot springs nearly two billion years ago.

Though humans are relative newcomers, the Ojibwe and their ancestors have lived in the region long enough to know the land intimately and weave their legends into its special places. It was they who created the Mountain Portage, which leaves the river below the falls at the bottom of a small ravine, then climbs the cliff and bypasses the torrent. When Europeans first came this way in 1688, they too followed the Mountain Portage Trail, just as today's time travellers can on its broad, well-trodden modern descendant.

Those interested in paddling this ancient river route in the wake of early French and later Nor'Westers (this was their main route west after 1803) will find it passable, even today. Though water levels in the Kaministiquia may be low after late June, determined travellers can follow it north through Dog Lake, over the height of land and through Lac des Milles Lacs to Quetico Provincial Park and the Historic Boundary Waterway.

Kakabeka Falls is hard to miss, since the Trans-Canada Highway (No. 11/17) crosses the Kaministiquia River just above the falls. Following the Ontario Parks signs, turn south off the highway east of the bridge to access the excellent interpretive centre, viewing areas, trails and campgrounds. To access the swimming area above the dam, turn north at the east end of the bridge. In winter, the Poplar Point Trail at the Upper Campground is open to cross-country skiers.

PETER ST. JOHN

The Legend of Greenmantle

Greenmantle, the lovely daughter of an Ojibwe leader, was captured by a Dakota war party. "Take us to the camp of your people," they commanded, and apparently obedient, she led them down the Kaministiquia River. Just above the Thundering Water, she sprang from her canoe and swam to safety, but the Dakota were swept over the falls and dashed against the rocks. Some say you can still hear their angry voices in the roar of the water.

Lake Superior to Lake Winnipeg

LINDA FAIRFIELD

*Blueberries, members
of the heather family
(Vaccinium), include
a variety of edible
species. Borne on
small shrubs that
grow along streams
and rivers, the blue-
black berries are
much sought by
bears in July and
August.*

*Wild asters catch the
sun by the shore of
Lake Superior.*

Though several place names between Lake Superior and Lake Winnipeg recall the fur trade – Ontario's LaVerendrye Provincial Park and Minnesota's Voyageurs National Park, for example – fur traders were only among the latest of a very long line of travellers to pass this way. A piece of handworked antler discovered near Morson, Ontario, on Lake of the Woods has been carbon dated to 8,000 years, one indication of how long people have lived in the region.

Trade between the Great Lakes and the Great Plains is also thousands of years old. Spearpoints and ornaments crafted of copper mined north of Lake Superior have turned up in archaeological excavations in Manitoba, hundreds of miles west.

These ancient trade routes followed even older pathways carved by water and ice. The route that served the fur trade for most of the 18th century begins at the Grand Portage Gap, a preglacial trough in the highlands along the northwestern edge of Lake Superior. From here, the route follows the international border to Rainy River and Lake of the Woods, before descending the turbulent Winnipeg River to Lake Winnipeg.

DENNIS FAST

Despite nature's efforts, this was not an easy route. The waterway was convoluted, with numerous portages. But it was, and still is in many places, beautiful and for westbound voyageurs, downstream almost all the way.

Though even today some parts of it are accessible only by water, highway travellers will find its combination of heritage reconstructions and natural beauty worth visiting. The route begins at Grand Portage, where one of the earliest fur trade reconstructions in the United States draws thousands annually, and follows the famous 8½-mile portage through the Gap to the upper Pigeon River. Hikers and skiers can follow this historic trail to Fort Charlotte, a small storage depot on the river, with its primitive campground. Motorists can access the trail near its midpoint on Old US 61 and the scenic lower Pigeon River from Highway 61. Parks on both sides of the border offer camping and information.

The next 70 miles of the route boasts some of the best canoeing in the United States, with deep gorges, 600-foot cliffs and island-studded lakes typical of the Precambrian Shield. Highway travellers can access the Boundary Waters via the Arrowhead, Gunflint

132

HOWARD SIVERTSON / FROM *THE ILLUSTRATED VOYAGEUR*

Setting off at dawn from Fort Charlotte, the hivernants or North West Company winterers, faced a journey that grew as the last two decades of the 18th century passed. For some, the watery road ahead would take them more than 1,500 miles northwest.

and Echo Trails; all head northwest from U.S. Highway 61 along the northwest shore of Lake Superior.

Farther west, the fur trade era is recalled at Fort St. Pierre, a replica of one of Pierre Gaultier de La Vérendrye's early posts in Fort Frances, Ontario, across the Rainy River from International Falls.

The shoreline between here and Lake of the Woods is largely agricultural and in places quite densely settled. This area is also archaeologically rich; the Manitou Mounds at Long Sault Rapids served as burial grounds of a civilization that existed here for more than 1,000 years.

Minnesota Highway 11 follows the Rainy River to Baudette, then heads west to Warroad, just south of the Canadian border. On the Canadian side, the Trans-Canada Highway (No. 11) goes west from Thunder Bay to the Rainy River, then turns north (on No. 71) to circumvent Lake of the Woods on the east side.

From the Rainy River the fur trade route crossed Lake of the Woods. The southern half of the lake to the Northwest Angle and the site of La Vérendrye's Fort St. Charles is shallow and demanding, though with unexpected delights.

Then the lake enters the shield and canoeing becomes a pleasure.

The final portion of the route to Lake Winnipeg bears little resemblance to its fur era predecessor. The once wild and beautiful Winnipeg River has been dammed in a number of places, but the upper reaches still draw paddlers today. Ahead stretches Lake Winnipeg, largely unchanged but for the cottages that line its southern shores. Shallow and tempestuous, it is still a continual challenge for boaters.

The Montrealers' mainline was not the only, or the earliest, fur trade route used. Before it came into regular usage, French traders travelled extensively along the south shore of Lake Superior, following the rivers west and south and establishing trade relations with the Ojibwe and Dakota. A reconstruction and nearby interpretive centre at Ashland, Wisconsin, recalls this era, when northern Wisconsin and eastern Minnesota were important trading regions.

Even during the heyday of the North West Company, Minnesota fur posts continued to do a brisk trade; the reconstructed North West Company Fur Post on the Snake River in Pine City recalls this era, transporting visitors to 1804.

Exploring the Fur Trade Routes of North America

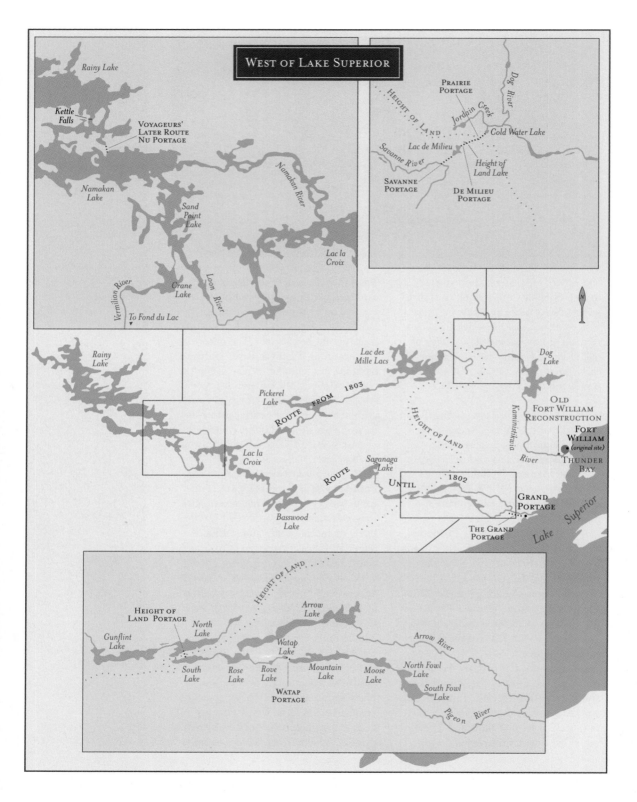

WEST OF LAKE SUPERIOR

Rainy Lake

Kettle Falls

VOYAGEURS' LATER ROUTE NU PORTAGE

Namakan Lake

Sand Point Lake

Namakan River

Lac la Croix

Vermilion River

Crane Lake

Loon River

To Fond du Lac

PRAIRIE PORTAGE

Dog River

Jordain Creek

HEIGHT OF LAND

Cold Water Lake

Lac de Milieu

Savanne River

Height of Land Lake

SAVANNE PORTAGE

DE MILIEU PORTAGE

Rainy Lake

Lac des Mille Lacs

Dog Lake

Pickerel Lake

ROUTE FROM 1803

HEIGHT OF LAND

Kaministikwia

OLD FORT WILLIAM RECONSTRUCTION

FORT WILLIAM (original site)

River

THUNDER BAY

Lac la Croix

Saganaga Lake

ROUTE

UNTIL

1802

GRAND PORTAGE

Basswood Lake

THE GRAND PORTAGE

Lake Superior

HEIGHT OF LAND

Arrow Lake

HEIGHT OF LAND PORTAGE

North Lake

Gunflint Lake

Watap Lake

Arrow River

South Lake

Rose Lake

Rove Lake

Mountain Lake

Moose Lake

North Fowl Lake

WATAP PORTAGE

South Fowl Lake

Pigeon River

134

South of Superior

Fifty years before the La Vérendryes pushed the fur trade out onto the western plains and a full century before fur brigades tapped the vast resources of the Athabasca country, the land south of Lake Superior was considered the richest beaver country in the world.

Médard Chouart des Groseilliers was looking for furs – and a safe place to trade – when he accompanied a returning Ojibwe trading party from the St. Lawrence, essentially a war zone at the time, to Superior's south shore in 1654. For two years, he ranged over the region, travelling west to Dakota country along the upper Mississippi. When he returned, it was with a fortune in furs and a plan to establish a string of posts on Superior's shores.

That plan was stymied by the colonial government of New France, which could never be accused of entrepreneurial thinking. Forbidden to leave

Image caption at left: DENNIS FAST

the colony, des Groseilliers and his young brother-in-law, Pierre-Esprit Radisson, crept away one night in August of 1659. With a party of Ojibwe, they slipped through the Iroquois cordon and reached Lake Superior in late October. Coasting

along the south shore, they arrived at Chequamegon Bay and built a small post. During the following months, the brothers-in-law cemented relations with the Dakota to the west and the Cree to the north. Back in Montreal with another fur armada, they were greeted with censure. Neither ever returned to the region.

Others had taken note, however. Daniel Greysolon, Sieur Dulhut, managed to obtain the requisite licences to trade legally and also spent time with the Dakota in 1678 and '79; Duluth, Minnesota, at the lake's western tip, is named for him.

Most French traders were unlicenced. Working from depots at Sault Ste. Marie and Michilimackinac, a veritable army of nearly 1,000 *coureurs de bois* carried on a profitable trade over a vast territory from the Ohio to the Mississippi Rivers. They left a legacy of place names – Fond du Lac, St. Croix, Eau Claire, Prairie du Chien and Dubuque, to list only a few – and in many places a mixed-blood population that fuelled the fur trade for generations. Five generations of the Cadottes of Lake Superior were employed in the trade between 1686 and 1840.

Even after the French period ended in 1763, the territory south of Lake Superior continued in importance. French-Canadian, English and New England free traders and later the North West Company established posts in the area. Today's time travellers can recapture the atmosphere of these smaller facilities at the North West Company Fur Post on the Snake River just west of Pine City, Minnesota.

PETER ST. JOHN

The 1659 wintering post of Radisson and des Groseilliers and Radisson is commemorated today in Ashland, Wisconsin; a tourism centre west of town provides an excellent overview of the area as well as information on Madeline Island, where a museum explores three centuries of island life.

All fur trade companies valued clear, even handwriting, such as is evident in this journal, left, at the North West Company Fur Post near Pine City.

The North West Company Fur Post

Miles south and west of Lake Superior, on a little river that flows into the St. Croix, a brigade of Nor' Westers established a small post in the fall of 1804. Beaver closer to the great lake must have been trapped out, for 1804 was a dry year and the voyageurs had a long slog inland up the Bois Brûlé River and down the shallow St. Croix to the tributary they called Rivière aux Serpents.

In some respects, Snake River Post was like many of the small, almost disposable trading houses the North West Company and its rivals threw up one year and abandoned the next. Low-slung and practical, it was just large enough to house a handful of traders and the goods they had carried inland.

But the region, at the western edge of Ojibwe territory, may have been more profitable or less populated by rival traders than expected, for archaeological excavations undertaken in the mid-1960s prior to reconstruction revealed far more artifacts than a winter or two would normally produce. It's therefore likely that the post operated for several years and perhaps as long as a decade.

The reconstruction, just west of Pine City, Minnesota, goes beyond a simple recreation of log buildings and a stockade. Here, interpretive guides recreate the dynamic era for the fur trade, when a cacophony of languages rang through the springtime air as trappers arrived with furs from the distant reaches of the watershed. Dressed for the period, they explain the impact of the trade on both the land and the people of North America and describe the pivotal role the Ojibwe and other native North Americans played as both trappers and traders.

Throughout the year, the post also holds a series of special hands-on sessions – maple sugaring, stone tool knapping and wild rice harvesting among them – to demonstrate the many skills possessed by people of the period, and largely lost today.

The post is located on Highway 7, 1 1/2 miles west of the Interstate 35 Pine City exit. It is open, free of charge, between 10 a.m. and 5 p.m. daily from the beginning of May until early September.

DENNIS FAST

The post at Pine City brings history to life with its interpretive staff, above, and displays, right, and offers a range of public programming that enhances understanding about early 19th century life.

DENNIS FAST

Grand Portage

DENNIS FAST

Just south of the Pigeon River, on a small bay on Lake Superior's northwestern shore, the North West Company built the first of its inland headquarters in the early 1780s.

PETER ST. JOHN

The site was not unknown; far from it. During the last quarter of the 18th century, the bay sometimes swarmed with people. Situated at the eastern end of an ancient portage to the interior that had become one of the main routes west to the fur country, the place had drawn free traders since at least the 1730s. By the mid-1770s, these fur rivals had built a series of small, fortified posts along the shoreline. Then in 1778, the British and Canadians found themselves competing not only with each other, but with Americans – troops from the Revolutionary Army who were operating in the Illinois country. To keep the trade in British hands, the commander at Mackinac sent a small regiment to build a fort, paid for by the traders. It was very likely this nucleus around which the newly formed North West Company built its great post in the years that followed.

In the space of a few short years, Grand Portage became (as had Michilimackinac before it) a place "famous in these regions". Here, every summer until

1802, the growing numbers of Nor' Westers gathered from far and wide for the "Rendezvous". Business and pleasure mingled as the furs from as far as the northern Rocky Mountains were exchanged for goods and supplies brought by canoe and ship from Montreal. At its height, in the late 1790s, the annual Rendezvous drew nearly 1,000 fur trade employees, hundreds of North American trappers and traders and more than 100 tons of trade goods, not to mention the furs.

The partners of the North West Company were mainly Highland Scots and the company was run like a clan chiefdom. The men were expected to work hard and play hard too. And nothing in the annual calendar rivalled the revelry at Grand Portage. In the Great Hall, up to 100 partners, clerks, agents and traders feasted on all the delicacies the land could provide: salt pork, beef and hams, fish and venison, bread and butter, peas, corn, potatoes, milk

DENNIS FAST

from the cows kept at the fort, along with freely flowing tea, spirits and wine. After all was consumed, the tables were pushed back and the bagpipes and fiddles and flutes appeared.

Knowledgeable interpretive staff at Grand Portage National Monument can make a visit seem like opening a door to the past.

As did its successor at Fort William, the Great Hall at Grand Portage, left, provided a comfortable, congenial atmosphere where NWC partners could meet to solve the challenges associated with operating a fast-growing, far-flung company. In 1788, those challenges included word that partner Peter Pond was suspected of killing a rival trader in the Athabasca country, the second time he'd been accused of murder.

AMANDA DOW

Grand Portage was at the end of a 1,300-mile canoe journey and even the least fastidious voyageur looked forward to cleaning up for their arrival and the Rendezvous. Just a mile or two east of the fort, the brigades stopped to wash, trim their beards and hair and don a clean shirt or sash they had toted all the way from Montreal.

Mountain maples color the slopes of Mount Rose in September and early October, affording a feast for the eyes. Year round the seeds, bark, buds, twigs, flowers and leaves provide birds and mammals with repasts of another sort.

As the music floated out over the bay, an observer might have had a glimpse of North America's remarkable multiracial future. Here, gathered together in common cause and celebration were French-Canadians, Ojibwe, Scots, Assiniboine, and New Englanders, along with some Cree, a few Germans and perhaps even a Spaniard or two.

But the music in the Minnesota wilderness did not last. The American Revolution that had prompted the fort's construction in the end spelled its demise. By the mid-1790s, it was clear the Canadian-based NWC would have to move its operations north of the American border which, following the "customary" trading route, most believed would fall along the Pigeon River north of Grand Portage. In 1798, as the Nor'Westers were casting about for alternative sites, the Ojibwe who lived along the boundary waters to the west reintroduced Roderick McKenzie to the old Kaministiquia route to the north. Within three years, the Nor' Westers had begun construction on new, even grander headquarters on the shore of Thunder Bay

The old post quickly moldered and by 1825 little was left of its former glory. But historians had not forgotten it and in 1922 members of the Minnesota Historical Society retraced the old portage trail and cleared the bush that had grown up on the site where Fort Charlotte, at the river end of the portage, once stood.

Excavation of the main fort site and the reconstruction of Grand Portage in the late 1930s was enabled by federal relief work programs and the Grand Portage Ojibwe, who provided crews to do the work. The reconstructed fort opened just before the United States became involved in World War II. The land was donated to the federal government by the Ojibwe and Grand Portage became a national monument in 1958.

That first reconstruction burned to the ground in 1969, but a second recreation of the fort, complete with the Great Hall, warehouse, kitchen, fur press, lookout tower and palisade allows thousands of visitors each year a window on a byegone era.

Grand Portage National Monument is located seven miles south of the U.S. – Canada border, off Highway 61. The buildings are open between mid-May and mid-October at a small admission charge. Interpretive staff in period dress help bring the period to life. Mount Rose (once known as Sugar Loaf Mountain) rises immediately

DENNIS FAST

west of the fort and an interpretive trail to the summit offers both an opportunity to learn more about traditional Ojibwe life and a grand view of Lake Superior.

138

The "Great Carrying Place"

It's not certain when the Grand Portage was first used by fur brigades, though La Vérendrye indicated the ancient trading route was generally known when he arrived in 1731. By 1775, the trail was wide, well-trodden and much dreaded, according to New Englander Alexander Henry, who was bound for the Saskatchewan River region. "The transportation of goods at this … Great Carrying Place was a work of seven days of severe and dangerous exertion," he wrote.

The portage leads to the Pigeon River, which French voyageurs called Rivière aux Tortes, an abbreviation of *tourterelles*, meaning turtledoves or pigeons. The trail begins innocuously enough, following a creek as it passes Mount Rose and the fields of the Grand Portage Ojibwe, who own the land on either side. Slowly it climbs, heading for a notch in the hills. Before it reaches Fort Charlotte 8 1/2 miles west, it will rise nearly 700 feet.

About every half-mile, the heavily laden voyageurs stopped at a *posé* or rest place, where their huge packs were stacked while they returned for more. Each voyageur's contract made him responsible for eight 90-pound packs of "such goods and provisions as are necessary for the interior country". Every additional pack he carried earned him one Spanish dollar. Carrying eight packs, two at a time, over the Grand Portage necessitated four round trips over every section of the trail, a total of nearly 70 miles.

Posés offered not only a chance to rest, but better protection for the goods, particularly during times of intense competition. Stacked together where men were coming and going, there was less likelihood of sabotage, as happened in 1802 when rivalry between the North West and XY Companies was at its height. While the "Potties" – a corruption of *les petites*, as XY employees were sometimes called – slept off their *régale*, the treat of liquor that accompanied to-ings and fro-ings at Grand Portage, their 30 kegs of "high wine" were bored with holes and drained.

There were usually 16 *posés* along the Grand Portage trail and the men were burdened by heat, flies, mosquitoes and often mud, in addition to the huge packs. The fur companies tried horses and oxen, but found them less efficient. Finally, with the end nearly in sight, the voyageurs could hear the cascading falls downstream of Fort Charlotte. Trotting faster, they could see the river through a break in the trees.

Fort Charlotte, named for King George III's queen, was never more than a supply depot, but for westward-bound brigades it was a sight for sore eyes. Only one portage in the entire system was longer and that evening they celebrated.

The *canots du nord*, carefully repaired and regummed since their arrival two or three weeks before, were lowered into the river and packed. Then with a song on their lips, the brigades left for the *pays d'en haut*.

Fort Charlotte can be reached only by the two traditional methods – by canoe or on foot. Backpackers, who must register in advance, can camp at the fort's primitive campground. In winter, the trail is open to cross-country skiers.

The voyageurs kept their smoking gear handy wherever they were, for a "pipe" offered a brief pause from their back-breaking work.

The Pigeon River has a split personality. At Fort Charlotte it is a placid, silty stream that flows between grassy banks. But less than a mile downstream, it suddenly plunges into a chasm 150 feet deep, the first of a series of cascades and rapids as it rushes toward Lake Superior. It was this impassable 20 miles of water that the Grand Portage was built to avoid.

DENNIS FAST

The Boundary Waters

Beginning on Superior's shore at the mouth of the Pigeon River and extending nearly 200 miles west over the height of land through Gunflint and Basswood Lakes and Lac la Croix to Rainy Lake, the boundary waters canoe route marks the international border between the United States and Canada. This magnificent region of still waters, wild rivers, thick forests and bountiful wildlife draws thousands of paddlers every summer. For them, this is the wilderness next door and both countries have taken steps to protect this precious heritage waterway.

The U.S. has designated much of the territory to the south as the Boundary Waters Canoe Area, while Canada has named the 150-mile (250-kilometre) stretch between Lake Superior and Lac la Croix a Canadian Heritage Waterway. Ontario's Pigeon River, Middle Falls, LaVerendrye and Quetico Provincial Parks line its north shore.

Those who come to paddle and portage are treading in ancient footsteps. In several languages, the names have stories to tell: at Portage Carrebeouf, woodland caribou once crossed the shallow Pigeon River, while A-ja-wa-wan Saga-ai-gon is the "Height of Land Lake". We know it now as South Lake, to differentiate it from North Lake across the barely perceptible watershed divide. For westward-bound brigades, the "road"

Moose, such as this watchful mother and handsome calf, are still found all along the boundary waters.

from here was downhill for hundreds of miles.

As the fur brigades reached this continental ridgepole, they engaged in a small ceremony. This was the place that separated *les hommes du nord* from everyone else. North West Company clerk John Macdonnell recalled it this way: "I was instituted a North man by *Batême* performed by sprinkling water in my face with a small cedar Bow dipped in a ditch of water and accepting certain conditions such as not to let any new hand pass by that road without experiencing the same ceremony which stipulates particularly never to kiss a voyageur's wife against her own free will the whole being accompanied by a dozen of Gun shots ....The intention of this *Batême* being only to claim a glass. I complied with the custom and gave the men ... a two-gallon keg."

West to Rainy Lake march the aquamarine lakes, embraced in granite basins, guarded by fissured cliffs, connected by narrow streams and the flow of history. The shores of Gunflint Lake, as expected, abound in flint, used by the voyageurs for their flintlock guns. At L'Anse de Sable – "the Handle of Sand" – the Ojibwe maintained a canoe factory at the end of the 18th century.

Saganaga Lake, studded with pine-clad islands, has been called by some the most beautiful lake in the world; others choose Cypress Lake,

BRIAN WOLITSKI

140

DENNIS FAST

Morning mist rises from one of many tumbling streams that feed this ancient waterway. Today's paddlers will find the route unchanged in many places, a timeless taste of wilderness.

to the west. There the clear water reflects 200-foot cliffs, painted with bright lichens and fringed with cedars and white pines. At Portage Rocher des Couteaux – the "Big Knife Portage" – the slates in the portage path stand on edge, ready to slice through a voyageur's soft moccasins.

Basswood Lake, where several French traders established posts during the 18th century, marked contested territory between the Ojibwe and Dakota. The trade, which relied largely on Ojibwe middlemen, was probably responsible, for it drew the Dakota north before eventually driving them south and west. A century later, in the mid-1900s, the Hudson's Bay Company operated several posts here, purchasing "water oats" or wild rice, fish and maple sugar from the Ojibwe, and hiring the men to hunt and build canoes, and the women to fish, net snowshoes and make and mend clothing.

At Crooked Lake, a fissured cliff rises 100 feet from the water. About 1730, a Dakota war party passed this way and shot a dozen feather-shafted arrows into the cleft about 20 feet above the water. Like the Ghurka, famed in India for slicing the shoelaces of enemy guards, their warning was unmistakeable. The arrows were still there more than 60 years later when mapmaker

David Thompson passed this way and in the end, it was the rock face, not the arrows that gave way. Quetico Park is also famous for its many pictographs.

Lac la Croix is where the Nor'Westers' old route crossed the "new" one from Thunder Bay, used after 1803. The junction at the east end of the lake was marked by Pointe du Mai, once identifiable at a distance by a lobstick or maypole, created by lopping all the branches of a tall pine that stood at the end of the point (thus "lopped stick"). For Frances Simpson, the HBC governor's 18-year-old English bride who came this way in 1830, the maypole was topped with purple ribbons and a red feather.

Lac la Croix drains into Namakan Lake (from the Ojibwe *Nah-ma* or "Sturgeon") by two routes; the voyageurs generally took the southern one, which also leads via the Vermilion River to Fond du Lac in today's Duluth.

Lodges and launch points along this ancient canoe route can be accessed by road or air on both sides of the border. Many outfitters are equipped to assist with longer trips. The region is also popular in the winter for skiing and snowmobiling.

Voyageurs National Park

The shield offered few choices for comfortable campsites, but early French and later NWC voyageurs could turn even a rocky shore and an overturned canoe, opposite, into a haven for the night.

Minnesota's Voyageurs National Park was established in 1975 to protect the ancient waterways that the fur brigades followed as they moved west during the 17th and 18th centuries. Extending from Sand Point Lake on the east, where three trade routes converged, to International Falls and Fort Frances (both originally fur posts) on the west, the park's 218,000 acres include 30 lakes and 506 islands.

The main fur route followed the Loon River into Sand Point Lake. Just to the south, a narrow opening leads between high rock walls through Crane and Vermilion Lakes to an alter-

This access made the lower reaches of Crane Lake, south of Voyageurs Park, a busy place in times past. A French trader named Bourassa built a small wintering post here in 1736, a post La Vérendrye believed was badly situated, given that the waterway was a favored route of the Dakota, who were enemies of both the French and Ojibwe. In fact, 1736 was the year that La Vérendrye's eldest son, Jean-Baptiste, and his companions were killed by a Dakota war party.

Recent archeological investigations on the site thought to be Bourassa's post revealed artifacts associated with North West and Hudson's Bay Company

Ojibwe paddlers, completely at home in this beautiful and rugged landscape, are caught shooting some rapids in this painting by Frederick Verner.

FREDERICK ARTHUR VERNER / NATIONAL ARCHIVES OF CANADA / C-114480

native route to Lake Superior. This route was used by both the Ojibwe and Dakota and later by French and American traders to access Superior at Fond du Lac ("Bottom of the Lake") in today's Duluth.

traders, but whether this indicates later posts on the same site or simply the existence of a regularly-used trading site is not clear. The NWC did operate a small post on Vermilion Lake to the south, which was managed by Dr. John

McLoughlin in 1811 and 1812. Though born in Canada, McLoughlin was not only Minnesota's first doctor, he was also later recognized as the "Father of Oregon" (see page 246). Hudson's Bay Company traders also camped on Crane Lake to trade in 1848.

Sand Point Lake, largely rocky, is named for a point that is not. Here, the Ojibwe sometimes manufactured canoes during the summer season, to sell to passing traders. At its north end, on the Canadian side of the narrows to Namakan Lake, is a long, serpentine fold of caramel-colored feldspar. Nearby are pictographs that originally included two painted in a rare white, rather than the usual rust pigment. The white paint was created by mixing white clay (the Ojibwe name for Sand Point Lake was Wa-ba-bi-gon or "White Clay") with sturgeon oil. Today, a slab with some of these pictographs is preserved at the Royal Ontario Museum in Toronto.

Sturgeon once abounded in Namakan Lake and were often speared by the Ojibwe at the foot of Kettle Falls between Namakan and Rainy Lakes. Early travellers portaged around this cataract, but later Nor' Westers preferred the Nu Portage, which bypassed the falls to the east. Today's boaters can bypass the dam at Kettle Falls using a transfer system that is available for a fee during the summer months.

Rainy Lake is the largest body of water the brigades encountered west of Grand Portage. Though no longer wild, the lake is still lovely and very popular.

Voyageurs National Park draws visitors year round. There are 160 official mainland and island campsites for summertime enjoyment; in the winter, the park maintains miles of cross-country and snowmobile trails. There are many public water access sites, with parking, as well as visitor centres on Rainy Lake's Black Bay just east of International Falls, on Kabetogama and Crane Lakes and at Ash River.

BRIAN WOLITSKI

Among those who traded in the area was Germain Maugenest, a French-Canadian who gave the Hudson's Bay Company one of its most enduring symbols. Maugenest sailed to London in 1779 to discuss terms of employment. Among his suggestions was to market "point blankets", which had been used by the French for nearly 70 years. These blankets had the price, in beaver skins, woven right into the wool in a series of bars. In 1780, point blankets worth 1, 1½, 2, 2½ and 3 beaver pelts were made for the first time in London. They're still made today.

TOO MANY CHANGES TOO QUICKLY

Originally people of the eastern woodlands, in the 17th century the Siouan-speaking Dakota occupied the region west of Lake Superior to the upper Mississippi. When the French first arrived in their territory in the 1660s, their lifestyle involved a seasonal round of hunting, fishing and harvesting, much like the Ojibwe to the north and east. For a time, the Dakota traded directly with the French, but this changed when the Ojibwe – well established in the trade – began to move west, pressing the Dakota on their eastern boundaries.

The name by which many know the Dakota likely comes from this period. The word *Sioux* is a French interpretation of an Ojibwe word for "snakes", meaning "enemies". By comparison their own word – Dakota – means "allies". However only the easternmost of the three branches of this family of cultures, the Santee, actually uses the word Dakota. To the west the Yankton and Yanktonai people – from whom the Assiniboine of the northern plains came – replace the "d" with an "n" sound and call themselves Nako'ta. Farther west still, an "l" sound is used; these are the Teton Lakota, who created a flowering of plains culture before suffering a tragic decline and final defeat in battle under Chiefs Sitting Bull and Crazy Horse.

About the same time the Ojibwe were moving west, the Assiniboine (see page 193), who had earlier split with the Nako'ta and moved north around Lake of the Woods and Lake Winnipeg's east shore, obtained European weapons from the English on Hudson Bay. For a time, the Dakota yielded to this superiority in weapons, then the tide turned as they, too, obtained guns and ammunition. By 1725, the Assiniboine had largely moved west to the plains.

The Ojibwe, however, were more formidable enemies and by 1750 the Dakota had been forced into what is now western Minnesota. From here, they struck back along the Red and Assiniboine River Valleys. Alexander Henry the Younger was warned several times about Dakota attacks by his Plains Ojibwe or Saulteaux companions. Such attacks did occur against the Cree on the Red River in 1800 and against the Plains Ojibwe at Portage la Prairie in 1806.

But the biggest threat to the Dakota came from American settlement. Forced to give up 24 million acres of land, confined to a small territory along the Minnesota River, expected to trade hunting for farming, starving as a result of delays of food and payments, the Dakota under Chief Big Eagle found "It seemed too sudden to make such a change." In 1862, they decided to fight instead. The resulting defeat at the hands of the United States Army is remembered at Lower Sioux Agency History Centre, east of Redwood Falls, and at other sites in southwestern Minnesota.

Some Santee fled west to join the Teton Lakota and several thousand moved north, where they live today in southwestern Manitoba and southeastern Saskatchewan.

The Dakota, such as this family photographed in the 1860s, were people of the Great Lakes forests when they first encountered Europeans. The fur trade and later settlement devastated their society and pushed the survivors north and west.

JACOBY / MINNESOTA HISTORICAL SOCIETY / E91.31/p21

International Falls

Though Fort Frances, Ontario, across the Rainy River is likely better known today for its fur trade past, the first fur post in the region may have been situated on what is now the Minnesota side of the river. At least that's what many have believed for years, based on a brief report by a Jesuit priest in far-off Québec. The report claimed that in 1688, French-Canadian trader Jacques de Noyon built a small wintering post on a site presumed to be just east of International Falls. Today, a plaque along Highway 11 marks the supposed site.

But Ed Oerichbauer, director of the Koochiching County Historical Museum in International Falls, feels there is little evidence that de Noyon came so far west. It would be easy, he says, to confuse locations along a water route that for much of its human history has been regarded as a single entity. *Koochiching*, an Ojibwe word for "Mist over the Water" was the name given to a waterway that today includes Rainy River, Rainy Lake and several other lakes to the east. Early European visitors took much the same tack. Lac La Pluie or Rainy Lake often referred to more than the large lake that bears the name today. So though de Noyon may have reached what he called Lac La Pluie, Oerichbauer feels it's unlikely he came as far as the outlet to Rainy River.

Further, the south riverbank does not facilitate easy launching or landing of canoes, as does the north shore. For anyone looking for a post site, it was an important consideration.

However far west de Noyon travelled, it seems to have been far enough to meet Assiniboine traders and learn of the route to the Red River. And on his return to Québec, his observations undoubtedly inspired others to push farther west.

For the next 140 years, however, the focus of the trade was mainly on the Canadian side of Rainy River, where a portage route took travellers around Koochiching (later Chute de la Chaudière and then Alberton) Falls. Here, where a dam now provides power for paper mills on both sides of the border, the Rainy River once poured over three ridges, dropping 20 feet.

Then in 1821, John Jacob Astor's American Fur Company established a post on the south side of the river overlooking the falls (and not incidentally Fort Lac La Pluie, the Hudson's Bay Company post on the north shore). Though Astor had deep pockets, the AFC was never able to make a real dent in the long-established Canadian trade. Nevertheless, the American competition was certainly noticed, and in 1833 the Hudson's Bay Company bought out the American traders. Astor, incidentally, sold the company the following year.

A plaque marking the site of Jacques de Noyon's reputed post is situated at the Rainy Lake Lookout on the Noden Causeway (Highway 11). The Koochiching County Historical Museum at 214 – 6th Avenue features an excellent overview of the fur trade in the region. Across the toll bridge, Fort Frances boasts several fur trade sites.

DENNIS FAST

After hundreds of miles of travelling through rocky, coniferous shield country, the fertile alluvial shores of the Rainy River were a welcome change. Here, large maples color the autumn landscape.

Grand Mound

People were travelling and trading along the Rainy River thousands of years before Europeans even dreamed of a world across the ocean. Just 17 miles west of International Falls, Grand Mound Centre – the largest burial mound in the Upper Midwest – allows a peek into the culture of the Laurel people, who lived along the river about the time the Romans invaded Britain.

Fort Frances

George III, whose profile graces this coin in the Fort Frances museum, occupied the English throne for 60 tumultuous years between 1760 and 1820. He presided over the loss of the American colonies as well as British expansion across what is now Canada.

A reconstruction of Christophe Dufrost de La Jemerais' Fort St. Pierre (1731) overlooks Rainy Lake at Pither's Point Park.

Fort Frances is among a number of cities in Canada named for a fur trade post, but one of only a few that bear a woman's name. In this case, the Hudson's Bay Company post – originally Fort Lac La Pluie – was renamed to celebrate the visit of Frances Simpson, Governor George Simpson's 18-year-old bride, in the summer of 1830. At the time Frances was en route to Fort Garry on the Red River and still excited about the adventure that lay ahead. Unfortunately, a combination of her husband's long absences, the relative isolation she endured – at the insistence of the governor she was almost completely cut off from female company – and the death of her first-born child quickly changed her mind about life in the "Nor'Wast".

The HBC post, by whatever name, was not the first, but the last of a long string of fur posts situated along the north side of the Rainy River. The earliest was established by Christophe Dufrost de La Jemerais, a nephew of Pierre Gaultier de La Vérendrye, who arrived in September 1731 with a small contingent of men. He built a wintering post on a point of land known today as Pither's Point, where Rainy Lake pours over a double set of rapids into the Rainy River. In honor of his uncle, La Jemerais named it Fort St. Pierre.

The elder La Vérendrye came up the next year and for more than a quarter-century, as the family of adventurer-traders pushed west, they returned again and again to the fort on the point, expanding its fortifications as their relationship with the Dakota to the south deteriorated.

DENNIS FAST

DENNIS FAST

But it was European, not North American, politics that spelled the end for this early family compact. The fur trade was always lucrative. In the autumn of 1759, Louis-Joseph La Vérendrye returned to Montréal accompanied by 1,200 Assiniboine and Ojibwe traders and an armada of canoes filled with furs, but New France fell the following winter and the La Vérendryes never returned.

The importance of Koochiching ("Mist over the Water"), as the Ojibwe called the waterway for the mist that often shrouded the falls, in the fur trade was still to come, however. First free

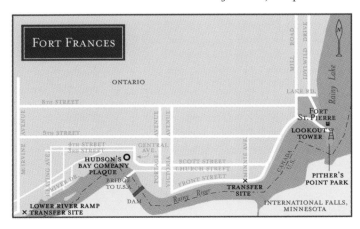

FORT FRANCES

ONTARIO

8th STREET

5th STREET

4th STREET
3rd STREET

HUDSON'S
BAY COMPANY
PLAQUE

BRIDGE
TO U.S.A.

DAM

LOWER RIVER RAMP
✕ TRANSFER SITE

MILL ROAD

IDYLWILD DRIVE

LAKE RD.

Rainy Lake

FORT
ST. PIERRE

LOOKOUT
TOWER

CENTRAL AVE.

SCOTT STREET

CHURCH STREET

FRONT STREET

✕
TRANSFER
SITE

Rainy River

CANADA
U.S.A.

PITHER'S
POINT PARK

INTERNATIONAL FALLS,
MINNESOTA

traders and then, in 1793, the North West Company established posts along the north shore of the river. The Nor'Westers' fort, known as Rainy Lake House, was located about 2.5

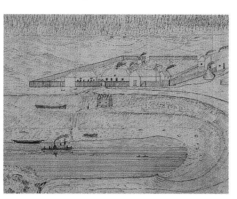

kilometres downstream from the falls. It was soon the most significant fur operation in the area and particularly important because of another NWC post far to the northwest. Fort Chipewyan, on the shore of Lake Athabasca in what is now northern Alberta, produced the richest, thickest furs in the entire trading system. But the fort was so far north that it was all but impossible for even the most dedicated fur brigades to reach Grand Portage on Lake Superior and return in one short season between spring thaw and freeze-up. So the Athabasca House depot was established at Rainy Lake House and a special brigade brought the trade goods and supplies for Fort Chipewyan down from Grand Portage. This cut more than 600 kilometres off a trip that was already dauntingly long. The only thing the Athabasca brigades missed was the Rendezvous at Grand Portage; very likely they made up for that on the shores of Rainy River.

Competing with the Nor'Westers, Alexander Mackenzie's XY Company built a post upstream of Rainy Lake House, near the falls, about 1800, but abandoned it four years later when the XY and North West Companies united after the death of Simon McTavish.

The Hudson's Bay Company, meanwhile, made several half-hearted attempts to establish itself in the region and finally built a post on or very near the old XY site in 1818. Three years later, when the HBC and the Nor'Westers merged, Rainy Lake House was closed and the combined operations were moved to Fort Lac La Pluie. The region soon declined in importance, however, for the HBC funnelled its main shipments of furs through Hudson Bay. Still, Fort Frances, as the HBC fort was known after 1830, remained open for business longer than any other fur establishment in the region; the last of its buildings burned in 1903. By then the community had adopted the name and new industries were driving the region's economy.

The fur trade at Fort Frances has not been forgotten. On Pither's Point, a community recreation of Fort St. Pierre (albeit not quite on the original site) recalls the earliest post. Downstream, near the centre of town, is Portage Avenue. Portage de la Chaudière – the portage around the falls – began near its foot. Just a block or so west at 259 Scott Street is the Fort Frances Museum, with fur trade displays and summer programming. And near the shore, just west of the bridge to International Falls, a plaque erected in 1998 marks the site of the HBC's long-standing post. West again, on the shore off River Drive, yet another plaque marks the site of the Nor'Westers' Rainy Lake House.

Manitou Mounds

On the north side of the Rainy River between Fort Frances and Rainy River is Kay-Nah-Chi-Wah-Nung, "the Place of the Long Rapids". Here, along three kilometres of shoreline on two glacial terraces are more than 30 village and camp sites and at least 17 burial mounds, with an occupation history of at least 3,000 years. Today, this fascinating history is interpreted at the Kay-Nah-Chi-Wah-Nung Historical Centre, which also has information on the outstanding birding opportunities along the rapids, which never freeze.

Tawny puffball mushrooms and golden maple leaves create an autumn tapestry.

The Historic Boundary Waterway

Intricate floral designs of the 19th and 20th centuries set woodland Cree and Ojibwe handwork apart from their western plains counterparts, as well as from their own earlier, geometric designs.

The deep fertile soil of the Rainy River Valley has long supported both thick mixed forests and a series of human cultures.

Flowing west and north from Rainy Lake into the southeast corner of Lake of the Woods, the Rainy River cuts through land that was, more than 11,000 years ago, part of glacial Lake Agassiz. Its banks, as a result, are of rich, alluvial soil, unlike the waterways to the east, which wind through the ancient rock of the Precambrian Shield. This fertile environment has fostered communities for thousands of years; a new interpretive centre at Kay-Nah Chi-Wah-Nung Manitou Mounds just south of Barwick, Ontario, offers a view of Laurel society 3,000 years ago.

For the fur traders who followed in the wake of these and other earlier travellers, the Rainy River was the first open, arable land many had seen since leaving the Ottawa Valley. Canadian-born voyageurs found the relatively flat, open land rather boring, but for those born in England or the Scottish Lowlands

DENNIS FAST

it looked like home and they were sometimes almost rapturous in their descriptions. Duncan McGillivray wrote

that it was "reckoned the most beautifull River in the North, a preference which it richly deserves."

DENNIS FAST

Several short-lived posts were built along the river during the 1790s, but none lasted more than two or three winters.

Today, though it is one of the most populated stretches of the Montreal mainline, the Rainy River continues to be a pleasant route for paddlers and other boaters. It is also part of the Historic Boundary Waterway, an association created in 1995 to encourage safe, enjoyable and informed use of the rivers and lakes between Atikokan and Minaki, Ontario.

Water levels in the river are controlled by the dam at Fort Frances and channel markers assist with navigation. For those travelling from Rainy Lake to the lower Rainy River, a boat transfer system, available by appointment for a fee, operates in Fort Frances between May 15 and the first weekend in September. The river can also be accessed at the smaller communities of Emo, Barwick and Pinewood, as well at Rainy River, in Ontario, and Baudette in Minnesota.

Lake of the Woods

Straddling the geological line between the Precambrian Shield and the western plains, Lake of the Woods has a split personality. On the north and for the North West Company with its sights on the distant north, and toward the end of the fur era, it was a trading area for the Hudson's Bay Company,

east, the Ontarian part of the lake, it is a place of deep water, rocky shores and thousands of islands. On the south and west, the Minnesotan and Manitoban part of the lake, it is relatively shallow and edged with marshes. The Sable Islands, long dunes of sand that provide critical nesting habitat for the endangered piping plover, edge the south basin. This varied environment has sustained people for at least 8,000 years and today draws visitors year-round.

During the fur trade era, Lake of the Woods served several purposes: for several years during the early 1730s, it was a headquarters for Pierre Gaultier de La Vérendrye's penetrations west; 60 years later, it served as a corridor

which had a post at Rat Portage (now Kenora) at the north end of the lake.

Lake of the Woods aficionados like to boast that their lake has more shoreline than Lake Superior, which may be true given its 14,000 islands. And it stands to reason that fur trade brigades leaving the mouth of the Rainy River at the lake's south end might have sought the shelter of these islands wherever possible. That was not their normal route, however, for distance was time and they had far to go. Instead, the usual route headed straight north, making what the French termed *la grande traverse* across what is now Traverse Bay, skimming the west side of Big Island.

Howard Sivertson catches a moment of tranquility in the otherwise gruelling days of the voyageurs in his painting, The Pipe, *in his lovely book,* The Illustrated Voyageur.

Sivertson points out that a tiny islet like this was the perfect place for such a stop, since it was usually free of bugs and open to the breezes. The north and east sections of Lake of the Woods contain thousands of such tiny islands.

Piping plovers require open beaches sprinkled with small round pebbles as nesting sites.

JERRY KAUTZ

Misconceptions about the source of the Mississippi River, which early travellers believed flowed out Lake of the Woods, resulted in a deviation of the international boundary. In 1823, surveyor David Thompson (see page 191), was asked to determine the most northwesterly point of the lake. He located three possibilities, but missed Ptarmigan Bay, which was north and west of all three. Based on his work, the boundary was determined in 1872, then adjusted slightly southward in 1927. The North West Angle, above right, therefore belongs to Minnesota.

When the wind – the voyageurs called it *La Vieille*, "The Old Woman" – blew too hard to contemplate a direct crossing of the open water, the canoes ducked slightly east and slipped past the other side of Bigsby and Big Islands.

In 1732, La Vérendrye and his relations established Fort St. Charles on the shore of the North West Angle, which belongs to Minnesota. Today, the old, partially reconstructed French post is separated from the mainland by a narrow stretch of wetland.

The North West Company brigades rarely stopped for more than a pipe, covering the 120 kilometres to the top of the lake in a day if possible. About halfway up, they were obliged to portage though a narrow channel that often lacked enough water to float their canoes. Today, the water level has risen enough to allow small craft to pass through French Portage Narrows.

The lake drops into the Winnipeg River by three channels, Kenora's Eastern and Western Outlets and a small passage at Portage Bay's west end that spills into

the river only at high water. The water in Portage Bay was often stagnant and foul, but the Nor'Westers chose it for one simple reason – it involved the shortest portage for their large loads. Later, lighter HBC canoes used a longer portage to the east.

Today, both are buried beneath the railway embankment north of the Trans-Canada Highway at Keewatin (the name means "North Wind" in several Algonquian languages), but boat ramps allow boat owners to transfer their craft from the lake to the river six metres below.

The fur traders may not have stopped to enjoy the scenery, but modern voyageurs certainly do. Studded with 14,000 islands, Lake of the Woods draws visitors year-round. Kenora, its largest community, swells to accommodate a huge summer influx. The Lake of the Woods Museum at 300 Main Street has more than 15,000 artifacts, including a substantial collection of Ojibwe art and many articles from the fur trade. Just east of the town, the Trans-Canada Highway (No. 17/71) splits and Highway 71 skirts the east side of the lake, providing access to some of the most scenic spots in the region and a trio of Ontario provincial parks. The lake can also be accessed from the western or Manitoba side, which leads to Buffalo Bay and Minnesota's North West Angle.

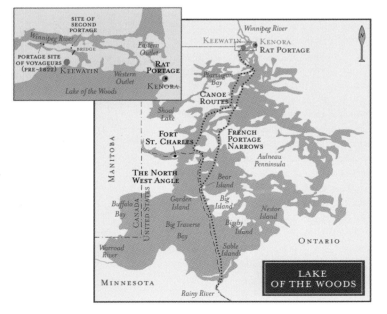

LAKE OF THE WOODS

Fort St. Charles

This post, on the west shore of Lake of the Woods, was one of the few at which Pierre Gaultier de la Vérendrye was actually present during construction. He was usually preceded in his travels by one of his four sons or his nephew, Christophe Dufrost de La Jemerais (see The La Vérendryes on page 204).

Fort St. Charles was built during the summer of 1732 as the family marched west in search of two not always compatible objectives – furs and the route to the mythical "Western Sea". The conflict between the two was particularly evident during the initial years at Fort St. Charles. The explorations required time, men and supplies; to pay for it, La Vérendrye needed to establish a profitable trade, but the fur trade also required the same things.

Focusing on the trade in 1733, the post soon ran out of supplies and by the following summer was also low on food. Sending La Jemerais and his eldest son, Jean-Baptiste, north to establish a new post at the mouth of the Winnipeg River, La Vérendrye made the long journey back to Montreal to meet with his patrons and partners. When he returned in September 1735, he had his youngest son, Louis-Joseph, with him.

The following spring, Jean-Baptiste arrived at Fort St. Charles with the news that La Jemerais, who was just 26, had died at Fort Maurepas. Since both posts were again running short, La Vérendrye sent the young man, along with a Jesuit priest, Father Jean-Pierre Aulneau, and at least 20 French and Ojibwe voyageurs to Fort Kaministiquia for supplies. They did not get far. Camping on a small island in Lake of the Woods they were surprised by a large Dakota war party.

For many years, it was believed the ambush was unprovoked, but now it seems that in addition to furs, La Vérendrye was trading heavily in Dakota and Pawnee slaves, purchased from the Ojibwe and Assiniboine to the south and west. The Dakota were also being pressured on their eastern borders by the Ojibwe and violence was increasingly common on both sides.

When discovered, the bodies were found to have been decapitated. The remains were returned to Fort St. Charles and buried. Nearly 175 years later, a group from St. Boniface College in Winnipeg rediscovered the site and the graves were exhumed. In one, 21 headless bodies were found; their skulls had been buried separately.

The site was marked with a plaque in 1950 and the Knights of Columbus have partially recreated the fort and marked the gravesites. Today, Fort St. Charles is a Minnesota Historical Site.

The reconstructed post is on the northwest shore of Magnusons Island, off the northeast shore of the North West Angle. This disparate part of Minnesota can be reached on Manitoba Highway 308 southeast from the Trans-Canada (No. 1) or northeast from Highway 12 to the junction of Highway 502. Take this gravel road northeast across the border and follow the fort signs to a cluster of lodges on the northeast point. In the summer, the island must be reached by boat; in winter it can be accessed by walking paths and snowmobile trails.

THE NINETEEN SKULLS AND BONES TO WHICH SKULLS PROBABLY BELONGED.

These two grim plaques mark the graves of the French who were killed on an island in Lake of the Woods in 1736. The island has been called Massacre Island, but that name today belongs, rather strangely, to an island that was not the site of the ambush.

HEADLESS BODIES OF REV. FATHER AULNEAU J. B. LaVERENDRYE SON OF THE EXPLORER

The Winnipeg River

A string of fur posts came and went along the lower reaches of the Winnipeg River after 1730 as this route to Lake Winnipeg was used by the French, the Nor'Westers and ultimately by the Hudson's Bay Company.

As big as today's plains bison are (and they can be nearly two metres at the shoulder), Bison occidentalis was much larger. Their skill at killing such an animal is testament to the courage and hunting expertise of early Manitobans.

AMANDA DOW

Dropping from Lake of the Woods in the Canadian Shield into Lake Winnipeg at the edge of the Manitoba Lowlands, the Winnipeg River the voyageurs knew was a wild, beautiful waterway that traversed Earth's most ancient mountains. Eric Morse, historian and discriminating canoeist, called it "unquestionably the grandest and most beautiful river the Montreal Northmen saw on their whole journey from Lake Superior to Lake Athabasca".

Over its 225-kilometre length it drops 100 metres and was once a river of spectacular falls and rapids. Today, though tamed by eight dams along its length, parts of the waterway still invite, even challenge, paddlers.

The river has long been a refuge. Some of the world's last ice age bison – *Bison occidentalis* – came here to escape drought on the Great Plains in a rapidly warming world. Archaeological excavations at the Jansson Site, three kilometres upstream from Great Falls on the east bank, revealed copper artifacts from the Lake Superior area, along with the skull of an extinct bison believed to be 4,800 years old. Elsewhere *Bison occidentalis* disappeared 3,000 years before.

Clearly, Europeans were latecomers here, but like earlier travellers, they had to circumvent a dozen cascading falls and many more rapids. Even with optimum water conditions, canoeing the length of the river required 26 portages. Today's paddlers can capture the wild spirit of the river best in the first 50 kilometres below Lake of the Woods. Here, cascading through the Dalles and winding north through Minaki, it is still an unfettered stream.

Below this stretch is the Whitedog Dam and farther along, the English River enters from the east. The

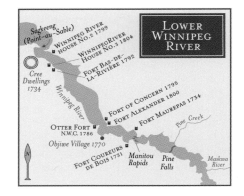

Cree often took the English River route east and north to trade their furs to the Hudson's Bay Company's Albany House on James Bay.

Beyond the junction, at Boundary Falls, an old portage trail crosses the larger of two islands. Most voyageurs portaged here but a canoe belonging to Alexander Henry the Younger was lost running the rapids along the north shore in 1800. In his diary, Henry catalogued the lost goods, including kettles, guns and shot. In 1966, the Royal Ontario Museum and the Minnesota Historical Society cooperated in an underwater search program, retrieving a huge haul of fur trade goods, among them the items Henry listed. Modern excavations along the south channel have made both main channels safer to run.

The river now turns west and drops in earnest, losing 50 metres over

GEORGE BACK / NATIONAL ARCHIVES OF CANADA / C-28251

George Back's A Part of the Upper Winnipeg Falls, *shows the wild, tumultuous nature of the Winnipeg River during the fur trade.*

the next 100 kilometres. Today, three dams are located along this stretch – at Pointe du Bois, Slave Falls and Seven Sisters. The last of these, below modern Pinawa, earned its name because of a succession of falls and cataracts. Alexander Mackenzie wrote, "Here are seven portages, in so short a space that the whole of them are discernible at the same moment."

Pinawa sits on the north side of the river, on a large island created by two channels that the fur traders treated as separate rivers. The north channel was the "Pinawa River", while the turbulent south branch was often called Rivière Blanche. High water in the spring rendered the latter impassable and the brigades opted for the sluggish Pinawa Channel, though Alexander Henry complained that "the mosquitoes were here in such clouds as to prevent us from taking aim at the ducks." Today the marshy channel draws birders in the spring.

There are three more dams below Lac du Bonnet, which have flooded several falls with picturesque names, including Cap du Bonnet, Terre Blanche and Eaux qui Remuent or "Moving Waters", now the much subdued Silver Falls. Then the river enters the Manitoba Lowlands, where sand beaches and clay banks replace the rocky shores. This fertile stretch has supported human habitation for millennia.

The first *coureurs de bois* appeared sometime after 1700, arriving in the spring with canoes filled with trade goods and departing in the fall with furs stacked between the gunnels. In the early 1730s, they constructed a small post on the west side of the river, near a now-drowned sandy point the Cree called *Sagkeeng*, the "Meeting Place". In 1734, Jean-Baptiste La Vérendrye and his cousin, Christophe Dufrost de La Jemerais, established a post – Fort Maurepas – upstream on the east side of the river, but it was not a success; La Jemerais died there early in 1736. After the French regime ended, both the North West Company and Hudson's Bay Company had a number of posts along the river, as did other smaller fur concerns, including the short-lived XY Company.

The upper Winnipeg River can be reached from both the Trans-Canada Highway (No. 17) and Lake of the Woods at Keewatin, Ontario, where boat ramps can be found on both the lake and the river. North of the lake, Highway 596 leads to Minaki and Highway 525 continues to cross the river near Whitedog. Paddlers putting in here could end their journey in Manitoba's Whiteshell Provincial Park. Pointe du Bois and many other points along the river can be reached from secondary roads off Highway 11, which traces the west side of the river from Traverse Bay to the dam at Seven Sisters.

Quiet beach-combers are likely to see a svelte river otter along the shores of the Winnipeg River. And paddlers along the upper reaches of the river tell of playful otter families that sometimes accompany their canoes.

BRIAN WOLITSKI

Hudson Bay to Cumberland House

LINDA FAIRFIELD

*Black spruce (*Picea mariana*) is a tall, hardy evergreen tree that grows throughout the Canadian Shield, often in wet habitats. Its twining roots provide a strong binding material (*watap*) that was used to "sew" birchbark canoes, while its gummy sap made the joints waterproof.*

Abundant water and rugged granite combine in many places in northern Manitoba to create scenes of remarkable beauty, as here at Pisew Falls on the Grass River. For early fur traders, such splendor meant arduous portages and the Grass River was soon abandoned in favor of the Hayes.

If the Ottawa-Mattawa-Lake Superior route was the Montrealers' mainline, then this waterway – southwest up the Hayes River to its junction with the Nelson, across the top of Lake Winnipeg, past the great rapids at the mouth of the Saskatchewan River and west through Cedar Lake to Cumberland House – was the Hudson's Bay Company highway.

Beginning almost immediately after the 1774 construction of Cumberland House, the company's first major inland trading post, this arduous route became the main supply line to what quickly grew into a vast trading territory in northwestern North America. The Hayes River route would eventually link York Factory, the enormous depot on Hudson Bay, to inland posts as far south as North Dakota and as far west as the Columbia River.

For more than a century, the portage paths were beaten smooth each summer and the posts and depots along the way rang with activity. In the early years, canoes were used to haul trade goods inland and furs to the bay. Like those of the North West Company, they grew in size over the passing decades, but by the early 19th century, the need to transport ever larger cargos brought York boats – long, wooden boats inspired by Orkney yoles – into service. The HBC boatmen were never happy with the decision to convert to these unwieldy craft, since it was they who were obliged to transport them over the nearly 40 portages between York Factory and Cumberland House and York boats never completely replaced the lighter, more manoeuvrable canoes.

The arrival of Scottish settlers bound for the Red River Valley in 1811 put even more pressure on the Hudson's Bay highway and a series of attempts were made to create a "winter road" of ice and snow parallel to the summer route.

Steamships and railways spelled the end of this important water route by the late 1880s. However its relatively low flow, which made it a preferred route over the mighty Nelson to the north, has also saved it from developers. Today it is still wild and attractive to canoeists.

There are no roads to York Factory, but visiting this National Historic Site is possible by air and the communities of Norway House and Oxford House, as well as several fly-in lodges along the Hayes River route offer accommodation, supplies or assistance with canoe trips. Highway travellers heading west can also visit a small park in Grand Rapids that features a section of the tramway built by the HBC, portages used for millennia, parks that commemorate the visits of early European travellers and the sites of several early fur posts.

MIKE GRANDMAISON

154

PARTNERS IN TRADE, IGNORED BY SETTLEMENT

Long a people of the northern woods and coastal lowlands of Hudson and James Bays, the Cree were the first North Americans that the English encountered when they established their bayside posts in the 1670s and 1680s. Adept at hunting and trapping, they became key partners in the fur trade and quickly assumed the role of middlemen with more distant nations.

Soon, a number of Hudson's Bay Company employees learned to speak Cree, an Algonquian language, and many Cree learned to speak English, cementing a relationship that lasted for 200 years. Moving west and north together with the trade, the HBC men quite naturally designated landmarks, rivers and other North American nations by the names the Cree gave them. Thus the Dene were known as *Chipewyan* (in Cree, "Pointy Coats") and the Inuit became *Eskimos* ("Eaters of Raw Meat"). Only in the past quarter century have these second-hand names been largely revised.

Yet ironically, "Cree" is not Cree at all, but Ojibwe. The word comes from the Anishinabe *Kiristinon*, which Lake Superior Ojibwe used to describe their northern neighbors around James Bay. To the ears of early French traders and missionaries, it sounded like *Kristineaux* or *Christinos*, which was shortened over time to Cree. The Cree called themselves *Nehiawak* – "the People", adding regional descriptors to this root as they moved west with the fur trade. The *Saka-wiyiniwak*, the "Forest People" lived north of the Saskatchewan River, while the *Katepwew-sipi-wiyinwak*, the "Calling River People" lived in what the French called the Qu'Appelle Valley.

The Cree were allies of the related Ojibwe and soon formed ties with the unrelated Assiniboine of the eastern plains. Their enemies included the Dene to the north and, as they moved south and west, the Dakota, Atsina and eventually the Blackfoot. Access to European weapons made them formidable adversaries.

The move west, from the eastern shield and coastal lowlands to the Great Plains, resulted in the evolution of the Plains Cree (*Paskwa-wiyiniwak*) in the late 18th and early 19th centuries. They adopted a lifestyle based on buffalo hunting, and many became excellent horsemen.

They also intermarried with European traders, particularly with the Orcadian, Scots and English employees of the HBC; entire communities in northern Manitoba and Saskatchewan can trace part of their lineage to the fur trade.

But disease (it's estimated that the smallpox epidemic of 1781-82 killed more than half the Cree in the Hudson Bay watershed), alcohol, racism and the pressure of European settlement took an enormous toll on the Cree. Though such towering leaders as Poundmaker and Big Bear rose during times of crisis, for many the past 125 years has been a time of poverty and hopelessness. Today, cultural revival, education and a renewal of the long-lost authority of women in Cree society are together working to begin the healing for this once-powerful nation of people.

COURTESY OF MANITOBA CULTURE, HERITAGE AND TOURISM

Cree beadwork and embroidery includes intricate and beautiful floral designs, as are evident here on the tea cozy, below.

COURTESY OF MANITOBA MUSEUM OF MAN AND NATURE

Cree women, above, had a strong voice in family and community affairs when Europeans first arrived on Hudson Bay; today, many are experiencing a revival of this influence and responsibility as Cree communities begin a process of cultural healing.

York Factory

by Michael Payne

Letitia Hargrave, wife of Chief Trader James Hargrave and one of the more astute commentators on fur trade life, called it a "great swell" and "by far the most respectable place in the territory," but other observers were less taken with York Factory. In his novel on Hudson Bay, R.M. Ballantyne described York as "a monstrous blot" set in a swampy landscape, while fellow 19th-century author and York Factory resident William Smellie wrote: "But oh! how tame and tiresome is the scene! Dreary, and dull, and cheerless, well I ween…"

Of course York Factory was intended as a fur trade post, not as a source of artistic inspiration, and most residents, not to mention the Hudson's

York Factory, seen here in an aerial photograph, grew from a small fur post in the late 1600s to become a substantial, multicultural community. For a good part of its history it was the virtual capital of the fur trade.

COURTESY PARKS CANADA

Bay Company shareholders, cared more about how many furs passed through the post than the aesthetic appeal of its location. In this respect, York was closer to Letitia Hargrave's description than Smellie's. For the better part of two centuries York Factory was the most important fur trade post in the HBC operations, and from the 1770s

to the 1860s it served as the administrative, warehouse and transshipment centre of the trade. It would not be an exaggeration to call it the capital of the fur trade.

Its prominence was a result of its strategic location on a narrow peninsula of land between the mouths of the Nelson and Hayes Rivers. The Hayes offered the best route into the interior from Hudson Bay and connected York directly with a massive hinterland. By the mid-19th century York's warehouses held trade goods bound for the Mackenzie River and New Caledonia along with furs traded beyond the Rockies and bound for market in London.

The first post was built at York in 1682, but it was not until 1714, following the Treaty of Utrecht, that the HBC assumed undisputed control of the site. Between 1714 and 1782 the HBC gradually built York into its largest and most profitable bayside post. For much of this period the average value of York Factory's annual trade was more than 30,000 Made Beaver.

Trade began to decline in the 1760s and early 1770s due to increased competition from Canadian fur traders based in Montreal. The HBC responded by building its own inland posts, beginning with Cumberland House in 1774. These posts could not be supplied directly from Britain, nor could the furs they traded be shipped directly to London. As a result, York acquired a new importance as the HBC's network of inland posts expanded.

In 1782 a French naval expedition captured York Factory and Prince of Wales Fort. Both were destroyed and trade was seriously disrupted, but the HBC reestablished the two posts the following year. A serious flood in 1787 convinced Joseph Colen, the officer in charge,

KEN GIGLIOTTI / THE WINNIPEG FREE PRESS

to move York about two kilometers upstream to higher ground. Work began that same year on the combined warehouse, residence and workshops that company employees thereafter called the "Old Octagon", after the shape of its courtyard. Archaeological excavations at York in the 1990s turned up the foundations of this remarkable building.

A combination of the expansion of the company's business and the growth of the Red River Settlement after 1811 strained the capacity of the Old Octagon. The merger of the Hudson's Bay and North West companies in 1821 added to the problem, as York took over most of the functions of the old NWC centre, Fort William. As York's duties grew, so did the number of men stationed there with their families. A growing number of Homeguard Cree also lived nearby, so that by the 1820s York looked more like a village than a conventional fur trade post.

The most significant change in this period was the construction between 1830 and 1838 of a huge warehouse roughly 1,675 square metres in capacity. This building is approximately 30 metres square and stands two stories high, with a smaller central section of three stories. It was the largest building undertaken by the HBC until the construction of retail stores in the 20th century and at its peak, it sat at the centre of a complex of more than 40 buildings, ranging from a school and a church to workshops and houses.

By the 1860s the HBC could bypass York, shipping goods directly to Red River from St. Paul, Minnesota, by rail and steamboat. The post began a long decline, until it really only served the local Cree population. Finally in 1957, after 275 years of operation, it was closed. It was declared a national historic site in 1960 and since 1968 has been operated by Parks Canada.

Important as York Factory was to the fur trade, its historical significance lies as much in the community it created as its economic reach. It is one of the best-documented communities in 18th- and 19th-century Canada. There are 181 surviving post journals in the Hudson's Bay Company Archives that describe day-by-day living at York for the period up to 1870, along with more than 100 correspondence books and about 1,500 account books that detail the business operations of the post. Combined with private letters from individuals such as James and Letitia Hargrave, books by R.M. Ballantyne, Andrew Graham and James Isham, and other archival records, it is possible to reconstruct life at York Factory in the 18th and 19th centuries with remarkable accuracy. If you visit York Factory, spare a thought for the two Dandie Dinmont terriers the Hargraves kept at York, or Joseph Colen's personal library of 1,400 volumes, or the men who played soccer there on New Year's in 1776.

While most canoeists on the Hayes choose to travel downstream from Norway House to York Factory, experienced canoeists Douglas and Wilfred Keam from Norway House undertook the much more arduous upstream journey in 1999. The trip from York to The Forks of the Red and Assiniboine Rivers took 52 days and the pair was joined by other paddlers and canoes along the way.

The Hayes River

During the heyday of the fur trade era, what we now know as the Hayes River went by not one but five names. For convenience, however, it was often simply called the "Lower Track" because two other routes to the north had been earlier used by both the Cree who brought furs down to the bay and the Europeans they guided inland. The northernmost of these alternate routes, the "Upper Track" went up the Nelson River to its junction with the Grass River, followed the Grass River system to Cranberry Portage and crossed to a tributary of the Sturgeon-weir system north of Cumberland Lake. This was the route Samuel Hearne apparently took when he went inland to construct Cumberland House in the fall of 1774.

The so-called "Middle Track", between the Hayes and Nelson Rivers, traversed five lakes and several river systems from the lower Hayes River through Utik and Cross Lakes to the Summerberry River, which flowed from the Saskatchewan below The Pas. Anthony Henday and Matthew Cocking both used this route in the mid-1700s

and it was very likely the route Henry Kelsey took in 1690.

Neither of the upper two routes was suitable for the fully laden freight canoes that were the HBC norm soon after 1775. The Hayes, though more a watery staircase than a navigable river – particularly in its well-named "Hill River" section – was at least passable. This simple fact endowed it with an historic importance equalled only by the Ottawa River thousands of kilometres east during both the fur trade and early European settlement eras.

Going upstream from Hudson Bay, the 610-kilometre journey began with days of "tracking" the loaded boats, hauling them with long lines to which the men were harnessed like oxen. The river's 37 portages (bypassing 45 rapids and falls) began nearly 200 kilometres upstream at "The Rock", now called Whitemud Falls. Here, where two large islands and several small ones block the river as it tumbles off the Precambrian Shield onto the Hudson Bay Lowlands, crosses paid tribute to bay-bound paddlers who made a fateful decision against one last portage. During the 1790s, a small supply post – Rock Depot – was built on one of the islands to cut the round-trip journey of men from the western posts by 400 kilometres; goods and furs could be ferried at leisure from York Factory.

From here to Knee Lake, a distance of about 80 kilometres, the riverbed climbs steeply, gaining almost three quarters of its total 218-metre rise in elevation. Full of rocks and islands, the waterway is tumultuous. En route is Brassey Hill, the highest point between Hudson Bay and Lake Winnipeg. The

Black spruce and morning mist combine to create a ghostly scene along the Hayes River.

MIKE GRANDMAISON

view from the top allows a panorama over 36 lakes.

Slogging on upstream, the brigades reached what was known as "the Dramstone", which marked the last of the worst of the rapids. Here the men often demanded to be treated with a wee nip for their toils. Ahead lay Knee and Oxford Lakes. A resort graces the scenic shores of the former; on the latter, the modern community of Oxford House dates its history to the fur trade. Both lakes are aligned with the prevailing westerlies. Though bay-bound travellers may find this an advantage, both lakes can be dangerous in high winds.

Above Oxford, the brigades passed through a scenic gorge (better appreciated going down than up) they called Hill Gates before reaching Robinson Falls and its accompanying portage. This "carrying place", as the HBC men called it, is more than 1.5 kilometres long – only the portage at Grand Rapids was longer on the route to Cumberland. Both eventually boasted tramways with flatcars to transport the York boats and their heavy loads past the falls or rapids.

From Robinson Lake the upper Hayes leads via Painted Stone Portage to the Echimamish River (in Cree, "the River-that-Flows-Both-Ways"). Here two streams originate in a flat, marshy meadow. One flows east and the other west and in the early years of the fur trade a succession of beaver dams kept the water level in this wetland sufficiently deep to float canoes. Then the beaver were trapped out and men were obliged to build the necessary dams. Fortunately the beavers are back, building again in just the right places. The westward flowing portion of the Echimamish leads to the upper Nelson River, Playgreen Lake and the modern community of Norway House.

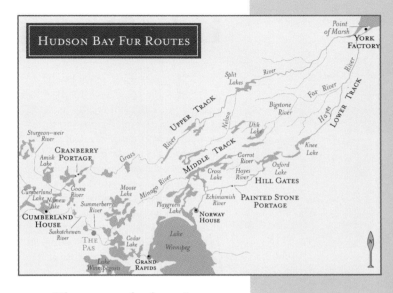

HUDSON BAY FUR ROUTES

Where many other large rivers in Manitoba, including the Nelson, have been dammed over the past 40 years, the Hayes is undeveloped. As Hap Wilson and Stephanie Aykroyd wrote in their excellent book of maps, *Wilderness Rivers of Manitoba*, "Past history combined with the thrill of whitewater and an ever-changing scenery make the Hayes an excellent choice for the discriminating paddler."

Norway House on the northeast tip of Lake Winnipeg can be accessed by road or air. Outfitting services are available here or in Thompson. Air transportation can also be arranged to Oxford House for a shorter journey to the bay. An airlift from York Factory must be arranged prior to departure. From Norway House to York Factory generally takes about four weeks for modern paddlers and the upstream journey is longer, though George Simpson – who almost never paddled himself, but drove his men mercilessly – once travelled from York to Norway House in less than a week.

Made Beaver

The tanned pelt of a prime winter beaver, termed Made Beaver or MB, quickly became the standard of trade for the Hudson's Bay Company. All other furs and goods were measured against it. The pelt of an arctic fox, below, might be worth two MB, while a gun could fetch 10.

DENNIS FAST

Lake Winnipeg

The heart of an enormous watershed, crossroads of half a continent, Lake Winnipeg has both enabled and frustrated transportation for millennia. A descendant of glacial Lake Agassiz, Lake Winnipeg is North America's seventh-largest lake. Proof that people have travelled its ever-varying shorelines for more than 10,000 years has been found on the Manitoba Escarpment (Lake Agassiz's western shore) in the form of an 11,000-year-old Clovis point crafted of Knife River flint from southern North Dakota.

In the footsteps of these early mammoth hunters came bison hunters from the west, mound-builders and copper traders from the south, hunter-gatherers from the north and the ancestors of the Cree and Ojibwe from the east. Europeans arrived only in the last 300 years.

French *coureurs de bois*, arriving via the Winnipeg River, were very likely the first Europeans to see Lake Winnipeg, though it's possible that Pierre Radisson reached Lake Winnipeg from Hudson Bay in the early 1680s.

They and those who followed all discovered the same thing. Though it provided access to an enormous territory – south through the Red River to the edge of the buffalo prairies, east to Lake Superior and beyond, north to Hudson Bay, and

west via the Saskatchewan River to the vast western plains – Lake Winnipeg was a monster. Many feared it more than Lake Superior, which was more than three times as large and much colder. Lake Winnipeg has a nasty habit of transforming itself from a beguiling calm to surging whitecaps in 10 minutes or less. The fur trade journals are full of bleak tales of waiting for days for the wind to abate, of being swamped or dashed against the rocks, of battling sudden storms and losing both men and supplies.

The north basin, larger and deeper than its southern counterpart, was particularly deadly, especially in a south wind. For 70 kilometres, the north coast is edged by high clay banks. When the wind blows from the south, it creates wind-driven tides that pile the water into the north basin, raising water levels by more than a metre and inundating the narrow northern shore. A brigade caught crossing this treacherous stretch had nowhere to land. Knowing this, the canoemen waited for promising weather and then sailed day and night with prayers on their lips. At the northwestern corner, a long ridge of sand – Limestone Point - shadows the shore for 25 kilometres. In bad weather, the canoes were portaged into calmer water on the other side.

Then the brigades hastened south along high limestone cliffs to the mouth of the Saskatchewan River. Ahead lay "the Large carrying place", as Joseph Smith called it in 1757, which gave access to the Saskatchewan River above Grand Rapids. At just over five kilometres, the portage route was gruelling, but west-bound brigades were probably delighted to see it,

Though they never quite reached the size of the North West Company's canots du maître, *the HBC's brigade canoes were sometimes large enough to warrant the shoulders of four or even five canoemen. Smaller canoes were generally portaged upright by two men.*

ROGER TURENNE

*Limestone cliffs,
best appreciated
in winter, soar
along the shoreline
of Lake Winnipeg's
north basin.*

for it meant Lake Winnipeg was behind them.

Not only the Hudson's Bay Company, but the Nor'Westers used the Grand Rapids portage, leading to desperate tactics on both sides. The North West Company brigades came this way en route to far-off Lake Athabasca; they may have been even happier to see the long portage than their HBC rivals were.

Arriving on Lake Winnipeg from the Winnipeg River, the Nor'Westers hugged the eastern shore as they paddled north. Not even they – as foolishly brave as they often were – would attempt to cross either basin. About a third of the way up the lake's 450-kilometre length was Black Island. Here, by island hopping, a crossing was possible, though wind-driven tides sometimes caused the water to roar through the narrow channels.

From Grindstone Point, they kept to the west side of the lake, traversing large bays to save time as they moved north. Just south of Grand Rapids, they were forced far out into the lake to circumvent Long Point (the voyageurs' *Le Détour*), a 40-kilometre finger of sand and gravel that is part of The Pas Moraine.

Two other fur routes used Lake Winnipeg. To access posts along the Red and Assiniboine Rivers (see page 192), the HBC brigades (and the later Selkirk Settlers) turned south, not west from the Hayes River and traced the eastern

shore of the lake to The Narrows, where they crossed the route taken by the NWC and followed the west shore of the south basin to the mouth of the Red River. The Nor'Westers, who also had posts on the southern plains, travelled from the Winnipeg River to the Red River along Lake Winnipeg's south shore.

Today, Lake Winnipeg is one of Manitoba's most popular vacation spots. The silty south basin (the Cree *Wi-nipi* means "Muddy Water") is ringed by beaches, including some, such as Grand Beach, that are truly magnificent, and cottage communities. The less populated north basin boasts clear water, soaring cliffs and abundant wildlife; for these reasons Long Point and parts of the northwest lakeshore have been included in the new Manitoba Lowlands national park.

Lake Winnipeg's south basin, located about 60 kilometres north of Winnipeg, Manitoba's capital, is easily accessed on the west by Highways 8, 9 and 234 and on the east by Highways 59 and 304. North of The Narrows, access is limited. Highway 6 leads through Grand Rapids (a side road south of town goes west onto Long Point) and Norway House can be reached via Highway 373 off the same major road. Norway House has regular air service.

ROUTES FROM
LAKE WINNIPEG

To York Factory &
Hudson Bay via
the Nelson River

To York Factory
& Hudson Bay
via the Hayes River

To the Rockies
via the
Saskatchewan River

*Lake
Winnipeg*

To western prairies
via the Assiniboine
& Qu'Appelle Rivers

To Lake Superior
via the
Winnipeg River

To the Mississippi River
via the
Red River

To Missouri Country
via the Assiniboine
& Souris Rivers

Exploring the Fur Trade Routes of North America

Grand Rapids

A two-kilometre-long portage bypassing the worst rapids, see map below, was built for the York boats. Partly unloaded at the lake landing, right, the boats were tracked on long lines from the cliff tops to the new portage, unloaded and run down the rapids for the rest of the load. The later tramway, a section of which is preserved in a town park, greatly eased the burden of the long portage.

PETER ST. JOHN

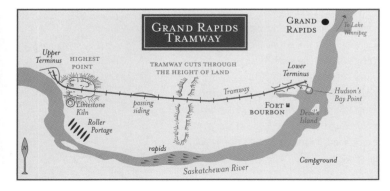

Before the Grand Rapids Dam was built in the 1960s, the mighty Saskatchewan River poured into Lake Winnipeg here, arcing between limestone cliffs, dropping 21 metres over the last seven kilometres. For at least 4,500 years, the falls had drawn people to fish for sturgeon and whitefish, but the bounty had a price. Though skilled paddlers ran the rapids coming down to the lake, going upstream meant a long portage.

Louis-Joseph La Vérendrye was likely the first European in the area, guided inland in 1739 by Cree traders who wanted a French trading post on the Saskatchewan River. Two years later he returned to build the first Fort Bourbon near the east end of the Grand Rapids portage.

After the French era, the portage saw increasing use and by 1780, both the Hudson's Bay and North West Companies came this way. As two rival brigades were passing, the HBC's Matthew Cocking noticed how the voyageurs carried their huge packs – balanced on a tump line that crossed

their foreheads. His own Cree porters used a breast strap, causing pain when the loads were heavy.

As the canoes grew larger and York boats came into service after 1797, alterations were made to the portage. Initially, the York boats were rolled over the 5.2-kilometre trail on logs, but the Nor'Westers, balancing their huge loads, complained that the rollers compromised their footing.

Neither the HBC nor the NWC had posts at Grand Rapids during the competition period, but both recognized the site's strategic importance. In June 1819, HBC Governor William Williams positioned an armed force on the portage trail and captured the crews of 10 NWC canoes as they came down from the Athabasca country. The following spring, the Nor'Westers countered by imprisoning Colin Robertson.

The HBC established a post on the lake in 1864 that briefly offered hotel space for lake steamer passengers heading up the Saskatchewan River. By 1877, traffic over the portage was heavy enough to warrant a tramway, which was profitable until railways expanded into the region.

Grand Rapids is on Highway 6, the main route through the Interlake. A section of the west's first railway has been preserved in Tramway Park. The magnificent rapids are gone, but from the campground on the south shore the rock-strewn riverbed and limestone cliffs can be seen, allowing a glimpse of a long and fascinating past.

MIKE GRANDMAISON

GRAND RAPIDS TRAMWAY

GRAND RAPIDS ● *To Lake Winnipeg*

Upper Terminus — HIGHEST POINT — TRAMWAY CUTS THROUGH THE HEIGHT OF LAND — *Lower Terminus*

Limestone Kiln — *passing siding* — *Tramway* — FORT BOURBON — *Hudson's Bay Point* — *Devil's Island*

Roller Portage

rapids

Campground

Saskatchewan River

The Early Parklands

Manitoba's Parklands region may be better known for its latter-day administrative and provisioning posts (see The Upper Assiniboine on page 210) than its earlier fur forts, but the region was important during the early trade and several sites are remembered with reconstructions or signage.

Louis-Joseph La Vérendrye constructed the first Fort Dauphin in 1741, likely at the mouth of the Mossy River on Lacs des Prairies, his name for both Lake Winnipegosis and Lake Manitoba to the south. Other French-Canadian traders, including Maurice Blondeau and François Le Blanc ("Old Franceways", many called him), continued trading here after the fall of New France. In the late 1760s, they encountered the first HBC men in the area, including William Tomison, who spent the winter of 1769 in the Riding Mountains and on Lake Dauphin. Five years later, Peter Pond, Jean-Baptiste Cadot (or Cadotte), Alexander Henry and the Frobisher brothers came north with a fleet of 30 canoes, intent on pushing the Montreal trade far to the north. Pond, a New Englander, wintered at "Fort Dauphin", which his map showed as being on the west shore of Lake Dauphin, likely at the mouth of the Valley River.

Both the North West and XY Companies had posts here, as did the HBC. The HBC's Fort Dauphin was constructed in 1815 on the Valley River and moved closer to the lake two years later. HBC surveyor Peter Fidler retired and died there.

To the north, competition was fierce in the Swan River Valley in the 1790s. The Nor'Westers built a post on the Swan River, 19 kilometres above Swan Lake, in 1787 and the HBC countered in 1790, sending Charles Price Isham into the region. Isham built less than a kilometre upstream from the NWC, established large gardens nearby (the region is famously fertile) and began training Orkney canoemen to build and repair canoes. Isham traded for 7,500 Made Beaver in 1792, but competition soon trapped out the area and made hunting problematic. Like other HBC post masters, Isham also faced employee unrest over the introduction of York boats in the 1790s, which cut the labor force dramatically and undermined the experience of the senior canoemen.

The many Fort Dauphins are recalled at Fort Dauphin Museum, a fur trade replica constructed on the northwest bank of the Vermillion River in Dauphin. From Highway 5A and 10A West, turn south on Jackson Street. The Swan River trade is recalled with a plaque located just off Highway 10, close to the Swan Valley Museum in Swan River.

This tin cup was among hundreds of artifacts recovered from an excavation of one of the many Fort Dauphins on the Valley River.

PETER ST. JOHN

The Mossy Portages

The Pas Moraine, a natural causeway left by the receding ice sheets, served for millennia as a highway between western Manitoba and Lake Winnipeg. Canoemen also used it to cross from Cedar Lake on the Saskatchewan River system to Lake Winnipegosis, and Lake Manitoba, below.

In their footsteps came fur traders, headed south to Lake Manitoba, left, or west to the Swan River region. One of two main portage trails, a four-kilometre path leading to Oskar Point and the clear waters of Lake Winnipegosis, is today marked with a Manitoba Historic Sites Plaque.

Henry Kelsey at The Pas

The Saskatchewan River Delta is not, as one might imagine, at the river's mouth on Lake Winnipeg. Instead, it is northwest more than 100 kilometres in a low-lying region on the Manitoba-Saskatchewan border. Here, the Pasquia and Carrot Rivers join the Saskatchewan as it winds though a network of marshes. Shaping this huge wetland is The Pas moraine, a huge glacial remnant that has served for millennia as a natural causeway. To the north is Clearwater Lake, with its crystalline water.

River, moraine, wetlands and deep, clear lakes; even today these distinct habitats draw an abundance of wildlife, and it's easy to imagine the Assiniboine, with young Henry Kelsey in tow, deciding to spend the winter of 1690 here.

Historians have never pinpointed the location of Kelsey's "Deering Point", where the 20-year-old HBC employee apparently wintered, but many think that it may have been where the river and moraine intersect, at the modern town of The Pas. For nearly a century, this is where the Assiniboine and Cree gathered each spring to make canoes from the large birch, in order to transport their furs to the bay. After 1775, the Pasquia Cree traded their furs upstream at Cumberland House until the terrible smallpox epidemic of 1781 all but emptied the countryside.

Recent archaeological excavations along the shore of the Saskatchewan River at The Pas failed to turn up any evidence of Kelsey's brief stay, but the search continues. His journal tells of burying "a Rundlett" containing a hatchet and six knives when he left to go south in the spring of 1791. Perhaps, like Champlain's astrolabe and Louis-Joseph La Vérendrye's lead tablet, Henry Kelsey's "rundlett" will someday be found.

Born the same year as the Hudson's Bay Company, Kelsey, just 14, arrived on the bay in 1684. Despite his youth, he could read and write and he showed both a facility for languages (he ultimately wrote a Cree dictionary) and a love of travel. Taking advantage of these talents, the company sent him west and south to promote the idea of travelling to trade with the English on the bay.

Though he became governor of York Fort before his death in the 1720s, by the mid-18th century many believed his journey had never happened. This may have been because people had trouble deciphering his journal or its rhyming introduction, but it was more likely due to the testimony of Arthur Dobbs, an Irish aristocrat and staunch critic of the HBC, before a parliamentary committee in London in 1749. Dobbs suggested that Kelsey had been a runaway and his version was believed for nearly 200 years. Then in 1926, Kelsey's original journal was inexplicably discovered in Castle Dobbs, the hereditary home of Sir Arthur, in Carrickfergus, Northern Ireland.

The Pas is on Highway 10 in northwestern Manitoba. Kelsey's visit is recalled on a plaque in a riverside park at the end of Fischer Avenue.

Rex Woods' painting of young Henry Kelsey and his party of Assiniboine guides conveys some of the wonderment he must have felt as they emerged from the parklands forests and Kelsey became the first European to see the herds of bison that had sustained life on the western plains for so many millennia.

REX WOODS / COURTESY ROGERS COMMUNICATIONS INC.

Cumberland House

When Samuel Hearne arrived with 10 men in the summer of 1774, Pine Island was a place of towering evergreens – spruce, not pine, but the English always had difficulty telling the difference – on the southern edge of a bountiful lake. Hearne had been charged with establishing the Hudson's Bay Company's first inland post west of the bay. He chose Pine Island, partly for its trees, after a lengthy search that took him through much of the Saskatchewan delta and east to the location of the modern town of The Pas.

The site on the north shore of the island overlooking the lake was better, he thought, and the men built a temporary "log tent", a kind of double lean-to, for the winter. They called the new post Cumberland House, after William, Duke of Cumberland, and the widening of the Saskatchewan River at its front door Cumberland Lake.

Though theirs was the first trading house on the island, the men were hardly alone. They had, in fact, been driven inland by the sheer numbers of Canadian free traders on the lower Saskatchewan River. It was no longer enough to sit, as the HBC had for more than a century, and wait for the Cree, Ojibwe and Assiniboine to make the long journey to the bay. Now, competition was damming the flow of beaver pelts as

effectively as the beaver themselves obstructed tens of thousands of streams across the great unknown north.

Hearne had come from York Fort on Hudson Bay by way of the "Upper Track", which led into the north end of Namew Lake and south to Cumberland Lake. Though he could not have known it in the summer of 1774, within a year the free traders would paddle past Pine Island, turn northwest up the route he had descended and take the Sturgeon-weir River to Amisk Lake. From there it was a short hop to the Churchill River and by 1779, Peter Pond would be over Methye Portage and into the Athabasca watershed.

To the west, the Saskatchewan and its tributaries stretched across the western plains from the Rockies. Pine Island would soon be a major crossroads of the fur trade and for the HBC and its nemesis, the North West Company, a hub of fur trade activity and competition.

Hearne's men began work on the post in the spring of 1775 and within two years it was doing a brisk trade.

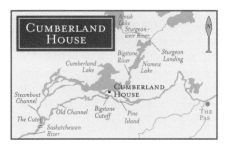

FRANKLIN ARBUCKLE / HUDSON'S BAY COMPANY ARCHIVES / P-416

Though the London Committee had tentatively selected Pasquia (modern The Pas), as the site for its first western inland post, on visiting the site, Samuel Hearne found that many people had wintered there before him, beginning with Henry Kelsey more than 80 years before. It was, Hearne complained, "entirely bare from all kind of woods"; he chose Pine Island instead. Here, he studies the plans as his men build the new post in the spring of 1775. The "log tent" they wintered in sits behind the rising structure.

William Tomison took over as post master in 1778 and was there in December of 1781, when the first horrifying epidemic of smallpox swept across the western plains, killing an estimated seven of every 10 people. Though Tomison and his men worked tirelessly for more than two months to feed and nurse the stream of men, women and children, they could not stem the tide of death. The Cree and Assiniboine and many Blackfoot and Kutenai to the west were devastated by the epidemic, which was compounded by a winter during which the game seemed to disappear. The plains had been burned the previous summer, driving the bison away, and even rabbits were scarce. To make matters worse the following summer, 1782, was the year the French captured and burned York Factory, and desperately needed supplies were late arriving. Tomison waited near York's charred shell until September 4th, before turning back inland empty-handed. The ship appeared a week later.

About 1790, Cumberland House was moved across a small bay and a larger post was erected. The North West Company immediately built right next door and until their amalgamation three decades later, the two companies co-existed in a kind of armed neutrality. Meanwhile, both were expanding. The HBC established both South Branch House on the South Saskatchewan and Manchester House on an island in the North Saskatchewan in 1786. The latter was largely supplanted in importance by

Buckingham House, built in 1792 and Edmonton House farther up-river in 1795. South Branch House was closed after it was attacked by the Atsina in 1793. Though the focus of the Nor' Westers was the rich fur-bearing region of Athabasca, they had enough manpower to precede or counter every move of the HBC up the Saskatchewan River with posts of their own.

Because of its location, Cumberland saw a stream of soon-to-be-famous names pass through its gates. David Thompson convalesced here with a broken leg in 1790. While it was mending, he studied surveying under the HBC's Philip Turnor; he later used this knowledge for the North West Company and the Government of Canada. Peter Fidler also studied under Turnor before accompanying him on a reconnaisance mission to Lake Athabasca.

John Franklin, George Back and John Richardson all spent the winter of 1819 at Cumberland; the latter two were artists and Richardson, a biologist, painted several species of birds and mammals that today bear his name.

After amalgamation in 1821, Cumberland House declined in importance as a fur headquarters, replaced by Norway House. The steamboat era briefly revived trade, but that too ended when the railway reached the north. Today, Cumberland House (population 14,000) is Saskatchewan's oldest community and boasts its oldest schoolhouse.

Cumberland House is on Highway 123, 134 kilometres northwest of the Kelsey Trail (No. 55), between Nipawin and the Manitoba border. The stone powder house, built in 1790, can be seen along with a plaque commemorating the founding of the first post in 1774.

Hearne followed the Grass River, below, to Cumberland Lake, but this "Upper Track" was soon abandoned for the Hayes River route. Now a popular provincial park, the Grass River draws canoeists and wildlife watchers, who may be rewarded with sightings of woodland caribou.

MIKE GRANDMAISON

BUILDING FOR TOMORROW ON TWO CONTINENTS

Few fur trade figures are as little understood as William Tomison, "chief, inland" or governor of the Hudson's Bay Company in North America from 1786 to 1811. Undoubtedly complex, he was a man who combined a good heart with a no-nonsense manner. But history has given him short shrift because the qualities he valued were largely unappreciated at the time. He believed in human equality in an era when the prevailing order was Eurocentric and hierarchical. He was self-effacing when self-aggrandisement was better understood and though he wrote volumes of letters and reports (and wrote well, though he always regretted his lack of formal education), he left no autobiography, no list of his many accomplishments.

PETER ST. JOHN

Tomison was born in Orkney about 1739. He signed on with the HBC in 1760, and spent 51 years in Western Canada. Initially posted on the bay, he soon learned Cree and was among a handful of men sent inland in the late 1760s and early 1770s to attract trade to the bayside posts.

His first senior posting came in 1778, at Cumberland House, the company's first major inland post. For nearly 25 years, though he travelled far and wide, Cumberland remained at the heart of his vision for the HBC, but the first years were a trial. Smallpox swept across the plains in December 1781, killing thousands. The Cree around Cumberland, weakened by famine, were particularly hard hit and many turned to the post for help. Tomison put his men on half-rations to feed the growing crowd and worked night and day to try to stem the tide of death. Yet typically, he did not neglect the business of the post. Death and business – they were two separate matters.

In the same way, he could be both generous and frugal and some found his habit of thrift annoying. David Thompson, fussed over and cared for by Tomison when he suffered a badly broken leg as a teenager, wrote decades later of Tomison's annoying habit of retrieving tiny beads or nails found on the floor.

Tomison has also been criticized for his focus on the Saskatchewan River trade when others had their sights on the Athabasca. Yet he knew better than most of his English colleagues how the company's workforce was stretched past its limit, particularly after York boats were put into service in the late 1790s. While other senior officers stayed by the bay, he went inland every year, taking a full share of the load as the brigades moved ever farther west.

But they were "English gentlemen" and he was an Orcadian who had begun his career as a laborer. He had a clear view of the other side of the street and for years waged battles for better treatment of his employees and against liquor as a trade item. Eventually, the fight wore him down and he retired in 1811 a wealthy but embittered man.

On leave in Orkney in 1790, Tomison endowed a small school in South Ronaldsay and before he died in 1829, he left half his estate, with instructions that it and interest for 20 years be used to enlarge the school or build anew. Tomison Academy, left, was built in 1851, on a hill overlooking Scotland. Still as solid as the rock on which it stands, it has become the Tomison Heritage Centre, to celebrate the ties between Orkney and Canada and the man whose life touched thousands on both continents.

North to the Athabasca

LINDA FAIRFIELD

The high-bush cran-berry (Viburnum edule) *is not related to wild cranberries we associate with Thanksgiving; rather it is a member of the honeysuckle family that grows in moist woodlands along northern rivers and lakeshores. Its bright red berries are an excellent source of Vitamin C and despite its tart taste, it was relished by the voyageurs.*

Amisk Lake on the Sturgeon-weir River, right, boasts clear water, granite cliffs, limestone points, as well as plenty of secluded beaches.

Often forbidding, at times and in places stunningly beautiful, the Athabasca was the Eldorado of the fur trade. Here, endless forests and innumerable lakes and rivers sustained enormous numbers of fur-bearing mammals, and the long cold winters produced incomparable pelts. But getting in and getting the furs out was a costly and dangerous business.

Just finding the way in took Europeans decades (though the Dene had been travelling through the region for millennia). Led by a small number of intrepid free traders, they worked their way north and west from the Saskatchewan River Valley in the 1770s. The Frobishers, two of three brothers from Yorkshire, England, were reduced to literally eating their deerskin shirts at the post they built on Trade Lake in the Churchill River in 1774. But by 1778, Methye Portage, the height of land between the Hudson Bay and Arctic watersheds, had been breached and word of the northern riches was out. Within five years, the North West Company was sending large brigades along the tortuous river route north to reap the harvest.

Today it is hard to imagine how companies based on the St. Lawrence River or in London could create a thriving business in northern Alberta without benefit of modern transportation or communications, yet that is precisely what transpired. For a century, first the North West Company and after 1821 the Hudson's Bay Company managed to mine the harvest of furs using a system of supply depots and thousands of indomitable (and largely undemanding) employees.

Today, this route north from Cumberland Lake in the Saskatchewan River delta, up the Sturgeon-weir and Churchill Rivers, across Methye Portage and down the Clearwater River to the Athabasca, seems off the beaten track. But in the 1800s it might have been the centre of the continent for all the famous faces that passed this way. Alexander Mackenzie, Simon Fraser, John Franklin and John Richardson all built international reputations here; others made their fortunes.

Time travellers today can find traces of this remarkable past in many places along the route, for the landscape is largely unchanged. Here, too, is a modern-day trading post that has successfully bridged two worlds. And those interested in tracing these waterways by canoe will find some of the best paddling North America has to offer.

CARIBOU HUNTERS OF THE NORTHERN FORESTS

These Athapaskan-speakers of the tundra and transitional forests or taiga of northern Canada were among the earliest North American nations the English encountered when they began to establish fur posts on northwestern Hudson Bay. Widely known as *Chipewyan*, a term that comes from the Cree *Chepawyan* or "Pointy Skins", referring to the distinctive tails on their long over-shirts, they were also called the "Northern Indians", as distinct from the Cree or "Southern Indians", by Hudson's Bay Company employees. Their own name for themselves is Dene, "the People".

Their language is distinct from the widely spoken Algonquian languages of southern Canada, as well as the Inuktitut of the far north, and their origins may reach back many millennia. They clearly have inhabited the vast northland for at least a thousand years; the Navaho of the American southwest, whose legends tell of a great migration from the far north about 1,000 years ago, speak a similar Athapaskan language and call them-selves Dinnie.

When Europeans first encountered them, the eastern Dene were hunters and fishers who mainly depended on the great migratory herds of barren-ground caribou for food, clothing and lodge covers. They also used caribou sinew for sewing and cut hides into long strips to make snowshoes, fish nets and snares.

Just as the plains cultures were remarkable buffalo hunters, the Dene had a myriad ways of hunting caribou. They ambushed the herds at strategic river crossings, drove them into huge empoundments and speared them from canoes as they swam across rivers or lakes. They were wonderfully adept at fishing as well, as David Thompson noted in 1785: "When the land is scarce of Deer [caribou] … they take to the Lakes to angle Trout or Pike at which they are very expert." Other animals were also hunted, but the northern tundra and taiga were harsh environments for survival and the Dene often faced shortages and sometimes starvation. To survive, they wintered in family groups, moving when necessary to hunt. During the summer, they often gathered in large summer villages by the shores of a lake or river.

Unlike the Cree, with whom they were often at odds, the Dene initially had little interest in the fur trade. Though determined efforts were made to encourage them and a post at Churchill was built to cater to them, furs were less abundant on the tundra and in the northern forests than they were farther south.

Farther east at Fort Chipewyan, geographic conditions were quite different, and the Dene played a larger role in the fur trade, trapping, hunting and fishing for the North West and later Hudson's Bay Companies. The western movement of the Cree pushed some related peoples – the Hare and Dogrib in particular – far-ther north, and an epidemic of smallpox killed large numbers in 1781, but on the whole the Dene were not as negatively impacted by the fur trade as were many southern cultures.

W. O. MATHERS IN *THE FAR NORTH*

This woman's beautiful parka demonstrates the distinctive tailoring used by both the Dene and the Inuit, which earned the Dene their Cree appellation, Chipewyan.

The Sturgeon-weir River

PETER ST. JOHN

Little Limestone Point, rich in fossils, stretches into Amisk Lake where it pours into the Sturgeon-weir River, offering a perfect spot to stop for lunch, as the Athabasca brigades often did whether they were heading north or south.

AMISK LAKE

This tributary of the Saskatchewan River begins in a lagoon at the northwest end of Wood Lake just south of the Churchill River and runs through the ancient granite of the Precambrian Shield to Amisk Lake. From Amisk ("Beaver" in Cree), it drops through ragged limestone into Namew (or "Sturgeon") Lake, which empties into Cumberland Lake.

Today, the Sturgeon-weir is an enticing downstream canoe trip for paddlers who delight in its nearly ideal gradient of about two metres per kilometre. For fur traders heading upstream 200 years ago, loaded with goods for the Athabasca region, the river was less than delightful. The voyageurs called it Rivière Maligne, the "Wicked River", for, as Alexander Mackenzie said, it was "an almost continual rapid". The name we know it by today comes from the Cree practice of trapping sturgeon with weirs across the shallow rapids.

Tough slogging or not, this was the gateway to the north country and, beginning with Joseph and Thomas Frobisher, who established the first post on the Churchill River in 1774, a trickle of traders soon became a flood. The Yorkshire-born Frobishers spent a horrendous winter on the Churchill, but were back for more the following autumn in the company of the veteran Alexander Henry the Elder and 43 men. It was late in the season as they headed up the Sturgeon-weir, and they were caught by winter on October 29th as they passed Little Limestone Point at the south end of Amisk Lake.

With food for just three days, they hurried across to Moody Bay, where Henry divided the men into two groups. One group began felling trees for the buildings – a "masters" house and store facing the lake and employees' cabins on the other three sides of the quadrangle – while the other group went fishing. Amisk is cold and deep and full of fish, which saw the traders through the months of cold. By early May when Henry noted "swans flying toward the Maligne River", they were undoubtedly more than a little sick of their piscine diet.

The post was maintained for two years; in 1778, Peter Pond crossed Methye Portage into the Arctic Ocean watershed and built the first fur post within spitting distance of Lake Athabasca.

Amisk Lake and the resort community of Denare Beach are on Highway 167, 19 kilometres southwest of Flin Flon. A further 30 kilometres south along the same road takes you to a picnic site at Little Limestone Point on the Sturgeon-weir River. Access to the river is also possible off the Hanson Lake Road (No. 106, which follows a glacial esker) and Highway 135, which goes north from 106 at the Jan Lake turnoff. The Denare Beach Museum has artifacts excavated from Fort Henry.

The Upper Churchill River

From the Sturgeon-weir River, the Athabasca-bound brigades crossed Frog Portage to the upper Churchill. During the fur trade, this section of the river was treated separately from its lower reaches, which pour into Hudson Bay at Churchill. However, its Cree name – Missinippi or "Very Big Water" – aptly describes the entire 1,600-kilometre river.

Draining nearly 300,000 square kilometres of northern Alberta, Saskatchewan and Manitoba, it crosses a forested landscape of glacially sculpted bedrock in a long series of quiet lakes connected by rapids or falls. In many places, outcroppings of rock rise from the water's edge, providing a canvas for one of the largest collections of pictographs in Canada. Entering the river at Trade Lake, the fur brigades turned west and, following the sometimes convoluted course, paddled and portaged upstream past the site of Stanley House, established in 1798 by the HBC (now Stanley Mission, where the first church in Saskatchewan was completed in 1856) and the Rapid River, which drains beautiful Lac La Ronge, now a provincial park.

At Otter Rapids, the river tears over a bed of large rocks nearly a kilometre long. Today, the Cree who live in nearby communities along the river roar up and down in motor boats, and paddlers usually shoot the rapids, but over the centuries many miscalculated and died. During the fur trade crosses were a common sight here and upstream near Pin Portage.

Continuing through Black Bear, Pinehouse and Primeau Lakes (the last named for Louis Primeau, who ascended the Churchill River from Hudson Bay in 1766), the brigades left the shield country just before Lac Ile-à-la-Crosse. The first post here was established by Thomas Frobisher in 1776 on a peninsula where the Cree sometimes played lacrosse. Catering to both Cree and Dene trappers, it was often a rather contentious place. From the northwest end of Lac Ile-à-la-Crosse, the brigades followed the river north and west to Peter Pond Lake and followed swift, shallow Methye River north to Lac La Loche.

Today, the upper Churchill River is a busy, beautiful waterway, largely unspoiled and used by both river residents and large numbers of visitors for travel and fishing.

Access to this part of the Churchill River is possible in several places across northern Saskatchewan. The two most popular routes are along Highway 102, which skirts Lac La Ronge Provincial Park to Otter Rapids, and Highway 155, which leads north past the town of Ile-à-la-Crosse, as well as Peter Pond and La Loche Lakes, to the Clearwater River. Lodges all along the river provide accommodation and canoe trip support.

DENNIS FAST

*Black bear (*Ursus americanus*) twins practise their climbing skills on a large poplar. Equally at ease in the water or on land and willing to dine on almost anything, they are perfectly at home in the north woods. They can sometimes be seen swimming across lakes or rivers such as the Churchill, left.*

MIKE GRANDMAISON

171

BRIDGING TWO WORLDS

These beautifully tanned black beaver pelts are fit for a queen. The Hudson's Bay Company charter required a gift of two black beaver pelts and two elk skins to be presented to the monarch or his descendants every time they visited Rupert's Land.

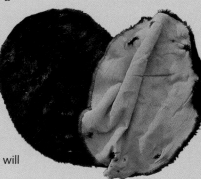

There are many who believe that the fur trade is over. In the last two decades of the 20th century, international pressure against trapping drove fur prices way down, putting many trappers and traders out of business. Alex Robertson is an exception, as he always has been. In Lac La Ronge, Saskatchewan, Robertson's Trading Post is thriving, thanks to a combination of business acumen, remarkable community relations and plain hard work.

Alex and his son Scott manage a business that combines a modern grocery, general store, camping supply centre, grocery warehouse and remote fly-in service with an old-fashioned fur trading post. Oh yes, and the Robertsons have one of the largest collections of Cree art in the country, and Alex can sometimes even be coaxed into selling a piece, but only if he believes a buyer will love it as much as he does.

The senior Robertson is one of the most knowledgeable fur traders in North America. He trained at a fur grading school in Montreal before going to work for the Hudson's Bay Company in the late 1940s. For 20 years, he worked as a fur buyer in the winter and a relief manager at HBC posts right across Canada during the summer months. By 1967, he was ready to make his own decisions. With his wife and four children, he moved from Prince Albert to Lac La Ronge, purchased a small grocery business and became a free trader – a modern-day *coureur de bois*.

A large part of his success over the past three decades has depended on building excellent relations with his customers, many of whom are Cree. Alex speaks some Cree, which he learned on his own, as does Scott, who studies it still. Both have developed relationships based on respect and understanding. One of the councillors of the Lac La Ronge band says of Alex, "He could probably walk on water if he wanted to … I don't know any other white man of his calibre."

To visit the trading post is to bridge two worlds. Outside, several Lac La Ronge seniors sit in the sunshine. A child wanders out of the store clutching a banana, one of dozens the Robertsons hand out daily to local youngsters. Inside, the walls and ceiling are hung with furs, carvings and paintings, interspersed with polar fleece jackets, down-filled sleeping bags and kitchenware. The soft murmur of Cree can be heard as a young man strides by, pushing a trolly laden with shipping crates. Alex, now over 70, hovers nearby.

"When I retire," he says with a knowing smile, for retirement is not really in Alex Robertson's vocabulary, "I'm going to just sit here on my balcony and watch the world go by."

At "Alex's desk", a small counter at the back of the store, Alex, left, and Scott are framed with furs and photographs, reflecting their individual passions.

PETER ST. JOHN

Methye Portage

The marathon 20-kilometre Methye (or La Loche) Portage, the longest in the entire system between Montreal and Lake Athabasca, begins about 1.5 kilometres up a small winding creek on the northwest side of Lac La Loche. Heading north, the trail gently climbs a low sandy ridge that separates the Hudson Bay watershed from that of the Arctic Ocean. This is an ancient travel route and it was the one Peter Pond took in 1778. What he found on the other side – furs without parallel – led a veritable army of others to follow in his footsteps and soon, this sandy track assumed almost mythic status.

Today's travellers might wonder: can this nearly level road through an open spruce and jack pine forest be the infamous trail that leads to the well-known panorama of the Clearwater Valley? From all the famous paintings of the trail, including the one above right, history buffs might assume that the portage is hilly, but they would be wrong. Apart from the steep climb to or from the Clearwater, Methye Portage more resembles a road than a portage trail.

About 13 kilometres into the crossing from south to north, the brigades came upon the first of two small lakes, both isolated from any source of water

GEORGE BACK / NATIONAL ARCHIVES OF CANADA / C-94110

and full of fish. One, Rendezvous Lake, is bordered by beaches of white sand and a parklike meadow. Here, for decades in the mid-1800s, the Mackenzie brigades met their counterparts from the south, exchanging plush northern furs for the coming year's outfit.

The trail winds between the lakes and, a couple of kilometres farther on, suddenly leads to the celebrated viewpoint. Almost no one was unaffected by the vista.

In the early years, the companies hired Cree porters to help with the arduous business of transporting the heavy packs, but by the 1850s the loads had become so large that pack horses and oxcarts were needed. The route continued to be used until 1886, when it was largely replaced by one that led north from Edmonton to Athabasca Landing on the lower Athabasca River.

Methye Portage is part of Clearwater River Provincial Wilderness Park. The jumping off point is the town of La Loche. From there a 20-kilometre trip by boat or canoe takes you to the north end of Lac La Loche and the trailhead.

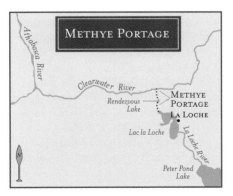

METHYE PORTAGE

Athabasca River
Clearwater River
Rendezvous Lake
METHYE PORTAGE
LA LOCHE
Lac la Loche
La Loche River
Peter Pond Lake
N

The reaction of Robert Hood, midshipman with Franklin's first expedition, to the celebrated view was typical, if better expressed than the norm. "We were prepared," he wrote, "to expect an extensive prospect, but the magnificent scene before us was so superior to what the nature of the country had promised, that it banished even our sense of suffering from the mosquitoes which hovered in clouds above our heads."

Canoeing
the Clearwater River

by Robin & Arlene Karpan

Canoeing the Clearwater makes it easy to understand why it was designated a Canadian Heritage River. It has everything – a rich history that helped define the fur trade, breath-

The Clearwater River thunders through Skull Canyon upstream from Methye Portage.

ROBIN KARPAN

*Sleek and playful, river otters (*Lutra canadensis*) are a delight and can sometimes be seen sliding down a snow bank or cavorting in the water. Even better, they seem to like an audience. During the fur trade, however, their lush fur was more appreciated in a fur press than on an otter.*

BRIAN WOLITSKI

taking landscapes, and a variety of river conditions that make it both a joy and a challenge to canoe.

The Clearwater begins in Broach Lake in northwestern Saskatchewan, heads southeast, makes an abrupt turn west and eventually joins the Athabasca River at Fort McMurray, Alberta. Along its 295 kilometres it descends 150 metres, sometimes gradually over numerous long boulder-strewn rapids, and sometimes abruptly as it plunges over waterfalls and races through steep-walled canyons.

Ancient pictographs attest to the river's age-old importance. People have lived here for thousands of years, and it was believed to have been an important area of contact between cultures of the boreal forest and the northern plains. The Athapaskan-speaking Beaver people

who occupied the area before Europeans arrived were later displaced by Cree and eastern Dene.

When Peter Pond crossed Methye Portage (also called Portage La Loche) to the lower Clearwater in 1778, the face of the fur trade changed dramatically. The 20-kilometre travel route that connected Lac La Loche with the Clearwater River provided a land bridge between the Churchill and Saskatchewan River systems that drain eastward to Hudson Bay, and the waterways that drain north to the Arctic Ocean. Pond's use of this route opened up the lucrative Athabasca country to the fur trade and led to the establishment of Fort Chipewyan, the famed "Emporium of the North" on Lake Athabasca.

For the next century, the portage was like a highway for voyageurs lugging canoes and later York boat brigades hauling furs and supplies across the land bridge using horses and oxcarts. Those using the route reads like a who's who

ROBIN KARPAN

of northern exploration – Alexander Mackenzie, Philip Turnor, Peter Fidler, David Thomson, John Franklin ... the list goes on.

The reason the fur traders chose this route is that it allowed them to by-pass the many rapids and waterfalls farther upstream on the Clearwater. Today's explorers have different priorities, so a canoe trip down the Clearwater is usually a combination of the historic lower reaches and parts of the upper river with its white-water thrills and spectacular scenery.

Upriver, the banks are lower, but interspersed with dramatic stretches. Here, paddlers will find the beautiful Virgin River pours out of Careen Lake just before it joins the Clearwater, and rugged, rock-lined Granite Gorge. Farther down-stream, as you work your way through long stretches of rock gardens and portage around waterfalls, you descend deeper and deeper into the massive glacial melt-water valley. The banks are cloaked with rich greenery as you look up almost 200 metres to see the valley rim.

A highlight is Smooth Rock Falls where the river narrows and twists as it thunders over impressive drops. It would be a toss-up to decide which campsite is more spectacular – the one high on a cliff above Smooth Rock Falls, or the site over-looking Skull Canyon where the water divides into two channels between a high-walled gorge with perfectly vertical cliff faces. If you use your imagination, the naturally-carved patterns in the rock resemble skulls.

Of course, history purists wishing to follow faithfully in the steps of fur

traders could paddle across Lac La Loche then carry across the 20-kilometre Methye Portage. It would provide a feel for this historic route, and most definitely provide a feel for the voyageurs' sore muscles.

Canoeists wanting to paddle most of the Clearwater usually start at Lloyd Lake, and take anywhere from 12 days to three weeks to get to Fort McMurray. Another popular put-in point is where the Virgin River joins the Clearwater, as the deep flat water can accommodate float planes. The main road access is at Warner Rapids where Highway 955 crosses the river northeast of La Loche. For those not wanting to paddle all the way to Fort McMurray, take-out points with float plane access include Contact Rapids north of La Loche, and White Mud Falls just across the Alberta border. Methye Portage and the Saskatchewan portion of the river create Clearwater River Provincial Wilderness Park.

The rapids that the fur traders went to considerable lengths to avoid draw pad-dlers aplenty today.

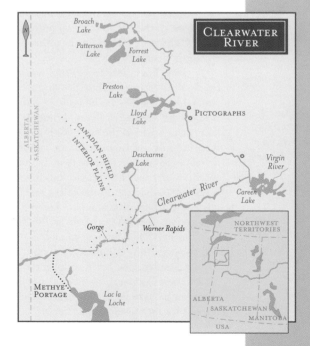

CLEARWATER RIVER

Broach Lake
Patterson Lake
Forrest Lake
Preston Lake
Lloyd Lake
PICTOGRAPHS
ALBERTA
SASKATCHEWAN
CANADIAN SHIELD
INTERIOR PLAINS
Descharme Lake
Virgin River
Clearwater River
Careen Lake
Gorge
Warner Rapids
NORTHWEST TERRITORIES
METHYE PORTAGE
Lac la Loche
ALBERTA
SASKATCHEWAN
MANITOBA
USA

Fort Chipewyan

Located on the northwest shore of Lake Athabasca, at a geographical crossroads every bit as important as the Straits of Mackinac

LORNE BOUCHARD / HUDSON'S
BAY COMPANY ARCHIVES / P–435

Philip Turnor, with his young assistant Peter Fidler, above, spent just one winter on the shores of Lake Athabasca, but his surveys greatly aided both the HBC and the rival Nor'Westers in mapping the northern reaches of the continent. Turnor's expertise also convinced Alexander Mackenzie to return to England for some training in surveying before setting out for the Pacific coast.

had been in earlier centuries, Fort Chipewyan quickly became "the Grand Magazine of the Athapiscow Country", as HBC surveyor Philip Turnor rather enviously described it in 1791.

New Englander Peter Pond was the first trader to penetrate the Arctic watershed. In 1778-'79, he built a small post on the Athabasca River about 70 kilometres south of the lake. With 25 men and just five canoes of trade goods, he managed to obtain more than £8,000 worth of furs that first season and this success soon had the Montrealers beating a path to the distant north. For the first decade, they operated out of Pond's fort, but by 1788 a number of factors had convinced the Montrealers, who by this time had combined to form the North West Company, to build a supply centre on the lake itself. One of the main reasons for establishing this "depot",

which was eventually stocked with at least two years of supplies, was the growing realization of the lake's strategic importance.

The Athabasca and Clearwater Rivers to the south provided access via Methye Portage to the Hudson Bay watershed and the upper Athabasca led to the western plains and the Rockies. In addition, as Alexander Mackenzie would shortly discover for himself, from the delta area at the lake's west end, channels led north via the Slave and Mackenzie Rivers to the Arctic Ocean and west via the Peace River to what is now the British Columbia interior. In other words, as remote as it seemed, Lake Athabasca was in fact a hydrological hub.

The first Fort Chipewyan (after the Cree name for the Dene to the north-east) was built by Roderick McKenzie (Alexander's cousin) in 1788 on a rocky point on the south shore of the lake, where the fishing was good. However less than a decade of trading there convinced the company to move not once but twice; by 1803 they were building on high ground on the northwest shore, where today's community of Fort Chipewyan still stands. One of

BRIAN WOLITSKI

the problems was that the Peace River had a habit of pushing spring ice out into the lake where it jammed around the old fort site, preventing the canoes or boats from embarking as early as they might. A position closer to the delta allowed an earlier departure for the brigades, a distinct advantage where the season was already short.

Over the years others tried to grab a piece of the lucrative Athabasca trade. In 1802, Peter Fidler built Nottingham House on English Island in the Peace River delta not far west of the second Fort Chipewyan and about the same time Alexander Mackenzie's XY Company built a post on Little Island, directly in front of the Nor'Westers' fort. This may have been what prompted the larger company to move farther west the following year, though in 1804, on the death of controlling partner Simon McTavish in Montreal, the XY Company merged with the NWC. Their combined dominance

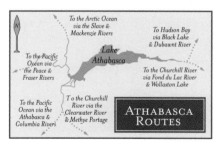

To the Arctic Ocean via the Slave & Mackenzie Rivers

To Hudson Bay via Black Lake & Dubawnt River

To the Pacific Ocean via the Peace & Fraser Rivers

Lake Athabasca

To the Churchill River via Fond du Lac River & Wollaston Lake

To the Pacific Ocean via the Athabasca & Columbia Rivers

To the Churchill River via the Clearwater River & Methye Portage

ATHABASCA ROUTES

drove the HBC from the area for more than a decade. The Hudson's Bay Company returned to the area in 1815, but their Fort Wedderburn was never a success.

Though company employees were often critical of the final incarnation of Fort Chipewyan, it was apparently superior to its antecedents (including the one

that had so impressed Turnor) and its adversaries. In the spring of 1821, just prior to the merger of the two companies, George Simpson at Fort Wedderburn found the Nor'Westers' Fort Chipewyan to be "a magnificent Establishment compared with this".

Later that year, the HBC abandoned Wedderburn and moved across to what is now often called "Fort Chip". For decades, the huge post headquartered the most productive region in the company's transcontinental empire.

Today, little remains of this "Emporium of the North", as Alexander Mackenzie once called it. The last of the old buildings was torn down in the 1960s, but visitors can still wander along footpaths to the high outcropping known as "the Rock", where the lookout tower once stood. Across the lake to the southeast is Goose Island, once the site of the fort's fishery, and beyond it, Old Fort Point, where the first post stood. This is a rugged, bountiful land. At the west end of the lake is Wood Buffalo National Park, with its abundance of large and small mammals, dense flocks of migratory birds and diversity of fish. This richness has earned the park a World Heritage Site designation. On the lake's south shore (in Saskatchewan) is Canada's largest active dune field, a legacy (as is the lake itself) of the last glaciation.

Access to Fort Chipewyan is by air from Edmonton or Fort McMurray or, from late December to approximately mid-March, by winter road from Fort McKay on the Athabasca River, a 215-kilometre trip. Or, of course, by canoe along the route the voyageurs took.

The Saskatchewan River Route

LINDA FAIRFIELD

Saskatoon berries (Amelanchier alnifolia) are often mistaken (by easterners, at least) for blueberries, but west- erners consider that these juicy, sweet dark purple berries are actu- ally superior. Excellent dried, they were often mixed with pemmican. The name "saskatoon", which comes from the Cree misass-ku-tu-mina, is also the name of one of Saskatchewan's major cities.

The dry South Sask- atchewan River Valley is very different than its forested northern sister. When Europeans arrived in the 18th cen- tury, its grassy slopes were home to vast herds of bison and the buffalo people who had lived among them for millennia.

Created by the combined waters of the North and South Saskatchewan Rivers, which join east of Prince Albert, the 1,939-kilometre Sask- atchewan River drains much of Canada's western prairies. From its source at the Columbia Icefield, the North Saskatch- ewan flows east through Rocky Mountain House, hugging the edge of the parklands through Edmonton, North Battleford and Prince Albert. The South Saskatchewan is formed by the junction of the Bow and Oldman Rivers and joined downstream of Medicine Hat by the Red Deer River, before flowing through Saskatoon to merge with its northerly sister.

Together, the rivers are longer than the St. Lawrence and provide access to most of the western plains. Between 1775 and 1845, they were at the heart of the most intensely competitive period between the HBC, NWC and American fur companies.

The river's musical name comes from the Algonquian *Kisiskatchewani – sipi*, "Swift- Flowing River," and during the spring when the snow melts in the Rockies, both branches can rise and flow very swiftly. Yet the rivers were navigable for almost their entire length and in the crucial section between Cumberland House (see page 165) and Edmonton, there were no rapids that could not be either lined up or run down, eliminating the arduous portages that were the norm in the Canadian Shield to the east and north. For most of their length, both branches have cut deeply into the earth, creating wide, panoramic valleys.

Though the South Saskatchewan provided access to both Montana and the Rockies, the North Saskatchewan was the main fur trade focus, particularly between 1786, when Manchester House and Fort de l'Isle were built on Pine Island just north of Paynton, Saskatch- ewan, by the HBC and NWC respectively, and 1799 when the two companies con- structed posts at Rocky Mountain House on the eastern slopes of the Rockies in Alberta. In between, a flurry of forts went up all along the river, including Fort Edmonton, the first incarnation of the trading centre that eventually became a provincial capital.

The furs from the North Saskatch- ewan never rivalled those of the Athabasca country, but the Saskatchewan River continued in impor- tance for decades as a transportation cor- ridor to and from the Pacific coast. Today, this intense period of competition is remembered with reconstructions and interpretive centres at Fort Carlton, Elk Point and Rocky Mountain House and at the Provincial Museum in Edmonton.

PETER ST. JOHN

Nipawin

The name of this picturesque community comes from the Cree *nepo-we-win*, "the viewing place". Located on a high ridge on the south side of the Saskatchewan River, this ancient lookout spot was where Cree families gathered in the fall to watch for canoes returning from York Fort on Hudson Bay. Though the river has been altered by dam construction, travellers today can still get a wonderful view of the water from the Nipawin and District Regional Park, adjacent to the town.

The first Europeans passed this way with Louis-Joseph La Vérendrye, who travelled upstream from his post on Cedar Lake to the Forks of the Saskatchewan River in 1748 to draw trade down to Fort Bourbon. Within five years, Louis de la Corne had established a post farther upstream and so successfully blocked the flow of furs to the bay that the HBC responded by sending Anthony Henday inland.

Over the next half-dozen years, French traders dominated the river and several veterans stayed in the area after 1763. One was François Le Blanc, also known as "Old Franceways" and "Saswe", who may have been with the La Vérendryes in the late 1730s and early 1740s. By 1768, apparently in the employ of James Finlay of Montreal, he established a trading house above Nipawin, just below Finlay's Falls. The palisaded post, built in the rectangular French style with the narrow end toward the river, was excavated in the 1930s. Today, both men are remembered in the name of the Francois-Finlay dam. The dam created Codette Lake, which, though wrongly spelled, recalls Jean-Baptiste Cadot, one of a famous fur trade family (sometimes spelled Cadotte) from the Straits of Mackinac. Upstream from Finlay's Falls were Cadotte Rapids.

Though they didn't build posts along the river until 1774, Hudson's Bay Company traders, including William Pink, Joseph Smith and Matthew Cocking, were active here in the 1750s and 1760s, but the region's fur trade heyday was in the early 1790s, when the NWC created Thorburn's House at the Nipawin Rapids five kilometres upstream from the town and a second post about three kilometres farther upstream to counter free trader David Grant in 1793.

The HBC's James Bird built a wintering house the following year, after the destruction of South Branch House by the Atsina, as did the "South Men", traders from the upper Mississippi.

In 1795 Bird moved again, upstream to La Corne, where he built the first incarnation of Carlton House; the NWC constructed Fort St. Louis nearby.

Nipawin and the regional park are located on the Kelsey Trail (No. 55), 141 kilometres east of Prince Albert. The park offers full services, including boat rentals.

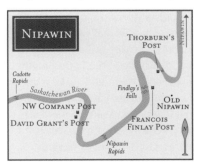

PETER ST. JOHN

From the viewing place in what is now Nipawin and District Regional Park, the Saskatchewan River stretches west, attracting boats of all sizes.

The Forks of the Saskatchewan

The North and South branches of the Saskatchewan River come together east of Prince Albert in a deep and dramatic valley. Depending on the season, the rivers are often quite different in color and both still harbor sturgeon, though very few are the giants that once inhabited both rivers.

From the hill, opposite, Fort Carlton sits in the sunshine on the bank of the North Saskatchewan River, just as it did in the early 1800s. The fort was built at a long-used ford in the river called La Montée. Here HBC officers often left their canoes or York boats in favor of horses and went hunting.

About 50 kilometres east of modern-day Prince Albert, the North and South Saskatchewan Rivers meet in a deep, dramatic valley. A small park above the confluence celebrates the first fur trader in the area, Louis de la Corne, who established a fur post below The Forks in 1753, a decade before the end of the French era.

Chevalier de la Corne was born at Fort Frontenac (now Kingston) in 1703. He joined the *troupes de la Marine* in 1722 and saw active service in Acadia and elsewhere before being appointed to oversee *les postes de l'Ouest* in the early 1750s. Travelling up the Saskatchewan River beyond Nipawin, he built a post on the south side of the river and called it Fort Saint-Louis, but it was soon known as Fort à la Corne. Another post, Fort la Jonquière, was occupied briefly farther west, but La Corne was the first place in Saskatchewan where grain was grown.

Fort à la Corne was in service for four or five years, but its founder returned to Quebec in 1755 to fight in the Seven Years War. At war's end, though born in Canada, he elected to be repatriated to France, but died when his ship, the *Auguste*, sank off the coast of Cape Breton.

A nearby site was later used by several posts, including the HBC's Fort à la Corne between 1846 and 1932. The Fort à la Corne Trail, linking Cumberland House and Fort Battleford, passed the post and continued south of the Weldon Ferry.

Upstream from The Forks on the North Saskatchewan is La Colle Falls, a

boulder-strewn stretch of rapids that once stalled fur brigades as they made their way upstream in the low water of autumn. Fortunately, the shores of the river are wide and sandy, allowing the fur traders good footing as they tracked the heavily loaded boats up river and today's paddlers fine places to camp.

The park at The Forks can be reached via Highway 302 east of Prince Albert to the sign for The Forks, follow the Weldon Ferry Road to about two kilometres before the ferry, where a gravel road to The Forks is signed. This park affords a wonderful panorama of the rivers, with trails that wind down the steep, forested valley wall to the river's edge. To reach the Fort à la Corne site, which is marked by a plaque, take the Weldon Ferry across the South Saskatchewan River, head south to the third turnoff (Highway 789) and travel 26 kilometres east, then north toward the river, following the signs.

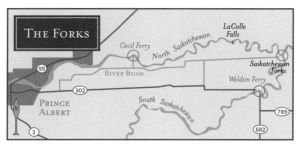

180

Fort Carlton

In the autumn of 1795, James Bird of the Hudson's Bay Company established a post called Carlton House below the junction of the North and South Saskatchewan Rivers. In 1804, it was reestablished 150 kilometers upstream on the South Saskatchewan River, but moved again six years later next to a rival North West Company post on the North Saskatchewan at La Montée, a shallow ford. After cohabiting in a common stockade – something that wasn't uncommon on the edge of Blackfoot territory – for several years, the Nor' Westers abandoned the post. The HBC stayed and called it Fort Carlton.

Location was everything during this intensely competitive period, and the fort was on a well-travelled trail between the North and South branches of the river. This trail eventually formed part of the Carlton Trail from Fort Garry to Fort Edmonton; another trail linked Fort Carlton to Green Lake and the Churchill River. These two waterways – the Saskatchewan and the Churchill – formed the major routes between the Rockies and Hudson Bay.

Fort Carlton was established to trade furs – beaver, muskrats, foxes and wolves, as well as buffalo robes and dressed deer, moose and elk hides, but over time the trade in furs was replaced by what the HBC called "country produce". These locally available foods included pemmican, venison, fish and berries and Fort Carlton gained importance as a provisioning post. As John Peter Pruden put it in 1819, "There is no convenient place either above or below so as to induce us to shift our situation ... as the Buffalo seldom go below this place."

Initially, York boats moved supplies by river from York Factory, but after 1860 most goods came by oxcart from Fort Garry. The completion of the railroad to St. Paul, Minnesota in 1859 made it cheaper to bring trade goods to Fort Garry through St. Paul, rather than York Factory. And so long trains of squealing ox carts hauled freight along the Carlton Trail, transforming a faintly etched track into a deeply rutted road.

In 1873, the fort became the headquarters for the Saskatchewan District, but its dominance was slipping. In 1874, the steamboat *Northcote* shifted attention to the settlement at Prince Albert and in 1882 the district headquarters followed. Fort Carlton was left with a skeleton staff. The North West Mounted Police occupied the buildings in 1884, but declared the fort indefensible during the Riel Rebellion a year later. A series of fires soon spelled an end to the era.

Fort Carlton has been partially reconstructed to recreate this era of carts and pemmican. Visitors can climb the hill east of the stockade to see the deeply rutted Carlton Trail or wander down to the river, where heavily laden York boats once docked.

From Prince Albert, go south 56 kilometres on Highway 11 to Duck Lake, then west 26 kilometres on Highway 212.

PETER ST. JOHN

The fur trade is only a small part of the region's long and fascinating history. At Wanuskewin Heritage Park in Saskatoon, time travellers are transported back thousands of years to an age of buffalo jumps and medicine wheels, while Fish Creek and Batoche, both national historic sites, relive the bloody battles of the 1880s between the Metis and the Canadian militia. The history of the region can also be seen in the murals of Duck Lake, above.

PETER ST. JOHN

Canoeing the North Saskatchewan

by Doug Taylor

PETER ST. JOHN

The North Saskatch-ewan is blessed in many places with wide sand beaches, such as this one at La Colle Falls east of Prince Albert, that invite paddlers to stop and stay awhile.

From the Alberta/Saskatchewan border, the North Saskatch-ewan River flows east, unfettered for 600 kilometres, first bending southeast for 300 kilometres then turning north-east for another 300 before slowing and widening into today's Codette Lake, the first of two large reservoirs marking the end of the river's natural configuration. Though this distance features two cities and a number of modern installations, including bridges and power lines, there are vast tracts of wilderness here. Yet this stretch of the river is often over-looked in favor of the North Saskatch-ewan's upper reaches or more dramatic (and crowded) northern rivers such as the Churchill and the Clearwater (see pages 171 and 174).

In several places, the river passes through boreal forest, for this is a tran-sitional ecoregion, where grasslands meet forests. Grassland ecosystems persist on many south-facing slopes (on the north side of the river), while the north-facing slopes are often covered with mixed wood or pure stands of deciduous or conifer-ous forests. These contain several more tree species than the northern boreal forest region resulting in a hybrid system that combines the biodiversity of each.

The main appeals of the North Saskatchewan are safe, unregulated naviga-bility, sweeping landscapes and a fascinating natural and human history. Each bend delivers new vistas; each hour has new excitement; each season brings special offerings. The river is navigable even in the seasonal extremes, allowing hardy canoeists extra months of paddling every year.

Perhaps the river's most notable attribute is its sheer numbers and diversity of migratory birds. Simply astonishing avian displays can be witnessed, with their associated clamor, such as the thun-derous ascension of a half-million water-fowl or clouds of snow buntings rolling in flashing spheres over the slopes. Turkey vultures soar by the hundreds over the sun-warmed valley walls, often tilting to avoid collisions with circling eagles, hawks and ravens as they too celebrate the joy of flight. Yet the val-ley's wildlife is not what it was before and during the fur trade era, when it was inhabited by cougars, wolves, plains grizzlies and bison. Today, these species are either very rare or extirpated.

Fed by a vast watershed that includes much of western Canada east of the Rockies, carved through deep glacial deposits, the North Saskatchewan is extremely changeable. Seasonal variations in water levels can range three vertical metres. Sustained rainfall in Alberta can cause the water to rise a metre or more in Saskatchewan overnight. Despite this, there is a built-in delay, caused by the

COURTESY VELMA FOSTER

vast watershed and gradual slope, that allows canoe trippers (and many of the valley's other creatures) to safely adapt to conditions. Depending on the season and the conditions, the water can be the color of strong coffee with cream or as clear as glass.

Because of these extremes and the river's power, it carries, deposits, then carries again a host of artifacts, both natural and man-made, large and small, ancient and new. Relentless hydraulic forces constantly transform the river course. Huge trees tilt precariously over the water on half-eroded root systems. Islands with old growth are cut and undermined by the roiling water; their thick carpets peeling in mats into the brown current, releasing their load of humus, roots, stones and bones. All this moves downstream to form new configurations of landscape in a constant cycle of change. Yet there is some predictability to this movement of unimaginable tonnage. Heaps of driftwood and lumber snag and tangle at the heads of islands. Silt is deposited in eddies behind glacial boulders and on gravel bars and islands. Lighter flotsam is deposited in bands along the banks.

For paddlers, the result is a long, uncrowded valley campground. Potential tent sites are too numerous to mention. You simply determine your priorities, invite consensus among your party and camp anywhere. But do pay attention to changing water levels; learn the clues and cues. If a strong wind is blowing along the valley, shelter under the sleepy applause of a cottonwood bluff. Bugs bad? Too hot? Camp on a sand spit or gravel bar.

And imagine, the valley has seen quarrels, struggles, terror and murder,

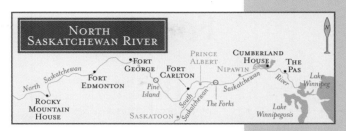

along with peace and prosperity. It has witnessed the rise and fall of nations.

Making daily distance is easy on the North Saskatchewan. The water moves at three to five kilometres per hour and paddlers will soon learn to navigate the lee bank, take advantage of tailwinds using an umbrella or a sheet, or simply drift, steer and relax for hours. Those dubious of their paddling skills can start with a short trip. More experienced canoeists can create their own longer journeys, for today's roads lead to the river's edge in many places and are nicely spaced for easy trip planning.

During the fur trade era, before highways and rail lines, the river and its associated overland trails were the heart of a continental network of transport routes. The valley sheltered a string of posts; many, including Fort Pitt, Fort Carlton and beautiful Pine Island north of Paynton, are marked along the river with reconstructions, interpretive exhibits or signage.

Most of Saskatchewan's main north-south routes cross the river, as do three ferries, which operate between April 15th and November 15th. Prince Albert and North Battleford have riverside parks and campgrounds and several regional parks or provincial campgrounds are located along its shores.

BRIAN WOLITSKI

Wapiti or red deer (Cervus canadensis) were called elk by the Europeans, who found them in abundance along the North Saskatchewan River. The fur trade and settlement periods devastated their numbers and it was to protect them that Elk Island National Park was founded just east of Edmonton in 1906.

Cloaked in mature spruce, Pine Island, opposite bottom, looks much today as it must have when William Tomison first saw it in the mid-1780s. Yet within a decade the island had been completely denuded of its thick forests as no less than five fur houses were built on it, including Manchester House, from 1786 to 1792 the HBC's most westerly post.

Exploring the Fur Trade Routes of North America

Fort George

The Lac la Biche Portage

For 30 years after 1792, the NWC brigades used the Beaver River and Lac la Biche as a connector between the Saskatchewan River, with its supply of pemmican, and the Athabasca fur trade to the northeast. The Athabasca also served points west though Yellowhead Pass, and allowed access through Lesser Slave Lake and the Peace River to New Caledonia. Lac la Biche's role was curtailed when George Simpson built a trail to Fort Assiniboine.

Located high on the north slope (where photo, right, was taken) Buckingham House had a grand view of the Saskatchewan River and neighboring Fort George below, but the NWC's post location on the hillside protected it. Archaeological excavations revealed thousands of artifacts, including this handsome brass button, above, with buffalo motif.

By the time the fur companies crossed the Alberta border, competition for furs was heated and occasionally nasty. In the late summer of 1792, Angus Shaw, a NWC partner, led a party of men up the North Saskatchewan River and constructed a large post, Fort George, near what is now Elk Point, Alberta. William Tomison, governor of the Hudson's Bay Company, responded within weeks, establishing Buckingham House on the hill immediately above it.

Both companies built on the north slope for defensive reasons that were to prove prescient. In the following two years, the Atsina, allies of the Blackfoot Confederacy who were feeling the squeeze from the trade's westward-moving Cree and Assinboine suppliers, attacked four trading posts and burned one, South Branch House, to the ground.

Shaw had 60 men at Fort George, most of them French-Canadians from Quebec; many had their wives and children with them. Tomison's post was smaller, with 38 men, all but four of them Orcadians, like himself. Perched high on the south- facing wall of the valley, Buckingham House was a long climb from the water, but it gave Tomison a grand view of the river in both directions and the comings and goings at the neighboring post below.

Knowledge of the opposition was important, for the Nor' Westers had been known to intercept furs bound for HBC posts and add them to their own haul. On more than one occasion Tomison, who was fortunate to trade for half of the number of furs the much larger Montreal company did, confronted his rivals over just such an occurence.

Both posts not only traded for furs, which were trapped in the forests north of the river and the parklands to the south, but also for pemmican, mainly from the Blackfoot Confederacy. As the routes grew in length, lightweight preserved food became an absolute necessity, allowing the brigades to concentrate on paddling, rather than hunting or fishing. The HBC was longer in adopting "travelling food" than the NWC, and on a number of occasions, including the surveying trip that Philip Turnor and Peter Fidler took to the Athabasca country in 1790, Hudson's Bay employees faced starvation while travelling on the company's behalf.

Though both posts were large, neither was expected to last longer than the time it took to trap out an area of its fur-bearing animals. By 1795, both companies were looking farther west and five years later both had abandoned the site.

Elk Point is located just north of the North Saskatchewan River on Highway 41, 63 kilometres north of the Yellowhead Highway (No. 16). The Fort George/Buckingham House Provincial Historic Site and interpretive centre are off Highway 646, east of Highway 41 and south of town.

BARBARA ENDRES

PETER ST. JOHN

THE BUFFALO HUNTERS

This union included three powerful nations who had united to gain control of the vast buffalo plains of Saskatchewan and Alberta sometime before Europeans arrived in the early 1750s. The confederacy included the Siksika (literally "Black Feet", from a legend of people who walked across the burned prairie); the Kainai (meaning "Many Chiefs", but also called by the English the "Blood" people) and the Pikuni (literally "Scabby Robes", after a legend about improperly prepared buffalo hides, but often called "Piegan"). The three were independent nations, but united by their Algonquian language and culture.

During the 18th and early 19th centuries, as fur traders arrived on the North Saskatchewan River (then Siksika territory), and Cree and Assinboine middlemen began to press their eastern borders, the confederacy grew to include the Athapaskan Sarcee from the north and the Atsina, a breakaway group of southern Arapaho who had drifted north to live in the Eagle Hills along the North Saskatchewan River.

FREDERIC REMINGTON / NATIONAL ARCHIVES OF CANADA / C–011198

COURTESY OF THE GLENBOW MUSEUM

Proud, independent buffalo hunters who obtained horses from the south after about 1730 and guns from the Cree in the east, the Siksika and their allies were initially uninterested in trade with the Europeans. The HBC's Anthony Henday, arriving at a huge Blackfoot camp in the mid-1750s, was impressed by the people and their hospitality, but largely unable to convince them to bring furs to Hudson Bay. Only a small group of young adventurers made the trip. The majority would not consider squeezing into tiny canoes and "starving on fish". They said, "it was far off and they could not live without Buffalo flesh," wrote Henday.

Descended from ancient buffalo cultures, the members of the confederacy were incomparable bison hunters. Running the massive creatures over cliffs or into pounds, hunting them by stealth, or later on horseback in displays of riding that left Europeans speechless, they had lived in freedom and plenty for thousands of years. The fur trade spelled the beginning of the end of this long era, presaging European settlement and the destruction of the once innumerable plains bison.

For a time, however, the Blackfoot Confederacy lived in uneasy peace with the Hudson's Bay and North West Companies, who planted posts ever farther out along the North Saskatchewan River (though always on the north shore) during the 1790s. They traded bison hides and pemmican, a food that archaeologists believe was invented on the Alberta plains.

By the early 1800s, the encroaching Cree and Assiniboine created hostilities that lasted for 70 years. The confederacy members were pushed south, until the Siksika occupied Pikuni territory along the Bow River and the others were pushed into southern Alberta and northern Montana (where they are known today as the Blackfeet).

After the Blackfoot acquired horses in the 1740s, their buffalo-hide lodges grew in size. By the time this watercolor was done more than a century later, some were large enough to seat more than 50 people comfortably. The tipis and many other articles were strikingly decorated with mainly geometric designs, illustrated by the quillworking on this pipe.

Fort Edmonton

Plains bison (Bison bison) *once lived in the tens of millions on the North American plains and sustained both the trade and the employees of many western posts. Though a bull may stand 1.8 metres (or six feet) at the shoulder, today's bison are small by comparison with their enormous ancestors that crossed Beringia during periodic migrations over the past 300,000 years.* Bison priscus, Bison antiquus *and* Bison occidentalis *were all much larger.*

BRIAN WOLITSKI

In the spring of 1795, a crew of Nor'Westers was sent up the North Saskatchewan River from Fort George to build a new post at the mouth of the Sturgeon River. The site is in what is now Fort Saskatchewan (named for a later NWMP post), but Angus Shaw, the NWC bourgeois or post master, called it Fort Augustus.

When William Tomison returned to the Saskatchewan from his arduous annual journey to Hudson Bay and learned that his neighbor was building upstream, he immediately ordered a crew to follow the Nor'Westers and build a new HBC post in the same vicinity. Tomison called the new post Edmonton House; the name would survive many incarnations and eventually become the Alberta capital.

The initial Edmonton House was relatively short-lived; in 1802, both companies moved upstream to a site on Rossdale Flats, where the Edmonton power plant now sits. But eight years later, they moved again, this time downstream 80 kilometres to the mouth of White Earth Creek. That location proved to be too far from the mountains for the fort's fur suppliers and in 1812, both companies moved back to Rossdale Flats. By this time, all the peripatetic behavior was beginning to vex the London Committee, which ordered Fort Edmonton either to stop moving about or to give new posts new names.

The important determinants in choosing the perfect site were these: Fort Edmonton should be located at the most westerly point that a brigade from York Factory could reach before freeze-up. The

HBC's Acton House at today's Rocky Mountain House was too far. The low water of autumn and early cold spells had forced brigades overland. The post also needed a large, flat site near a ford in the river. The site at Rossdale Flats met those criteria and was almost equidistant from two southerly bends in the Athabasca River – Fort Assiniboine and Athabasca Landing – allowing overland connections.

Fort Edmonton therefore stayed put, for a time. On the amalgamation of the two companies in 1821, some thought was given to closing it and moving south, to the heart of the bison plains, but this was considered dangerous. In 1824, George Simpson, always a great promoter of the Athabasca Department, also considered closing Fort Edmonton at the company's annual meeting at Norway House. He believed the Churchill, Beaver and Athabasca Rivers might provide a speedier route to the mountains. Intending to make a final decision en route, he told John Rowand, (after 1826 chief at Fort Edmonton) to take the fall outfit inland along the North Saskatchewan, then go overland to meet him at Fort Assiniboine on the upper Athabasca. He himself would take the northern route. Simpson left Norway House on August 26th, travelling, as he would for decades, in an express canoe, with hand-picked voyageurs. Rowand went inland with the fall brigade of heavy York boats, delivering the winter's supplies to posts along the way. Yet when Simpson arrived at Fort Assiniboine on October 2nd, he found that Rowand had long preceded him and had finally left after waiting for three days.

Even for Simpson, who disliked being proven wrong, the decision was

186

J.D. KELLY / COURTESY ROGERS COMMUNICATIONS INC.

J.D. Kelly's painting of Governor George Simpson's visit to Fort Edmonton in May 1825 conveys the pagentry that accompanied the departure of the York boats for York Factory in the spring.

easy. Fort Edmonton would stay and the Saskatchewan, not the Athabasca, would serve as the principal supply route. This, of course, is exactly what William Tomison had believed nearly 40 years before.

Fort Edmonton was to move once more, but at the behest of Mother Nature, not the officers of the HBC. The river flooded twice in the 1820s and Rowand moved the post to a higher river bench just below the site of the present Alberta Legislature. There, he turned Fort Edmonton into "a fur trade *entrepôt*". Breaking the fertile ground, he successfully grew large crops of potatoes and barley, and experimented with wheat, trying to develop a shorter-season strain. Fort Edmonton also raised horses and supplied the pack trains over the Rockies, as well as other posts, and produced York boats by the dozen. The months-long trip to York Factory was hard on the boats and most lasted only a season or two, though old, recaulked boats were filled with water and placed strategically about the fort as fire prevention aids. The best of the Orcadian boatbuilders could produce up to eight boats a year.

But mainly, Fort Edmonton produced pemmican and other bison products, including pickled buffalo tongues, considered a delicacy in London (as well as at home). Fresh and frozen meat was also consumed in great quantities at the fort itself, for its population ranged between 120 and 150 and until 1870, when the vast herds were rapidly hunted to near-extinction, the entire community lived mainly on buffalo meat.

Rowand built a large residence, often called "The Big House" but sometimes dubbed "Rowand's Folly", in 1835 and a string of well-known personages passed through over the years: Paul Kane, the artist, stayed twice and John Palliser, the geographer, and his entire expedition spent Christmas there in 1858.

After the HBC turned over its rights to Rupert's Land to the British government and in turn sold them to Canada in 1870, the store at Edmonton served the growing community. Finally in 1915, shortly after the Alberta Legislature was built on the valley rim above, Fort Edmonton was dismantled. Today, it is remembered with a reconstruction and living history museum at Fort Edmonton Park, three bends of the river upstream, and in displays at the Provincial Museum and Archives.

Fort Edmonton Park is located on the south side of the river just west of Whitemud Drive, while the Provincial Museum of Alberta is located south of 102 Avenue, west of Groat Road.

The Naming of Edmonton House

by Robert Pruden

There is little doubt that Edmonton House was named for the town of Edmonton in Middlesex County, England, but there are questions as to how this came about. Was it in recognition of a wealthy family of Hudson's Bay Company shareholders, or was it named as a tribute to a 17-year-old apprentice, John Peter Pruden?

One view is that Edmonton was named for the deputy governor of the HBC from 1782 to 1799, Sir James Winter Lake. Members of the Lake family, which had an estate in Edmonton, England, held the position of governor or deputy governor for more than 90 years. Sir James served the company for 45 years, from 1762 to 1807.

Naming posts and geographical features for members of the upper classes was a common practice and in a period of expansion there were many posts and features to be named. For example Lake House, built before Edmonton, was named for Sir James. Given that, would William Tomison, who built Edmonton House, have felt an obligation to pay him further tribute?

There was another native of Edmonton, England, among the ranks of the HBC. In 1791, the company took on a 13-year-old apprentice named John Peter Pruden, who was born and raised there. By 1795, Pruden had worked at

York Factory for four years and spent a year at Carlton House under James Curtis Bird. He made a favourable impression for in 1798 he was described as: "A Steady Young Man promises fair to make a Valuable Servant ..."

In later years Pruden rose through the ranks of the company, becoming a chief factor prior to his retirement in 1837. His long and distinguished career would certainly have been worthy of the recognition given to his birthplace then, but in 1795 that career had just begun.

Pruden was known to Tomison when Edmonton House was built. In fact, less than a year later, Pruden was transferred there, and remained until 1799. At the time, the majority of HBC employees came from Orkney. In 1795, of the 138 inland workers, 119 were Orcadian, while only 19 were English. Of those, six were from London and only Pruden was from Edmonton.

It's not known how Pruden came to be hired, but he may have been recommended by the headmaster of the local school or the vicar of the local parish. It is also possible that he came to Sir James' attention through direct contact.

Other posts had been named for employees' birthplaces. In 1800, James Bird named Acton House after his hometown. We can't know what was in William Tomison's mind when he named Edmonton House, but in doing so, he paid tribute to two individuals who together worked for more than 90 years for the HBC, in completely different capacities. While Sir James lived a life of relative affluence in England, John Peter Pruden forged a life in a new land. The naming of Edmonton, Alberta is a fitting tribute to both of them.

York boats were used by the Hudson's Bay Company on all of Canada's major rivers and lakes east of the Rockies after 1797. Though company boatmen didn't care for the switch, for the boats were much heavier to portage than canoes, the increased loads and decreased manpower needed dictated their use on many routes until the end of the fur era.

JERRY KAUTZ

Rocky Mountain House

At first glance, Rocky Mountain House – the name given to all but one of five posts established on the North Saskatchewan – Clearwater River junction between 1799 and 1875 – might be considered a fur trade success. David Thompson used it as a base of operations for his attempts to reach the Pacific. The nearby town was named for the post and today, 76 years of fur trade history are recalled at Rocky Mountain House National Historic Site, which offers programming and information from an excellent visitor centre. Yet despite its long history, interesting personalities and many incarnations, Rocky Mountain House never lived up to expectations.

The first posts were established in the late summer and early fall of 1799, side-by-side as usual by John McDonald of Garth for the NWC and James Bird for the HBC. Both companies hoped to entice the Kutenai, members of an isolated Rocky Mountain culture that some anthropologists believe may be related to the ancient Aztecs, to trade at the post. That this never happened may have been because the K'Tunaxa (northern Kutenai) had been decimated by smallpox and were subject to periodic attack from the Siksika of the Blackfoot Confederacy.

Instead, the original posts and their successors mainly dealt with the Blackfoot, Cree and Assiniboine and the trade focused on provisions rather than furs. Still, production was never consistent. In some years, "Rocky" was the continent's leading supplier of pemmican; in others famine reigned. It was closed at least five times because of a lack of provisions.

David Thompson and his wife Charlotte were often at Rocky Mountain House. The first of their 13 children was born there in 1801 and the family returned in 1806, after Thompson, by this time a NWC partner, had been charged with finding a practical route to the Pacific. In 1807, he crossed the Rockies over Howse Pass and built Kootenay House on the upper Columbia River. Yet he seemed in no rush to reach the Pacific

until ordered to in 1810, to counter the Astorian expeditions to the mouth of the Columbia. Thompson accomplished his mission in 1811, arriving behind Astor's ship, but took a route that passed north of Rocky Mountain House.

And as it did in many places, the fur trade here brought disruption, disease and death for native North Americans. In 1837-38, an epidemic of smallpox all but destroyed the nations of the Blackfoot Confederacy, killing three of every four people. Rocky Mountain House National Historic Site is dedicated to an accurate portrayal of the fur trade era, and in this, it succeeds without reservation.

Rocky Mountain House National Historic Site is located off Highway 11A, seven kilometres west of town. The site offers hiking trails, a buffalo paddock, a canoe launch and a display herd of bison.

Paul Kane was not certain whether he was painting a Cree or Assiniboine encampment on the plain in front of Rocky Mountain House, when he visited there in April 1838. A playfort, a three-quarter scale replica of the post shown above, has recently been constructed to cater to youthful history buffs.

Jasper House

JERRY KAUTZ

Among bighorn sheep (Ovis canadensis), horn size denotes rank. The male on the right, above, is in his prime, likely six or seven years old, but he may sire few offspring for human encroachment threatens bighorn sheep almost everywhere. Now found in the Rockies between Yukon and Colorado, mountain sheep number less than a tenth of what they did when Europeans arrived.

The Columbia express brigades must have been delighted to see the braided flats of the Athabasca River and the ramshackle huts of Jasper House, for they meant that the arduous journey over the Rocky Mountains was at an end. Their journals indicate that one really can get too much magnificent mountain scenery.

On the heels of David Thompson's successful journey to the mouth of the Columbia River in 1811, the North West Company quickly realized that pack trains crossing the Rockies over Athabasca Pass would need a supply post on the eastern side. Two years later, a small post was built at the outlet of what was then called Brûlé Lake, but is now known as Jasper Lake, in actuality a widening of the Athabasca River.

Briefly named Rocky Mountain House – a rather confusing title since it was the same as the large NWC fort on the Saskatchewan River to the southwest – the post was known by 1815 as Jasper Hawse's House (or sometimes, as a pun, Jasper's Hawse).

Despite its spectacular surroundings, the post was, according to an early visitor, "a miserable concern of rough logs, with only three apartments, but scrupulously clean inside". In short, there was little to hint at the luxurious accommodation that would one day be the norm at Jasper.

This rough collection of huts served first the Nor'Westers and later the Hudson's Bay Company until about 1828, though largely as a summer house "for the convenience of the Columbians", the express brigades that carried mail and personnel east up the Columbia and over the snowy pass (see page 237).

In 1829, Jasper House II was rebuilt a small distance downstream, on the left bank of the river at the junction of the Snake Indian River. In so doing, the HBC settled in the same place that earlier travellers had thousands of years before. Archaeological excavations in the area indicate at least three separate pre-fur trade occupations of the site – the earliest perhaps 8,000 years ago.

The second incarnation of Jasper House was mainly used to raise and supply horses for the mountain brigades, though it did trade furs as well. It was used sporadically and rebuilt at least once more, before an early settler in the area took possession of the post in the 1890s.

Nearby, at the mouth of the Miette River, another early post, Henry House (1811-25), was built by Nor'Wester William Henry, the son of Alexander Henry the Elder, about 1812. It too supplied horses for the brigades, but closed about the time Jasper House II was built.

A plaque on the west side of the Yellowhead Highway (No. 16), at the north end of Jasper Lake, marks the site of the first Jasper House. The post gave its name not only to the lake, but also to the nearby town of Jasper and popular Jasper National Park.

PETER ST. JOHN

A LIFE OF MAPMAKING

Born of Welsh parents in Westminster, England, in 1770, David Thompson's fur trade career was sealed by the premature death of his father. His penniless mother sent him to Grey Coat Hospital (see page 47), where the serious-minded seven-year-old studied maths. At 14, he was apprenticed to the Hudson's Bay Company and assigned to clerk for Samuel Hearne, chief at Churchill on the bay. The events of that first winter and the 30 years that followed were recounted (though not always accurately) in his *Narrative*, written after he was 75.

In the next years he travelled widely, as he would for the rest of his life, but in December 1788, on a steep slope in the North Saskatchewan River Valley, he fell and broke his right femur. The break hobbled him for 18 months, but transformed his life, for while convalescing he was apprenticed to Philip Turnor, the HBC's first surveyor. Henceforth, surveying was his life and though he spent 13 years with the HBC, by 1797 opportunities to do this chosen work, as well as a chance at a partnership, lured him to the rival North West Company.

His first assignment, completed with an alacrity that was missing in later years, took him from the Mandan Hidatsa villages of the Missouri to Minnesota's headwaters of the Mississippi and on to Grand Portage on Lake Superior. From there he went northwest, where he met his life partner, 14-year-old Charlotte Small. A measure of his dedication is his note about the wedding: "The event took place on June 10, 1799 at Lat. 55.26.15N, Long. 107.46.40W." Though their location thereafter changed almost daily, Charlotte and their family were almost always with him.

Made an NWC partner in 1804, he was charged in 1807 with finding a way through the Rockies to the lower Columbia River. In retrospect the need for speed seems obvious, given the American interest in the region and the just-completed Lewis and Clark expedition. Despite this, Thompson spent three years in a virtual cul-de-sac that today comprises parts of Montana, Idaho and Washington, building trading posts and looking for a navigable connection with the Columbia.

Finally aware that the Columbia flowed north before turning south, but still in no rush, he headed east on furlough. At Rainy River, he was told to return west and reach the Columbia before the Americans did. Blocked from using his accustomed access at Howse Pass, he went north along the Athbasca River and followed the Whirlpool River to its source in midwinter, mapping the route that would become the "Okanagan Trail" (see page 221).

A pious and sometimes rather sanctimonious teetotaler, Thompson was appalled at the use of liquor as a trade item and forbade its use on the west side of the Rockies, despite NWC policy. After retiring in 1812, he surveyed part of the Canada-U.S. border and completed a widely used map of Western Canada. Despite his accomplishments, he died in penury in 1857.

AMANDA DOW

Thompson's achievements are remembered with a plaque on a cairn in the Athabasca Pass. At the height of the pass are two small lakes or tarns that George Simpson would later dub "the Committee's Punchbowl".

South to the Plains

When most of us think of the fur trade, we think of boreal forests, rushing rivers and beaver meadows. But there was another fur trade landscape, one that fuelled the trade for decades as it stretched across the continent. The Great Plains, a sea of grasses in the heart of North America, quickly became almost as important to the fur trade as were the northern forests. The plains were inhabited by vast herds of bison (or buffalo, as they are often called) and the plains peoples whose lives depended on them. Both were crucial; one provided the meat that stoked the trade, the other hunted and prepared it.

Beginning with the first posts established on the Red and Assiniboine Rivers by La Vérendrye in the 1730s, the trade in provisions – buffalo meat and pemmican, as well as corn traded from the south by the Hidatsa and Mandan – made travelling the trade's huge distances possible.

Transportation on the plains relied on two methods,

boats or canoes and the two-wheeled Red River cart. Together they opened the Great Plains, initiating the fur trade, introducing disease and western settlement, and ultimately leading to the destruction of both the bison and the proud plains people who lived among them. But for a century between 1760 and 1860, despite two devastating epidemics of smallpox, western plains cultures flowered. Their unfettered way of life drew a number of eastern peoples – the Cree, Assiniboine, Anishinabe and Dakota, as well as the Metis – to develop a lifestyle based on buffalo hunting.

Meanwhile, the fur companies battled for goods and furs. On the Red and the Assiniboine Rivers, mid-18th century free traders' posts gave way to the North West and the Hudson's Bay Companies and both found competition from the rapidly growing American fur trade. In 1811, departing radically from its long-held opposition to settlement, the Hudson's Bay Company sponsored the first of what would, by the end of the century, be a flood of homesteaders. The needs of these settlers gradually fuelled the trade and after the two Canadian companies merged in 1821, the importance of the plains grew for the enlarged HBC. In the 1830s, the company established two large forts on the Red River.

South of the border, a lucrative trade in furs and provisions spawned a network of trails and the development of international trade, sowing the seeds for the capitals of both Minnesota and Manitoba.

LINDA FAIRFIELD

Sweet grass (Hierochloe odorata) *is one of several fragrant grasses used to make baskets. When dried, it also burns with a lovely odor and was used by plains people for ceremonial purposes.*

The Qu'Appelle Valley, with its grassy hills, wooded coolies and abundant water, was long a favored wintering site for bison.

PETER ST. JOHN

AT HOME ON THE PLAINS

Related to the Yanktonai Nako'ta of the Minnesota woodlands, the Siouan-speaking Assiniboine broke away after an internal clash sometime before 1640. Anthropologists believe the ancestral Dakota were agrarian, a people who farmed the fringes of the Mississippian mound-building society. By the 16th century, however, they had become hunters of the Great Lakes woodlands.

After their split with the ancestral Nako'ta, the Assiniboine moved north and west, occupying the area around Lake of the Woods and the eastern shore of Lake Winnipeg about the time the French extended the fur trade into the Upper Great Lakes. Accomplished hunters and trappers in a bountiful fur-bearing region, they soon became involved as suppliers to the French trade and joined their Cree allies in making the long journey north to trade on Hudson Bay.

Henry Kelsey accompanied a trading group of Assiniboine when he left York Factory in 1690. In fact, the name "Assiniboine" comes from the Algonquian; the Cree called them *Usinne pwat*, "Stone Sioux", while in Ojibwe they were known as *Assiniboël*. Like their relatives to the south, the Assiniboine called themselves Nako'ta.

Their involvement with the fur trade and continued conflict with other Siouan-speaking nations pushed the Assiniboine west out onto the plains. By 1800, they had left the woodlands behind and were moving across the southern prairies from western Manitoba to Alberta and Montana. Becoming superb bison hunters, they developed great expertise in building buffalo pounds. By 1850, they had moved into the eastern slopes of the Rockies, where they are known as the Stoney.

Their relations with European fur traders were generally friendly and Assiniboine hospitality was widely esteemed. But the contact period also brought disease, which impacted the Assiniboine disastrously. Estimated to number more than 10,000 in the late 18th century, there were only about 2,600 in 1890.

The move west also brought them into conflict with the three nations of the Blackfoot Confederacy (see page 185). With fewer horses than their powerful enemies, the Assiniboine became skilled horse raiders. David Thompson described a remarkable raid on Rocky Mountain House in which the Assiniboine, disguised as antelope, made off with 50 horses.

Today the Assiniboine, their numbers substantially revived, live on small reserves in Saskatchewan and Montana, while the Stoney have a large oil-rich reserve near Morley, Alberta. Manitoba's Assiniboine River and the town of Assiniboia in Saskatchewan are among many places that bear their name.

Before horses (which originated in the Americas, but died out after the last glaciation) were returned to North America by the Spanish, bison were hunted in many different ways by plains people. One of the most difficult, approaching the buffalo on foot, required stealth, caution and a favorable wind. Some hunters wore wolf skins as a disguise.

These modern tipis, pitched outside Lower Fort Garry, recall the buffalo hide lodges used by many plains nations, including the Assiniboine after they moved west and north to become buffalo hunters.

Lower Fort Garry

J ust 32 kilometres from downtown Winnipeg on the lower Red River, Lower Fort Garry has been called "the most elegant example of Hudson's Bay architecture on the continent". The fort dominates the west bank of the river a few kilometres below the St. Andrews Rapids, high above the reach of flooding.

These attributes – easy navigation from Lake Winnipeg and a site safe from flooding – undoubtedly contributed to Governor George Simpson's decision on the location of the fort, for the terrible Red River flood of 1826 had destroyed the first incarnation of Fort Garry at The Forks of the Red and Assiniboine. But for Simpson, the site on the lower Red River had another advantage. It was reasonably distant from both the Red River Settlement and the growing colony at St. Andrews, where a number of fur traders had settled their mixed-blood families. Simpson had just married his young cousin Frances in England and he was anxious to keep her apart from his North American wives and families.

With its massive limestone walls now shaded by large elms, Lower Fort Garry does not dominate the banks of the lower Red River as it once did. But the history of the place is perhaps more evident today, thanks to a varied and informative interpretive program.

Work began on the fort in 1831. Pierre la Blanc, a stonemason from York Factory, was hired at considerable expense (£75 per annum) to build a large stone house-cum-administration building facing the river. Though it was the first structure finished, in 1832, the Simpsons resided there only a brief time. Both were ill during the following winter and their infant son died in 1833.

After the family tragedy, the zest Frances had once had for Rupert's Land disappeared; she returned to England and eventually settled in Lachine. Others were also disillusioned with the sprawling new fort. The day-long journey down the river was irksome to farmers and hunters who were in the habit of selling their goods at The Forks. The reality was that The Forks was already established as the settlement's economic centre and not even George Simpson could reverse that.

Simpson had been thinking strategically; supply brigades heading for the distant north would get a jump on the long trip by departing from the Lower Fort. Each spring, the York boats filled with supplies and trade goods set out on the torturous journey to Lac La Loche and Methye Portage. There, at the divide of the Hudson Bay and Arctic Ocean watersheds, the Red River brigade met its northern counterpart laden with pelts from the rich Athabasca and Mackenzie districts. With the crucial rendezvous accomplished, the Hudson's Bay "trip men" headed east to York Factory, dragging their York boats over the thirty-odd portages of the Hayes River. Once at the bay, they retrieved the newly arrived "outfit" – the coming year's goods and supplies – that had come by ship from London and hastened back up the Hayes. Depositing some of the goods at Norway House, they raced back to Red River ahead of the advancing winter.

Despite its advantages for the brigades, the Lower Fort was never really

DENNIS FAST

PETER ST. JOHN

viable and in 1836 the HBC was forced to rebuild at The Forks. Lower Fort Garry never became a major centre of trade; instead, it catered mostly to the local parishes of St. Peters, St. Andrews and St. Clements. On occasion during the 1840s, the annual council of the Northern Department, normally held at Norway House, took place at "the Stone Fort", as the locals dubbed it, but for the most part it was a quiet place.

The fort's industrial heyday came in the 1860s, when it possessed a boat building shed, a malt house, a distillery and lime kilns. Its operations also included a large farm and a sales shop, where trappers and farmers received credit, not cash, for their furs or produce; the HBC feared that money might be spent at a free trader's store.

Free traders gradually became a problem for the company as Red River became a permanent settlement. By the 1840s, its multiracial community of Metis, Orcadians, Scots, Cree and Ojibwe peoples harbored genuine resentment at the HBC's attempt to monopolize trade. In order to suppress the free trade movement, the company brought in 150 men of the Royal Warwickshire Regiment (the Sixth of Foot) from England. Quartered at the Stone Fort, the bored soldiers never fired a shot, but they did complete the unfinished third of the outer walls and gave strong impetus to both the ale-making industry and the overall local prosperity. The regiment returned to England in 1848, but a year later the free traders won a legal victory over the company, effectively breaking the HBC trade monopoly.

Beginning in the early 1820s, when the first Anglican minister arrived at St. Andrews, the community around the Lower Fort suffered serious racial divisions. George Simpson's questionable marital relations were reflected in increasingly racist inclinations on the part of a number of the company's senior officers. Despite the crucial role that native North American women had played in the fur trade, they were ever more ostracized as the century wore on. Yet the economic relationship between the company and the local Cree and Saulteaux continued. The Saulteaux of St. Peter's parish not only netted and dried fish, selling them to the company in exchange for provisions, they also provided laborers for the farm and the York boat brigades.

In 1870, the Lower Settlement became part of the Province of Manitoba and in the years following the fort served a variety of capacities from penitentiary to country club. The HBC closed its operations in 1911 and in 1951 deeded the fort to Canada. Today, Lower Fort Garry, the oldest intact stone fort in North America, is a national historic site and has been restored to reflect life in the 1850s.

Lower Fort Garry National Historic Site is 32 kilometres north of Winnipeg, east of Highway 9. The Visitor Centre and complex of buildings is open from mid-May to the first weekend in September, from 9 a.m. to 5 p.m. daily.

The "Big House", left, built for Governor George Simpson and his bride Frances in 1831, has been restored to reflect a later period, when Governor Eden Colvile and his wife Anne lived here after 1850.

The furloft and sales shop, also completed in 1831-32, was the business centre of the fort. Here, trappers brought their furs and farmers their crops, to be exchanged for goods or credit. Laborers employed at the fort were also generally paid in credit at the sales shop, to avoid transactions in cash (which might have been used elsewhere).

PETER ST. JOHN

Fur Trade Communities

Just as its well maintained river trails draw Winnipeggers today to skate and walk, the frozen Red and Assiniboine Rivers drew the region's early settlers. Peter Rindisbacher's Winter Fishing – 1821 *shows one favored activity. The rivers were also used as highways by dog trains and snowshoers.*

St. Andrews Church, below, the oldest church west of the Great Lakes, continues to serve the local population today.

PETER ST. JOHN

Though the Hudson's Bay Company tried for years to discourage its Orcadian (and later Canadian) employees from liaising with North American women, from the outset it was obvious the policy would be almost completely ignored, even by company officers. By the early 18th century, most bayside posts had an associated community of wives and families and the company was soon hiring the mixed-blood children of traders. The number of fur trade families grew as the trade did and by 1800, the company was beginning to ponder the idea of authorizing a "retirement community" somewhere in its vast territories.

Retiring French and Canadian fur traders had already created several such communities along Quebec's St. Lawrence River and Michigan's Straits of Mackinac, as well as in Manitoba's Red River Valley. The resulting multiracial communities not only provided excellent employees for the fur trade, but developed cultures of their own. In the Red River Valley, a community of Metis buffalo hunters had begun to develop by the first decade of the 19th century. Though some also farmed the east side of the Red River near The Forks or traded, many families lived largely for the winter bison hunt. Initially, the hunt was accomplished on the nearby plains of Manitoba and North Dakota, but as the herds began to decrease, the buffalo brigades pushed ever farther west. By the 1850s, these brigades numbered dozens, even hundreds of oxcarts, which set off in the fall in a long line of shrieking vehicles and patrolling ponies. The French-speaking communities attracted settlers from Quebec and soon included a Roman Catholic cathedral and convent.

After 1812, the valley was also home to the Selkirk Settlers, victims of Scotland's Highland Clearances, who were trying to build a new life. These Scots initially settled in Kildonan on the

PUBLIC ARCHIVES OF CANADA / C-001932

west side of the Red River below The Forks, around Fort Douglas; Selkirk's later Swiss and German settlers claimed land along the Seine River.

The Red River Valley therefore seemed the perfect place for the glut of fur trade employees created by the merger between the HBC and the NWC in 1821. Within two or three years, a substantial number of English-speaking fur trade families had settled on the west side of the Red, above the rapids in St. Andrews. A decade later, the community boasted an Anglican church as well as the intended headquarters of the Hudson's Bay Company, Lower Fort Garry.

St. Andrew's Church and nearby Kennedy House, a restored mid-19th century manor built by William Kennedy, son of Chief Factor Alexander Kennedy and his Cree wife Aggathas, are located on River Road, off Highway 9, about 25 kilometres north of Winnipeg. Kennedy House boasts a popular tea house that is open from late May to early October.

THE SELKIRK SETTLERS' SAVIOUR by Doug Whiteway

In 1816, when the Red River colony was in grave danger of annihilation capped by violence between partisans of the North West Company and the Hudson's Bay Company, Peguis, chief of the Saulteaux, once again gave the Scottish settlers his material protection and the benefit of his great influence, taking the homeless farmers to his village at Netley Creek, 60 kilometres north of present-day Winnipeg.

It was not the first time Peguis and his people had lent assistance to the troubled settlers, nor would it be the last. Indeed, it might be said that Peguis played one of the key roles in nurturing the settlement by defending the beleaguered Scots against antagonists and showing them how to survive in a landscape that was to them harsh and alien.

Adapting to a new landscape was something Peguis, who was born circa 1774, and the Saulteaux had had themselves to do. They came to the plains in the late 1700s from Sault Ste. Marie in the Lake Superior region and had to modify tool-making methods, hunting and gathering patterns, and other skills that had been developed over centuries of life in a woodlands environment. Their adaptation was quick and far-reaching. By the time an advance party of Selkirk settlers entered the Red River valley in 1811, Peguis and the Saulteaux were regarded as the region's primary landlords.

Adaptability may also lie behind Peguis's alliance with the HBC and the Selkirk settlers, though there may have appeared little to gain from helping the white man gain a toehold in another part of North America. When the second party of weary settlers arrived in Red River in late summer 1812 with no food to last the winter, it was Peguis who helped them to better-supplied posts southward at Pembina. He signed a treaty with Lord Selkirk in 1817, believing that a bond of trust would better serve his people, but toward the end of his long life in 1864, he became disillusioned with the violations and trespassing on reserve land.

Chief Peguis is buried at St. Peter's Dynevor Church in East Selkirk, off Highway 59, and a plaque is dedicated to his memory in Kildonan Park, on Main Street in Winnipeg.

PETER ST. JOHN

To see Chief Pequis's grave, visit St. Peter's Dynevor Church, above, located five kilometres north of East Selkirk. Take Highway 508, then follow the signs to the church, which was built in 1836.

WILHELM KAUFMANN IN *THE CITY OF THE RIVERS*

Four Forts at the Forks

by Doug Whiteway

Fort Douglas, shown below in 1815 and named for Thomas Douglas, Earl of Selkirk, was at the centre of some of the most brutal confrontations Winnipeg has known. The battle was between the fur trade and settlement. By the time this interior scene was painted at Upper Fort Garry in 1848, opposite, it was clear that settlement would be the ultimate victor.

Tucked away in a tiny park just off the corner of Broadway Avenue and Main Street in downtown Winnipeg is a splendid crenellated Tyndall stone gate, a remnant of what was once a formidable fort with four large bastions and five-metre-high walls – a visual demonstration of the Hudson's Bay Company's commanding role in the Red River Valley in the early 19th century. Built in 1836 and named Upper Fort Garry to distinguish it from Lower Fort Garry built five years earlier, it was the second so-named fort built near the strategic confluence of the Red and Assiniboine Rivers, and the last of four forts that rose and fell within a century of the first European contact with the aboriginal inhabitants of the Red River Valley.

ERNEST J. HUTCHINS / NATIONAL ARCHIVES OF CANADA / C-018184

The first was Fort Rouge, established in 1738 by a French-Canadian named Louvière for Pierre Gaultier de la Vérendrye, as one of a network of trading posts from Lake Superior to Lake Winnipeg. Though the timbers of this fort are said to lie today beneath the junction of Winnipeg's two major thoroughfares, Portage Avenue and Main Street, no visual evidence of the

structure lingers. La Vérendrye, more absorbed in the mythic quest for a route to the "Western Sea" than with the practicalities of the fur trade, built his forts in relative haste. Fort Rouge was likely a crude wooden structure, a European oddity on the boundless prairie, and destined to deteriorate. The name lingers today only in the name of Winnipeg's first suburb – Fort Rouge – that stretches southwest of the forks of the Red and Assiniboine.

It was not until the turn of the 19th century, when rivalry between the HBC and the North West Company intensified in Red River, that fort building at The Forks began in earnest. In 1806, the Nor'Westers built Fort Gibraltar within 50 metres of the Red River's west bank to handle its fur trade business, stand in opposition to the HBC, and, within a few years, lead the attack on the Scottish settlers brought in by the HBC's majority shareholder, Thomas Douglas, Earl of Selkirk.

Its stockade made of oak trees split in two, its picketing as high as five metres, Fort Gibraltar shielded eight houses within its walls and lasted until March 1816 when HBC officers and men seized and destroyed it. To stake their claim in Red River, the HBC had built Fort Douglas nearby in 1813, and with the destruction of Fort Gibraltar seized control of the Red and denied passage and provisions to the Nor' Westers. In June 1816, some Nor'Westers and their allies captured Fort Douglas after killing the local HBC governor and 20 of his men at Seven Oaks, a few kilometres north of the fort.

Lord Selkirk restored order with the help of disbanded Swiss mercenary

HENRY JAMES WARRE / NATIONAL ARCHIVES OF CANADA / C-017936

soldiers and the Nor'Westers rebuilt Fort Gibraltar. But in 1821, after an epic struggle, the two fur trading companies merged and Fort Gibraltar, better situated at The Forks, was taken over by the HBC and renamed Fort Garry, after Nicholas Garry, a London Committee member who had been sent to oversee the amalgamation. Fort Douglas was sold to a Red River settler in 1825 and vanished the next year in one of the severest floods in the Red River Valley's recorded history.

The 1826 flood so damaged Fort Garry that the HBC constructed a new post, Lower Fort Garry, 32 kilometres north along the river, as its administrative centre. But by 1836, with the Red River colony clearly settled and growing at the junction of the Red and Assiniboine, the HBC returned to The Forks

and built a new fort, Upper Fort Garry, an impressive structure with barracks, officers quarters, chief factor's residence, general store, fur store, pemmican store and governor's residence. In the early 1850s, with trade increasing, the fort was extended to the north. The North Gate, the only surviving remnant of the fort, was a private gateway that led to the governor's house and gardens.

The fort remained the seat of government for the District of Assiniboia and the Red River settlement until 1870 when the Province of Manitoba was created. With the decline of the fur trade and the rapid growth of the city of Winnipeg, incorporated in 1874, Upper Fort Garry soon became an anachronism. By 1882, a burgeoning city, wanting to extend Main Street to the south, had the fort demolished. All that remains is a charming remnant to hint at Winnipeg's fur trade origins.

The remnant of Upper Fort Garry is tucked behind a service station just south of Broadway Avenue between Main and Fort Streets. The Seven Oaks Massacre is commemorated by a monument at Main Street and Rupertsland Avenue in present-day West Kildonan and a reconstruction of Fort Gibraltar with interpretation is open to the public on the east side of the Red River at Whittier Park, located on the river at the north end of Rue St. Joseph N, in St. Boniface.

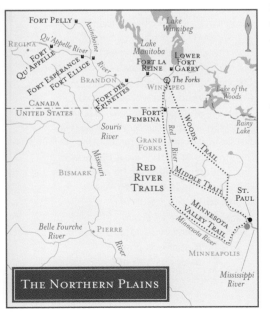

THE NORTHERN PLAINS

Exploring the Fur Trade Routes of North America

The Pembina Posts

Perfectly adapted to the North American plains, bison seem almost oblivious to even the worst weather. Bison will turn their well-protected heads and forequarters into the wind and ride out even the worst of blizzards.

Rising in South Dakota at Lake Traverse on the continental divide between the Hudson Bay and Gulf of Mexico drainage basins, the north-flowing Red River is shared by the Dakotas, Minnesota and Manitoba. Long before Europeans established their political boundaries, the river marked ecological boundaries in an area of great diversity. To the east are the pine forests of the Upper Mississippi and to the west, the Great Plains.

Ojibwe and Metis trappers and traders began working this bountiful area in the 1730s, trading at posts on the Winnipeg and Assiniboine Rivers. In the early years, it was mainly furs they brought to the forts, but by the 1780s, when the recently created North West Company began to expand across the continent, the trade had grown to include pemmican.

In 1793, Nor'Wester Peter Grant established the first post on the upper Red River, locating it on the west bank across from the mouth of the Pembina, near today's St. Vincent, Minnesota. But fear of the Dakota (see page 144), who had been at war with the Ojibwe and their Montreal-based allies for more than 30 years, caused the post to close within three years.

The NWC tried again in 1797, ordering Charles Baptiste Chaboillez to build another at the mouth of the Pembina. Chaboillez built on the east side of the river, just below the Pembina and called the post Fort Pambian, which may have

been a corruption of the Ojibwe *Anepeminan sipi*, the "Redberry River", after the highbush cranberries that grow along its banks. An alternative meaning comes from two Ojibwe words, *pam bian*, meaning "a place of meeting for all around". For two years, Fort Pambian was just that, as Chaboillez traded south, east and west, but again the threat of Dakota attacks convinced him to retreat to the north.

The following autumn, Alexander Henry the Younger paddled up the Red past the Pembina and began construction of what he hoped would be a regional headquarters near the mouth of the Park River, south of Drayton, N.D. But his Ojibwe suppliers soon made it clear the trading house was located too far into Dakota territory and in the spring of 1801, he moved to the north side of the junction of the Pembina and Red. For several years Henry's men fanned out over the area, building a series of wintering houses as far south as the Grandes Forches of the Red and Red Lake Rivers (today's Grand Forks), east to Red Lake and west to the Pembina Mountains.

To counter the Nor'Westers, the XY Company built on the south side of the Pembina in 1801 and the Hudson's Bay Company established a post on the east side of the Red in 1803. With such competition, the region was quickly trapped out and when, in 1808, the Dakota attacked Henry's headquarters, he lost little time in leaving.

South of this hub of competition, Robert Dickson, a Scot with flaming hair, had arrived in the region via the Minnesota River. Unlike the Nor'Westers and HBC men, he allied himself with the Dakota, marrying the sister of Waneta, leader of the Yanktonai Nako'ta. About 1800, he built a post on Lake Traverse and began pressing the Pembina traders on their southern flank. The War of 1812 ruined his business, but he bounced back to become an agent for Thomas Douglas, Earl of Selkirk, who in 1811 had brought the first shipload of impoverished Scottish settlers to North America via Hudson Bay.

The Selkirk Settlers arrived in the Red River region in late August of 1812. Though Selkirk's family controlled the HBC and though he had been granted a huge territory centring on The Forks of the Red and the Assiniboine, his weary group was less than welcome, for food was short. Too late to plant crops and facing a long, hungry winter, they moved south to Pembina, with its proximity to the buffalo plains. To accommodate them, Fort Daer was built on the south side of the mouth of the Pembina River, where Chaboillez's fort had once stood. But the Metis buffalo hunters viewed the settlers as a threat to their way of life. Caught between the hostility of the Metis and Nor'Westers to the north and the War of 1812 to the south, the colony clung to survival in hunger and isolation. The merger of the HBC and the NWC in 1821 dampened the hostility, and two years later the establishment of the international boundary just north of Pembina forced the HBC to relocate.

In the late 1820s, the American Fur Company established a post just south of the border. The Hudson's Bay Company countered by outfitting Metis traders to trade in the U.S. When John Jacob Astor proposed to sell his Pembina operation to free traders, the HBC backed down and in 1833, proposed that Astor close his posts from Pembina to Lake

Superior in return for a payment of £300 a year for five years. Astor, about to sell out anyway, agreed.

Over the next decade, St. Louis fur trader Pierre Chouteau, Jr., purchased most of Astor's holdings and in 1843, sent Norman Kittson to establish a trading house on the upper Pembina River near today's Walhalla, N.D. A year later, Kittson built another post on the Red River just below the border. Kittson was so successful that in 1846, the HBC brought in a regiment from England to try to police the trade. Still, Kittson's higher prices pulled traders south, but the end was near, for the great buffalo herds were nearly gone and settlement was replacing the fur trade.

One of the many incarnations of Fort Pembina sits on the Red River.

Pembina, N.D. is located just south of the U.S.-Canada border east of Interstate 29. An excellent museum and travel information centre is within sight of the border, while the actual sites of the old fur trade posts are marked with a cairn in a community park just south of the confluence of the Pembina and Red Rivers. About 30 miles farther south on I-29, a rest area commemorates Alexander Henry's early post on the Park River.

The Red River Trails

In winter, the waterways became highways of ice and dog trains were used to take mail and supplies from one post to another. The dogs are harnessed, opposite, for the long journey from Red River to St. Paul, Minnesota.

By 1815 the North West and Hudson's Bay Companies had been trading along the upper Red River for more than two decades, but the river itself had never been used as a major commercial route. Both companies had well-established supply routes, the Nor' Westers' west from Montreal via the Great Lakes and the HBC's south and west from Hudson Bay.

It was Thomas Douglas, Earl of Selkirk and founder of the Selkirk Settlement at the junction of the Red and Assiniboine Rivers, who first raised the possibility of a third commercial route to the south and east. In the fall of 1817, he travelled up the Red to its source at

WILLIAM ARMSTRONG / NATIONAL ARCHIVES OF CANADA / C-10502

Buffalo meat drying on the racks, Red River carts nearby and a fire ready to make tea, these were the delights of the plains for the buffalo hunters of the Red River Valley, above.

Lake Traverse on today's South Dakota-Minnesota border, across the continental divide and east along the Minnesota River to the Mississippi en route east to negotiate with the American government.

The Americans had put trade restrictions on goods passing from the Selkirk Settlement to the Mississippi through more than 500 miles of unmapped Ojibwe and Dakota territory. Though the land belonged to native North

Americans and the boundary between Canada and the U.S. would not be established for another half-dozen years, the U.S. was suspicious of any attempts by fur traders or settlers to trade goods south. The Hudson's Bay Company, of course, had trade restrictions of its own, and was in the midst of a trade war with the NWC. But Selkirk knew that his colony must be able to import and export goods if it was to survive. And the closest markets and supply sources were southeast, via the Mississippi.

Like his visions for settlement in western North America, the idea was prescient, though initially largely unappreciated. His plea to American Secretary of State John Quincy Adams simply reinforced Adams' desire to fortify the region (in 1819, Fort Snelling was constructed at the mouth of the Minnesota River), but over time, Selkirk's dream became a reality. Beginning tentatively in 1820, a series of overland trails were soon worn deep into the prairie (see map, page 199).

The traffic that shrieked over them by oxcart enabled the western pemmican trade, sowed the seed for the city that became St. Paul, Minnesota's capital, and greatly aided the growth of Manitoba's capital, Winnipeg. Between 1820 and 1878, when the railways put the cart trails out of business, an enormous diversity of goods flowed north and south. In 1832, 10 Red River farmers travelled all the way to Kentucky to buy 1,400 sheep and herd them home. Though more than 1,100 animals died en route, the remainder provided the nucleus for herds in Manitoba. In 1849, a piano was shipped over the trails and literally millions of dollars worth of furs and trade goods travelled the rutted roads.

The original Red River Trail followed the valley south along the ancient, sandy beaches of glacial Lake Agassiz about 20 miles west of the river, crossed to the east bank at one of several fording places and continued south to the source of the Minnesota River, following that valley to the Mississippi. Though the cart drivers preferred the open plains for travel, wood and water were needed at each campsite, so the trails kept to the river valleys. In time, this route was replaced by two others: the Middle Trail, which cut across country from what is now Breckenridge on the upper Red to St. Paul, and the Woods Trail, which followed the east side of the Mississippi north to the Crow Wing River and then turned north on the east side of the Red.

At the peak of their use, as many as 2,500 Red River carts used the trails in a single year, carrying 600 tons of freight for the HBC alone. In 1859, entrepreneur Anson Northup managed to haul sections of a tiny steamer from the Mississippi to the Red in response to a $2,000 challenge. The boat, named for its owner and described as "a lumbering old pine-basket", was purchased by the Minnesota Stage Company in a secret partnership with George Simpson and the HBC and operated between a terminal on the upper Red (named Georgetown, for the governor) and the Red River colony. In the next decade, until the HBC territories were transferred to Canada in 1869, nearly a million dollars worth of furs were hauled over the routes.

BUILT FOR THE PLAINS

Two-wheeled carts pulled by horses or oxen had been long used in French Canada and it was likely Canadian voyageurs who expanded on the idea to create the sturdy, versatile Red River cart. Nor'Wester Alexander Henry the Younger wrote of such an early contraption in 1801, when he was stationed at Pembina. His men had fashioned a cart with solid wheels, sawed from tree trunks, which he said were "worth four horses to us, as it would require five horses to carry as much on their backs as one will drag in each of these large carts."

Though to an outsider, the descendants of these carts looked like "ramshackle, squeaky" affairs, in truth they were perfect for the job. Built of oak where available, with five-foot-high, deeply dished wheels for stability, and an open box lashed together with dampened buffalo hide that dried to a tight, strong connection, a Red River cart could ford streams, plow through marshes, and even be quickly dismantled and converted into a scow. The buffalo hide scow cover could also be thrown over the top of the cart at night to make a tent. And broken axles or pieces were easily mended along the routes.

To protect the axles from being choked with ever-present prairie dust, most cartwheels used no grease and the shriek of the wheels on the ungreased oaken axles sounded, according to one observer, "like a disgruntled panther". Pulled by an ox, often tied by the horns to others fore and aft, one driver could handle a brigade of several carts.

Used by Metis buffalo hunters, as well as in commercial brigades, Red River carts were symbolic of the plains economy for decades, both here and on other major routes across western Canada.

THE SEARCH FOR THE WESTERN SEA

Between 1730 and 1750, the French-Canadian fur trade family of Pierre Gaultier de Varennes, Sieur de La Vérendrye, pushed far out onto the western plains, spurred by the search for the *Mer de l'Ouest*, the hypothetical "Western Sea".

La Vérendrye was born in 1685 in Trois-Rivières, entered the army as a cadet at 12 and fought the English in North America and Europe for 15 years. Returning from France in 1711, he married and settled near Trois-Rivières, where his four sons – Jean-Baptiste, Pierre, François and Louis-Joseph – were born. But La Vérendrye found the life of a farmer tame and when the boys were half-grown he followed his brother Jacques-René to Lake Superior.

A. H. HIDER/ NATIONAL ARCHIVES OF CANADA / C-6896

Shown here striking an heroic pose at Lake of the Woods, Pierre Gaultier de La Vérendrye was in reality an enigmatic figure who struggled with conflicting goals and on a number of occasions made and paid for poor decisions.

Wintering on Lake Nipigon and at Michipicoten, he heard tales about the Western Sea from Ojibwe and Cree travellers. In 1730, he returned to Québec to petition the government to fund an expedition west. Maurepas, the French minister of the marine, refused financial backing but awarded La Vérendrye a three-year fur trade monopoly, on condition that he seek the route to the sea. To obtain supplies he, his eldest son Jean-Baptiste and his nephew Christophe Dufrost de La Jemerais formed partnerships with Montreal merchants. In the spring of 1731 they headed west with a fleet of canoes and a crew that also included La Vérendrye's two middle sons.

Though the conflict between trading (which required establishing posts and creating relationships with local trappers) and travelling greatly slowed their westward progress, the family built posts at Rainy Lake, Lake of the Woods and the mouth of the Winnipeg River by 1734. That year La Vérendrye journeyed to Montreal for supplies and an extension on his monopoly, returning with his youngest son late in 1735.

The following spring both La Jemerais and Jean-Baptiste died, (see page 151) causing a retrenchment at Lake of the Woods and it wasn't until 1737, when Maurepas demanded action, that La Vérendrye again looked west. In May 1738, he and his men descended the Winnipeg River, crossed Lake Winnipeg to the Red River, ascended to The Forks and headed west up the meandering Assiniboine to a point almost directly south of Lake Manitoba. There, they constructed Fort La Reine, while a smaller crew sent back to The Forks built Fort Rouge.

That autumn, with 20 Frenchmen and hundreds of Assiniboine, La Vérendrye set out southwest for the country of the storied Mandan and the great *Rivière de l'Ouest* (see page 216). Arriving in November on the upper Missouri in today's North Dakota, they were conducted to a village by a Mandan delegation. Though impressed by the well-fortified settlement, La Vérendrye was disappointed to find that the Mandan were not, as myth had made them, Welsh.

Deserted by his Cree interpreter, he had difficulty communicating. Using sign language, he learned that the Mandan lived in large villages along the Missouri and had enemies downstream. Farther south and east, where the river was very large, lived a tribe of white men. Clearly, this was the Mississippi, where Spain held sway, but of the land to the west he could learn very little. Leaving two of his men to learn the Mandan language, he set out in bitterly cold mid-December weather for Fort La Reine.

During 1739 La Vérendrye's third son, François, went north to establish posts at Fort Dauphin on Lake Manitoba, Fort Bourbon on Cedar Lake near the mouth of the Saskatchewan River and Fort Paskoyac at what is now The Pas. That fall, the two Frenchmen returned from the Mandan villages with tales of a western people who rode horses and strangers, perhaps Europeans, who had been seen on the shores of a great salt lake.

Unable to make the journey himself, La Vérendrye first sent Pierre with a small party in 1740 and then François and Louis-Joseph with two others in 1742. All had instructions to contact the Horse People. The younger boys had more success than their brother. They returned to Mandan country, then travelled south along the valley of the Little Missouri River to the edge of the Black Hills before turning west into the Powder Hills.

This was Crow country, and their Mandan guides, understandably nervous in enemy territory, decamped for home. The French were determined to stay and finally, guided by a passing party of Crow, they reached the Horse People. The Crow in turn led the seekers west to join a war party against the Snake who, the La Vérendryes were told, lived in the mountains near the sea.

The expedition reached the Big Horn Mountains in January, 1743, but found the Snake camp deserted. As the war party headed home, it's unlikely the La Vérendryes needed much convincing to do likewise. Before them the mountains stretched west; here was no "Western Sea". In March, en route to Fort La Reine, Louis-Joseph buried a lead tablet, claiming the territory for France, on a hill on the west bank of the Missouri. In March 1913, 170 years later, a young girl found the tablet on a hill across from Pierre, South Dakota.

La Vérendrye lived until 1749, but control of the trade passed to others. Of family members, François stayed longest in the west, returning to Québec with 1,200 Ojibwe and Assiniboine and a flotilla of fur-laden canoes in 1759, just before the French regime fell.

PETER ST. JOHN

Despite his failings, La Vérendrye and his sons covered an astonishing amount of territory and gave Europeans that followed a better sense of the vastness of North America. This cairn on the Assiniboine River at Portage la Prairie, Manitoba, recalls the post from which they journeyed south and west to the mountains.

FORT LA REINE

Near here, in October 1738, Pierre Gaultier de La Vérendrye built the fourth and most important of his western posts, which he named Fort La Reine. The site was chosen, in part, to intercept the trade of Indians crossing the portage to Lake Manitoba en route to the English posts on Hudson Bay. Fort La Reine served as the base for the explorations of La Vérendrye and his sons south to the Missouri and north to the Saskatchewan. Ordered abandoned in 1749, the post was reconstructed by Jacques Legardeur de Saint-Pierre, in 1751. During his absence in 1752 it was burnt by Indians, and was probably not rebuilt.

Près d'ici, Pierre Gaultier de La Vérendrye éleva, en octobre 1738, le quatrième et le plus important de ses postes de l'Ouest, qu'il nomma fort La Reine. Il fit choix de ce lieu pour intercepter le trafic des Indiens qui franchissaient le portage vers le lac Manitoba afin de se rendre aux postes anglais de la baie d'Hudson. Le fort servit de base aux explorations de la Vérendrye et de ses fils au sud du Missouri et au nord de la Saskatchewan. Le poste fut abandonné en 1749. Jacques Legardeur de Saint-Pierre le rebâtit en 1751. Incendié en son absence par les Indiens en 1752, il n'aurait pas été reconstruit.

Historic Sites and Monuments Board of Canada.
Commission des lieux et monuments historiques du Canada.

Fort des Epinettes

Fort des Epinettes' focus was on the plains, right, and on attracting Assiniboine buffalo hunters and their families to produce and trade pemmican. Its name, however, comes from the surrounding forested hills, below. Though the conifers are spruce, not pine (epinettes), these relics of a cooler age are worthy of note, for this is the only spruce forest within a hundred kilometres.

PETER ST. JOHN

P ine Fort, as some called it, was one of the earliest fur trade posts established west of Portage la Prairie, and the first permanent site within what is now Manitoba's Spruce Woods Provincial Park. The first of three incarnations of the post was constructed at the junction of Epinette Creek and the Assiniboine River by a trio of Montreal traders, Thomas Corry, Forrest Oakes and Charles Boyer, in 1768. Built mainly as a provisioning post, it relied in the early years on the Assiniboine, who had earlier come into the area from the south, to hunt bison and make pemmican. A near-perfect travelling food, pemmican fuelled the early fur brigades as they pushed west and north up the Assiniboine, Qu'Appelle, Shell and Swan Rivers.

The post was also a distribution centre for corn and tobacco, traded from the south by the Mandan of the upper Missouri River. Peter Pond made reference to this trade on his map of 1785, with the legend: "Here upon the Branches of the Missury live the Maundiens who bring to our Factory at Fort Epinett, on the Assinipoil River Indian Corn for sale. Our people go to them with loaded Horses in twelve days."

It appears that the first Fort des Epinettes was abandoned for a short time about 1781 or 1782, perhaps as a result of the smallpox epidemic that raged through the country (see Cumberland House on page 165), and rebuilt by the North West Company on or near the same site about 1785. The second post lasted almost a decade before it was abandoned, according to Alexander Henry the Younger. "From the scarcity of wood, provisions and other circum-

stances, it was abandoned," Henry wrote in 1805, "and built higher up river, where the settlement is now, at Rivière la Souris." The "other circumstances" he referred to included the founding of the HBC's

Brandon House near the mouth of the Souris River in 1794.

The old post was briefly reestablished in 1807, and appeared on Arrowsmith's 1832 map, likely as a result of dated information, but Fort des Epinettes was in fact just a memory by that time. In 1890, geographer Joseph Burr Tyrrell found the site, partly washed away by bank failure along the Assiniboine, and mapped the remains of the fort.

Today, the post is remembered with a plaque in popular Spruce Woods park. Nearby, the Epinette Trails, and the remarkable dunes of nearby Spirit Sands, draw hikers, bikers and wildlife watchers.

Spruce Woods Provincial Park is about 70 kilometres east and south of Brandon. Take the Trans-Canada Highway (No. 1) east to Highway 5 and turn south for 28 kilometres to the park entrance and information centre on the east side of the road. Spruce Woods park has a full-service campground and many other facilities.

Brandon House

Between 1793 and 1832, Hudson's Bay Company posts in three different locations on the Assiniboine River bore the name Brandon House; all were located near the junction of the Souris River, downstream from the modern city of Brandon. In addition, the North West Company's Forts Assiniboine and Rivière la Souris, independent trader Peter Grant's Fort Souris and an XY Company fort were all clustered in the same vicinity.

Though both the Brandon Hills to the west and the Carberry Hills to the east were (and still are) wooded havens for wildlife, the posts were built with food rather than furs in mind. Situated near the buffalo plains, they were pemmican posts, and carried on a regular corn and tobacco trade with the Missouri River Mandan to the south.

The first incarnation of Brandon House was established in 1793 by "Mad" Donald McKay. Eyeing the Mandan trade, he built above Grant's Fort Souris. It seems the Mandan objected, either to the HBC or to European traders generally, for they attacked Brandon House a year later.

Meanwhile, the Nor'Westers abandoned Fort des Epinettes and moved upstream to locate their new post, Assiniboine House, nearby. Until 1811, the companies coexisted and even cooperated. Trade with the Mandan was regular enough that the Assiniboine posts were quickly aware of the arrival of Lewis and Clark at the Mandan villages in 1804.

The creation of the Selkirk Settlement downstream at Red River in 1812 changed these amicable relations. Provisions were suddenly in short supply and increased tensions led to the "Pemmican War". In 1814, claiming a right to regulate bison hunting and pemmican production in Rupert's Land, the HBC seized pemmican belonging to the NWC and stored it at Brandon House. The Nor'Westers, led by Cuthbert Grant, countered by looting and sacking the post in 1816. A fire a year later completed its destruction so Peter Fidler, in charge at the time, moved across the river in 1818 to the south bank and built "a small new house ... 30 by 14 feet", with two stables for the horses needed for the Mandan trade.

Brandon's heyday was nearly over. In 1824, Fort Pelly was established upstream on the Assiniboine as the region's headquarters. Five years later, the last Brandon House was built on the river 16 kilometres below modern Brandon as a deterrent to the rapidly growing Missouri trade.

Today little in Manitoba's second-largest city, other than its name, recalls a period of free trade that predated NAFTA by nearly 200 years. In nearby Wawanesa on the Souris River, a plaque at the Lions Club Park recalls the international trade and the seven forts in the area.

BARBARA ENDRES

Pemmican

Invented on the plains more than 4,000 years ago, pemmican was an almost perfect travelling food. Made of dried and pounded buffalo meat mixed with rendered fat and sometimes dried berries, it was lightweight and nutritious, would keep for months or years, and could be stewed, fried or eaten cold.

Jumping buffalo is another ancient art that was practised in Manitoba as well as farther west and south. Several jumps have been found in the Brandon area. Unlike those on the Alberta plains, some were not high enough for the fall itself to kill the bison; animals that survived found themselves in a pound, where they were quickly dispatched.

The Qu'Appelle Valley

Ten thousand years ago, meltwater from the Rockies poured from the South Saskatchewan River through this valley into glacial Lake Agassiz. The torrent scoured deep into the prairie sediments, creating a steep-sided glacial spillway. As the water receded, a series of lakes connected by a meandering river formed along the valley and a protected mix of habitats – grassy hills, wooded coulees, lakeshore forests and streamside marshes attracted both wildlife and people. A stream of cultures inhabited the valley over the millennia, including people from the south who created a large burial mound on the hillside above Crooked Lake west of the Manitoba border about 1,000 years ago.

The fur trade was a late chapter in this long history, drawing Europeans here in search of pelts and provisions. Before and after the end of the French era in 1763, the focus of the trade, which was mentioned in the journals of Fort des Epinettes on the Assiniboine River

The earliest posts in the valley were just upstream of the junction of the Qu'Appelle and Assiniboine Rivers, below. By the mid-1860s, Fort Qu'Appelle, opposite top, was located well upstream in what is now central Saskatchewan. The Hudson's Bay Company store that succeeded it, opposite bottom, is the oldest known company store in Canada.

after 1768, was on the lower valley and from 1787 to 1820, a series of posts was located around the junction of Big Cutarm Creek, just west of today's Saskatchewan border. The first of these, the North West Company's Fort Espérance, was located on the south side of the valley below the creek. From the outset, it was a highly productive pemmican post, for the valley was a favored wintering site for bison. Every year, the post sent large numbers of *tareaux* – hide sacks filled with pemmican – down the Assiniboine and Red Rivers and across the lower part of Lake Winnipeg to the Nor'Westers' provisioning depot at Bas de la Rivière at the mouth of the Winnipeg River. Depots such as this allowed voyageurs heading east and west to stock up on provisions en route.

Between 1801 and 1804, the breakaway XY Company located about 1.5 kilometres downriver from Fort Espérance, closer to the Assiniboine. In 1810, John McDonald of Garth moved the NWC department headquarters upstream to a site on the lakes (perhaps at the eastern end of Round Lake), but the fort was moved back downstream to just above Cutarm Creek four years later. It was from this post, called Fort John and located near a Hudson's Bay Company post, that Cuthbert Grant planned and launched his attack on the Selkirk Settlers at Red River. The Nor'Westers also burned the nearby HBC post before moving back to their original 1787 location in 1816. The second Fort Espérance, built higher on the hillside than the first for security reasons, was closed in 1819 because of hostilities.

This early fur era on the Qu'Appelle is recalled in Fort Espérance National

PETER ST. JOHN

208

Historic Site, which is marked by a fort-like arrangment of sculptures and plaques.

After 1819, there were no posts on the river for more than 30 years, until

Administered and supplied from Fort Pelly until 1872 and thereafter from Fort Ellice, Fort Qu'Appelle was, like its predecessors, a pemmican post.

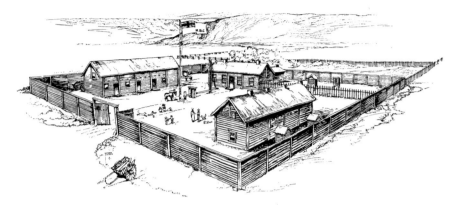

the first incarnation of the Hudson's Bay Company's Qu'Appelle Lakes post was built in 1853 between the second and third Fishing Lakes (now Echo and Mission) more than 100 kilometres west. A year later this post was moved 29 kilometres south to the "Squirrel Mountains" at today's Qu'Appelle.

In 1866, the HBC moved back to the south side of the river at the present site of Fort Qu'Appelle and established a post that included a substantial farming operation, according to a visitor in 1872. "The company," he wrote, "have about 25 acres under cultivation in the Valley, where they grow Wheat, Barley, Potatos and Garden Vegetables." Nearly 100 head of horses and 80 cattle were also kept at the fort.

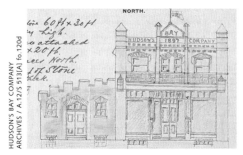

From its walls a web of trails, like the spokes of a wheel, led east to Fort Ellice, west to Chesterfield House on the South Saskatchewan River and north through the Touchwood Hills to Fort Carlton.

As settlers poured into the area, the fort became more general store than trading post. In 1897, a new brick and fieldstone Hudson's Bay Company store was built southeast of the fort on what is now the corner of Company Avenue and Broadway Street. Today privately owned, the handsome building is the oldest known Hudson's Bay Company store in Canada and houses several shops.

Fort Espérance National Historic Site is located on the south side of the Qu'Appelle Valley just off highway 8. From the Trans-Canada Highway (No. 1), turn north on No. 8 at Moosomin and follow the signs. Fort Qu'Appelle is northeast of Regina at the junction of Highways 56 and 10; both go north from the Trans-Canada Highway.

Who Calls?

The Cree living in the Qu'Appelle Valley during the fur trade gave the region its name. They called it Katepwewsipi, *the "Calling River", after the legend of two young lovers. Betrothed to a beautiful girl, a young man set out one autumn to wed her. Paddling without ceasing, he descended the river, his head full of dreams.*

At nightfall he entered the last lake. As his paddle flashed over the silent water, he heard someone call his name. "Who calls?" he answered, his voice drifting across the water. Again, he heard his name and as the moon rose, he knew it was his beloved. Paddling frantically, he reached her camp, but even before he had beached the canoe he knew the truth, for death fires and wailing greeted him. Rushing to her tipi, he found her still and lifeless.

„She called you twice as she died," the weeping women said, "just before the moon rose." Captivated by the legend, French traders translated the valley's name to Qu'Appelle – "Who Calls?".

The Upper Assiniboine

Fort Pelly was erected near the elbow of the Assiniboine River in 1824, three years after the union of the Hudson's Bay and North West Companies, by Chief Trader Allan McDonnell and named for Sir John Henry Pelly, governor of the Hudson's Bay Company from 1822 to 1852.

Established as the headquarters of the Swan River District, it was initially one of the most important trading posts

ALFRED J. MILLER / NATIONAL ARCHIVES OF CANADA / C-000432

Fire on the prairies was widely used by plains nations to manage the grasslands, attract and direct bison and sometimes even hasten the seasons. Burning in early spring, when the ground was still frozen, could hasten new growth by as much as three weeks, attracting the buffalo. But for fur traders and later settlers, prairie fires were terrifying, often destructive and battled furiously whenever they occurred.

in the Northwest and a major supply and distribution centre for outposts north, south and west, including Touchwood Hills and Fort Qu'Appelle.

The first Fort Pelly was built "on a rising ground at a small distance East of the elbow of the Assiniboine River". But for periodic flooding, it was a well-chosen site. A short portage to Snake Creek led to the Swan River, which in turn flowed into Lake Winnipegosis. Another portage took brigades into the lower Saskatchewan River, where they joined the main fur highway to York Factory on the bay. Alternatively, the Assiniboine River connected Fort Pelly with Red River and points north and south.

This first of two forts at the elbow location was a substantial post

with a store, a trading shop, an officer's quarters, a forge, a workshop, a stable and a boat yard. The last of these was a busy place; the first York boat was completed here in January 1825 and they were still being built nearly a half-century later.

In 1830, Chief Factor Colin Robertson, an experienced senior officer, settled into Fort Pelly with his family and rolled up his sleeves to take on aggressive competition from American and other free traders to the south. Robertson, a former Nor'Wester, was no stranger to competition, and he likely realized that Fort Pelly was too far from the disputed territory to be effective. The following year, the company built Fort Ellice.

Fort Pelly was destroyed by fire in 1842 and though rebuilt, it was then flooded, rendering it unservicable. In 1856, a new post, known as Fort Pelly II, was built on higher ground less than a kilometre to the southeast. The Swan River District headquarters moved to Fort Ellice in 1872, but Pelly remained a store and trading centre till 1912.

Beginning in 1971, thousands of artifacts were uncovered in a three-year dig at Fort Pelly I, giving valuable insight into the differing trade goods and styles over time. Among the artifacts retrieved and taken to the Museum of Natural History in Regina were "a Jew's harp, two dog-harness bells, two baling seals, several keys and parts of locks and large spun glass beads."

The Swan River District was enormous, extending 400 kilometres south from Fort Pelly to the American border and west to the South Saskatchewan River near the Alberta border. In the 1830s, this huge district was challenged by both the American Fur Company and independent traders. Fort Union, built at the forks of the Yellowstone and Missouri Rivers in 1828, (see page 218) had created a base from which the Americans could challenge the HBC in a manner reminiscent of the competition between Michilimackinac and Sault Ste. Marie (see The Fur Trade in Old Michigan on page 102) years earlier.

To meet this competition and check the infiltration of what the HBC called "the smugglers from the Pembina and Turtle Mountain region", Fort Dauphin was reopened in 1827 and the third incarnation of Brandon House was built in 1828. But the most important post was Fort Ellice, which was constructed in 1831 on the Assiniboine near today's St. Lazare, much closer to the American border.

Until Fort Ellice was built, Brandon House had served the Cree and Assiniboine, as well as the Mandan of the upper Missouri, who traded buffalo meat and Indian corn. (The urban habits of the Mandan had prompted Eurocentric speculation that they might be descended from a group of Welsh adventurers who centuries earlier had set sail from the British Isles and disappeared.) Fort Ellice was created in order to "protect" the trade of the Assiniboine and Crees from American opposition. Company traders from both it and Fort Pelly vigorously pursued the trade war with Fort Union until the Cree and Assiniboine peoples returned to the Hudson's Bay posts in 1835.

Fort Ellice was named for Edward Ellice, member of parliament for Coventry, England, who was instrumental in pushing through the 1821 Act of Parliament that merged the HBC and North West Companies. It was "beautifully situated at a point on the level of the Prairie where the deep and picturesque valley of the Beaver Creek joined the broad valley of the Assiniboine River," according to one visitor.

A disastrous smallpox epidemic in 1837 and 1838, carried aboard the American steamboat *St. Peter's*, killed nearly 18,000 Assiniboine, Cree, Mandan and Blackfoot. Not surprisingly, this had an enormous impact on the fur trade as well. Over time Fort Ellice superseded Fort Pelly in importance, mainly because of its strategic location on the transportation routes that subsequently developed through Fort Garry via the American railway, the Red River barge and oxcart caravans.

Both Fort Pelly and Fort Ellice were rebuilt in the late 1850s and early 1860s, heralding a more cooperative commercial society.

Both Fort Pellys were located about 13 kilometres southwest of the village of Pelly, SK on the north side of the upper Assiniboine River. Pelly, located on Highway 49 about 24 kilometres west of the Manitoba border, has scale models of the forts in its museum at 305 – 1st Avenue South. Fort Ellice is located just south of St. Lazare, MB. Take Highway 42 just west of the town, turn onto a winding municipal road and follow it south about three kilometres, climbing the valley slope to the fort site, which is marked with a cairn.

BRIAN WOLITSKI

Mule deer, such as this velvet-antlered buck, were once widely found in Manitoba. They have been replaced in the past century by white-tailed deer from the east.

The broad, fertile Assiniboine River Valley spreads below the site of Fort Ellice. The large post had an outpost at Horod where lovely rich furs were obtained from the Saulteaux, who trapped in the lush forests of the Riding Mountains.

PETER ST. JOHN

211

Over the Shining Mountains

LINDA FAIRFIELD

Many species of wild roses (Rosa L.) grow across North America, establishing themselves at the margins of forests. Borne on prickly shrubs, the five-petalled flowers are showy and fragrant, blooming in early summer. The fruit or hips, which ripen in the summer, are fat and red and very high in Vitamin C. Several parts of the plant are edible; the petals can be used in salads and the fruit makes delicious jelly, syrup and tea. The hips were widely used by native North Americans.

Shining blue in the sunshine, right, the Fraser River at Quesnel gives little hint of the tumult it will soon become as it thunders south through the Fraser Canyon.

The Louisiana Purchase by the young American republic in 1803 had an immediate and obvious impact on the fur trade in the United States, but its repercussions were also felt much farther afield, in what is now Canada's northwest.

A year later, both the North West and Hudson's Bay Companies were aware of the Lewis and Clark expedition up the Missouri, even as the Corps of Discovery settled in for its first winter at the Knife River Villages (see page 238). The Americans, they realized, were aiming to lay claim to the territory west of the Rockies and north of California.

More than a decade before, Alexander Mackenzie had reached the Pacific on foot, becoming the first European to cross the continent north of Mexico, but despite his achievement even he realized this was not a practical commercial route. So the Nor'Westers responded to the American challenge of 1804 with a two-pronged assault on the mouth of the Columbia, beginning in 1805. David Thompson, backed by John McDonald of Garth at Rocky Mountain House, was assigned to find a way over the Rockies from the upper North Saskatchewan River and young Simon Fraser was charged with

finding a route west and south by way of the upper Peace River.

As it turned out, neither route proved to be the way to the Columbia; that wasn't sorted out until 1811 (see David Thompson on page 191), by which time the Americans had already built a post on the Pacific shore. But the Nor'Westers did establish Fort Dunvegan about midway up the wide, bountiful Peace River Valley, and by 1808 Fraser and his men laid claim to a large area of what is now the interior of British Columbia, where the furs were reckoned to be as good as or better than those of the Athabasca country.

Fraser called B.C.'s intermontane territory New Caledonia, recalling his mother's tales of Scotland, "a land of brown heath and shaggy wood". He established a string of posts along the water routes between the Peace and Fraser Rivers; several grew into northern British Columbia's towns and cities. Though the Hudson's Bay Company battled for decades to extend this territory south to the Columbia, using the fur trade as a weapon of politics, in the end Washington state went to the Americans (see The Columbia Department on page 226).

Today, the New Caledonia fur trade is recalled at picturesque Fort

JERRY KAUTZ

Dunvegan Provincial Park in north-western Alberta, Fort St. John, at Hudson's Hope and McLeod Lake in northeastern B.C. and at Fort St. James National Historic Site in the town of the same name. The "grease trail" that Alexander Mackenzie followed from the Fraser River to the sea has been marked and nationally recognized and draws hundreds of hikers every year. The route that Thompson mapped to the Columbia was, with some adjustments, used to convey express brigades over the Rockies. Farther west, Thompson's River Post grew up at the forks of the North and South Thompson Rivers (today's Kamloops) and became an important staging post for HBC horse brigades.

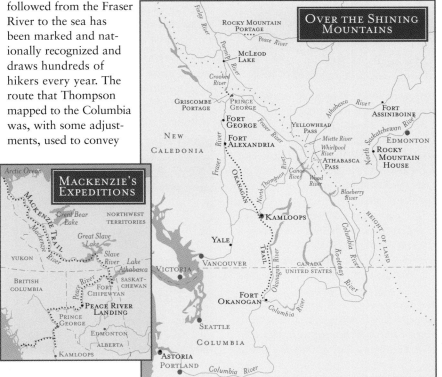

MACKENZIE'S EXPEDITIONS

OVER THE SHINING MOUNTAINS

The Rainbow Mountains soar above the Chilcotin Plateau, a wild and beautiful upland area that is home to a multitude of wildlife, including grizzly bears (Ursus arctos). Grizzly means "grayish" and "inspiring horror." Both meanings apply, for these bears often have a frosting of gray or blonde hair on their backs and shoulders and adult males can weigh up to 400 kilograms and are enormously strong. By contrast the tiny cubs, born in the winter, weigh about 400 grams (less than a pound) each.

Exploring the Fur Trade Routes of North America

Fort Dunvegan

by Michael Payne

The fur trade in the Athabasca-Peace River area proved so lucrative for the North West Company that it attracted rival traders almost immediately. By the early 1800s the NWC

NATIONAL ARCHIVES OF
CANADA / C–21296

An unknown artist captured the wide Peace River Valley looking east from Fort Dunvegan in this late 19th-century woodcut. Today, a provincial park and heritage site recall the days of the fur trade when the river served as a much-travelled highway.

Farther downstream, north of the town of Peace River, the forces of nature have carved the cliffs of the river valley into delicate bas-relief columns.

PETER ST. JOHN

was aggressively expanding its posts to meet the XY and Hudson's Bay Companies' challenges. In 1805 Archibald Norman MacLeod selected a site at roughly the midpoint on the Peace River for a new post. He called it Fort Dunvegan after the MacLeods' ancestral home on the Isle of Skye.

Fort Dunvegan served three main purposes for the NWC and then the HBC between 1805 and 1918 when it closed. It was a center for trade with the local Beaver or Tsatinne, as well as neighboring Cree, Metis and Iroquois families. It was also an important source of provisions. Dunvegan's gardens were renowned for their fertility. In fact the river flats are still used as market gardens

– two centuries after the first crops were planted there. Post hunters also provided bison and moose meat for other posts and canoe and boat brigades. Finally Dunvegan served as a transhipment centre for furs and trade goods en route to and from New Caledonia in the interior of British Columbia.

The combination of the river, wooded flats and high hills make Dunvegan one of the most picturesque of all fur trade sites. Even hard-bitten traders commented on the beautiful location of the post. For example, in 1884 William Traill wrote, "I am quite in love with the place which I think is the prettiest I have seen in the Country."

Fort Dunvegan Provincial Park and Historic Site, with its excellent interpretive centre, is located at Dunvegan Bridge, where Highway 2 crosses the Peace River. The serviced campground lies along the river, and the valley is just as picturesque as it was when Archibald Norman MacLeod chose the site two centuries ago.

PETER ST. JOHN

Fort St. John

Though today's visitors come mainly via the Alaska Highway, Fort St. John owes its origins to the Peace River. During his 1793 trip to the Pacific on behalf of the North West Company, Alexander Mackenzie (see page 222) noted attributes that made this stretch of river right for a fort. First, the banks and mid-stream islands were crowded with mature evergreens and birch, needed for construction and canoe building, and the streams flowing into the Peace were crowded with beaver. Moreover, he wrote, "as for the other animals, they are in evident abundance, as in every direction the elk and buffalo are seen in possession of the hills and plains."

Mackenzie should not have been surprised. The Dene had lived here for generations and knew the Peace as the "river of beavers". But by the mid-1700s they and the Awokanak – the "timid people" or Slavey – were being displaced by well-armed Cree, who were moving west even faster than the traders.

The year after Mackenzie's journey, John Finley founded a fort, which he called Rocky Mountain House, at the junction of the Peace and Moberly Rivers about ten kilometres from the present city. This first post in mainland British Columbia was abandoned in 1805, when Simon Fraser and John Stuart built Rocky Mountain Portage upstream, at the foot of the Peace River Canyon near Hudson's Hope.

The name, Fort St. John (pronounced Fort **Sin**-jun in the early days, reflecting the common British pronunciation), was given to a second post at the mouth of the Beatton River, also built in 1805. Subsequently, the name was used for four other posts.

The Hudson's Bay Company took over the earliest of these when it and the NWC were amalgamated in 1821, but two years later announced its intention to close it. This was unacceptable to the local people, who had given up their traditional lifestyle to become trappers for the fur companies, and now depended on European goods. The threatened post closure was seen as nothing less than a breach of contract and they reacted by destroying the fort and killing five company employees. The HBC retaliated by closing all the Peace River forts for three years, causing widespread hardship and starvation.

Subsequent forts were built in part to serve gold seekers who trickled into the Peace River in the 1860s and, after 1897, poured past en route to the Klondike gold fields.

Today, Fort St. John is the largest city in the region, thanks to gold of a different color. Dubbed the "energy capital of B.C.", the surrounding forests of evergreens and birch have been replaced with a forest of oil derricks.

Fort St. John is located on the Alaska Highway, 73 kilometres north of Dawson Creek. Though nothing remains of the sixth and final fort, the North Peace Museum traces the fur trade history and jet boat tours of the Peace River allow a glimpse of the view the traders had.

PETER ST. JOHN

This view of the broad valley of the Peace, which shows the location of one of the later forts, was taken from the outskirts of the modern city of Fort St. John.

Wherever possible, fur trade posts incorporated at least some of the practical accoutrements of home. In the fertile Peace River Valley, that invariably included gardens.

McLeod Lake

At the north end of McLeod Lake, the North West Company built Trout Lake Post – later McLeod Lake Post – in 1805. The post was constructed to trade with the Tsek'ehne (or Sekani) people who, some say, "have lived in the area

since before Adam and Eve". The Tsek'ehne then included the two southern-most groups of Sekani, lake people who fished for trout and carp in the lakes in the low mountains north of the Continental Divide.

Though never large, McLeod Lake has the distinction of being the oldest continuously occupied European settlement in British Columbia.

Like others to the north and east, McLeod Lake became a Hudson's Bay Company post in 1821, but unlike the others, it continued to operate every year for the next 131 years on the same site.

Finally, in 1952, the store was moved across to the Hart Highway (No. 97) to a building that had been constructed nine years before. The company store continues today as a general store with a gas bar.

At the original site, a nearby Tsek'ehne cemetery marks the site of a village that was created in the mid-1800s, after Oblate missionaries arrived in the area. Prior to that time, the Tsek'ehne people believed that burials should be scattered across the land, so that the spirits of the dead could roam the forest hunting the spirits of the animals.

It's easy to miss the turnoff to the original fort site. About 300 metres north of the McLeod Lake General Store, turn west off Highway 97 onto the Carp Lake Road and go down the hill to a flat grassy area on the Tsek'ehne Reserve at the north end of the lake. Several HBC buildings still stand; they are well signed and in good condition. The cemetery is just west and south of the old fort site.

At the north end of McLeod Lake, above, several buildings mark the site of a post that operated continuously here for 147 years, before moving a short distance away to the nearby highway.

PETER ST. JOHN

PETER ST. JOHN

PETER ST. JOHN

Fort St. James

Fierce competition with the Hudson's Bay Company and the continuing push to find a navigable route to the Pacific induced the North West Company to send Simon Fraser and a party of 20 men up the Peace River in 1805. Following the upper Peace and Parsnip Rivers, they wintered at McLeod Lake and early in the spring of 1806, Fraser sent James McDougall to explore the surrounding country. During his travels, McDougall visited a Carrier village on Sturgeon Lake (later called Stuart Lake after company clerk John Stuart), promising to return. Accordingly Fraser and his men arrived there on July 20th and established Stuart Lake post, later called Fort St. James. Within two years the Nor'Westers had created four trading posts in the region – Rocky

called New Caledonia, after the stories his mother told him of her Scottish homeland.

Fort St. James soon emerged as the administrative centre of the Caledonia trade and was subsequently an important commercial centre for the province of British Columbia, as well as its gateway to the north. Despite its early importance, the region's harsh climate earned the fort a reputation as a punishment post, sometimes called "Naboth's Vineyard", a sort of Siberia.

The area was rich in thick, lustrous furs, however, which were mainly trapped by the Carrier, a western Dene people also known as the Dakehl or Yinka Dene. The relationship between the traders and the trappers was an often uneasy one, based on mutual misunder-

JERRY KAUTZ

The well-stocked trade store at Fort St. James recalls the days when this was the hub of a fast-growing region of British Columbia, as settlers and prospectors replaced the fur traders that had made the fort their regional headquarters for nearly a century.

JERRY KAUTZ

Looking northwest from the fort, Stuart Lake awaits autumn in the setting sun.

Mountain Portage, Fort McLeod, Fort St. James and Fort George, later Prince George. Constructed of stoutly built log houses surrounded by picket stockades, these forts became the collective nucleus for a rich fur-bearing district Fraser

standing. This cultural gulf was particularly obvious after the HBC took over the post in 1821. In 1824, for reasons that may have had to do with a woman, two Carrier men killed two HBC employees. One of the Carrier was killed soon

JERRY KAUTZ

The warehouse at Fort St. James, right, was built in a style termed Red River frame (but also called poteau sur sole, pièce sur pièce or post and sill). With origins in both Europe and New France, the buildings had notched uprights into which shorter squared horizontal logs were fitted. The men's house, above, was a more typical log cabin style, with dovetailed corners.

after but the second disappeared for nearly four years. Finally in 1828, young James Douglas – then a clerk at the post but later governor of the colony of British Columbia – and a party of HBC employees found the second man hiding in the lodge of Chief Qua. Dragging him out, they brutally killed him, some say hacking him to death with hoes.

Qua, who was away at the time (as was the chief factor of Fort St. James), was furious on his return. Carrier tradition protected anyone who sought refuge in the chief's lodge, rather like the protection given to people who seek sanctuary in churches. With some of his men, Qua marched on the fort, intending to kill Douglas and soon had him splayed on a table with a knife at his throat.

At this point, the various versions of the story diverge, indicating the gulf that still exists between native North American and European cultures. The "official" version of the story is that Douglas's wife Amelia saved her husband by pleading for his life and throwing gifts down from a balcony. The Carrier version says that it was Qua's grandsons who convinced him to let Douglas go, reminding him that killing was the job of the warrior chief, not the clan leader, and would have tarnished his position. Amelia's "gifts" were left lying where they fell.

The incident does seem to have propelled Douglas's career (and that of Amelia), and later in the year it provided an opportunity for George Simpson, who was visiting the fort, to harangue and threaten the Carrier people for their "misbehavior".

Fort St. James was used continuously into the 1930s, gradually converting to sales based on cash rather than trade as it catered to prospectors, miners and settlers who poured into the area after the 1880s.

In the 1950s, the Fort St. James Historical Society used the old general warehouse and fur store for its local museum and in 1971, the fort was recreated as a national historic site. Restored to the year 1896, Fort St. James National Historic Site commemorates an important chapter in the history of the province.

Fort St. James National Historic Park, the fourth incarnation of the post, sits on the southeast end of Stuart Lake, about 160 kilometres west and north of Prince George, British Columbia.

JERRY KAUTZ

Follow the Yellowhead Highway (No. 16) west for 107 kilometres, turn north at Vanderhoof and follow Highway 27 55 kilometres north to the town. After crossing the Necoslie River turn west on Kwah Road to the fort.

MOUNTAIN PEOPLES OF INTERIOR BRITISH COLUMBIA

Related by language and culture, the four Interior Salish peoples – the St'at'imc (the British called them "Lillooet"), the Okanagan, the Secwepemc (or "Shuswap") and the Nlaka'pamux (the "People of the Canyon", or "Thompson") – occupy much of intermontane British Columbia. They are also related to other Salishan-speaking people of Washington state.

JERRY KAUTZ

When Europeans first came upon them in the early 1800s the four groups differed somewhat in their lifestyles, mainly due to variations in geography and climate (the region encompasses the almost desert-dry upper Fraser River area as well as the densely forested Thompson River watershed). But they also shared many aspects of culture and lifestyle, including winter villages of distinctive round semi-subterranean homes, sometimes called "pit houses", a reliance on salmon as a primary food source, and intricate and sophisticated artwork.

Trade had been part of Interior Salish life for thousands of years and the people had a vast network that extended from the Pacific coast to the eastern slopes of the Rockies (where the remains of subterranean houses nearly 3,000 years old have been found in several valleys) and from the southwestern United States to northern Canada.

When the North West Company's Simon Fraser arrived at the confluence of the Thompson and Fraser Rivers in 1808, a Salishan village of more than 1,200 people sat on the site now occupied by the town of Lytton. This was the largest Nlaka'pamux community, strategically located at the heart of the salmon runs. Downstream during the spawning runs, the rivers shone silver with leaping fish, which were netted, speared or trapped in great numbers, often from small platforms along the canyon walls. The fish were eaten fresh, smoked or dried and pounded for use during the winter months. Fur traders called the resulting preserved food "salmon pemmican", and on many occasions it kept them from starvation.

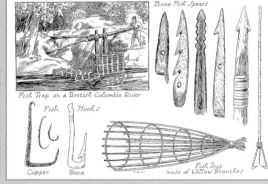

C. W. JEFFREYS / NATIONAL ARCHIVES OF CANADA / C-69760

The Salish had many means of preparing and preserving salmon, a mainstay of life. Two, which were quickly adopted by incoming European fur traders, were to dry or smoke the fish. Dried salmon, above, hangs in the fish cache at Fort St. James.

During the spawning runs, salmon were trapped, netted and speared. Freshwater fish were also caught with hooks and nets in the region's many lakes and rivers.

The people also hunted, gathered berries and plants and fished for freshwater fish. The fur trade came relatively late to this area, but disease and pressure from miners and settlers greatly diminished their numbers. They also experienced growing pressure along the northern edge of their territory during the 19th century from the Dalkehl (also known as Yinka Dene or Carrier), Athapaskan speakers who were involved in the fur trade and moved south with it.

The Alexander Mackenzie Heritage Trail

by John Woodworth C.M.

The trail that today bears Alexander Mackenzie's name was one of dozens of "grease trails" that once linked the northwest Pacific Coast to the mountainous interior. The trails are so named because of a thriving trade in rendered fat from the herring-like eulachon. These fish were so oily that they were also called "candlefish". Their silver schools spawned in early spring in British Columbia's coastal rivers, where the coastal peoples rendered the catch into an edible greasy gel. This "grease" was then backpacked in carved cedar boxes – like old fashioned butter boxes – to trade in the interior.

HÄLLE FLYGARE

Looking west toward the Coast Mountains across a carpet of flowers in Tweedsmuir Provincial Park, Stupendous Mountain (named by Alexander Mackenzie) is the highest peak in the range.

Evidence of the antiquity of the grease trail between the port village of Bella Coola and the Fraser River – now designated the *Alexander Mackenzie Heritage Trail* – can be found in the many pit-dwelling sites tucked along its winding foot paths. These semi-underground *kikulis* yield a 4,000-year-old record of use, including charcoal-covered cooking stones once used to boil foods in tight-woven baskets. Volcanic glass chips are found at former campsites, providing clues to a network of trade in obsidian that spread well beyond Canadian borders.

As the Pacific terminus of Canada's sea-to-sea *Alexander Mackenzie Voyageur Route*, this trail achieved recognition and a degree of preservation in the 1980s when its long-hidden overland route was painstakingly uncovered by Hälle and Linda Flygare of Canmore, Alberta. Its 350-kilometre passage over the Chilcotin Plateau and through the Rainbow Mountains commemorates Mackenzie's extraordinary journey of 1793 – the first recorded crossing of continental North America.

In 1801, Mackenzie recorded his travels in a 400-page book with a rambling 26-word title that is easier on the tongue if shrunk to *Voyages from Montreal … to the frozen and Pacific Oceans … 1789 and 1793*. When U.S. President Thomas Jefferson read the book, he responded to Mackenzie's fervent claim to British autonomy over the Pacific Coast from Russian Alaska to Oregon by mounting the Lewis and Clark expedition up the Missouri and through the Rockies to the mouth of the Columbia River (1804–1806).

Central British Columbia is corrugated by mountain ranges that feed snow runoff to major coastal rivers such as the Fraser, Skeena and Columbia. Mackenzie's crew had first to fight their way west through the Canadian Rockies via the upper Peace and Parsnip Rivers. On one stream at the continental divide, the 10-man party smashed both ends of the fragile 10-metre freight canoe and had to rebuild it.

An aerial view of the upper Fraser south of Prince George clearly shows the 250-kilometre Blackwater River trench (Mackenzie called it the "West Road"), draining west to east from the coastal Rainbow Mountains in Tweedsmuir Park, across the 1,300-metre Chilcotin volcanic plateau to the Fraser. Mackenzie, upon learning that downstream from modern Quesnel the Fraser drops south through chasms to the Lower Mainland and

HÄLLE FLYGARE

Vancouver, paddled back upriver to the mouth of the Blackwater to locate the established grease trail. The crew members, by now rebellious, cached their canoe and supplies and with heavy hearts and packs turned west. For these heroes of the paddle, how humbling to *walk* – in skimpy hide moccasins – the 350 kilometres to the coastal Bella Coola River.

Ten tedious days later at the Rainbow foothills, the trading family they had joined en route pointed the party south west to an alpine pass – a tiny 'V' on the horizon. The men struggled forward through July snowbanks to the pass of which Mackenzie later wrote, "… Before us appeared a stupendous mountain, whose snow-clad summit was lost in the clouds. Between it and our immediate course flowed the river to which we were going. Our guide … informed us that it was no great distance."

It was, in fact, a beautiful 30-kilometre alpine hike and a 1,300-metre plunge to the river. There at dusk, at an unexpected reception, they were plied with roasted Pacific salmon and welcomed into the seasonal fishing station Mackenzie later named "Friendly Village". They still faced another 40 kilometres downstream by dugout canoe to salt water (the site of modern Bella Coola), passing en route the valley's major landmark, glacier-topped Mount Stupendous.

Meanwhile, back on the east slopes of the Rainbows, the helpful trading family had detoured right instead of left to savor the much-closer Dean River salmon and steelhead runs. Why yield their trade secrets?

In the footsteps of the Flygares, volunteers formed the Alexander Mackenzie Voyageur Route Association, sponsored a trail reclamation program and moved to gain national recognition of the trail's historic value.

Today the 350-kilometre hiking trail and the Bella Coola River portion caters annually to several thousand day or weekend hikers and campers who come in from the Fraser or the Dean or up from the Bella Coola Valley; only a few stalwarts tackle the entire route in the steps of Alexander Mackenzie, an 18-day backpack from the Fraser to the Bella Coola valley. Those who do may see mountain caribou in Tweedsmuir Park and tiny spirithouses that mark gravesites in earlier settlements.

The trail's west end at Bella Coola can be reached on Highway 20, 456 kilometres west of Williams Lake. A connecting overnight ferry can take you back to Vancouver Island. The east end of the trail can be reached via the Blackwater Road (old Highway 97) on the west side of the Fraser from Prince George or Quesnel.

HÄLLE FLYGARE

The Blackwater River, seen here at Blackwater Canyon, goes by another name that recalls Mackenzie's journey as well as all the travellers who crossed the high plateau for millennia before him: the West Road River.

These fine petroglyphs or rock carvings, left, were created along Thorsen Creek in the Bella Coola Valley.

A TRANSCONTINENTAL VOYAGEUR by Doug Whiteway

O f all the Europeans to penetrate the North American continent, few have the rank of Alexander Mackenzie. His journeys – the first from Lake Athabasca to the Arctic Ocean in 1789 and the second from Peace River to the Pacific Ocean between 1792 and 1793 – are epic, earning him the distinction of being the first European to cross the continent north of Mexico. He completed these journeys before he was 30 years old.

ALEXANDER MACKENZIE
and his EXPLORATIONS

ARCTIC   OCEAN

GREAT BEAR
LAKE

Sir Alexander Mackenzie
from portrait by Sir Thomas Lawrence.

GREAT
SLAVE
LAKE

YUKON

BRITISH

COLUMBIA

LAKE
ATHABASKA
FORT CHIPEWYAN

PEACE RIVER
LANDING

PRINCE RUPERT

ALBERTA

SASKATCHEWAN

EDMONTON

PRINCE
ALBERT

SASKATOON

PACIFIC   OCEAN

CALGARY

Born in Stornoway in northern Scotland in 1764, Mackenzie travelled with his father to New York as a 10-year-old. But in 1778, during the American Revolutionary War, he went to Montreal, where he entered the employ of a fur trade firm. That firm merged with the North West Company in 1787 and Mackenzie, now a partner in the NWC, was assigned to Lake Athabasca in what is now northern Alberta. It was here that the ambitious 23-year-old conceived a plan to find an overland route to the Pacific, where, it was hoped, NWC furs could go west by water to sailing ships on the Pacific Coast. Based on charts indicating that a large river flowed westward out of Great Slave Lake, Mackenzie, with Dene guides, paddled a route that eventually carried him northward 3,000 kilometres and deposited him at the edge of the Arctic Ocean. Little wonder he named the waterway River Disappointment. We know it today, of course, as the Mackenzie River.

However disappointing this first venture was, Mackenzie remained undaunted, and three years later, having returned to England in the interim to study surveying, he planned a second expedition. In the spring of 1793, he ascended the Peace River and its tributary, the Parsnip, and broke through the Rocky Mountains to the Fraser River. Finding himself stymied by tales of the lower Fraser's deadly cataracts, he followed an ancient grease trail across the Chilcotin Plateau and down the Bella Coola River to the Pacific – an arduous but beautiful trip that cemented his reputation.

Alexander Mackenzie immortalized his transcontinental journey with an inscription on this rock in the Dean Channel on the Pacific: it read "Alex Mackenzie from Canada by land 22nd July 1793". The inscription has been permanently recreated on the rock for all to see.

Mackenzie left the West in 1795 and resigned from the North West Company four years later after disagreements with its senior partner, Simon McTavish. He went to England to write an account of his travels, was knighted by George III and returned to Canada in 1802 as head of the new XY Company, often known as "Sir Alexander Mackenzie & Co", composed of traders disgruntled with the NWC. For the next two years, rivalry between the XYC and the NWC was intense. Then, in 1804 McTavish suddenly died and a coalition was quickly negotiated.

Mackenzie's ambition was to form a trading company that would span the continent and involve the union of the NWC and the HBC, but he died in Scotland in 1820, a year before the historic merger took place.

HÄLLE FLYGARE

Kamloops

by Ken Favrholdt

Simon Fraser travelled the river named after him in 1808. His colleague David Thompson followed the Columbia River to the east. Neither ever spent any time on the Thompson River, but Fraser named it for his friend, whom he thought was on it.

At Kamloops, the North and South Thompson join to form the main Thompson River. The first Europeans to arrive at the ancient Secwepemc (or Shuswap) settlement of Kamloops were fur traders from John Jacob Astor's Pacific Fur Company. They arrived at the place "called by the Indians Cumcloups (sic)" in November 1811. This may have been a misprint, meant to read "Cumeloups".

The Secwepemc were so eager to trade that the Astorians came back the following year and built a post here, called Fort She Whaps. A short time later, the Nor'Westers also arrived at the river forks and set up a post "alongside" the Astorian operation. Following the War of 1812, the North West Company took over Fort She Whaps. The location of this post was likely on the site of the former Kamloops residential school on the Kamloops reserve.

The fort went by many names over the years, including Thompson's River Post and Fort Kamloops. In fur trade parlance, these forts were also known as "posts" or "houses".

In 1821, the Hudson's Bay Company took over the entire fur trade across western North America and the Kamloops post was likely rebuilt at a site closer to the forks of the rivers. Here the fort stood until 1841, when Chief Trader Samuel Black was killed there by a nephew of Chief Tranquille, whose untimely death had been attributed to a trade transaction with Black.

The following year, the fort was relocated to a more secure location on the northwest corner of the river junction. Here, though flooding was an occasional problem, the company had a large farm and raised horses for the brigades.

In 1863, following the gold rush that swept through the interior of B.C., the post was relocated to the south side of the Thompson River, just west of the present Overlanders Bridge. The bridge was named after a party of gold seekers who came through Kamloops; a few stayed to help construct the new HBC fort.

After the arrival of the Canadian Pacific Railway in 1885, the Hudson's Bay Company moved into the growing town of Kamloops and became a strictly mercantile operation. The days of the fur trade had by then faded from the scene.

Kamloops is on the Trans-Canada Highway (No. 1) in south-central B.C. The Kamloops Museum and Archives has many fur trade artifacts, including part of an old fort in the "piece-sur-piece" style. The museum is at 207 Seymour Street.

PETER ST. JOHN

Situated just east of the junction of the North and South Thompson Rivers, (the latter shown above), Thompson's River Post (left) was established in 1821. Recent archaeological excavations have revealed a Plateau pithouse village adjacent to the post, not surprising since this is land that has been inhabited by the Secwepemc for millennia.

The Brigade Trails

by Ken Favrholdt

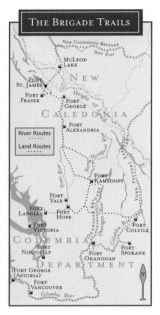

THE BRIGADE TRAILS

Okanagan/Okanogan

Though it's the same stream on both sides of the border, the river's name is spelled with an 'a' on the Canadian side, and with an 'o' on the U.S. side.

The brigades passed along the west side of Lake Okanagan.

PETER ST. JOHN

Unlike the fur trade in eastern Canada, waterways west of the Rockies could not always be used. Rapids and canyons limited water travel to only some stretches of major rivers, so to provide a continuous trade route from the Pacific to the interior, trails used by aboriginal peoples were adopted by the fur trade companies.

After 1821, the Hudson's Bay Company developed an overland route that linked the posts of New Caledonia (in northern B.C.) to the Columbia District (in Washington state). By 1826, a trail linked Fort Alexandria on the upper Fraser River to Fort Okanogan on the Columbia River (near today's Brewster, Washington).

From Fort Alexandria, boats were used on the Fraser River to provide links to the New Caledonian posts. From Fort Okanogan, bateaux – smaller versions of the York boat used east of the Rockies –– were used for transportation along the Columbia River to Fort Vancouver, the limit of navigation for ocean-going ships.

The outbound brigade left New Caledonia in May, arriving at Fort Vancouver in mid-June; after a short stay there, the inbound brigade would reach New Caledonia in mid-September.

Midway along the brigade trail, Kamloops, a major native settlement of the Secwepemc, became an important post where horses for the pack trains were raised. Originally, the route went along North Thompson River from Kamloops, west across the Interior

Plateau to Horse Lake and north from Bridge Creek (present 100 Mile House). At Alexandria, goods were transferred to canoes and bateaux for the journey to Fort George (Prince George), Fort St. James and other New Caledonian posts. After 1842, another route was used from Kamloops north: west past Kamloops Lake, north to Loon Lake, and connecting to the older route at Bridge Creek.

South of Kamloops, the trail skirted the west side of Okanagan Lake, which had proven to be too unpredictable for boat transport.

Known as the Okanagan Brigade Trail, this long overland route between the Fraser and the Columbia rivers was the main artery of the fur trade in British Columbia until the Oregon Treaty of 1846 established the boundary between British and American territories, bisecting the former Columbia Department. Although the HBC retained trading privileges south of the border, customs duties made the operations uneconomic and the arrival of American immigrants led to conflict with native Americans in the region. The Okanagan route was abandoned after 1849.

Although the Okanagan Brigade Trail was the main route for New Caledonia's inbound goods and outbound fur returns, Athabasca Pass (at 1,748 metres on the British Columbia-Alberta boundary) was used for express journeys across the Rockies between York Factory and Fort Vancouver. The express route carried departmental accounts and letters as well as new recruits or replacements for the various western outposts. The brigade set out every spring from Fort Vancouver on a breakneck journey to

Hudson Bay, usually taking three months and 10 days, and returning in early winter.

David Thompson of the North West Company (see page 191) traversed Athabasca Pass to the Columbia River in January 1811 and descended to the Pacific Ocean, only to find that the Pacific Fur Company owned by American John Jacob Astor had arrived by ship several months earlier. Athabasca Pass was first used as a main route by the Astorians returning east in 1814. From the west, it was reached via a point at the Big Bend of the upper Columbia called Boat Encampment, where canoes were cached and the arduous ascent of the "Big Hill" from the Wood River began. On the eastern slope, this pass was reached by a more gradual ascent from Jasper and the Whirlpool River. Horses could be used to a limited extent on the east side until snowfall.

The rapids of the Columbia River, such as The Dalles (see page 281), made this an expedient but hazardous route. Artist Paul Kane, who accompanied the express in 1846, wrote that the Columbia had claimed 68 lives to date. The route was also last used on a regular basis in 1849.

After the boundary between British and American possessions west of the Rockies was established along the 49th parallel, a new route was sought by the Hudson's Bay Company that would avoid the Columbia River route through American territory. Fort Langley (see page 234) became the principal entrepôt for incoming goods and outgoing furs en route to New Caledonia. From Fort Langley to Fort Hope (established in 1848), the Fraser River could be used by bateaux. Several routes were explored including a steep trail from the Fraser Canyon north of Fort Yale (also established in 1848), across the mountain ridges to the Nicola Valley. Finally, in 1849, a route was chosen that crossed the Cascade Mountains from Fort Hope to the Tulameen River across Manson Ridge, named after the HBC chief trader at the time.

Tulameen, the site of an aboriginal summer village, became an HBC campsite as well. At Tulameen the trails branched, one heading east along the Similkameen to the Kettle River, providing a "back-door" for the Hudson's Bay Company to supply Fort Colville in Washington Territory.

The other trail headed north through the Otter and the Nicola Valleys to Fort Kamloops. The Hope-Tulameen route was used until 1861 when a trail through the Fraser Canyon was made into the Cariboo Wagon Road, but some miners still used the Cascade route to go directly to Kamloops. Others used the old Okanagan trail from Washington Territory to get to Kamloops and the Cariboo goldfields to the north.

Sections of all of these routes are preserved today, including one a few kilometres east of Little Fort along Highway 24, another on the west side of Lake Okanagan where a plaque at Westbank marks the trail, and the trail through Athabasca Pass. Many place names commemorate the routes. There are Brigade Lakes north and south of Kamloops, and Hudson Bay Springs northwest of Kamloops. Unfortunately, the site of historic Boat Encampment was drowned by Kinbasket Lake.

The "express route" went up and over the Rockies through Athabasca Pass, left.

Pack Horses

Between 200 and 300 horses were used in the brigades, manned by a dozen voyageurs. Each horse carried two 40-kilogram packs and travelled an average of 30 kilometers a day between campsites. Horse Lake near 100 Mile House is named for an incident where several horses drowned crossing the mouth of the creek in 1827.

The Columbia Department

LINDA FAIRFIELD

The lodgepole pine (Pinus cortorta) is a tall, slender, long-needled conifer that was extensively used for the uprights of tipis from the eastern slopes of the Rockies west into the intermontane area of western North America.

From the heights of the Astoria Column, 164 steps above Cox-comb Hill in Astoria, Oregon, Youngs River winds to its junction with the Columbia. The history of the area spirals up the exterior of the column, which also allows a breath-taking view of the Columbia to the north and the altered cone of Mount St. Helens to the east.

This was the mecca of the North American fur trade, the long-sought gateway to the Pacific. But as the 18th century passed, there was a growing awareness that when and if such a gateway was discovered, it would not permit easy passage across the continent.

The journeys of the La Vérendryes to the eastern slopes in the early 1740s and the remarkable sea-to-sea crossing by Alexander Mackenzie 50 years later, confirmed that even when the mountains were surmounted, the land beyond was fraught with obstacles.

Yet, by the first decade of the 19th century there were many reasons to confront the challenges. British, Russian and American ships reported a wealth of furs (not to mention fish and forest products) on the Pacific coast. The North West Company, pushing west along the Peace River, found furs to rival those of the Athabasca. And the Louisiana Purchase of 1803 put an enormous new territory into the hands of the United States. Though the young republic lacked the population to colonize it and many believed Louisiana was largely a desert, President Thomas Jefferson was determined to discover what the country held and whether it was suitable for the fur trade. The Lewis and Clark expedition between 1804 and 1806 created a

snapshot of the "Trans-Missouri West" and opened the fur trade floodgates.

So by 1810, though the Corps of Discovery's main observation about its winter at the mouth of the Columbia had been that it rained almost every day, the major players in the fur trade were seriously intent on establishing a presence there. That year the NWC's David Thompson tried a new route over the Rockies (see page 191) and John Jacob Astor launched a two-pronged assault on the Columbia from New York.

In the end, both companies arrived in 1811, the Americans beating the Nor' Westers by less than four months to establish Fort Astoria. But international politics soon decreed that neither would be the major player on the coast, in the short term at least. Britain's Hudson's Bay Company dominated the trade in a huge region to the north and east for more than two decades. Then American settlers decided the issue, pouring over the Oregon Trail – an old fur route – by the hundreds of thousands in the 1840s to settle what are now Oregon and Washington.

Today, recreations on both sides of the 49th parallel allow time travellers to experience this last bastion of the fur trade in a setting that, despite the winter rain, is nothing short of magnificent.

PETER ST. JOHN

226

THE PEOPLE OF THE CEDAR FORESTS

The magnificent coastal areas of Washington and Oregon have been inhabited for thousands of years by cultures which thrived on the bounty of the sea. From the whale-hunting Makah or Kwih-dich-chuh-ahtx – the "people who live by the rocks and seagulls" – at the northwest tip of the Olympic Peninsula to the Umpqua of southern Oregon, a host of tribes lived and traded along the edge of the Pacific.

Contact with Europeans came early, when Spanish galleons arrived off the coast about 1560. With them came the first waves of disease, but real dislocation did not occur until 250 years later, when American fur traders built their first posts at the mouth of the Columbia River in 1811.

The Chinook people dominated the confederacy of Columbia River tribes in the early 19th century. A nation of traders, they had developed an international dialect that the British (who took over from the Americans in 1813) called Chinook Jargon, which was understood by many tribes. By the 1820s, the Chinook political leader Concomely was the most powerful man in the confederacy. His people lived in large, elegant longhouses constructed of western red cedar, which was also used for furniture and canoes. Cedar bark was made into hats, weirs, rope and even clothing.

Concomely allied himself with the British through his daughters, two of whom married traders. His grandson, Ranald MacDonald, the son of the Hudson's Bay Company manager at Fort George (Astoria), was a bright young man who theorized that a racial link must exist between his people and the Japanese who sometimes manned the ships that came from Japan. Though Japan was off limits to foreigners, at 24 he was hired as a deck hand on a trader to Japan in 1848 and marooned himself on an island off Hokkaido. While awaiting deportation, he conducted English classes, becoming the first teacher of English in Japan.

As a whole, however, the contact period was disastrous for the people of the Pacific Coast. Disease took a huge toll and settlement and the lust for gold pushed many nations from their lands. More than 24 separate bands were forcibly removed from their homelands and crowded into one reservation in the 1850s, which was then diminished over time. By 1860, only 3,000 people remained in what is today known as the Confederated Tribes of Siletz and in 1954, the confederation was "terminated" by a federal act. The remaining lands were confiscated.

Those who survived had been forced to adapt, becoming farmers or loggers, but the memory of their ancient culture remained. Finally in 1980, the U.S. federal government set aside 3,660 acres of land in scattered sites across Lincoln County, Oregon. In the past two decades, the federation has begun to rebuild its culture, educate its people and provide job training.

Cedar was widely used by the nations of the Pacific coast for housing, furniture, clothing and art, as well as for magnificent canoes, such as this 60-foot long Haida war canoe from the northwest coast of British Columbia. Carved from a single log, it carried between 16 and 20 warriors.

THOMAS WESLEY McLEAN / NATIONAL ARCHIVES OF CANADA / C–69781

Haida Sea-going War Canoe

Fort Astoria

Charged with establishing a post, the Astorians who arrived in the spring of 1811 found themselves all but stymied, not by the weather or the local people, but by the size of the trees, below. Douglas firs (centre), western hemlock and Sitka spruce soared hundreds of feet into the air, defying their tiny axes. But America's claim to the lower Columbia River was at stake and by summer, Fort Astoria, above right, rose in a small clearing in the forest.

AMANDA DOW

This outpost of the American dream was begun in April of 1811 by members of John Jacob Astor's two-pronged fur trade expedition to the Pacific. They arrived on the *Tonquin*, which had sailed from New York in the fall of 1810 (see Astor on page 111). After great difficulties crossing the bar at the mouth of the Columbia, the ship deposited its 33 passengers, their building supplies and seeds and sailed north to trade at Nootka Sound on Vancouver Island. Despite warnings about the vulnerability of both his ship and his men, Captain Jonathan Thorn did not believe that the Nuh-Chah-Nulth people were capable of overcoming his crew. He did not live to regret his mistake. After several days of trading, the Nootka people ambushed and killed Thorn and most of the crew, leaving just five men alive. Four escaped in a small boat while the fifth, who was injured, lured many Nuh-Chah-Nulth aboard again and blew up the ship. The escaping Americans were caught and killed.

At Astoria, meanwhile, as the company men struggled to build a post where many of the trees were larger than houses, the members of Astor's overland expedition began to straggle in, each with a tale of incredible hardship. By the time David Thompson and his North West Company men arrived from Canada in mid-July, 1811 (see page 191), the Americans were well ensconced. But as they had so often before, international events intruded. The War of 1812 stopped supplies from reaching Astoria and its inhabitants decided in 1813

to sell the fort and several outposts to the Nor'Westers and head for home, though the prospect of crossing the mountains again was undoubtedly daunting.

PARSONS, *ILLUSTRATED LONDON NEWS* / NATIONAL ARCHIVES OF CANADA / C–23570

The Nor'Westers ran the fort, which they renamed Fort George, for eight years – though never profitably. Three years after the NWC merged with its Hudson's Bay Company rival in 1821, Governor George Simpson arrived on the Pacific and decided that a new Columbia Department headquarters was in order, but on the north side of the river. In 1825, Fort Vancouver was begun 100 miles upstream.

But Fort Astoria was not the first American post at the mouth of the Columbia. That honor went to Fort Clatsop, a small wintering post built by Meriwether Lewis, William Clark and their Corps of Discovery in the winter of 1805. The little band moved in on Christmas Day, endured a very wet winter and left on March 23, 1806.

Astoria, Oregon is a picturesque city on the south shore of the Columbia. A partial reconstruction on the corner of 15th Street and Exchange Avenue marks the site of old Fort Astoria. Fort Clatsop National Memorial, a reconstruction of Lewis and Clark's post, is located six miles southwest off Highway 101.

THE LITTLE EMPEROR

The man who served as governor of the Hudson's Bay Company in North America for nearly 40 years and ran the company with such ruthless efficiency that many called him the "Little Emperor" was born in Loch Broom in western Scotland in 1792. His parents were not married and soon after his birth, he crossed the country to live with his grandfather, a Presbyterian minister, and an aunt, Mary, in Avoch and Dingwall near Inverness. His family looked after him well, ensuring that he had a good education and securing an apprenticeship in London for him when he was 17. Though he did take his cousins Aemilius, Alexander and Thomas Simpson into the HBC, the last as his secretary, Simpson did his utmost to erase his background from the official records, with the result that even his biographers know remarkably little about his early years.

During his years in London, he came to the attention of Andrew Colvile, an influential member and later governor of the HBC. At Colvile's behest, Simpson was sent to the Athabasca country in 1820, when he was 28. Arriving at the tail end of nearly 40 years of bitter rivalry between the HBC and the North West Company, Simpson saw the combatants up close, but was untainted by the conflict when the companies merged the following year. Still, he seems an unusual choice to be named co-governor of the new company.

Simpson grabbed the opportunity and within two years had put his stamp on the company in a way that would be very familiar today. He downsized and rationalized, closing posts and slashing staff, his eye always on the bottom line. He liked to see things for himself and by 1830 had a continent-wide reputation for setting speed records for travel. Of course, Simpson himself never lifted a paddle, saddled a horse or put up a tent. But he did rise long before dawn and drove his men mercilessly. Efficiency and order were his watchwords, at least where the company was concerned. His cousin Thomas, his secretary for seven years, called him a "severe and most repulsive master". Yet his personal life, at least until he was nearly 40, was disordered in the extreme. He had one mistress after another, fathering at least one child in Britain before 1820 and several more in Canada. When in 1830, he brought his young bride, Frances, back to North America, one of his country wives had to be hurried from a company post as the couple arrived.

His view of the Oregon Country was colored by politics. He believed the HBC was an extension of Britain. By building posts in the territory, he was making a case for British control. The Americans, on the other hand, believed Oregon was theirs by right of discovery; Lewis and Clark had wintered there in 1804 and the Astorians had built the first fur post.

Knighted in 1841, Simpson toured the world, but he was losing his sight and may have been suffering from syphillis. After 1850, he fought a losing battle against the forces of change and died in 1860, just after playing host to the Prince of Wales, later Edward VII, in Montreal.

PETER ST. JOHN

George Simpson was just 32 when he made his first visit to the Pacific coast in 1824, but his instincts for improving his company's bottom line were already evident.

Mount Baker rises above an autumn landscape. Simpson could hardly be unaffected by the beauty of the Pacific coast, but his delight in the scenery was eclipsed by the inefficiencies he discovered at the department's posts.

Fort Vancouver

For more than half its 35-year history (1825-1860), Fort Vancouver was the fur trade capital of a vast area that stretched from southern Oregon to the northwest coast of British Columbia and from the Pacific Ocean east to Idaho. It was also a bastion of British interests in a huge territory known as the Oregon Country, a region that Britain and the United States had temporarily agreed to share when they could not agree where to draw the boundary between them. Yet because Fort Vancouver's extraordinary chief factor, Dr. John McLoughlin, was a man who was fair and firm, the people of the region were all treated the same way, whether they were British, Chinook, French-Canadian, Hawaiian or American.

For more than two decades, this even-handed approach kept peace in a rapidly changing territory and earned McLoughlin wide respect. Among the people of the Columbia River confederacy, he was called "the White-Headed Eagle" and for many Americans, who often arrived half-dead at the end of the 2,100-mile Oregon Trail, he was nothing short of a life-saver. But toward the end of his tenure in the mid-1840s, McLoughlin's egalitarianism brought censure from all sides. The Hudson's Bay Company, which employed him, believed he was damaging Britain's cause by assisting the settlers that were pouring into the area.

And the Americans, despite his generosity, saw him as a representative of British imperialism in a territory they believed was theirs by right. Tales of his terrible treatment of the coastal peoples and the company's virtual slavery of its employees grew in luridly imagined detail as they were told and retold back in the United States. The tribes of the Columbia River confederacy, watching their land being gobbled up by homesteaders and their forests emptied of wildlife by trappers, devastated by disease and a destruction of their cultural values, would soon turn against all Europeans in the region.

Initially, however, Fort Vancouver was a great success. The fort was established in 1825, when the Hudson's Bay Company decided for several reasons to move from Fort George (originally Astoria) at the mouth of the Columbia. The older post was on the south side of the river and Britain, hoping to extend its territory to the Columbia, needed a post on the north shore. Though Fort Vancouver was 100 miles farther upstream, and therefore more difficult to supply from the sea, the land surrounding it was level and fertile, very different than the heavily treed, steeply inclined area around Fort George.

McLoughlin chose the site himself, and his men immediately began clearing the land. Within 15 years, Fort Vancouver was surrounded by 2,500 acres of fenced gardens and fields, along with the first orchards on the West Coast. The fort,

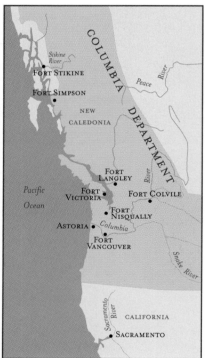

A long string of visitors passed through Dr. McLoughlin's large and comfortable home, from Chinook chiefs and rival traders to troublesome clergymen and the first of what would be a flood of settlers by the mid-1840s.

PETER ST. JOHN

which was almost completely self-sufficient, also kept cattle, horses, sheep and hogs.

The fort's physical presence grew as well; in addition to buildings found everywhere – the trade shop, kitchen and bakehouse, carpenter's shop and smithy – Fort Vancouver had a large and quite elegant factor's residence and huge warehouses. Because most of its supplies came by sea, it was obliged to store at least two years of trade goods, and serve as the main distribution centre for New Caledonia to the north (see page 228) and a series of smaller outposts. Just beyond the palisade a village grew up to house the more than 300 men and their families who worked at the fort.

McLoughlin's vision was that Fort Vancouver would headquarter a string of coastal posts as far north as Russian Alaska and as far south as modern San Francisco. He was well into his plan by

1841 when HBC Governor George Simpson, recently knighted, arrived. After a whirlwind tour, the governor ordered all but one of McLoughlin's coastal posts closed. Instead, he decreed that furs would be collected by the *Beaver*, the company's steamer, and ordered that a new company headquarters be constructed on Vancouver Island.

Furious, McLoughlin was marshalling arguments to present to the company's governing committee in London when the final blow came. Arriving in Stikine, on the far northwest coast, Simpson discovered that McLoughlin's 23-year-old son John, who had been left in charge of an unruly staff, had been murdered by his own men. Rather than conduct a thorough investigation, which might have made Simpson himself responsible for putting the young man in a dangerous position, the governor decided that young McLoughlin had precipitated his own death.

At Fort Vancouver, Dr. McLoughlin refused to accept the verdict. His final four years with the HBC were consumed in an attempt to discover the truth, clear his son's name and prove Simpson wrong.

Life at the fort was changing as well. Settlers were pouring into the Willamette Valley to the south and in 1846, Britain and the U.S. signed the treaty that divided the Oregon Country along the 49th parallel. The U.S. Army soon created a military outpost just north of the fort and the company finally closed its doors in 1860. Six years later Fort Vancouver burned to the ground and was quickly turned into fields used by the army.

Following archaeological work on the site, much of Fort Vancouver was re-created in the 1960s and '70s. Today, the fort looks much as it did in the mid-1830s, when it was the most important settlement on the Pacific northwest coast.

Fort Vancouver is located on the river in Vancouver, Washington, just east of Interstate 5. Turn east off I-5 at Mill Plain Boulevard and follow the signs to the excellent visitor centre on East Evergreen Boulevard.

Bald eagles, the symbol of the American republic, have wintered along the northwest coast for millennia. Their numbers were dramatically reduced during the mid-20th century as a result of pesticide use, but have rebounded in recent years.

The restoration of Fort Vancouver includes period gardens and an orchard, allowing visitors a glimpse of life here 180 years ago.

THE CANADIAN FATHER OF OREGON

Dr. John McLoughlin was a man who built bridges, but the Oregon Country of the early 19th century was a place where compromise often looked like concession. Unlike George Simpson, who was small in stature and prone to petty recriminations, McLoughlin was large in every way. A giant both physically and morally, he was given to great compassion as well as violent (though fortunately rare) oubursts.

Born in Rivière-du-Loup on Quebec's St. Lawrence River in 1784, he studied medicine in Montreal and on certification went to work as a physician for the North West Company at its new headquarters in Kaministiquia, later Fort William (see page 128). He enjoyed the life, but by the time the NWC amalgamated with the rival Hudson's Bay Company in 1821, he was tired of the aggressive competition.

After his first wife died giving birth, he married Margarite Wadin McKay, the daughter of Swiss trader Jean Etienne Wadin, an original Nor'Wester who was murdered in 1782. Margarite was the widow of Alexander McKay, a partner in John Jacob Astor's Pacific Fur Company, who was aboard Astor's *Tonquin* when it was attacked and sunk in 1811. Left with four young children, Margarite soon married the young doctor, producing four children of their own.

Despite orders to the contrary, "Dr. John" as many called him, rescued many groups of Oregon trekkers. Here, he greets Jason Lee, the leader of the first group of Methodist missionaries to reach the Columbia Department. Lee became a friend, but over time the missionary could not control his land-hungry followers.

CHARLES F. COMFORT / HUDSON'S BAY COMPANY ARCHIVES / P–405

Three of their children travelled with them to the Columbia in 1824. En route, they were overtaken by George Simpson, travelling with his hand-picked crew. Simpson made much of the fact that he had made up 20 days on McLoughlin, and of the doctor's rumpled appearance, but failed to mention that McLoughlin was travelling with young children.

On the Columbia, McLoughlin was named chief factor of Fort Vancouver, which he planned and built. He held the position until the boundary between the United States and Canada put the fort in American territory in 1846, then retired to Oregon City, where he died in 1857.

During the intervening 20 years, he put his stamp on the entire territory. He made Fort Vancouver a thriving, prosperous place that produced not only tons of furs, but grain, cattle, pigs and dried salmon. And he extended a compassionate hand to all who asked for help. Rival traders, starving settlers, the local Chinook and Klikitat people in distress, no one was turned away, though McLoughlin's assistance often contravened company policy.

But it was a tragedy involving McLoughlin's son and namesake, who was murdered at a company post in Russian Alaska, that completed the rift with the company. Simpson, arriving just days after the killing, decided the young man had precipitated it, though later investigations showed he was understaffed and blameless. McLoughlin was beside himself and took the case all the way to London. Several members of the Committee were sympathetic, but they stood behind their governor.

Fort Nisqually

Because of its personnel, location and timing, Fort Nisqually was a welcome contrast to many fur forts. In 1833, Archibald McDonald was sent from Fort Vancouver to build a post, named for the local Nisqually people, to take the Puget Sound fur trade from American sea traders. Constructed on a high bluff overlooking the Nisqually River Valley and the sound, it was the first European settlement in the region, which probably explains why it blew over in a gale during its first winter. Fortunately the Nisqually and other Puget Sound Salish people were friendly and helpful and a good trading relationship soon ensued.

In 1839, HBC Governor George Simpson created the Puget Sound Agriculture Company, a subsidiary aimed at encouraging farming north of the Columbia River. He also tried but failed to lure Red River families to Nisqually to work for the company and farm. In 1843, Dr. William Tolmie, whose son was later premier of British Columbia, was given charge of Fort Nisqually and instructed to expand it. He built a larger trading post about a mile inland, put

1,500 acres under cultivation and developed herds of 10,000 sheep and 6,000 cattle.

Bastions with cannon and swivel guns were installed at the new fort, but Dr. Tolmie's real interest was in expanding relations with the people of the region. Soon, he had established trade with the Yakima and

Klikitat of the Cascade region between the Fraser and Columbia Rivers and by 1849 as many as 250 fur-laden horses would arrive annually from Fort Colvile with huge quantities of furs to be cleaned, repacked and sent on to Fort Victoria.

Dr. Tolmie and his second-in-command Edward Huggins, a young immigrant from the HBC offices in London, were widely respected for their fair dealings. When in 1855 the coastal tribes responded with riots and attacks to the confiscation of their territory by land-hungry settlers and gold-hungry miners, the HBC post and supply lines were untouched. As had Dr. John McLoughlin at Fort Vancouver before them, Tolmie and Huggins also welcomed exhausted or starving survivors of the Oregon Trail, often feeding and clothing them at the fort.

In 1859, Huggins took charge of Nisqually, remaining there until its demise in 1869 and becoming an American citizen. Huggins then took over the old post and built up a farm of 1,000 acres. Puget Sound had been ceded to the U.S. under the Oregon Treaty of 1846, but a financial settlement between the U.S. and the HBC was not reached until 1869.

In 1933, local and federal work relief agencies moved the original granary and factor's house, with their typical squared timbers and mortised joints, to a park in Tacoma and embarked on a major restoration.

Today, the restored fort is located in Point Defiance Park in Tacoma, Washington, where it looks over Puget Sound, much as the 1833 original did. A monument marks the site of the inland fort near Du Pont, Washington.

MEL WOODS / COURTESY FORT NISQUALLY HISTORIC SITE

Interpretive guides pose near a reconstructed bastion, above, at the Fort Nisqually replica in Point Defiance Park in Tacoma. The reproduction is a faithful copy of the original, shown at left in an 1865 photograph.

DARMER PHOTO / COURTESY FORT NISQUALLY HISTORIC SITE / 288-95-5

Fort Langley

Like Fort Ellice on the Assiniboine (see page 210), Fort Langley was built for international political reasons. Since the 1700s, sea otter pelts had been harvested along the Pacific coast, but by 1821 the Hudson's Bay Company faced stiff American competition for furs in the whole Columbia District. So in 1824 Governor George Simpson decided to end American competition by initiating a policy of intensive trapping and underselling – a "scorched earth" policy in effect. To consolidate this trade a new post would have to be created at the mouth of the Fraser River.

James MacMillan was sent out from Fort George (Astoria) with 40 men to establish a fort on the Fraser River. Named for Thomas Langley, a member of the London Committee, the post was begun on the south bank of the Fraser near the mouth of the Salmon River on an 8,000-year-old site at the entrance to Sto':lõ territory, in 1827. It boasted two bastions with artillery and a wooden palisade for defence.

With the mouth of the Columbia River 500 kilometres south and the Kamloops depot 500 kilometres east, Fort Langley was an isolated spot from which to take on the Yankee fur pedlars. Nevertheless, between 1827 and 1833 it played a major role in the British offensive against American traders. At the same time, more than half the 3,000 beaver pelts collected in the district in 1831 were from the Fraser River establishment. Archibald McDonald, chief factor during this period, traded throughout the Fraser River and Puget Sound. After the region's furs were exhausted, Fort Langley became an important provisioning post. The Sto':lõ people caught and salted up to 2,000 barrels of salmon annually for local consumption and for export. The Sto':lõ also worked in the potato fields and transported goods by river.

In 1833, James Murray Yale became chief factor and the next year the fort's trade crested at 2,000 beaver skins, after which it declined. A new fort was built seven kilometres upstream in 1839. It immediately burned down but was quickly replaced by an establishment that soon boasted 15 buildings. Between 1845 and 1854, grain, beef, pork and salted salmon were produced annually in the growing metropolis.

The Fraser River had put paid to Governor Simpson's fervent hopes for a water route to the interior. An alternative developed after 1848, when a horse brigade trail was cut from Kamloops through the Cascade Mountains to Hope. Furs then came by boat to Fort Langley.

In 1858, 30,000 gold prospectors converged on the region and in November, Britain proclaimed British Columbia a Crown colony with James Douglas as its first governor. The restoration of Fort Langley began in 1955.

Fort Langley National Historic Park is 6.5 kilometres north of Langley, B.C., off the Trans-Canada Highway (No. 1).

PETER ST. JOHN

Shaded by huge trees on the south shore of the Fraser River, the cooperage or barrel-making shop was one of Fort Langley's key buildings in the 1830s and '40s. Barrels of salted salmon were shipped to markets as far away as the Sandwich Islands (Hawaii) and Australia. In the 1860s, the cooperage was turned into a sales shop as settlers and miners poured into the Fraser Valley.

234

Fort Victoria

PETER ST. JOHN

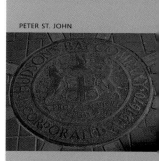

A fort with a strange beginning, Fort Victoria grew out of a longstanding argument between George Simpson, governor of the Hudson's Bay Company and the chief factor of Fort Vancouver, Dr. John McLoughlin. The disagreement lasted from the late 1820s to 1843, when Fort Victoria was finally constructed on a bay on the southern tip of Vancouver Island.

Simpson favored the use of steamboats along the northwest Pacific coast, while McLoughlin felt a string of forts on the coast was the only way to service the region. Simpson was convinced that the Americans would ultimately control a large area north of the Columbia, including Puget Sound. McLoughlin defended the Columbia route, pointing out that the Fraser River, which Simpson favored, was unnavigable into the interior, but Simpson argued that the sandbar at the mouth of the Columbia was a continual hazard to navigation. Both men visited London to make their cases.

Finally in 1841, Simpson pulled rank and the following year James Douglas was dispatched with 40 men from Fort Vancouver to establish a depot on the island. Needing a safe harbor, plenty of timber, land for tillage and a source of water, he chose a location on Camosack Harbor, or Camosun, as the local people called it. The post was initially called Fort Adelaide, then Fort Albert, before finally being named for the reigning monarch, Queen Victoria.

Construction began in June 1843. Douglas hired the local Songhees people to assist with the stockade, which measured 90 by 100 metres and ultimately enclosed eight buildings. The pallisade stretched from today's Wharf Street to the corner of Bastion and Government, now known as Bastion Square. Trading began immediately, and that summer 300 beaver and sea otters were obtained.

In 1846, the community at Fort Victoria expanded to absorb people from Fort Vancouver, which, following the Oregon Treaty, was in American territory. In 1849 Douglas too moved from Fort Vancouver to take charge at Victoria. Initially unhappy with the move, he found himself governor of the new crown colony of Vancouver Island just 18 months after arriving. Outside the walls of the fort, the community had grown to number several hundred people.

The post was enlarged in 1847, but the fur trade did not last long at Fort Victoria, for in 1858 gold was discovered in the British Columbia interior and thousands poured into the posts along the Fraser River, converging on the island as well. In 1862, the City of Victoria was incorporated and quickly became the supply centre for the coastal region and much of the interior.

The fort was demolished in 1864, to make way for the modern city that became the capital of British Columbia.

The construction of the HBC post at Fort Victoria, shown below in an 1848 painting, only briefly predated the settlement era. In just two decades, the harborfront land the post occupied was wanted for other uses. Today, visitors can trace the outlines of the fort and read the names of many of its employees on the brass plaques and brickwork of the surrounding streets. The story of the post can be found in the nearby Royal British Columbia Museum and Archives.

JOHN TURNSTALL HAVERFIELD / BRITISH COLUMBIA ARCHIVES / PDP-4464

The Lewis and Clark Trail

LINDA FAIRFIELD

*Reed grasses
(Calamagrostis spp.)
are tall, slender per-
ennials with jointed
stalks and long,
narrow leaves. There
are many species
worldwide and
all reach optimum
height in moist
areas and wetlands.*

*Imagine the emotions
at the first sight of
the mighty Columbia
River, pictured here
near Washington's
Maryhill State Park.*

Winding from the Mississippi River to the Pacific Ocean, the route taken by Meriwether Lewis and William Clark between 1803 and 1806 has become synonymous with American destiny and national sovereignty. Though the river routes and mountain passes taken by the expedition leaders and their Corps of Discovery had been trav-elled for millennia by many cultures, this epic journey at the behest of President Thomas Jefferson fired the imagination of the American people and opened the Rocky Mountain and western fur trades. These in turn ultimately spurred the settlement of the Oregon Territory and helped to establish the U.S.–Canada bor-der on the 49th parallel, rather than far-ther south along the Columbia River.

Even prior to 1803, Jefferson had apparently con-templated a west-ern expedition. As a member of the American Philosophical Society, he had been involved in at least three plans to send Americans to the Pacific coast between 1783 and 1800. His election as president, followed by the rather unexpected sale of the enormous Louisiana Territory, which effectively doubled the land at least nominally under American control, gave him both the means and new reasons for going ahead. It also seems that his

choice for the initial leader of the expe-dition was decided well in advance, perhaps as early as 1801. Early that year, as he was about to be inaugurated, Jefferson wrote to the 26-year-old Lewis, offering him a position as secretary-aide. In his letter, he made references to Lewis's knowledge of the "Western country", as well as his army training.

Less than two years later, on February 28th, 1803, as Congress appro-priated funds for the expedition, Lewis was commissioned as its leader. He in turn asked William Clark, his friend and former commanding officer, to be his co-leader. It turned out to be a part-nership made in heaven (see page 239).

In addition to geographic infor-mation, which was basically nonexistent as far as the territory between the head

JERRY KAUTZ

of the Missouri and the coast was con-cerned, Jefferson was interested in the resources and inhabi-tants of the territory. He asked the party to observe and collect, if possible, plant, ani-mal and mineral specimens, to record the weather, to give detailed information on the people they met, to map the permanent features of the route and to keep a daily journal. The co-captains were meticulous about doing this, often both writing in the journal and sometimes spelling one another off.

236

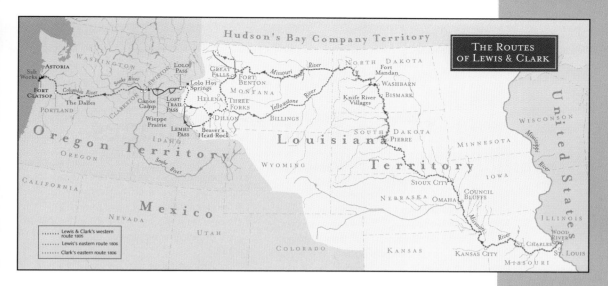

For Lewis, the expedition began in mid-1803, when he started collecting the various supplies that would be needed in Washington, Pittsburgh and Philadelphia. In a specially-built keelboat, with 11 men, he sailed from Pittsburgh down the Ohio River, collecting other recruits along the way. After meeting Clark and his black servant York at Clarksville, the party made camp at Wood River, on the east side of the Mississippi above St. Louis, opposite the mouth of the Missouri. They were there from December 12th, 1803, to May 14th, 1804. Though urbanization and river migration have destroyed the site of this camp, a model of the expedition's route can be found at the Lewis and Clark Center on Riverside Drive in nearby St. Charles. And the Confluence Greenway, a 40-mile trail, connects key sites along both rivers.

In May 1804, the expedition camped at St. Charles for five days before heading upstream on a trip that would last two years, four months and nine days. During the first season of travel, as the party traversed territory that was relatively well known, they discovered (as would many others after them until the invention of the steamboat) how arduous was the business of towing a keelboat against the powerful current of the Missouri. They also suffered the only death the entire expedition would experience when Sergeant Charles Floyd

suddenly became ill near present-day Sioux City, Iowa. Modern physicians, reading the journals, believe Floyd likely died of appendicitis. Today, an obelisk marks his grave and a welcome centre and small museum interpret the site.

Following the route the party took to its first remote wintering site is easy and enjoyable today. Between St. Charles and the site of Floyd's death are more than a dozen recognized sites on the Lewis and Clark National Historic Trail. All provide information and often add exhibits or interpretive programming that enhance the experience for modern travellers. A National Parks brochure is also available.

Having covered approximately 1,500 miles in 164 days, the party arrived at the Mandan-Hidatsa villages (see page 238), clustered around the Knife River near today's Washburn, N.D., north of Bismark. With autumn progressing rapidly, the co-captains decided this was the right place to winter and on November 3rd, the men began constructing a triangular post across the river from the Mandan villages. The choice was fortuitous, for it was here that a 16-year-old named Sakakawea (or Sacagawea or Sacajawea – the Shoshoni teenager's name was spelled more than 10 different ways in the journals and continues to be spelled in three ways in different parts of the U.S. today) joined their party.

William Clark gave Hat Rock its name in October 1805, as the Corps of Discovery travelled along the south side of the Columbia River just east of today's Umatilla, Oregon.

JERRY KAUTZ

The Knife River Villages

This beautiful Clovis point of Knife River flint was found on Manitoba's Western Escarpment, more than 250 miles north of the Knife River. At least 10,500 years old, it provides a good indication of how long humans have been mining and knapping this exceptional stone.

The earthlodge villages of the Hidatsa and Mandan people, who occupied the Knife River Valley in the centuries before Europeans arrived, were a clever response to a largely treeless plains environment.

At least 11,000 years ago, someone discovered that rough cobbles found along the Knife River and Spring Creek in western North Dakota could be fashioned into almost incomparable spearpoints. When the outer surface was chipped away, the cobbles revealed a centre of dark translucent brown that could be crafted into points sharper than today's surgical steel. It was a revolutionary discovery and it put the Knife River, which flows into the Missouri north of Bismark, at the heart of a vast trade network.

About 600 years before Europeans arrived on the upper Missouri River, the Awatixa, a band of the Hidatsa, created a village nearby. Accomplished agriculturalists who cultivated corn, beans, squash and sunflowers, they lived in large dome-shaped earthlodges, between 35 and 40 feet in diameter. (Mandan ceremonial lodges could be 70 feet across.) By 1525, they were living in what is now called Lower Hidatsa, a village on the lower Knife River.

Soon, other related peoples joined them along the tree-lined valley. The Hidatsa-proper, for example, created Big Hidatsa village about 1600. When Europeans arrived, it was a town of about 1,000 people, housed in 100 huge lodges. Lower and Big Hidatsa, as well as Sakakawea Village, are protected today by Knife River Indian Villages National Historic Site, which includes trails, exhibits, a full-scale reproduction of an earthlodge and an excellent interpretive centre. Elsewhere, most of the many earthlodge villages that once lined the Missouri have been drowned by the river's huge dams or plowed under by farming.

Among those that are gone is the Mandan village that stood near the mouth of the Heart River (in today's Mandan, North Dakota) when Pierre Gaultier de La Vérendrye and his French and Assiniboine delegation arrived in December 1738 (see page 204). More than half the town's residents were killed by smallpox in 1781 and 1782; the rest moved north to the Knife River near the modern town of Stanton, just south of the Hidatsa villages.

Beginning in the mid-1780s, Canadian fur traders established a provisions trade with both the Mandan and Hidatsa (see Fort des Epinettes on page 206), while the Arikara, Dakota and Omaha prevented St. Louis-based traders from ascending the Missouri. In 1794, the North West Company's René Jessaume built a post in the midst of the Knife River villages. He was still there in late 1804, when Meriwether Lewis and William Clark wintered there en route to the Pacific.

Another smallpox epidemic in the 1830s, Dakota raids and American settlement took a huge toll on the Hidatsa, Mandan and Arikara. The survivors moved north to create Like-A-Fishhook Village; today, they live on the Fort Berthold reservation around the western end of Lake Sakakawea.

Knife River Villages National Historic Site is one-half mile north of Stanton, N.D.

ALFRED JACOB MILLER / NATIONAL ARCHIVES OF CANADA / C–000408

PIONEERS OF AMERICAN DESTINY

It should not surprise that Meriwether Lewis and William Clark were friends before they undertook the epic journey that made both famous. It's more surprising, perhaps, that they were also friends after it.

They were young men of very different temperaments. Burdened by command, weighed down by expectation and facing countless unexpected challenges, one might expect disagreements, mistrust or jealousy to have colored their intense three-year collaboration. Yet there appears to have been not even a hint of dissent between the two. Their commitment to the enterprise and to each individual member of the expedition, their cool heads in crisis, their self-reliance and resourcefulness meshed to make them among the most successful adventure teams in North American history.

Yet the two were very different. Both were Virginians, but Clark, born on August 1, 1770, was four years older. Lewis was born on August 18, 1774, and as a child was a neighbor of Thomas Jefferson. In 1794, Lewis joined the militia and was attached to a sublegion commanded by Clark, then a lieutenant. During the years that followed the two became firm friends. When President Jefferson commissioned Lewis to command the Corps of Discovery in 1803, the young man wisely asked him to make the leadership role a dual one and offered it to Clark.

Perhaps even then Lewis knew his own limitations, for he was introverted and moody, with a tendency to depression that seems to have increased with age. Clark was the perfect foil – extroverted, even-tempered and gregarious. Together they struck exactly the right balance.

The journey was an incredible test of all their resources. They and their party, which totalled 31 men, one woman and an infant, ran into almost every eventuality one can imagine. Weather of all kinds, terrain of almost every description, encounters with many different peoples, threats from wild animals, mosquitoes and fleas, sickness and accidents were all part of the job. Somehow, they managed not only to face everything with equanimity, but they never forgot the all-important job of keeping the journal and brought everyone home safely and in good spirits. The only negative aspect of the whole operation was a deadly encounter that Lewis had on the return journey. For reasons that have never been well explained, it appears he killed two Piegan warriors before beating a hasty retreat.

Back in St. Louis in 1806, both men were given a hero's welcome. Lewis was made governor of Louisiana Territory and Clark was promoted to brigadier general and appointed superintendent of Indian Affairs. He also became a partner in Manuel Lisa's Missouri Fur Company. But Lewis's depression soon worsened and on October 11, 1809, just 35 years of age, he apparently committed suicide.

Clark lived a long and productive life, which he shared with two children whom he had come to love – Sakakawea's little son, Jean Baptiste Charbonneau, who was born at Fort Mandan in 1805 and who had travelled 8,000 miles with the expedition before he was two, and his younger sister, who lost her mother shortly after her birth.

William Clark, above left, came from a family of activists and American patriots. His older brother, George Rogers Clark, was a military leader who led many successful raids against the British during the American Revolution. Meriwether Lewis's introspective nature made him an excellent journalist; his entries at Fort Clatsop sparked an enduring interest in the American West.

Fort Mandan

The first incarnation of Fort Mandan was not really a fur trade post at all, though its creators opened the floodgates of the American fur trade. It was built by Meriwether Lewis and William Clark's Corps of Discovery in November 1804, on the east bank of the Missouri River seven miles south of the mouth of the Knife River. It was an unusual construction, with a triangular palisade enclosing a double row of cabins and two storerooms.

The Mandan village on the opposite bank gave the post its name, but the trading that winter was mainly done by Canadians. Officially, the Nor' Westers were trespassing, but in practical terms the land still belonged to the Mandan and though Lewis and Clark disapproved, the Mandan continued to trade north, as they had

Fort Mandan's unusual triangular shape was much quicker and easier to build than the usual rectangular post.

for nearly two decades.

Unable to speak Mandan, the co-captains hired Nor'Wester René Jusseaume as their interpreter. However, when one of his young colleagues asked to join the Corps of Discovery, Lewis and Clark refused, fearing that the information they uncovered on their journey west would be relayed to the Canadian fur traders. Instead, the pair hired Toussaint Charbonneau and his young Shoshoni wife, Sakakawea (see page 242).

The winter months were cold, likely colder than most of the party had ever experienced, but the snow and cold did force the men to gel as a unit and allowed them to plan the crucial next stage of the journey.

None of them had any real idea of the distance to be covered, or of the hazards that lay beyond the mountains, for beyond the upper Missouri, the western interior was a mystery to EuroAmericans. That the party succeeded in reaching the Pacific coast before the end of 1805 was a major achievement.

The return of the Corps of Discovery to St. Louis in 1806 resulted in the creation of the Missouri Fur Company led by

BOTH IMAGES: MARY ANNE NYLEN

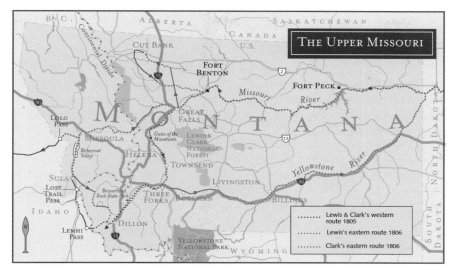

THE UPPER MISSOURI

..... Lewis & Clark's western route 1805
.... Lewis's eastern route 1806
.... Clark's eastern route 1806

Manuel Lisa, an ambitious Spanish-American. Initially interested in a Trans-Missouri – Santa Fe trade, by 1809 he had focused on the upper Missouri. His strategy was two-fold: trade with experienced trappers on the lower Missouri and send his own men into the hinterland of the upper reaches of the river. With this goal, he sent a huge force (350 men and 13 keelboats and mackinaws) up the Missouri and established a second Fort Mandan (a.k.a. Fort Lisa) a few miles above the Knife River. Though he established solid relations with the Hidatsa and Mandan, the War of 1812 and the vagaries of the fur markets kept the Missouri Fur Company on the edge of insolvency until Lisa died in 1820.

In 1821, the merger of the two huge Canadian fur companies under the Hudson's Bay Company banner led to the emigration of several key Nor' Westers, including Kenneth McKenzie and William Laidlaw. The two became partners in the Columbia Fur Company, which constructed a post on the Knife River in 1823. Despite Blackfoot and Arikara resistance that drove Astor's

American Fur Company from the upper Missouri, they maintained a presence there until they were bought out by Astor in 1827.

Four years later, McKenzie built another Mandan post on the west side of the Missouri below the Knife River and named it Fort Clark, after William Clark. It became the No. 3 post in the region, after Fort Union and Fort Pierre, though over time, buffalo robes replaced the beaver and other furs as the main trade items. Then, on June 19th, 1837, the steamboat *St. Peter's* landed at Fort Clark with the annual outfit, and a deadly cargo of smallpox. By the time the resulting epidemic had run its course, the Mandan and Hidatsa people had been devastated.

A replica of the Lewis and Clark fort is located on the north side of the Missouri, three miles west of Washburn, ND, about 10 miles downstream from the original. From US 83, turn south on Highway 200, then immediately west onto the county road to the Lewis and Clark Interpretive Center. Signs lead to Fort Mandan.

Mindful of their mission to obtain as much information as possible about the lands through which they travelled, the co-captains split up on occasion to cover more territory. Returning from the Pacific in 1806, they took separate routes through what is now western Montana. Lewis's divergence got him involved in the only hostilities the expedition experienced with any of the many cultures they encountered. In fact, it is unlikely that the undertaking would have been the success it was without the respeated generous assistance of native Americans.

A TRUE GUIDING LIGHT

For good reason, this remarkable young woman was recently chosen to adorn the American one-dollar coin. Though her short life was filled with hardship and unexpected challenges, she rose above adversity with courage, intelligence and perceptiveness to aid the success of the first American expedition to cross North America by land. She may even have been the first woman to vote in the United States.

Sakakawea was born about 1788 in what is now western Montana in a community of Lemhi Shoshoni people, who have lived along the continental divide for millennia. She was educated as a child in a wide range of essential skills, from food gathering, preserving and preparing, to the building of shelters and the manufacture of clothing. Like many Shoshoni girls of the time, she probably also learned to ride. Her people called her Sacajawea.

When she was 11, her family's camp was raided and she and several other girls were taken as hostages and carried off. At least one of the others escaped from their captors, but Sacajawea did not and was traded west, like a commodity, ending up in a Hidatsa village on the Missouri River. There, now known as Sakakawea or "Bird Woman", she apparently worked as a servant until a visiting French-Canadian trader by the name of Toussaint Charbonneau took her as his second wife the year she turned 16.

That year happened to be 1804. In late October, Lewis and Clark and the Corps of Discovery came to spend the winter. Within days, Charbonneau had offered his interpretive services – and hers, for she spoke Shoshoni – to the Americans. The offer made sense, so the two were hired and soon moved into the American post. Over the winter months, though Charbonneau dithered and fumed over this commitment, Lewis and Clark began to realize that his pregnant young wife was a completely different personality – calm, resolute and capable. It was an initial judgement that would be borne out again and again over the next two years.

On February 11, 1805, in the evening, Sakakawea gave birth to a son, whom the new parents called Jean Baptiste. Just two months later, the tiny boy, nestled in a cradleboard on his mother's back, would set off for the Pacific.

Throughout the journey, the Charbonneau family shared a tent with one or both co-captains; who had ample opportunity to see that, though her husband was sometimes temperamental and occasionally truly troublesome, Sakakawea was always cool and resourceful, particularly in difficult circumstances. The only occasion on which she showed unfettered emotion was when the expedition met her people – the Shoshoni – near the Continental Divide.

Both Lewis and Clark grew to admire her greatly and Clark became enormously fond of little Jean Baptiste, whom he called Pomp or Pompey. When the expedition ended, he asked whether he could adopt the boy. Sakakawea, likely aware that Charbonneau would not be a stable influence, agreed to consider the idea. In the end, Clark raised both Jean Baptiste and his little sister, who was born in 1812. Sakakawea, who had been ill following her son's birth, fell ill again after the birth of her daughter that year and died of what was described as "putrid fever", possibly a postpartum infection. She was perhaps 24.

JERRY KAUTZ

A statue of a radiant Sakakawea and her infant son adorns the state capital grounds in Bismark. It's one of several that honor this remarkable young woman.

The Upper Missouri

On April 7th, 1805, after a week of warmer weather, the Missouri was finally free of ice. The expedition – 33 people and Meriwether Lewis's dog, Seaman – embarked in two pirogues, canoes hollowed from tree trunks, and six regular canoes.

Almost immediately, the expedition experienced two things that would be with them throughout the journey: Sakakawea's remarkable ability to find food where none was apparent, and mosquitoes.

By April 20th, the canoes were close to today's Montana border and the captains reported an abundance of bison, elk, deer and antelope, as well as the first of many "whitebears" or grizzlies they were to encounter. Five days later, they made camp at the junction of the Yellowstone River, not far from where Fort Union (see page 252) would be built a quarter-century later. A small group was sent up the Yellowstone to investigate; the rest kept to the Missouri, as President Jefferson had ordered.

May began cold, snowy and often windy. Progress was slow and the pirogue carrying the co-captains and the Charbonneaus, as well as most of the technical equipment, nearly capsized one afternoon. Toussaint Charbonneau, unable to swim, was paralysed with fear, but as the boat filled with water, Sakakawea calmly went about catching the precious bundles as they floated away.

By mid-May, the weather turned. Today, this stretch between Fort Benton and Fort Peck, designated a "Wild and Scenic River" is one of the least changed sections of the Missouri.

A month later, on June 13th, Lewis rose at sunrise and, after hiking several miles, saw "the grandest sight I ever be-held", the Great Falls of the Missouri. Continuing upstream, he found a second, Crooked Falls, a third, today's Rainbow Falls, and a low, wide cascade, now called Coulter Falls.

There was a price for all that scenery, a gruelling month-long portage around the cascades; for much of this time, Sakakawea was ill, running a high fever. The cause of her illness is not known, but her little son was four months old. Four months after her daughter's birth in 1812, she died following a similar illness.

On July 15th, the expedition finally moved on, and a week later, Sakakawea saw landmarks she recognized. The three forks of the river, the land of her people, was just ahead. When Lewis announced this to the men, they broke into loud cheers. The mighty Missouri was almost behind them.

Though the Great Falls have been dammed, the original cascade can still be seen and the spectacle is impressive, particularly when viewed from the Ryan Dam Overlook. Rainbow Falls is much as it was, however Coulter Falls has been obliterated by Rainbow Dam. From the Visitor Information Center on 10th Avenue South in Great Falls, a paved river trail extends more than 10 miles along the river to the Crooked Falls overlook. En route it passes the Lewis and Clark Interpretive Center, where films, dioramas and interpretive programming help to bring the past alive. Nearby is Giant Springs, also called the world's shortest river, which pours 388 million gallons of water into the Missouri every 24 hours.

The scenic but troublesome Upper Missouri.

THE GREAT FALLS OF THE MISSOURI

Over the Continental Divide

Moving west at last beyond the Great Falls, the company began to realize just how formidable the Rocky Mountains really were. They were nothing like the "mountains" Lewis and Clark had known in Virginia. These peaks towered, snow-covered even in summer, to the west as the party travelled upriver to the headwaters of the Missouri, passing through a spectacular canyon that Lewis named the "Gates of the Mountains".

Heading southwest on a tributary, they passed the place where Sakakawea had been kidnapped five years before and, a little farther on, Beaver's Head Rock, where the Lemhi Shoshoni summered. This was familiar territory for the young mother and she was almost overcome on meeting her brother, Chief Cameahwait, and others of her people at a place Lewis called Camp Fortunate. As he had hoped, Lemhi Shoshoni were able to provide nearly 30 horses needed by the party to cross the mountains.

Led by a Shoshoni guide, the expedition then crossed the Continental Divide at Lemhi Pass, and headed north over 7,014-foot Lost Trail Pass into the Bitterroot Valley, which was Salish country.

Travelling north along the river, they were welcomed by a Salish leader, Three Eagles, and his village of 400. The journals record that the Salish were friendly and generous. Salish tradition describes the strangers as "pale, cold and poorly dressed", people to be pitied and treated with generosity. On September 11th, aware that winter was looming, the expedition continued west through Lolo Pass.

Travelling along a mountain trail both the Salish and Nez Perce had used for millennia, the former to visit their neighbors and the latter to reach buffalo country, the party experienced some of its worst privation of the entire journey. Though the region is lush and beautiful, with hot springs along the way, food was scarce. To make matters worse, their Shoshoni guide became confused by the many trails from the hot springs. Instead of staying on the main route, he led them on a detour that took them, almost faint with hunger, to the Lochsa River. Ill-equipped to fish, they were forced to kill a colt to stave off starvation.

Finally, on September 20th, they reached Wieppe Prairie and stumbled into a camp of Nez Perce from the nearby

Lolo Pass, right, provided a way through the Rockies, but looking west in mid-September made it clear to all that much more territory still lay ahead.

BOTH IMAGES: JERRY KAUTZ

Clearwater River. Though understandably anxious about this sudden appearance of strangers, the Nez Perce were convinced by two women to give them the benefit of the doubt. One was a Nez Perce elder who had long before prophesied the coming of white men; the other was Sakakawea. The fact that a woman and a baby were travelling with the expedition went a long way toward persuading everyone they met that the Corps of Discovery had peaceable intentions.

Armed with a map and guides, Lewis and Clark reached the Clearwater River six days later and began to build dugout canoes to carry them down to

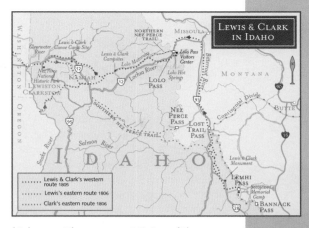

the coast via the Snake and Columbia Rivers. Watching the Americans trying to hollow the green logs with their axes, their hosts showed them a quicker method: first burn the log with pitch and dry grass, then hollow out the charred area with a specially shaped tool of obsidian, proven now to be sharper than surgical steel. On October 6th the canoes were finished and the following day the expedition set off, leaving the horses in the care of the Nez Perce until spring.

This is a circuitous and beautiful route through northern Idaho and western Montana. Well signed and littered with sites from this era, along with some from the Oregon Trail, it is worth the departure it requires from the main

highways. The canyon at Gates of the Mountains is easily accessed off I-15, just north of Helena, Montana. Beaverhead Rock State Park is located along Highway 41, about 14 miles north of Dillon; there is an interpretive sign just south of the rock. Lemhi Pass is on Back Country Byway, which crosses into Idaho. Even 200 years later, this is an often challenging, rough road, closed during the winter months. Interpretive signs tell the story of the expedition. From Lemhi Pass, take Highway 28 north to 93 or take 93 south from Missoula to Lost Trail Pass. North of the pass, 93 goes through the Bitterroot Valley, where the party camped just north of Sula and was treated so hospitably. At Lolo, interpretive signage at the junction of Highways 93 and 12 describe the place the expedition camped on the trip to the Pacific and their return. The unpaved Lolo Motorway (Forest Service Road 500) follows the original Lolo Trail up the ridge; Highway 12 parallels it. Lolo Hot Springs, now commercially operated, are just off No.12. There is a Visitor Center at Lolo Pass. Continue on No. 12 west along the Lochsa River. Near Kamiah, an interpretive sign indicates Long Camp, where the returning expedition was forced to lay over while awaiting spring in the mountains. The highway continues west past Canoe Camp and the Nez Perce National Historical Park Visitor Center in Spalding.

For nearly two weeks in the fall of 1805 the expedition camped here on the Clearwater River, at a place they dubbed "Canoe Camp", while five canoes were constructed for the journey down the Clearwater, Snake and Columbia Rivers.

The Corps of Discovery probably appreciated Lolo Hot Springs, near this distinctive outcropping, below, even more than bathers do today.

JERRY KAUTZ

The Columbia River

Though the Columbia River, below, has been so substantially altered by dams over much of its length (except for a short stretch near Hanford, Washington) that it might be more accurately described as a series of reservoirs, the surrounding countryside remains much as it was when Lewis and Clark passed this way. A host of interpretive signs and centres provide a wealth of information for those on the trail of this remarkable expedition.

After the difficult passage over the mountains, the first part of the journey to the sea must have seemed like a holiday. Travelling at last with the current, the Corps of Discovery sped down the Clearwater River to the Snake and down the Snake to the mighty Columbia. En route they passed landmarks still notable today, including Hat Rock.

Reaching the thundering cascade of Celilo Falls, now submerged beneath a reservoir, the party portaged and continued on down to The Dalles (see page 281). At The Narrows, they camped on the north side of the river, and visited a village of some 20 houses. Nearby, testament to the importance and antiquity of this meeting and fishing place, were many pictographs.

Soaked by a cold rain that fell almost every day, the party continued down the great river in late October and early November 1805. Historians believe they camped one night on the shore below what would later be one of the great posts of the fur trade, Fort Vancouver (see page 230).

Finally, on November 7th, Clark sighted the ocean and wrote in his journal, *"Ocean in view! Oh, the joy!"* The party was on the north (or Washington) side of the wide river

mouth and for the next two weeks travelled from place to place trying to find a suitable site for a winter encampment. Finally, the question was put to a vote; for undoubtedly the first time in U.S. history, both a black man and a woman voted with everyone else.

On November 27th, they crossed the river and 10 days later settled upon a site just west of today's Astoria, Oregon. Work began on the winter post on December 7th.

At the confluence of the Snake and Columbia Rivers, just west of Highway 12, is Sacajawea State Park, with her name spelled as Lewis and Clark usually did. Following Highways 12 and 730 on the Oregon side of the Columbia brings today's travellers to Hat Rock State Park, near Umatilla. I-84 continues west to Celilo Park, where the falls are now under water, and The Dalles. Here are a visitor centre, murals adorning the downtown and the nearby Columbia Gorge Discovery Center, which covers the whole history of the region. Across in Washington, petroglyph tours can be taken by appointment. A little farther west, on Highway 14 in Washington, there are Lewis and Clark exhibits, as well as a multi-media presentation on the history of the gorge at the Columbia Gorge Interpretive Center. Follow Highway 14 west to Fort Vancouver. From Vancouver, Washington take 1-5 to Longview, then Highways 4 and 401 to Cape Disappointment and Fort Canby State Park on the Pacific. To visit Fort Clatsop, the party's 1805 wintering site, cross the bridge toward Astoria and continue south on Highway 101, following the signs.

246

Fort Clatsop

For the Corps of Discovery, Fort Clatsop was likely remembered for the rain. During their stay of more than 100 days, from the first week of December 1805, when construction began at a site where elk were numerous, to the third week of March 1806, there were only a dozen days without rain and the sun shone on just eight. The result was depressing, to say the least.

On Christmas Day, despite everyone's best efforts, the menu featured rancid boiled elk, spoiled fish and roots, altogether a "bad" Christmas dinner, according to William Clark. Yet the men had roused their leaders with a volley of rifle fire and later sang and celebrated.

After all the tribulations of the enormous journey west, this was a cohesive, well-integrated unit. They cared about one another and looked out for everyone else's welfare. And the co-captains kept them busy, despite the rain.

Three days after Christmas, south of the fort on the seacoast near a village of Clatsop and Kilamox people, a second camp was built and for about six weeks a large fire was kept burning to render seawater for its precious salt. Generally three men were assigned here, though the numbers were sometimes larger. One can imagine, despite the rain and wind off the ocean, that tending the salt must have been a relatively sought-after duty, with a roaring fire that never went out.

The result, according to the journal, was "fine, strong & white" salt. When the party left in late March, they carried three bushels of salt with them.

In January, Clark spotted local people stripping blubber from the enormous carcass of a blue whale that had washed up on the beach. With 14 others, including Sakakawea, he hiked to the carcass to bargain for some blubber.

During their stay, the local people came almost daily to trade. Proving to be astute dealers, they quickly depleted the party's store of gifts and manufactured goods.

The co-captains sent men out to hunt almost daily, though not always with success, as Christmas dinner demonstrates. They took 131 elk and 20 deer, mainly during January and February when the animals moved down out of the hills. Still, along with the fleas, which infested clothing and bedding, the main complaint was boredom. Everyone counted the days until spring.

Finally, when the entire party was at its wits' end over the ceaseless rain, the day of departure drew near. On Sunday, March 23, 1806, the group headed upstream to begin the return journey. There would be trials and tribulations ahead, to be sure, but everyone made it home, including little Jean Baptiste, who was a toddler by the time the expedition reached the Knife River once again.

In addition to Fort Clatsop National Memorial, a small site in Seaside, Oregon, demonstrates how the men managed to make about three quarts of salt a day. Highway 101 leads to both sites. Farther south is Ecola State Park, where the whale was sighted. A 7.5-mile trail retraces the route Clark and the others took.

PETER ST. JOHN

Fort Clatsop National Memorial features an excellent reconstruction of the expedition's wintering post, above, as well as a living history program, visitor centre and gift shop.

The Missouri River Route

LINDA FAIRFIELD

Sagebrush (Artemisia tridentata) *is an aromatic shrub found on the southwestern plains. It has small gray-green leaves and tiny white flowers.*

As it does over much of its length, the Missouri River sprawls across the landscape near Fort Benton, Montana in a shallow, twisting braid.

The Missouri River fur trade, though initiated by the French, coincided with the fall of New France. Maxent Laclède and Company of New Orleans had been awarded the exclusive trade to a large area of the upper Mississippi in 1762. It was a great opportunity and, planning a large and costly expedition that would essentially create a centre for the fur trade, the company sent to France for supplies. It was not, therefore, until the summer of 1763 that Pierre Laclède Liguest, a partner in the company, was able to embark on the long journey upriver. When he and his party left New Orleans, news of the Treaty of Paris had not reached the city.

Progress by keelboat was notoriously slow and it was autumn by the time Laclède reached the junction of the Ohio River. There he discovered that the entire east shore of the Mississippi now belonged to the hated English. The rest of Louisiana, a vast territory that stretched from the Gulf Coast northwest to the Rockies (see map on page 38), had been ceded to Spain. Laclède therefore decided to locate his little community, St. Louis, on the west or Spanish side of the Mississippi, rather than the east shore. In its first year, it attracted nearly 500 French settlers who were loath to live under British rule.

Located on a high limestone bluff just below the junction of the Missouri and Mississippi, St. Louis quickly became the centre of the 19th-century American fur trade. Laclède and young Auguste Chouteau, the son of his common-law wife, traded on the lower Missouri for years, with Auguste's younger half-brother, Pierre. In their footsteps, Pierre's sons, Auguste and Pierre Jr., were involved in the trade for decades after Louisiana was sold to the United States.

Neither the French nor the Spanish had any real idea as to the extent of the territory included in the Louisiana Purchase of 1803, but President Thomas Jefferson was determined to find out, for he had grand plans for the young nation. Immediately, he sent Meriwether Lewis and William Clark and their Corps of Discovery up the Missouri River with instructions to reach the Pacific. Along the way, he told Lewis, the expedition was to take note of the fur-bearing animals, assess the attitudes of native North Americans to the fur trade and "determine the most direct and practicable water communication across the continent, for the purposes of commerce".

The latter two aims were completed less than satisfactorily; by causing the death of two members of the Blackfoot Confederacy (see page 185),

JERRY KAUTZ

ALFRED J. MILLER / NATIONAL ARCHIVES OF CANADA / C-000429

the Corps of Discovery initiated nearly three decades of Blackfoot hostility, and of course there was no practicable water communication across the continent. But the expedition's reports on the numbers and quality of fur-bearers greatly increased interest in the fur trade. A Spanish-American by the name of Manuel Lisa took the lead in 1807, the year after Lewis and Clark returned to St. Louis. Organizing an expedition of nearly 60 men, he ascended the Missouri and the Yellowstone Rivers to the confluence of the Bighorn. Trading over a large area, they accumulated a huge haul of furs and Lisa returned to St. Louis to form the first incarnation of the Missouri Fur Company, which served as the prototype of the upper Missouri trade until the mid-1820s, when John Jacob Astor's American Fur Company took control.

Lisa's vision was to trade with North Americans accustomed to the trade, particularly along the lower Missouri, but to hire EuroAmericans to trap the headwaters areas in the Rockies. This strategy angered the Blackfoot and others, but was employed a decade later in the Rocky Mountain fur trade. The War of 1812, the opposition of the Blackfoot and the problems of distance worked against the Missouri Fur Company until Lisa's death in 1820.

That same year, a group of powerful St. Louis merchants including Pierre Chouteau, Jr., initiated the French Fur Company and in 1822, William Ashley and Alexander Henry created the Rocky Mountain Fur Company. Shortly after, Astor, who dominated the trade at Michilimackinac (see page 111) extended his company's operations onto the Upper Missouri. Other companies also vied for the trade, but by the late 1820s, the American Fur Company controlled the upper Missouri and was rapidly buying out its competitors.

Astor sold his interests in the company in 1834. Pierre Chouteau purchased the Upper Missouri Outfit and continued to run a chain of huge posts. The most important were Fort Union (1828) at the confluence of the Yellowstone, Fort Pierre Chouteau (1832) near the confluence of the Teton River and Fort William (1834, later Fort Laramie) just south of the North Platte River. Trading for furs and later, buffalo robes, they continued to be active until the land was opened to settlement and the remaining herds of bison were exterminated.

Today, visitors can relive this turbulent time at excellent reconstructions at Fort Union and Fort Laramie, as well as Lewis and Clark's wintering post, Fort Mandan, near the Knife River Villages, north of Bismark, North Dakota. Nearby, the Knife River Villages National Historic Site (see page 238) features a fine interpretive centre that explains the long and fascinating history of the region.

To the west, the Museum of the Fur Trade (see page 270) in Chadron, Nebraska provides a superb overview of the entire fur era, and supports ongoing research. A small trading house, Bordeaux's Post, is located nearby. Two later posts in Montana – Fort Benton on the upper Missouri, and Fort Owen on the Bitterroot River at the western edge of the state – recreate life at the tail end of the trade.

When Europeans first arrived on the Missouri, they were captivated by the sight of mounted hunters in pursuit of the great herds of plains bison. The Plains people were magnificent horsemen, who often rode right into the herds to take their quarry.

The market for buffalo robes and bison by-products was increasingly important on the western plains during the 1830s. Between 1828 and 1834, an average of 25,000 buffalo robes were produced every year; by 1840 that had risen to 90,000 annually. Little wonder the great herds began to decline.

MARY ANNE NYLEN

The Hidatsa and Mandan people developed many strains of corn and beans, above, around their earthlodge villages along North Dakota's Knife River.

WORKHORSES OF THE AMERICAN TRADE

While the northern fur routes were being plied by lissome canoes and chunky York boats, until about 1830 the Missouri River fur trade relied on a much more stalwart workhorse – the keelboat. These craft, like the bull boats, mackinaws and dugout canoes also used along the southern trade routes, were fashioned for the conditions that faced them.

For most of its great length and for much of the year, the Missouri meanders over a wide flood plain, running broad and shallow across the Great Plains. But during the spring, from about mid-March to late June, melting at its mountain sources causes the river to rise and creates strong and unpredictable currents. Keelboats, with their shallow draft and unique methods of propulsion, suited the river's many personalities, though their progress was painfully slow. They made up for this torpid pace with an ability to carry huge loads.

Though largely human powered, these were not small boats. They averaged about 70 feet long, with a beam of about 16 feet and three or four feet of hold. True to its name, a keelboat had a keel running from bow to stern, while on deck most of the available space was taken up by a cargo box. Generally this space was filled with enough supplies and goods to last each fort on the river (and often its regional posts as well) for a year, but some keelboats were fitted out to take passengers and some served a combined function. Fully loaded, a keelboat could handle between 20 and 30 tons of goods.

This huge load was usually powered by oars, poles or a cordelle. When the wind was right – and it didn't happen often – the boats could also be sailed, giving the long-suffering crews a brief respite.

The cordelle – a long line attached to a central mast and pulled by men who walked the shores – was most frequently used. At other times, the boats were poled by men walking a narrow walkway down the sides of the boat, or rowed. Little wonder keelboats averaged less than 15 miles a day and took the entire season to reach the mouth of the Yellowstone River.

Manufactured at shipyards in Pittsburgh and Louisville, keelboats were not inexpensive vessels, averaging about $2,500 apiece. But unlike mackinaw boats, the flat-bottom craft that were hammered together at upstream posts to ride the June rise downstream to St. Louis (covering about 100 miles a day) where they were sold for firewood, keelboats were expected to last for years. Some did, but only a few, used on the very shallow upper reaches of the river, survived the coming of steamboats to the Missouri after 1831.

Agonizingly slow, but with a huge capacity, keelboats opened the Missouri River to the fur trade. They were used on all the main routes for more than a half-century, from the 1760s to the early 1830s, and even after they were replaced by steamboats, a few continued to be used on the upper Missouri and some of the river's shallower tributaries.

AMANDA DOW

Fort Pierre Chouteau

South Dakota's fur trade past goes back well beyond the first traders that struggled up the Missouri from St. Louis. Instead, it begins with the brief visit of Louis-Joseph La Vérendrye in 1743. Returning from an 18-month journey that conclusively proved there was no easy access to the Pacific, the young man buried a lead tablet on a hill overlooking the Missouri in what is now Fort Pierre (see the La Vérendryes on page 204).

Both Fort Pierre and the state capital, Pierre, across the river got their names from a post that was built nearly a century later. Constructed between 1832 and 1833 to replace the American Fur Company's Fort Tecumseh, which began washing into the river in the spring of 1831, Fort Pierre was enormous. Its palisades enclosed an area of more than 100,000 square feet and its accoutrements outdid even Fort Union at the mouth of the Yellowstone.

Located three miles upstream from the confluence of the Missouri and Teton Rivers on the right or west side of the Missouri, the huge fort was originally named Fort Pierre Chouteau, for Pierre Chouteau, Jr., manager of the AFC's Western Department. A year after its completion, Chouteau and his partner Bernard Pratte, Jr., purchased the American Fur Company's Missouri assets from John Jacob Astor. In 1837, Chouteau shifted his new company's headquarters from Fort Union to Fort Pierre, the centre of the Teton Lakota trade.

By the mid-1850s, the huge post was showing its age. With wood in very short supply, Chouteau and his son Charles debated about the wisdom of restoring it. Before they could make a decision, unrest among the Dakota convinced the American army to look for a place to garrison troops in the region. Seizing a golden opportunity, the Chouteaus sold Fort Pierre for $45,000 in April 1855, but the army also soon discovered the shortage of wood. Two years later, they dismantled the fort and rafted the lumber downstream to build Fort Randall.

In 1859, the Chouteaus constructed Fort Pierre II about a mile and a half north of its namesake, but it was abandoned in 1863. The precise location of both posts has been a mystery until recently. Now, thanks to a series of excavations in the late 1990s, archaeologists have a good idea where Fort Pierre was.

Interstate 14 goes through Pierre and the South Dakota Cultural Heritage Center at 900 Governors Drive is well worth a visit. Across the river, a plaque marking the site of Fort Pierre Chouteau is at the north edge of the Fort Pierre city limits, just east of Highway 1806 (to the Oahe Dam). On Verendrye Drive, atop Verendrye Mountain, a monument marks the place where Louis-Joseph de la Vérendrye buried his lead tablet. La Framboise Island, a natural area in the centre of the river, was used as a campsite by Lewis and Clark in 1804, when an initial meeting with the Teton Lakota went less smoothly than expected.

The large tipis of the Teton Lakota were often beautifully painted. These toured the United States with Buffalo Bill's Wild West Show.

Archaeologists have begun excavations at the site of Fort Pierre Chouteau, where a fur post that rivalled Fort Union once stood.

MARY ANNE NYLEN

251

Fort Union

Few places in North America demonstrate the international trade aspect of the fur business better than Fort Union, superbly resurrected as a national historic site on its original foundations at the junction of the Yellowstone and Missouri Rivers. Despite the efforts of both governments and companies, for much of its 300-year history the fur trade ranged across North America without regard to boundaries or allegiances. Fort Union's construction and early years, as well as its trading patterns demonstrate a predilection to free trade that predates the North American Free Trade Agreement by more than 150 years.

The fort was built in 1828 by the American Fur Company, founded and still headed at the time by German-born John Jacob Astor, who had become America's first millionaire. Construction was overseen by Kenneth McKenzie, a Scot who had been employed with the Montreal-based North West Company until it was absorbed in 1821 by its rival, the London-based Hudson's Bay Company. In the reorganization that followed, McKenzie and others (including William Laidlaw, later bourgeois of Fort Pierre) headed south. After forming a partnership for several years, they were bought out by the American Fur Company, which was rapidly expanding west.

By 1828, McKenzie was the senior partner in the AFC's Upper Missouri Outfit. Having been involved with the western trade in Canada, he knew that he would face stiff competition from the Hudson's Bay Company, which had been trading with the Assiniboine on the southern Canadian plains for decades (see South to the Plains on page 192). He was also aware that a wealth of furs could be found on the eastern slopes of the Rockies. His vision for Fort Union was to expand its authority far to the west, but American relations with the Blackfoot Confederacy, which reigned supreme along the Missouri headwaters, were nothing short of poisonous.

This bad blood had begun with the Lewis and Clark expedition; one of its members killed two Piegan, members of the Blackfoot Confederacy. The resulting animosity was aggravated by repeated attempts on the part of Americans to trap and build posts, without permission, on Blackfoot land. To make matters worse, Manuel Lisa's Missouri Fur Company had established trade relations with the Crow, traditional enemies of the Blackfoot.

Beginning in 1810, the Blackfoot retaliated, harrassing and killing intruders and for more than two decades, to venture into Blackfoot land was to court disaster, but McKenzie was determined to change all this. Among Fort Union's employees in the fall of 1830 was Jacques (sometimes called Jacob) Berger, who had worked for the Hudson's Bay Company on the South Saskatchewan River and spoke Blackfoot. Berger knew that diplomacy, not force, was needed to

Fort Union, below, at the confluence of the Yellowstone and Missouri Rivers, was a showpiece of the American Fur Company. The reconstructed residence of its bourgeois, above, shows the house after it was enlarged in the late 1830s to include expansive balconies and porches.

COURTESY FORT UNION
NATIONAL HISTORIC SITE

MARY ANNE NYLEN

convince the Blackfoot to trade and McKenzie agreed, sending him west with an invitation to trade at Fort Union.

With a handful of men, Berger set out in October, heading far upriver on horseback. As they reached the Marias River in central Montana, they were met by a party of Blackfoot warriors. Fortunately, they recognized Berger and invited the group back to their camp. Still, it was early December before Berger convinced the elders to allow a party to accompany him east (into enemy territory) to meet with McKenzie. In a manner reminiscent of the Dene who followed Thanadelthur to York Fort more than a century before (see page 56), 40 Blackfoot agreed to return with Berger to Fort Union.

The trip back was long and cold and the farther they went, the more ambivalent the Blackfoot were. At last, fearing a trap, they refused to go on. Desperate to keep them from deserting, Berger promised that if they did not reach the fort the following evening, they could have all his horses and his scalp. Reluctantly, they continued and in storybook fashion, just before dusk the next day they arrived at Fort Union.

Lavishing them with gifts and promises, McKenzie convinced them to allow him to establish a post in Blackfoot territory. The following summer, James Kipp took a crew upriver and built Fort

Piegan on the north side of the Missouri just above the Marias, not far from today's Fort Benton. (The post lasted just a year before being burned to the ground, but in that time it did an enormous trade in beaver.)

At Fort Union, meanwhile, McKenzie was trading with the Crow to the south and the Assiniboine to the north, building himself a substantial reputation and a fort to match. Having once served as bourgeois or master at Fort William, the palatial inland headquarters of the North West Company (see page 128), McKenzie knew the effect a "wilderness emporium" could have. His residence boasted eight glass windows, a novelty at the time; later, under his successors, it was enlarged to become one of the most imposing buildings in the west, with an upper-story balcony and a widow's walk. The fort was just as impressive, with stone bastions, a bell tower and, after a government embargo on liquor as a trade item came into effect in 1832, a distillery.

A parade of distinguished visitors – the artists George Catlin and Karl Bodmer and the naturalists Prince Maximilian of Wied and John James Audubon, among them – passed through the gate. Fort Union continued to do business into the 1860s, but was finally sold to the U.S. Army and dismantled in 1867.

Almost a century passed before archaeologists began to excavate the grassy mounds on the river, discovering a treasure trove beneath. Portions of the fort were reconstructed between 1985 and 1991 and today Fort Union Trading Post National Historic Site is open to the public year-round.

Fort Union is located 25 miles southwest of Williston, N.D., just north of the river and Highway 1804.

Fort Union traded not only for furs, but also for buffalo robes. Though the vast herds of plains bison are gone, these majestic animals can be seen, unfettered and in their natural surroundings, along the Little Missouri River, in Theodore Roosevelt National Park (South Unit), south of Fort Union.

PURVEYORS OF PROFIT AND LOSS

The Missouri, below, with its shallow, shifting channels, provided a constant challenge for riverboat pilots. In the decades after they were introduced in 1831, the boats were modified to improve their shallow draught and allow them to penetrate the river ever farther upstream. In 1860, a specially designed boat travelled the upper Missouri all the way to Fort Benton, making it the world's innermost port, more than 3,400 miles from the Gulf of Mexico.

Shortly after Fort Union was completed, Kenneth McKenzie began pressuring American Fur Company partners Pierre Chouteau and Ramsay Crooks to try steamboats on the upper Missouri. In 1831, the company purchased the 130-foot sidewheeler *Yellow Stone* and sent her up to Fort Pierre. The following year, she climbed the river to Fort Union. Both journeys were successful and steamboats were soon a regular feature of the Missouri fur trade.

In many ways they suited the river. They were flat-bottomed and drew less than four feet of water, with most of the boat's accoutrements – boilers, engines and cabins – above deck. They could haul a huge cargo compared to their keelboat predecessors; one ship could carry the outfit for an entire year and as many as 100 passengers. But they were demons to navigate in the Missouri's shifting, braided channels and gluttons for fuel. Within 15 years their constant demand for wood to fuel the engines had denuded the banks of the river and its tributaries well north of Fort Union. Each post kept men whose sole employment was cutting wood for the post fireplaces and the annual arrival of the steamboat from St. Louis.

While the *Yellow Stone* at least initially demonstrated the positive aspects of steamboating, the *Assiniboine*, purchased by the AFC in 1834 and sent up the Missouri above Fort Union, demonstrated its negative aspects. On its first trip, it was marooned by low water near the mouth of the Poplar River. Ever practical, McKenzie decided that since the boat was there for the year, the company might as well use it to trade with the Assiniboine and Plains Cree. He had his men build a wintering house,

JERRY KAUTZ

Fort Assiniboine, on the north bank near today's Poplar, Montana. In March, when the water began to rise, the boat floated from its prison, descended to Fort Union and picked up a large load of buffalo hides. Heading downstream, it was grounded again for a time and forced to wait again for the spring rise to catch up with it.

Finally free, it made good time down the river and at Fort Clark took on more buffalo robes and a large assortment of animal specimens that had been collected by Prince Maximilian, a German scientist who was touring the west. Then, just south of today's Bismark, ND, the fully loaded boat caught fire and burned, destroying between $60,000 and $80,000 of goods. It was a costly lesson. From then on, Pierre Chouteau chartered and insured the company's vessels.

But the 1837 journey of the *St. Peter's* was much more catastrophic, for in addition to its cargo it carried smallpox when it left St. Louis. Stopping at Fort Clark, it all but destroyed the Mandan, Hidatsa and visiting Arikara, and at Fort Union, it swept through the ranks of the Assiniboine and Cree and devastated the Blackfoot. Had the firm been willing to burn the boat and quarantine its passengers, the death toll – estimated at more than 17,000 – could have been much less.

Fort Benton

by Jerry Kautz

Following a succession of, for the most part, unsuccessful fur trading forts in the area, Fort Clay (now Fort Benton) was established on the north banks of the Upper Missouri River in 1846. The present site of Fort Benton was preferred over Fort Lewis, built in 1845 and located only a few miles upstream. It seems that when Alexander Culbertson (agent for the American Fur Trade Company) was establishing Fort Lewis for Pierre Chouteau, Jr., & Co. they neglected to take into consideration one of their major trading partners – the Blackfoot. The fort was located on the wrong side of the river, making it difficult for the Blackfoot to cross and conduct business.

So Fort Lewis was dismantled, floated down the river, reassembled and named Fort Clay. The relocation of the fort was not the only change during this time. Due to the vagaries of European fashion, the primary trade was in buffalo robes, replacing the tons of beaver pelts that had earlier been shipped back east.

Returning from a trip to Fort Laramie where Culbertson had seen adobe buildings, he became unhappy with his cottonwood log fort. He figured that adobe bricks made of Missouri River mud would provide much better protection from the area's extreme weather. So in the fall of 1848 the reconstruction of the fort using adobe bricks began. After completion of Major Culbertson's residence and one of the first large buildings, the post was rechristened Fort Benton during a Christmas Party in 1850 – in honor of Missouri Senator Thomas Hart Benton, a good friend of the American Fur Company.

It took until 1860, to complete the restructuring in adobe. The same year, specially designed steamboats made their way up the river to Fort Benton, which, in turn, became the head of navigation on the Missouri River, making it the world's innermost water port: 3,485 miles from the Gulf of Mexico. This opened up a whole new era in Benton's colorful history.

With the waning fur and robe trade came the discovery of gold in 1862. Steamboats readily moved thousands of tons of freight and people up and down the river. The fur trappers had already established routes throughout the region, making it easier for gold seekers and settlers to penetrate and lay claim to lands previously left to only the hardiest. Fort Benton became the hub of commerce and travel, opening up the western United States and southern Canada. Two major ground routes were established during the 1860s – a western route (Mullan Trail) connecting the Army's Fort Walla Walla in Washington State and the northern Whoop-up Trail to a fort of the same name that siphoned off Canada's wealth in exchange for whiskey. Of course, the

This replica of a keelboat, the Mandan, *created for the 1952 movie,* Big Sky, *is on display in Fort Benton.*

Perfectly colored to blend into the surrounding snowy plains, the pronghorn antelope (misnamed Antilocapridae, *the "antelope goat") is neither antelope nor goat. Rather it is the sole member of an ancient mammalian family and the only large North American mammal to have originated in this hemisphere and survived the coming of humans.*

Fort Benton, Montana's birthplace, sits in the sunshine along the Missouri River.

sudden influx of people combined with gold and whiskey proved to be less than a harmonious mixture. It doesn't require much of an imagination to figure out why a block in Fort Benton was dubbed the "Bloodiest Block in the West" when 12 of the 13 business were saloons, dance halls and brothels. Disputes erupted continuously with many ending in bloodshed. This, coupled with strained relations with the native tribes, saw most living in constant fear.

Going out of business in 1865, the American Fur Company sold the fort to the Northwest Fur Company, which allowed it to fall into disrepair. In 1869 the U.S. Army took over the fort intending to bring law and order to the area. With their efforts and the arrival of the Northwest Mounted Police in Canada (1874) this once wild area was tamed, allowing homesteaders and merchants to concentrate on the business at hand, eventually turning the area into the state's largest wheat producer, known as the "Golden Triangle". With the arrival of the railroad in 1883, river trade came to an abrupt halt, bringing an end to one of the most colorful periods in Montana's history.

The post was closed and the sun-dried adobe bricks were no match for the region's harsh climate. By the early 1900s all that remained of the original fort were the northeast bastion and a partial wall of the *engagés* quarters. During the ensuing years souvenir hunters pilfered countless artifacts, water and electrical lines were laid through the grounds, while sprinkler systems and even a paved roadway dissected the quadrangle that was once glorious Fort Benton.

Although early efforts did manage to save the oldest building in Montana – the original blockhouse – it wasn't until 1965 that the significant historical value was realized and Fort Benton was designated a National Historic Landmark. Where steamboats once lined up on the boat levee there is now an impressive interpretive walkway explaining Fort Benton's past. On one end of the levee an old firehouse is home to the information centre; at the other end and across the street is the museum and site of Fort Benton. Recently the local historical society undertook rebuilding the fort in its original location after extensive archaeological exploration, using the original blockhouse as a cornerstone.

Fort Benton is now a farming and ranching centre, but many of its grand old buildings have also been restored and once again beckon all to enter. Today, however, instead of walking into a saloon, dancehall or brothel, visitors are welcomed into stores and quaint tea houses offering antiques, collectibles, local handicrafts.

Fort Benton is located at the intersection of Montana Highways 87, 80 and 223. Old Fort Benton and the Museum of the Upper Missouri are situated at the east end of Front Street, which parallels the north bank of the Missouri River and the Boat Levee. The museum is open daily from late May to early September (an admission fee is charged). Fort Benton is open year-round.

Fort Owen

In the early days of the French fur trade (see page 24), trading posts were often built beside Catholic missions. This happened much less frequently in the American west, but with a small twist, that is how Fort Owen came about.

Established by Father Pierre Jean DeSmet, a widely travelled Catholic priest, Fort Owen was built in 1841 as a mission, sawmill and grist mill on the scenic Bitterroot River in today's Montana. Eight years later, John Owen, a sutler or licensed trader who peddled provisions to the army, came west to Fort Hall (in today's Idaho) with the U.S. Mounted Riflemen. At Fort Hall he met a Shoshoni woman named Nancy. In 1850 he resigned his army commission and travelled west with her to the Bitterroot Valley where he bought the mission, turning it into a trading post. For a time, Owen served as agent to the Flathead nation, but he had problems with government indifference and growing numbers of white squatters and was often forced to draw on his own funds to serve the people in his region. He finally resigned as agent in 1862.

Over the next decade, he served gold miners pouring into the territory, but competition and the death of his wife in 1868 proved too much for him.

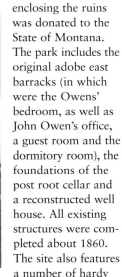

JERRY KAUTZ

He descended into alcoholism and in 1871 was diagnosed as suffering from dementia. Eventually, he was deported and, with a stalwart friend, returned to Philadelphia where he died in 1889.

The post was sold in 1872, but allowed to molder. In 1937 an acre enclosing the ruins was donated to the State of Montana. The park includes the original adobe east barracks (in which were the Owens' bedroom, as well as John Owen's office, a guest room and the dormitory room), the foundations of the post root cellar and a reconstructed well house. All existing structures were completed about 1860. The site also features a number of hardy plants and bushes cultivated by early settlers, including buffaloberry, currant and yellow rose bushes.

To reach Fort Owen State Park, take US 93 to the Stevensville Junction, then turn east on Highway 269 for just under a mile.

ALFRED J. MILLER / NATIONAL ARCHIVES OF CANADA / C–000406

The south entrance gate of Fort Owen, left, frames a panorama of mountains and high plains. Was it the view that drew John Owen and his Shoshoni wife Nancy here in 1850? She was a strong, capable woman, perhaps like the Shoshoni woman on horseback, above, captured by Alfred Miller a decade or so later. She kept the post, below, and her husband on a solid footing until her death in 1868.

JERRY KAUTZ

The Rocky Mountain Fur Trade

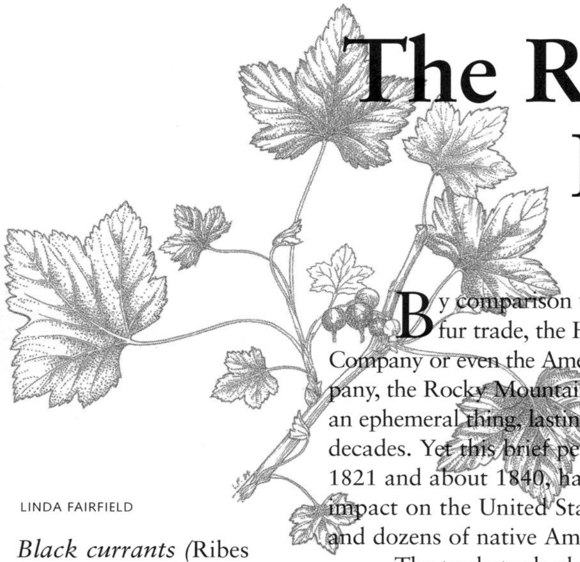

LINDA FAIRFIELD

Black currants (Ribes americanum) grow along the edges of aspen woodlands and in wooded ravines. Used worldwide for millennia, currants were eaten fresh, dried and stewed in many places and on the plains were added to dried buffalo meat to make pemmican.

The magnificent peaks, rushing rivers and deep forests of the Rockies, seen here near Alpine, Wyoming, produced a breed of "mountain men" that still exists today.

By comparison with the French fur trade, the Hudson's Bay Company or even the American Fur Company, the Rocky Mountain fur trade was an ephemeral thing, lasting less than two decades. Yet this brief period, between 1821 and about 1840, had a significant impact on the United States, Canada and dozens of native American cultures.

The trade took place largely in what are today the western states of Wyoming, Idaho, Utah and Colorado but its repurcussions were felt far beyond the region. By 1810, western North America was being claimed by competing European interests.

Spain had declared dominion over a huge area that stretched from the Pacific to the high plains and north almost to the Snake River. The U.S. and Britain were vying for control of the Oregon Territory, which stretched north from the Snake River well up into what is today British Columbia. And to the east, France had recently sold the vast Louisiana Territory to the U.S.

Much of this country was wild and rugged, with intersecting mountain ranges and great arid basins. In other words, it was a region of complex geology and difficult terrain that even today is relatively sparsely populated.

The Rocky Mountain trade had its earliest beginnings in myth and imagination. On their trip to the Pacific in 1804-06, Lewis and Clark (see page 236) had expounded on the incredible resources and diversity of the country (while conceding the difficulties of passage); the search for a western Utopia did the rest.

The first attempts to mine the wealth of furs began soon after the Corps of Discovery returned to St. Louis, but the parties of Manuel Lisa and Joshua Pilcher were rebuffed by the Blackfoot on the upper Missouri. Then the War of 1812 intervened. By the time the nation had recovered, a decade had passed and the Santa Fe trade had begun (see page 262). Checked again on the Missouri, this time by the Arikara who stopped William Ashley's large party, the traders began to look for other ways to reap the bounty of the mountains.

In 1824, Ashley sent Andrew Henry and the intrepid Jedediah Smith west, the former to establish a fort on the Bighorn River and the latter to scout possibilities in the central Rockies. But the fort did poorly, thanks to interventions by the Blackfoot, and by 1825 it became clear that the best way to harvest the region was to have no central base at all, nor to rely on native trappers, as most of

JERRY KAUTZ

the previous fur companies had, but rather to organize a series of independent American trapping parties that could be resupplied annually. They soon came to be known as the "mountain men."

The result was the first official rendezvous of the Rocky Mountain trapping system, in early July 1825, on Henry's Fork of the Green River. From that time until 1840, these rendezvous took place every year. In between, the trappers scouted almost every valley and mountain pass.

Over time, other companies evolved. Among the most successful, at least in the early years, was Smith, Jackson and Sublette, who managed to combine the talents most needed for the enterprise. Smith, as indicated earlier, was an adventurer, always, even to his death, searching for new horizons; David Jackson was the man on the spot, managing the teams of trappers during the winters in the mountains, and William Sublette, one of several brothers involved in the trade, was the supplier who travelled annually to St. Louis and back. Others, including the American Fur Company and Smith, Jackson and Sublette's successors, the Rocky Mountain Fur Company, controlled the trade after 1830.

The biggest returns were, not surprisingly, in the early years before the streams were trapped out and the competition became intense. Between 1838 and 1840, the rendezvous system collapsed and most of the trappers, who had numbered in the hundreds in the early 1830s, left the trapped out streams for Santa Fe, California and Oregon. Some, who liked the lifestyle, continued on. They and the era they championed are remembered in the Museum of the Mountain Man in Pinedale, Wyoming.

But perhaps the biggest contribution of the Rocky Mountain fur era

was not economic, but geographic. The mountain men used the routes that became the Oregon Trail (see page 268) and many of them were among the earliest American settlers in Oregon and California. They also established the American presence in both the Oregon Territory and the northern provinces of Mexico, and helped to create the boundaries the U.S. knows today.

The period was not all positive, however. The intensive trapping and the resulting wave of immigration destroyed the resource base, introduced disease and displaced many cultures, from the Pueblo and Mojave peoples of the south to the Blackfoot, Flathead and Chinook peoples of the north and west.

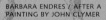

The archetypal mountain man — it's almost a contradiction in terms, since the trade drew men who were such rugged individualists.

THE QUINTESSENTIAL MOUNTAIN MAN

Jim Bridger was the quintessential mountain man. His life neatly bracketed the period of the Rocky Mountain fur trade and he was one of its finest hunters, guides and mountaineers, always seemingly able to adjust to new conditions.

Bridger was born in Virginia in 1804, but moved with his parents to Missouri when he was eight and apprenticed to a blacksmith at 13. In 1822, when he was 18, he joined Andrew Henry's expedition west. Over the next eight years, he wandered widely, reporting on valley trails and mountain passes, on well-stocked rivers and streams and on places no EuroAmerican had ever seen, among them Great Salt Lake, which he visited in 1824.

In 1830, he became one of the founding partners of the Rocky Mountain Fur Company and continued to lead expeditions in every direction. Less audacious, perhaps, than Jedediah Smith, or maybe just luckier, he was in a number of skirmishes and was seriously wounded, with an arrow in the back, in 1832. It remained there for almost three years until missionary Marcus Whitman removed it in 1835.

The year before, the Rocky Mountain Fur Company was absorbed by the larger American Fur Company. Bridger continued to work as a guide and hunter; in 1840 he was one of three men who served as guides for the last caravan to leave Missouri for the mountain rendezvous.

JERRY KAUTZ

BARBARA ENDRES

At the 1837 Rendezvous, Bridger donned a steel breastplate and plumed helmet, a gift from a wealthy Scots sportman, William Drummond Stewart.

The beautiful Flathead River, above right, was an area of fierce competition between the Rocky Mountain Fur Company and the HBC.

Approaching his 40th birthday, he embarked on a new career in 1843 as a trading post owner and manager with the creation of Fort Bridger. In December of that year, he wrote to Pierre Chouteau Jr., his former boss, with an order for supplies: "I have established a small fort with a blacksmith's shop and a supply of iron in the road of the emigrants on Black's Fork of Green River. They, in coming out, are generally well supplied with money, but by the time they get there are in want of all kinds of supplies. Horses, provisions, smith work etc., bring ready cash from them, and should I receive the goods hereby ordered will do a considerable business in that way with them."

This and the increasing guide work that he did for the army paid him well for more than two decades. In his 60s, he retired to a farm in Missouri, where he died in 1881.

Appropriately, Jim Bridger's name lives on in association with the Museum of the Mountain Man and the Sublette County Historical Society, in Pinedale, Wyoming. Both are dedicated to preserving the memory of this brief but crucial period of American history and encouraging scholarship about its many facets.

Museum of the Mountain Man

For a corps of dedicated fur trade enthusiasts, the era of the mountain men has never ended. On the second Saturday in July, every year, many of them can be found at the Green River Rendezvous Pageant – just as their predecessors Jim Bridger, William Sublette and Jedediah Smith could be found 175 years ago. The only difference is that the 21st- century rendezvous always take place in the same place – at the Museum of the Mountain Man in Pinedale, Wyoming – whereas their 19th-century equivalents moved from place to place every year.

In fact, six of the first 16 rendezvous were held on Horse Creek on the Green River, not far from Pinedale. Like those that followed, they drew American and native American trappers, as well as representatives of the fur companies laden with supplies for the coming season. As the year's haul of pelts was exchanged for provisions, things usually got rowdy.

One poetic description of the period goes this way: "The Rendezvous was the spillway for the flood accumulated by months of constant vigil and hardship. A time of relaxation, fun and frolic, of utter abandon."

JERRY KAUTZ

Today's rendezvous may be a little less abandoned, but they do echo the original in their buffalo feast, rodeo, and demontrations of mountain man prowess, held over several days at sites throughout the region. There's a fast-moving pageant with horses, mules, wagons and tipis, as well as more sedate pursuits including art shows, a street fair and exhibits at the museum.

During the rest of the year, the museum houses exhibits on the fur trade, native cultures of the region and early settlement history.

The Museum of the Mountain Man is open from 10 a.m. to 5 p.m. daily from May 1st to September 30th, and by special appointment during the winter months. The museum is located at the northeast edge of Pinedale on the road to Fremont Lake, which can be accessed from Pine Street in Pinedale or from Highway 191. Pinedale is about 120 miles south of Yellowstone National Park.

JERRY KAUTZ

The museum is dedicated to preserving the memorable exploits and enduring contributions of a rugged American breed.

Though not related to French sage (genus Salvia), the silvergreen sagebrush (Artemesia) of western North America, left, fills the air with the smell of sage.

The Santa Fe Trail

LINDA FAIRFIELD

Juniper, (Juniperus) with its aromatic berries and strong, sinewy wood, was used for a variety of purposes, from roof rafters in Pecos to curing meat in many places. And as they are elsewhere, the bluish-gray berrylike cones were used to flavor stews and other dishes.

Travelling along the Cimarron Cutoff through what is now northwestern Oklahoma and north-eastern New Mexico (right), the wagon trains were often desperate for water. It was here that Jedediah Smith (see page 258) was killed as he dug beneath the nearby Dry Cimarron River for water in 1831, the year that he and his partners had entered the Santa Fe Trade.

During the twilight of its colonial tenure in North America, Spain discouraged trade between the people of its northernmost Mexican province and the Americans in St. Louis to the east or the British and Americans in the contested Oregon Country to the northwest. New Mexico was ruled with an authoritarian hand by officials from church and state. Though the Red and Arkansas Rivers provided potential arteries to and from the Mississippi, there was very little traffic west of what is now the Texas border. For more than a half-century after 1763 the major supply lines all ran south to Mexico City. Only a few independent-spirited American entrepreneurs dared undertake expeditions to Santa Fe.

Then, in 1821, Mexico won a hard-fought independence from Spain and the doors opened to Americans, who were not shy about taking advantage of the new circumstances. Even as word of the change reached Mexico's far-off northern province, William Becknell, the first of a flood of traders happened to be on the road to Santa Fe. The path he carved, from Arrow Rock, Missouri, through Kansas and the Raton Pass to Santa Fe, is celebrated today as part of the Santa Fe Trail, with 20 certified sites open to the public.

In his footsteps Americans poured into New Mexico, though admittedly not in the numbers that subsequently took to the Oregon Trail. For the next 60 years, even after Texas was annexed by the United States in 1845, they rolled west, soon carving two trails into the territory. The southernmost, the Cimarron Cutoff that Becknell took a year later, in 1822, with a train of wagons, led down an old buffalo trail from the plains across the dry Cimarron Valley to the Pecos River, past the ancient town of Pecos and through the Glorieta Pass in the Sangre de Christo Mountains to Santa Fe.

The second, the Mountain Route, was to the north. It followed the Missouri and Arkansas Rivers, crossing the latter at an ancient fording place and angling southwest through the Sangre de Christos to join the lower route at Santa Clara Spring, near Wagon Mound. About 1830, Charles and William Bent and their partner Ceran St. Vrain built an adobe trading post on the north shore of the Arkansas River near the crossing place. Over time it came to be known as Bent's Fort (and eventually as Bent's Old Fort); in its heyday, it was the largest American-owned commercial

BARBARA HUCK

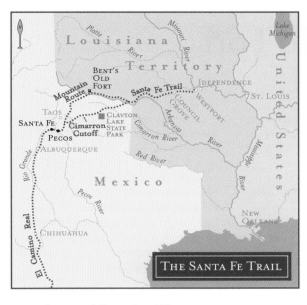

THE SANTA FE TRAIL

Christopher (or Kit) Carson, who arrived in Taos at the age of 17 in 1826. Carson had run away from an apprenticeship in Missouri and joined a wagon train heading west on the Santa Fe Trail. The life of a roving trapper-trader-interpreter struck his fancy, as did Taos. Though he travelled widely and ultimately had more careers than six average men, he never really left Taos. In 1845, he purchased a 20-year-old adobe house for his bride and lived there until he died in 1868. Today, both La Hacienda de los Martinez and the Kit Carson Home and Museum are open to visitors year round.

In the early years, furs made up a big part of the goods traded at all the posts. Like their northern counterparts who gathered annually at the Green River in Idaho, the New Mexican trappers were mountain men. Only their access was different. They entered the Rockies via an ancient trail through Raton Pass. That pass was too rough for wagons until 1866, when a mountain man and scout named Dick Wotton blasted a road through the pass and set up a toll gate. In 1879, the Topeka and Santa Fe Railway bought the toll from Wotton and opened the area to rapid settlement. Today, parts of Highway 64 from Raton to Taos follow the old trail.

centre between Missouri and Taos, New Mexico.

Of course, then as now, Taos played second fiddle to Santa Fe, which was the centre of New Mexico, politically, economically and socially. But Taos, perched at an elevation of 9,000 feet in the midst of the mountains, was an ancient place and a significant hub of the fur trade, even before Mexican independence.

In 1804, trader and rancher Severino Martin (later Martinez) built a "great house", La Hacienda de los Martinez, in the Spanish colonial tradition. Located at the northern terminus of El Camino Real, "the royal road" that connected New Mexico with Mexico City, the huge fortress-like building almost immediately came an important centre of trade. With massive adobe walls encircling two courtyards, the Hacienda has 21 rooms where Martin did his business and raised his large family. Mexican independence only broadened his horizons; after 1821 his home buzzed with Americans.

One of those was very likely

The bell tower of the Old Mission Church in Taos clearly shows its adobe construction.

New Mexico is well known for its magnificent archaeological and historical sites, but its paleontological treasures are less celebrated. One that should not be missed is the dinosaur trackway at Clayton Lake State Park. Here, along the spillway, are more than 500 petrified footprints, including those of a baby dinosaur.

Bent's Old Fort

In the beginning, of course, it wasn't old at all, but a bold and innovative commercial enterprise that was, for a time, the largest between the Missouri River and Taos, New Mexico.

Located on the north shore of the Arkansas River about 80 miles northeast of Taos, across from what was then the Mexican border, Bent's Fort was founded by Charles and William Bent and Ceran St. Vrain. The trio had hatched the idea of a trading post on a trip to Santa Fe in 1829 and soon began building the huge post. At first it was called William's Fort, because the younger of the two brothers was in charge there, while Charles and St. Vrain lived in Taos, the former directing the New Mexican trade and the latter running the company's stores.

Constructed of adobe in a huge parallelogram, the fort was almost completely self-contained. It included blacksmith and carpenter shops, kitchens and warehouses, trappers', hunters' and laborers' quarters, a large dining room, quarters for guests and even a billiard room. Inside, an ever-changing mix of American, Cheyenne, Arapaho, Mexican, French and English mingled in the quadrangle.

This was a much anticipated stop on the Santa Fe Trail and the fort did a booming business from the outset. As one of the few posts in the lower half of the Louisiana Territory, it was also an oasis and refuge on the high plains. One visitor compared the fort to a castle and certainly the walls lived up to that description. Six or seven feet thick at the base, they soared almost 18 feet high. Huge plank doors were located on the east wall and at the northwest and southeast corners were cylindrical bastions, complete with cannons.

Just upstream was a ford in the river; from here the Mountain Trail went southwest through Raton Pass to join the Cimarron Cutoff east of Pecos.

Charles Bent was named provisional governor of New Mexico in 1846, the same year the U.S. army took over the fort as a base for its invasion of New Mexico. That move disrupted regular business, anticipated a cholera epidemic, and ended the trade. When Charles was killed the following year, William sacked the post and moved 40 miles downriver to build Bent's New Fort.

Bent's Old Fort National Historic Site, beautifully recreated to reflect its heyday, is located eight miles east of La Junta, Colorado on Highway 194. It's open year round, with hours that change seasonally.

Throngs of people of all kinds passed through the gates of Bent's Fort during its heyday. They included scientists and adventurers, soldiers and mountain men, even white women like 18-year-old Susan Magoffin, who miscarried during her journey to Santa Fe and convalesced at the post. As she recuperated, she wrote in her journal that the post "fills my idea of an ancient castle".

BARBARA ENDRES

Pecos

This remarkable site was not, strictly speaking, a fur trade site, though it likely saw more trading during its long history than almost anywhere on the continent. Further, the Santa Fe Trail goes right by its south side and many traders on the trail camped nearby or even within its walls from 1821 until the coming of the railways in the 1870s. Even today, the deep furrowed ruts left by the great spoked wheels of the Conestoga or Pittsburgh wagons can be seen south of Pecos, filled with grass and flowers in the spring.

Established as a fortified mesa-top town as early as 1100, Pecos evolved from an earlier pithouse village near the river. Strategically located at the east end of Glorieta Pass, by 1500 the town had a population of at least 2,000 and boasted buildings five stories high.

The high-rise fortress community may have been in response to the arrival of Apaches on the neighboring plains. An Athapaskan-speaking people that had gradually moved south from northern Canada over the preceding centuries, the Apache were consummate plainsmen who, about 1525, apparently attempted to conquer the eastern pueblos. With Pecos at least, that strategy failed and soon the newcomers had decided on a "if you can't beat them, join them" strategy that lasted for more than two centuries.

Even before they became superb horsemen, the Apaches followed the herds of bison during the spring and summer and, laden with hides and pemmican to trade, sought the shelter of the mountain verges in the autumn. When the Spanish arrived on the scene about 1540, they reported that the Apaches were wintering under the "wings" of the pueblo. A century later the fall trade fairs included traders from all three nations. In the 1630s, Franciscan missonaries reported that hundreds of Apaches, with as many as 500 dogs loaded with meat and hides, were attending the fall fair.

This trade went on until about 1770, when attacks by mounted Shoshoni-speaking Comanches spelled their end. Whether the Comanches' targets were the Apache, the Pueblo people or the Spanish is not clear, but they were enough to convince the Spanish to take military action that finally climaxed in a peace treaty, signed at Pecos in 1786. From that time on, the Comanches too traded at Pecos.

Meanwhile, the population of the pueblo was declining. In 1730, it was about 530 as disease swept through the community again and again; waves of smallpox were recorded in 1738 and again 10 years later. In 1760, Pecos numbered only about 350 people.

By the time the first wagon train rumbled by in a haze of dust in 1822, the houses were still there, "well built and [showing] marks of comfort and refinement", according to one observer, but the end was near. The last residents left in 1838, and the village lay abandoned, except for curious traders, who typically camped at a spring about a half-mile southeast of the village.

There is more to the history of Pecos, including the story of its rescue. Today a National Historic Park, it is located 25 miles southeast of Santa Fe, off Interstate 25. The park, with a visitor centre and self-guided ruins trail, is open year-round.

A view of Pecos, with its church and mission buildings, as it might have appeared in the 18th century.

Santa Fe

New Mexico's capital is one of the three or four oldest European cities in the United States, but for more than 200 years after its founding, it was virtually closed to Americans. Established by the Spanish in 1609 to serve as the seat of government for the northernmost province of Spain's colonial empire, it sits on the Santa Fe River, which runs into the Rio Grande about 12 miles

BOTH IMAGES:
DENNIS FAST

Chilis, drying in the high mountain air, are seen everywhere in Santa Fe. New Mexico's beautiful capital, (right), has taken pains to maintain its unique mix of Pueblo and Spanish traditions.

west. New Mexico, of course, boasts much older cities, founded by the Anasazi and their descendents, the Pueblo people.

As it does today, Santa Fe served as the regional seat of government from the outset and one of the oldest buildings in the city is the Palace of the Governors, built in 1610. Trade in a variety of goods always played a major part of its economy, but for centuries, the fur trade was

almost entirely Spanish, with trails that ran south and west. Santa Fe was not only the main northern stop on the Camino Real from Mexico City, but formed the eastern end of the Old Spanish Trail to Los Angeles.

Beginning as early as 1739, when a small French expedition under the Mallet brothers travelled from the Mississippi to Santa Fe, periodic attempts were made to trade with the Spanish in New Mexico. Most such enterprises made one trip and never returned, usually because their goods were confiscated or they were marched back across the border of New Mexico by Spanish soldiers. One emissary, a French trader named Batiste Lalande, who arrived in Santa Fe about 1804 on behalf of the fur trading firm of Lisa, Morrison and Menard, chose to stay in New Mexico and apparently made Santa Fe his permanent home.

But until 1821, such forays were few and far between. And it appears that William Becknell (see page 262) was the first American trader to take wagonloads of trade goods into New Mexico a year later.

Others were not far behind. By 1824, Missouri traders were able to make the return journey in just over four months. That year, a party of 81 traders with 156 horses, 25 wagons and about $30,000 worth of merchandise set out from Franklin, Missouri, for Santa Fe. Arriving there on July 28th, they traded their goods and

turned for home. They were back in Franklin by September 24th, with $120,000 in gold and silver and $10,000 in furs. It was one of the most profitable ventures in the history of the Santa Fe trade.

The goods the American caravans carried included a great variety of things needed for everyday living, including dry goods, hardware, materials – especially domestic cotton – and many other manufactured items. On the return journey, the caravans were loaded with large quantities of minted gold and silver, as well as copper, which was mined in New Mexico, sometimes by Americans.

The total value of the trade rose as high as $450,000 per annum at its height and averaged $130,000 between 1822 and 1843.

In the early years, the traders met no particular opposition. By 1828, however, the plains people, particularly the Comanche and Cheyenne, could see that the wagon trains were disrupting their way of life and usurping their roles as trappers and traders. That year, three Americans were killed on the trail and the following season, the wagon trains began using armed escorts.

Despite this, the Santa Fe trade continued to be an enterprise of small businessmen. There were no large companies dominating this trade as there were in other parts of the continent. In part, this might have been because the trail was a remote, rugged one that crossed more than 700 miles of territory, most of it devoid of settlements and low on supplies of water. It appealed most, perhaps, to rugged individualists, the same characters who became mountain men.

Though not New Mexico's largest city – Albuquerque claims that honor – Santa Fe is its capital, a beautiful city that has been called the most successful blend of native, Spanish and Anglo cultures on the continent. Among its treasures are the Palace of the Governors, now a museum, and nearby Cristo Rey Church with its walls up to seven feet thick.

Santa Fe also boasts the Oldest House in the U.S.A., the lower walls of which date from the period of the

North and west of the capital, the Jemez Mountain Circle (Highway 4) is a must-see route for visitors. It leads to Bandelier National Monument in Firjoles Canyon, with its fascinating thousand-year-old cliff dwellings (left). Here, too, are the Valdes Caldera west of Los Alamos and the volcanic tuff, hot springs and "soda dam" along the Jemez River (below). All are remnants of New Mexico's volcanic past.

Analco Pueblo, about 1200. The rest of the house is about 400 years younger, having been built on the ancient foundations by the Spanish.

Exploring the Fur Trade Routes of North America

The Oregon Trail

LINDA FAIRFIELD

Throughout most of North America, golden-rod (Solidago), above, with its deep yellow flowers, signals that the height of summer has passed. For wagon trains on the Oregon Trail, it was a warning to hasten their pace, lest they be caught by snow in the western mountains. There are almost 100 species of this herb and most are native to North America. It may be that footsore emigrants used this herb as a soothing ointment, as Britons did in Tudor times.

The trail ruts can be seen in many places along the lengthy route, including here, at Flagstaff Hill in Oregon. As the travellers toiled up the hill, they caught their first glimpse of the Blue Mountains, and knew their journey was nearly at an end.

For almost 30 years, between 1841 and 1869, the Oregon Trail was synonymous with American desire, dreams of destiny and death. Lured by the promise of a new life, prompted by economic depression and unemployment east of the Mississippi River and provoked by fears that Britain would expand her North American empire to include what is now the Pacific Northwest, the first of an eventual 350,000 emigrants left Independence, Missouri, in 1841 to tackle the 2,170-mile journey to Oregon.

This initial group of 70 had little idea of what lay ahead. Some had been spurred by the glowing tales of Jason Lee, a Methodist missionary to Oregon who toured the eastern U.S. in 1838 promoting the idea of western settlement. Lee had travelled west in 1834 and established a mission in the Willamette Valley. Presbyterian missionaries Marcus and Narcissa Whitman and Henry and Eliza Spalding made the trip two years later, establishing missions farther east and proving, among other things, that white women could make the journey

west. All these early parties received substantial assistance from the trappers and fur traders who had preceded them.

The would-be trekkers who gathered in 1841 were another matter. Many of them underestimated the difficulties in store, and the group lacked a knowledgeable guide to take them across the plains and parched deserts, over the mountains and down the treacherous rivers. More than half soon abandoned the journey and only 30 actually reached Oregon, having been rescued and guided by fur trappers and missionaries.

This considerable lack of success did little to dampen enthusiasm, however, and in the spring of 1842 a hundred people under Dr. Elijah White set out from Independence led by a guide from Fort Hall (see page 277). Travelling a route used by John Jacob Astor's traders and trappers, they reached Oregon's Willamette Valley, proving that the apparently impossible could in fact be accomplished.

In 1843, the Great Migration - 900 men, women and children, 100 wagons and 700 oxen and cattle - encouraged thousands to follow.

JERRY KAUTZ

JERRY KAUTZ

Over the next five years, nearly 14,000 people completed the trek, but it was the conjunction of faith and fortune hunting that opened the floodgates of western emigration. Seeking religious freedom, Mormons began heading west in large numbers in 1847, veering southwest at Fort Bridger (Mile 1026) to what is now Utah. And in 1849 a tidal wave of more than 30,000 would-be gold miners headed west, mainly for California.

This wave of opportunists was accompanied by a wave of death, for cholera swept through St. Louis in 1849, killing more than 5,000, and quickly spread among the wagon trains on the trail. Strong men would develop a fever in the morning and be dead by nightfall.

Others died in droves of thirst or cold or the hundreds of dangers that lurked around every bend. In the end, at least 20,000 deaths were recorded on the trail, an average of 10 per mile. Most of the graves are unmarked.

Today's trekkers can explore many of the sites and much of the trail by automobile, for highways trace most of the route from the Missouri River to Oregon City. The trail corridor contains nearly 300 miles of discernible ruts and 125 historic sites. What follows are just some of the highlights.

On the Oregon Trail

The Oregon Trail crossed landscapes of almost every description, from grasslands to mountain passes and presented challenges ranging from a severe lack of water to thundering rivers to be crossed. Today, it winds through portions of six states; in most of those the ruts left by the great wagons can still be seen, while its history can be traced in a number of fine museums and interpretive centres.

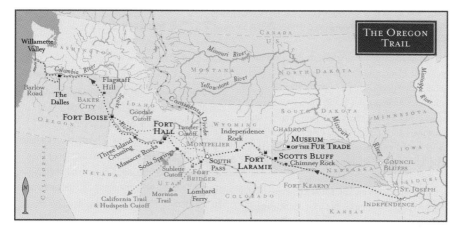

The Museum of the Fur Trade

With a remarkable collection of more than 6,000 fur trade artifacts, including one of the largest collections of trade guns in the world, an impressive record of research and a painstaking attention to detail, the Museum of the American Fur Trade in Chadron, Nebraska is a jewel.

Located on what were once the grounds of Bordeaux Trading Post, a small wintering house built on the bank of Bordeaux Creek in 1837, the museum was the inspiration of Charles Hanson. Growing up on a Nebraska farm during the Depression, Hanson found excitement and romance in tales of the American West. Those stories and associations led him to an interest in native North Americans and the fur trade. One of the books, *From Furs to Furrows*, had in it an outline for the establishment of a museum to celebrate the story of the American fur trade. Hanson was just the man to bring the idea to life.

In 1949, he was instrumental in incorporating an association to develop the museum, which opened in 1955. And for nearly a half-century, he devoted his time, energy, money and family to the project.

Housed in a Spanish colonial revival building that has been enlarged and extended over the years, the museum includes not only a huge variety of trade goods (including the oldest known "point" blanket [see page 143], dating to 1775) and furs, but also artwork and crafts of the Lakota, Mandan, Tlingit and other North American nations.

In addition, the museum is involved in propagating rare plants, including primitive Mandan tobacco, midget corn and early types of pumpkins, beans and squash obtained decades ago from the Hidatsa, Mandan, Dakota and Omaha. It publishes a scholarly quarterly magazine and has provided research funding to hundreds of individuals and publications.

Nearby, the Bordeaux Trading Post has been painstakingly reconstructed on its original foundation stones, which were unearthed in archaeological excavations in the mid-1950s. The interior has a remarkable authenticity, due in part to the recollections of two elderly sons of Joseph Bissonette, a contemporary of Bordeaux in the 1870s. The Bissonette brothers had visited the post many times and recalled details of its interior that would otherwise have been lost.

MARY ANNE NYLEN

Heritage seeds, such as Assiniboine Flint Corn, are among the many treasures that the Museum of the Fur Trade has managed to protect and preserve.

Located just north of the Oregon Trail, the museum provides a fascinating overview of the fur trade era.

MARY ANNE NYLEN

The Museum of the Fur Trade is located three miles east of Chadron on Highway 20. Just nine miles south of Chadron off Highway 385 is Chadron State Park, Nebraska's oldest, located on a beautiful pine ridge just south of the site of another fur post, built in 1841 by Louis Chartran. Widely respected by both the Dakota and his fur trade colleagues, Chartran gave his name (albeit slightly adapted over time) to the town, the park and a nearby creek.

Scotts Bluff

The Oregon Trail and its California counterpart were comprised of three distinct geographical sections, each occupying approximately a third of the total distance of about 2,100

WILLIAM HENRY JACKSON / COURTESY OF SCOTTS BLUFF NATIONAL MONUMENT

miles. Scotts Bluff, one of two remarkable geological formations in western Nebraska, was located at Mile 596, and signalled to weary travellers that the first third of their long journey was nearly complete.

Departing from Independence (Mile 0 on the trail), St. Joseph or Council Bluffs, the trekkers gathered at a site on the Platte River where in 1848 the U.S. Army established Fort Kearny, to provide protection for the wagon trains. From there, the first third of the trail followed the wide valleys of the Platte and North Platte Rivers.

The journey, which took between four and six months, typically began in early spring for no one wanted to be caught in the mountains when winter came. Spring also promised good grazing for the animals and waterholes not overly fouled. Though a mystery at the time, contaminated water proved to be the greatest hazard on the journey, for cholera lurked beneath the surface.

By the late 1840s, the Oregon Trail had developed its own etiquette, key to the survival of the greatest number of emigrants. The trekkers learned to agree on rules, to spread out in several columns and rotate positions daily to minimize the impact of the choking dust, and to travel every day but Sunday.

By the time they reached Chimney Rock, which rises 500 feet above the river at Mile 561, each had a good idea of whether or not they would make it. Here, and at the equally recognizable Scotts Bluff, which soars 800 feet above the river 35 miles west, were large campgrounds.

Both formations are isolated remnants of the Ogallala caprock that creates the High Plains section of the Great Plains.

Today, it's easy to imagine the encircled wagons at the base of the bluff. Contrary to popular belief, the wagons were generally circled to control and protect the trekkers' herds of animals, not for security reasons. Remnants of the trail can be seen in several places in the vicinity.

Today, this 3,000-acre national monument is marked by an excellent museum and interpretive centre that features both the human and natural history of the area. Interpretive panels mark the trails, a shuttle can take visitors to the summit and living history programs are shown daily during the summer and on weekends during the rest of the year. Scotts Bluff is located three miles west of Gering on Highway 92. The town of Scottsbluff is 10 miles northwest.

This painting by William Henry Jackson, left, not only captures the striking landscape of Scotts Bluff, but perfectly evokes the atmosphere of the trail, with its endless line of wagons and choking dust.

The High Plains extend southward from near the South Dakota-Nebraska border. They were created by Ogallala sediment which was deposited between 20 and 30 million years ago, as the young Rocky Mountains began to erode. Much later, the Platte River gnawed away this sediment, which had turned to rock, leaving the buttes of Scotts Bluff isolated from the High Plains farther west.

DAWN HUCK / AFTER GEOLOGIC SURVEY BULLETIN 1993

THE EMIGRANTS' GUIDE

Entrepreneurial publishers were quick to take advantage of the westward movement, producing a series of guidebooks and pamphlets for the trekkers. Some were almost evangelistic in tone and contributed to the "Oregon Fever", but others laid out sensible advice from those in the know. *The Emigrants' Guide to Oregon and California* by Lansford Hastings, the leader of the 1842 expedition, was published in Cincinnati in 1845 and included descriptions of the landscape and the travails encountered by parties headed for both territories.

Four years later, *The Emigrant's Guide to California*, published in St. Louis, recommended the following for a party of three heading west:

Five barrels (1,080 pounds) of flour
Six hundred pounds of bacon
One hundred fifty pounds of sugar
One hundred pounds of coffee
Seventy-five pounds of rice
Fifty pounds of lard
Fifty pounds of dried fruit
Fifty pounds of salt and pepper
Ten pounds of saleratus [or baking soda]
Five pounds of tea
Thirty pounds of lead
Three rifles
Three pairs of pistols
One tent
Forty-five pounds of bedding
Cooking utensils
Matches
Fifty pounds of candles and soap
Personal baggage

The supplies, it was reckoned, would weigh about 2,505 pounds and cost about $225. On top of that, a wagon (about $85) and team – either six mules (about $600) or eight oxen ($200) – were needed. Finally, a nest egg was necessary to get the newcomers through the first year at the other end. The total, generally at least $1,000, was a significant sum at the time and many families raised the necessary capital by selling their farms in the east.

Oregon or Bust! The cry was on the lips, in the hearts and painted on the wagons of hundreds of thousands of Americans for three crucial decades in the mid-19th century.

JERRY KAUTZ

272

Fort Laramie

Built as a fur post, this national historic site on the Laramie River had a number of identities. For starters, it went by three other names – Fort William, Fort Lucien and Fort John – until time, custom, and the U.S. Army intervened. It also served several functions.

The first post on the site – Fort William – was constructed in 1834 where the Rocky Mountain trappers' trail crossed the Laramie River. It was built of cottonwood by Edwin Patton and a dozen *engagés* for the St. Louis firm of Sublette and Campbell, which hoped not only to trade with the nearby Teton Lakota and northern Cheyenne, but to supply and outfit the Rocky Mountain trade. That didn't work out, however, and a year after the post was built William Sublette sold it to another small St. Louis concern, Fontenelle, Fitzpatrick and Co.

In accordance with the custom of briefly immortalizing the partners of these shifting fur companies, Fort William became Fort Lucien, for Lucien Fontenelle. But Fort Lucien was inaugurated at an inauspicious time, for fur prices were falling in Europe as fashion-conscious gentlemen turned to nutria and silk for their headwear (see page 23). In 1836, the post was sold yet again, this time to Pratte, Chouteau and Company, which had recently purchased the bulk of the American Fur Company assets from John Jacob Astor.

In 1841, the old wooden post was replaced with one of adobe construction, a few hundred yards upstream from the original. Adobe, an idea that had emigrated from New Mexico, made sense as this arid land had few trees. Chouteau named the new post Fort John, after one of his partners, John Sarpy.

The Rocky Mountain fur trade was largely a thing of the past by the early 1840s, but Fort John never lacked company, at least during the spring and summer months, for the old trappers' trail had become part of the 2,100-mile Oregon Trail from Missouri to the lower Columbia River. Every spring day hundreds, even thousands of covered wagons lumbered past the fort and every evening the surrounding area was dotted with dozens of fires, as the tired and dusty wagonners bedded down for the night. In total, more than 350,000 people crossed the continent on the trail between 1841 and 1870.

As the number of travellers on the trail grew, the need to assist and protect them grew as well and in 1849 the U.S. Government purchased Fort John for $4,000 and officially changed the name to what it had long been called colloquially – Fort Laramie.

The restored Fort Laramie is located three miles southwest of Fort Laramie, WY. Take Highway 26 to Highway 160 and follow the signs to Fort Laramie National Historic Site.

Fort Laramie, shown here in its earliest incarnation as Fort William, got its name from a French-Canadian trapper, Jacques Laramie, who had been killed along the headwaters of the Laramie River in 1821 by an Arapaho war party.

The bull boat, widely used on western rivers, was made of willow branches, over which was stretched a buffalo hide. Similar to the wicker coracle of early Britons, it was small and clumsy, but perfectly suited to the shallow tributaries of the Missouri.

Alternative Trails

On the shores of the Snake River, shown below, 10 emigrants were killed in a series of skirmishes with the Shoshoni in early August 1862. Soon the area, which included a section of the trail that passed through a narrow break in the rock, was being called the "gate of death" and "devil's gate", though the site of the actual violence took place to the east. Today, despite its name, Massacre Rocks State Park is celebrated more for Register Rock, where many travellers inscribed their names, as well as for the area's trail ruts and the site's rich geological history.

Many of the hundreds of thousands who embarked on the Oregon Trail took routes other than the main one, or were bound for destinations other than Oregon. These included those who for reasons of time or dwindling supplies opted for one or more of several shortcuts or "cutoffs", as well as the Mormons headed for Utah, and those bound for the gold fields and fertile valleys of California, particularly after 1848 (see map on page 269).

Sublette Cutoff is named for William Sublette, a partner in the Rocky Mountain fur trade company Smith, Jackson and Sublette. One of the best-known of the mountain men, who carved out a lucrative fur business in the 1820s and 1830s in Wyoming, Idaho and Utah, Sublette travelled regularly between St. Louis and the mountains. The route he used, by way of South Pass and the Platte River became the eastern segment of the Oregon Trail. But Sublette's name is given to a shorter route west of South Pass that crosses the dry interior of western Wyoming and the Green River. This was the heart of the territory of the mountain men and the general region of their annual rendezvous (see page 258).

Those who chose Sublette's Cutoff could save 85 miles and a week of travel, but the route was rugged and arid, including a stretch of nearly 50 miles with no water and little grass.

To the north, between South Pass and Fort Hall, was the Lander Cutoff, which was usable after F.W. Lander's road builders improved the grade in the 1850s. The road crossed the beautiful Wind River Range just south of today's Pinedale, Wyoming, the site of the Museum of the Mountain Man (see page 261).

Goodale Cutoff, also known as Jeffrey's Cutoff, went northwest of Fort Hall. Initially travelled by Donald McKenzie's fur trade party in 1820, it came into use for wagons in 1852. That year the Shoshoni began to react to the destruction of their land and the deaths of some of their people, creating fear among emigrants travelling the main southern route.

Timothy Goodale brought a large party this way in 1862, after which it was named for him. Idaho Highways 20 and 93 follow much of this route; where the trail skirted the remarkable lava fields of what is now the northwest corner of Craters of the Moon National Monument, the wagons were sometimes damaged, leaving broken parts in their wake.

Another departure from the main Oregon Trail was the Barlow Road, which opened in 1846 after Sam Barlow constructed a rugged toll road to the Willamette Valley around the southern flanks of Mount Hood. This gave emigrants an alternative to the dangerous, often deadly Columbia River for the last leg of their journey.

JERRY KAUTZ

Over the Great Divide

After weeks of following the broad, silty Platte and North Platte Rivers, the emigrants sighted a huge, gray-white mound of rock in what is now central Wyoming.

Turning west again, they followed the Sweetwater River, crossing and recrossing it a total of six times, before leaving it behind as they headed

WILLIAM HENRY ARMSTRONG / DENVER PUBLIC LIBRARY / WESTERN HISTORY DEPARTMENT / F-34321

Many described it as "looking like a great beached whale", but the sight was greeted with celebration for as summer began in earnest, the rock marked their first encounter with the cool, clear waters of the mountains. One such celebration took place on the 4th of July and earned the landmark the enduring name of Independence Rock.

As they had at Register Cliff, many emigrants carved their names into the face of the rock and most stopped to rest and water their animals for a time. Though more than half the distance to Oregon lay ahead, there was a pervasive feeling that Independence Rock marked the mid-point of the journey.

for South Pass and the Pacific watershed. At 7,550 feet, South Pass marks the Continental Divide and was the highest point on the Oregon, Mormon, California and Pony Express Trails, but for the travellers, the climb to the summit was almost imperceptible.

Cloaked in grasslands, watered by the Sweetwater River to the east and Pacific Springs to the west, this gentle approach to the Wind River Mountains had been the main passage between east and west for millennia. For the heavily-laden wagon trains headed west after 1840, the pass made the journey possible.

Now the main trail headed southwest to Fort Bridger, crossing

Independence Rock: the huge mound of granite at Mile 815 heartened the weary travellers. Just ahead were the Granite Mountains and, not far to the west, the Rockies.

The Lombard Ferry

Twenty-six miles southwest of Farson on Highway 28, a ferry crossed the Green River between 1852 and the early 20th century. The river was some 300 feet wide and Oregon Trail traffic was usually heavy during the summer and fall. The ferry helped to alleviate some of the difficulties in crossing the river. Nevertheless, historians estimate there was an average of a drowning a day at the crossing during peak periods.

the ill-fated Donner Party in 1846, the Mormons turned west and south across the Bear River, bound for the region around Great Salt Lake.

Others, bent on California, followed the Bear River north, then took the Hudspeth Cutoff from Soda Springs southwest across what are now southern Idaho and Nevada.

In Montpelier, Idaho, the Oregon/California Trail Center allows visitors to relive the history of these epic treks with living history and hands-on educational experiences.

Independence Rock, now a rest area with signage, is 55 miles southwest of Casper on Highway 220. To the west, South Pass is largely unchanged. Stone monuments mark both the pass and the crossing of the first white women, Narcissa Whitman and Eliza Spalding. From Highway 28, take the dirt road south from the summit of the first hill west of the Sweetwater Bridge. Watch for historic markers and trail ruts in 2.8 miles. Four miles southwest of the bridge on No. 28 is an interpretive site with a panoramic view of Pacific Springs, South Pass and the Oregon Buttes. The National Oregon/California Trail Center is located in Montpelier, at the junction of Highways 89 and 30. North on No. 30, following the Bear River, is Soda Springs, now the world's only captive geyser and once an oasis on the Oregon Trail.

Soda Springs, above, and Lava Hot Springs, both located southeast of Fort Hall in Idaho, are indicators of the region's complex geology. Soda Springs was sometimes called "Beer Springs" by Oregon trekkers because one spring had water that tasted "like lager beer ... only flat"; another, called Steamboat Springs, sounded like a high-pressure steam engine. Nearby Lava Hot Springs was a favored wintering site for centuries before the emigrants arrived; the endless hot water not only provided superb winter bathing and hot water for cooking, it was also perfect for processing hides.

the Little Sandy, Big Sandy and Green Rivers en route. Since the 1820s, this area of southwestern Wyoming had been the territory of the mountain men, an independent breed of American trappers and traders that defied the established conventions of the fur trade.

Ahead lay Fort Bridger, established in 1843 by mountain men Louis Vasquez and Jim Bridger (see page 260), who saw an opportunity in the growing tide of travellers. Located at Mile 1026, it quickly became a major supply point on the trail and, after 1847, the departure point for Mormons heading southwest for Utah.

Following a route pioneered by

Fort Hall

The story of this establishment, which was by turns an American supply post, a Hudson's Bay Company trading post, a provisioning stop on the Oregon Trail and a way station on a regional stage coach road, is a microcosm of the story of the American West between 1830 and 1870. It was a turbulent time, a period of just four decades in which the timeless rhythm of the western half of the continent was forever transformed. Land that for thousands of years had belonged to the Shoshoni and Bannock people was suddenly invaded in the early 1830s by fur-hungry EuroAmerican trappers and traders. In their wake came hundreds of thousands of American settlers. Idaho, like all the western states, would never be the same again.

The fort's founder, Nathaniel Wyeth, didn't set out to build a fur trade post. Instead, he had a contract with the Rocky Mountain Fur Company to bring $3,000 worth of trade goods to the 1834 Green River Rendezvous, to be held that year just west of the Green River in Wyoming.

It was a commitment he took seriously. To obtain the supplies, between August 1833 and April 1834, he travelled to Boston, New York, Philadelphia and Baltimore, then returned to St. Louis to marshall the party that would transport the goods. They included his two partners, Methodist minister Jason Lee, who would later make the trek across the mountains to Fort Vancouver, four of Lee's companions, two naturalists and 75 men with 250 horses to haul the supplies.

Despite his best efforts, however, his large supply train was passed by a smaller one directed by William Sublette, a partner in a rival fur company. And by the time Wyeth's supply train arrived at the rendezvous site in mid-June, Thomas Fitzpatrick of the Rocky Mountain Fur Company had decided not to accept Wyeth's goods, paying a penalty instead. Wyeth wrote, "I think he has been bribed to sacrifice my interests by better offers ..."

Angry and dismayed at the turn of events, Wyeth headed north and west with his men and goods, reaching The Bottoms, a sheltered bend of the Snake River that had been a favored gathering place for millennia, in mid-July. There, he began construction on a trading post, which he named Fort Hall, after Henry Hall, the most senior member of the New England Trading Company, which had financed his enterprise.

With Jason Lee and others, Wyeth continued on to Oregon in early August, leaving a contingent of men at Fort Hall to organize the business and encourage trapping and trading. However, among those who visited as the post was being built had been Thomas McKay of the Hudson's Bay Company. Displeased

This replica of Fort Hall owes it existence to the efforts of many determined history buffs over a period of almost seven decades.

Glenn's Ferry at Three Island Crossing

THREE ISLAND CROSSING

Buffalo & Longhorn Pasture

Indian Hole Pond

VISITOR INFORMATION CENTER

Interpretive Area

Picnic Area

Group Shelter

Snake River

Madison Ave extension

To I-84 exit 120

Overlook

(follow Slick Ranch Road, accessed from bridge west of Three Islands Crossing)

Three Island Crossing

West of Fort Hall, Mile 1398 marked the best place to cross from the south side of the Snake River. Here, the difficult crossing could be made via a series of islands to a shorter, well-watered route on the north side. Many emigrants had help from Shoshoni guides. In later years a ferry, for which the nearby town of Glenns Ferry is named, made the crossing safer for those who could afford it. Today, a state park features trail ruts, artifacts, a reenactment of the crossing, an interpretive centre and a full-service campground. The park is just south of I-84 at the Glenns Ferry exit.

278

with the idea of a permanent American post and intent on driving him out of the disputed territory, McKay was soon building upstream at the junction of the Boise and Snake Rivers.

Backed by the huge resources of the London-based company, McKay was able to undersell Wyeth, who soon found his business unprofitable. In 1837, he sold out at a reported loss of about $30,000. The post continued to be operated by the HBC for almost a decade, until the Oregon Treaty of 1846 gave the southern half of the Oregon Territory, to the 49th parallel, to the U.S. Fort Hall played a role in that, too.

Beginning in 1843 with the Great Migration to the Willamette Valley, Americans were pouring into the Oregon Territory. That year, missionary Marcus Whitman led a train of about 100 wagons and nearly 900 emigrants with hundreds of head of livestock over what would soon be the Oregon Trail. En route, they stopped at Fort Hall. The trader in charge, Richard Grant, tried to pursuade the emigrants to leave their wagons at the fort, but failed.

The travellers continued on their way. Weeks later, the arrival of so many with their "mobile homes" at The Dalles of the Columbia River (see page 281) went a long way to establishing

JERRY KAUTZ

the American claim to at least part of the Oregon Country.

For the next six years, people poured past Fort Hall en route to Oregon, Utah and the gold fields of California. That traffic lessened substantially after 1849, with the creation of the Hudspeth Cutoff, which diverted the Utah and California traffic south of the fort.

The tide of newcomers caused great concern and increasing hostility among the original people of the territory and in the mid-1850s, the HBC withdrew from the region, leaving the fort to be used for the next decade by independent trappers and traders.

In 1864, much of Fort Hall was dismantled to provide timbers for the construction of a stage station a short distance southeast, which was also named Fort Hall. That name was also given to a reserve that was established in 1868 for the Shoshoni, Bannock and Lemhi tribes of the region. And Fort Hall is the name of the town in which the reserve offices are located.

Today, a replica of the fort as it was during its Hudson's Bay Company years can be found in southern Pocatello, just west of Interstate 15 on the upper level of Ross Park. Take Exit 67 to 5th Avenue and turn north toward the city. Then turn left onto 4th Street and left again onto Terrill Ifft Park. Turn right on the first paved road on the right and follow it to the top of Lava Cliffs, then go right about 200 yards. The Fort Hall replica, maintained by the city, is open from 10 a.m. to 2 p.m. Tuesday through Saturday between mid-April and Memorial Day and between Labor Day and the end of September. During the summer the fort is open from 10 a.m. to 6 p.m. daily. The original site is located at the east end of the American Falls reservoir north of Pocatello.

Old Fort Boise

Early in Idaho's fur trade era, several attempts were made to build a trading post near the confluence of the Boise and Snake Rivers on what is now the boundary between Canada at the Columbia River.

In 1834, Thomas McKay established a post for the Hudson's Bay Company on the east bank of the Snake, just south of the forks. Intended to

IDAHO STATE HISTORICAL SOCIETY / 1254-D

Idaho and Oregon. The Shoshoni people, whose ancestors are believed to have inhabited much of Idaho for the past 8,000 years, were opposed to these developments and violently thwarted the first two attempts, by Astorian John Reid and Nor'Wester Donald McKenzie, in 1813 and 1819 respectively.

McKenzie was in the region as part of the North West Company's effort to "trap out" a broad band of territory south and east of the Columbia River. When the Hudson's Bay Company absorbed the NWC in 1821, the strategy was even more assiduously pursued. By attempting to deplete the region of fur-bearing animals, the British believed they might discourage Americans from penetrating the northern Oregon Territory, which was jointly held between the two nations, and thereby eventually draw the border between the U.S. and

counter the trade at Nathanial Wyeth's Fort Hall to the west, the initial cottonwood construction was soon replaced by adobe, unusual so far north. Backed by the resources of the HBC, the post operated successfully for two decades.

In its early years, it was a fur trading post, but within a decade it became even more famous for its hospitality to American emigrants travelling the Oregon Trail. Under Francois Payette, for whom a city in Idaho was later named, Fort Boise became an oasis in the wilderness. One traveller, passing through in 1845, wrote that the fort boasted "two acres of land under cultivation ... 1,991 sheep, 73 pigs, 17 horses and 27 meat cattle".

The Snake River flooded in 1853, washing away many of the adobe buildings; two years later, the HBC abandoned the post.

In this 1849 lithograph, Fort Boise looks remarkably like its larger, more enduring limestone relative on the Red River in Canada – Lower Fort Garry (see page 194).

Today, a cairn marks the spot where the HBC fort stood, about five miles by road northwest of Parma.

JERRY KAUTZ

Flagstaff Hill

If South Pass was the entrance to the vast arid interior of the American West, Flagstaff Hill marked the conclusion of 1,000 miles of landscape beyond the imagining of many Oregon Trail emigrants. Residents of the meadows and woodlands of the eastern U.S., they found the sagebrush

steppe a great test of will. Daytime heat often topped 100°F, even summer nights could be chilly, dust swirled around the wagons and scorpions and rattlesnakes were a continual worry.

Following the Snake River for much of the journey was both a blessing and a curse. Clear and filled with fish, it beckoned the thirsty travellers. But for much of its length, it swirled at the bottom of a deep canyon of its own making, and at fords its roaring waters often took a terrible toll.

The trail left the Snake River at Farewell Bend, heading northwest toward the mountains. As they toiled past the bluffs of Flagstaff Hill, 1,600 miles from the trail's beginning on the Missouri River, they caught their first glimpses of the Blue Mountains, and knew the journey was nearly at an end.

In the early days, the travellers all moved on, climbing into the highlands where wood and water were plentiful, heading for the treacherous Columbia River or, after 1846, for the Barlow Road to the south of it. And over the years, the huge wheels of their covered wagons wore ruts deep into the

The National Historic Center at Flagstaff Hill, Oregon, includes an encampment with the wagons circled as they were every evening, stretches of deep trail ruts and an excellent interpretive museum.

dry earth as an estimated 100,000 emigrants passed Flagstaff Hill en route west.

After 1862, when gold was found in the Blue Mountains, people began to settle near Flagstaff Hill and along the fertile banks of the Powder River to the north. Baker City grew up just west of the trail and the trail was largely forgotten. But here, as in many other places, some of it survived.

Today, the National Historic Oregon Trail Interpretive Center at Flagstaff Hill overlooks more than four miles of the original trail. A series of signed loop trails explains the history of the emigration and encourages exploration. The interpretive centre houses both permanent and changing exhibits, as well as a theatre, gallery, sales shop and rest rooms. A pioneer encampment operates on a seasonal basis and brings the great migration to life with a living history interpretation.

Equally fascinating is the Tamastslikt Cultural Institute, just northeast of Pendleton below the Blue Mountains. The only native-owned interpretive facility on the Oregon Trail, it provides an excellent overview of life on the Columbia Plateau prior to the coming of Europeans, as well as the story of how the Cayuse, Umatilla and Walla Walla people adjusted to the huge influx of newcomers in the 19th century.

The Flagstaff Center is located six miles east of I-84, just north of Baker City. It is open from 9 a.m. to 6 p.m. daily from April 1st to October 31st and from 9 a.m. to 4 p.m. the rest of the year, except Christmas and New Year's. The Tamastslikt Institute is east of Pendleton, off I-84 at exit 216.

The Dalles

The Dalles earned its name because of its turbulent water. In French *les dalles* referred to the way the water literally turned sideways as it churned through the rocky chasms. In earlier times, the river had been known by an equally descriptive Sahaptin name, Nch'i-Wana or "the Great River". The name it bears today – Columbia – was bestowed by someone who never saw the gorge area or the great falls. Sailing past the huge mouth of the river on a coastal trading voyage in 1792, American Captain Robert Gray named it for his ship, the *Columbia Redviva*.

The stretch between The Dalles and nearby Celilio Falls, now inundated, has served as a focal point for human populations for at least 11,000 years. Some believe it has been a centre of population for much longer. During the construction of The Dalles Dam, what appeared to be traces of an ancient hearth were found *beneath* the deposits left by the last glaciation; the ice sheets disappeared from the area almost 13,000 years ago.

People were drawn to the Columbia Gorge because of its celebrated salmon runs. As one of the most important fisheries in North America (huge sturgeon were also found here), the site had served as a strategic gathering place for millennia. When Lewis and Clark stopped at the churning 20-foot Celilo (pronounced Seh-*lie*-lo) Falls in October 1805, they counted 107 stacks of dried salmon, which they estimated weighed about 10,000 pounds.

Archaeologists have also found artifacts here that originated as far away as the Great Lakes and in the surrounding rocks and cliffs is a gallery of rock art that rivals any in North America.

But even as Captain Gray was nosing about at the mouth of the river,

JERRY KAUTZ

On the north side of the Columbia, in Washington's Horsethief Lake State Park, is a gallery of rock art. Both petroglyphs and pictographs are found here in the Columbia Hills, including Tsagaglalal, "She Who Watches", above. Tours along the pictograph trail are available during the summer months.

This view of Mount St. Helen's, left, was painted in 1845, just downstream from The Dalles.

HENRY JAMES WARRE / NATIONAL ARCHIVES OF CANADA / C-26343

JERRY KAUTZ

JERRY KAUTZ

Washington's Horsethief Lake State Park, at right with the campground in the trees, is just one of many places to visit along the 100-mile corridor of the Columbia River Gorge National Scenic Area, the first such designated region in the U.S.

things were changing at The Dalles. To the east, the plains people were being forced west into the mountains and to the north, the mountain people were being pushed south to the Great River. In their wake came the fur traders from Canada – David Thompson of the North West Company in 1811 and later, the great fur brigades of the Hudson's Bay Company. And with them came disease. By the 1830s, Dr. John McLoughlin, chief factor of Fort Vancouver (see page 230) estimated that some of the inhabitants of the Columbia River had lost nine of every 10 people to European diseases like smallpox and dysentry. This is a percentage that is accepted by most anthropologists and archaeologists in North America today, and refers not only to the people along the Columbia River, but to native North Americans as a whole.

Wherever contact occured, disease inevitably followed and the people of North America had virtually no resistance to the terrible scourges of Europe: smallpox, typhoid, bubonic plague, influenza, mumps, measles, whooping cough and, by the time of the Oregon Trail emigration, cholera, malaria and scarlet fever. By the 1840s,

when the emigrants first appeared along the Oregon Trail, The Dalles was a very different place than it had been even 50 years earlier.

The power of the river was unchanged, however, and the weary emigrants approached with trepidation, for they had been forewarned. The thundering rapids and deep gorges could be killers, but until 1846, when the Barlow Road was constructed, they had little alternative but to take their chances. Attempting to raft their goods and animals downriver, many lost their lives almost within sight of their goal.

The great rapids that gave The Dalles its name were drowned beneath a series of locks and dams between 1938 and 1971. The dramatic beauty of the gorge can still be seen however, in the Columbia River Gorge National Scenic Area, which stretches 100 miles east from Portland. An excellent overview of the region's history is found at the Columbia Gorge Discovery Center, located on Crate's Point, just west of The Dalles on Old Highway 30. In the community of The Dalles, a series of large downtown murals tells the story of the region.

The Willamette Valley

The first fur trade post in the Willamette Valley was Fort Astoria (see page 228), established near the mouth of the Columbia River in 1811. A decade later, the centre of the trade was moved inland to the north side of the Columbia across from the mouth of the Willamette River. Under Chief Factor John McLoughlin, Fort Vancouver quickly became the regional centre of commerce, but elsewhere, relations between traders and the local native tribes deteriorated.

In May 1828, Jedediah Smith was leading a band of Rocky Mountain trappers north from California. Nearing the Willamette Valley, they were attacked by a party of Umpqua. Only four, including Smith, survived and their furs and supplies were stolen. It was the second such ambush; earlier in California, the Mojave, incited by the Spanish, had killed 10 of Smith's men. The survivors reached Fort Vancouver in August; McLoughlin took them in, retrieved their furs and put them up until spring.

Despite this setback, others were drawn to the bountiful region. In 1834, another former mountain man, Nathaniel Wyeth, established a post called Fort William on Savies Island at the mouth of Willamette River. His vision was a combined business of trapping, trading and farming, but the HBC dominance was too powerful and by 1837, he had sold out and moved back east. The farming, however, proved prescient. Within a decade, thousands were pouring into the valley, securing their own futures and ensuring that the Oregon Territory south of the 49th parallel would go to the U.S.

Among the earliest of these were mountain men like Robert Newell and Joe Meek. In 1840, with the Rockies trapped out, Newell wrote to his brother-in-law, "We are done with this life in the mountains – done with ... freezing or starving alternatively ... Let us go down to the Wallamet and take farms."

By 1846, John McLoughlin had joined them, founding Oregon City on land he had earlier claimed. But the newcomers resented his wealth. His claims, even to his own home, were not recognized, though McLoughlin fought these decisions until his death in 1857. Oregon became a state two years later and by the early 1860s, its inhabitants were beginning to appreciate McLoughlin's part in their history. In 1862, his land was returned to his daughter Eloisa and today, he is recognized as the "Father of Oregon".

For millennia, people gathered each year below Willamette Falls to fish the whirlpools for salmon and other fish. Though he may not have realized it, in 1841, as Joseph Drayton painted this perspective he was witnessing the end of an era. Within 10 years, the falls had been harnessed for waterpower and "the American settlement" (later Oregon City) was growing up around them.

JOSEPH DRAYTON / OREGON HISTORICAL SOCIETY / OrHi 969

The Willamette Valley, Oregon's chief producer of wine, Christmas trees and cut flowers, is home to its capital, Salem. Oregon City, located southeast of Portland, has fine examples of the state's earliest buildings, including Dr. John McLoughlin's home, now a National Historic Site, at 713 Center Street.

Glossary

Adobe: The terms refers to sun-dried bricks made from clay, and the structures built from them. They are very common in the arid western U.S., Mexico and Central America.

À la façon du pays: A French term literally meaning "in the manner or custom of the country". The phrase was used to describe marriages between aboriginal North Americans and Europeans, which took place following the customs of a region or culture, without the sanction of European clergy. The British, in particular, had difficulty accepting the validity of such marriages, but many fur traders considered them just as valid as church-sanctioned ceremonies and eventually even the courts were obliged to acknowledge their legality.

Lake Huron, Ontario MIKE GRANDMAISON

Algonquian: (Or Algonkian) This is a major family of more than 50 North American languages spoken by people who lived, at the time of European contact, from Newfoundland to western Alberta and from Labrador south to Tennessee. It includes such groups as the Innu, Anishinabe, Cree, Siksika, Fox, Illinois and Algonquin, from whom the word came originally.

Algonquin: (Or Algonkin) A member of one of several Algonquian-speaking peoples that lived during the contact period along the Ottawa River and several northern tributaries of the St. Lawrence. The term also refers to the language spoken by these groups.

Anishinabe(g): Meaning "person" or "first man" ("people" or "first men" in the plural) this collective term is increasingly preferred by a large group of people who speak a variety of mutually intelligible Algonquian dialects including the Ojibwe, Saulteaux, Odawa and Potawatomi. The languages of the Nipissing, Mississauga and Algonquin are closely related.

Arquebuses: Variant of "harquebus", a heavy, portage matchlock gun invented during the 15th century and also called a "hackbut".

Astrolabe: A medieval instrument consisting of a graduated vertical circle with a moveable arm, used to determine the altitude of the sun or other celestial bodies for astronomical or navigational purposes.

Atsina: A breakaway group of Arapaho, an American plains people, the Atsina moved north into Canada prior to 1750. Europeans called them *Gros Ventre* or "Big Bellies", though not because they had over-sized stomachs. Instead, the sign for this nation was to place a hand on one's abdomen.

Basaltic: A dark or gray rock supposed to constitute the bulk of the earth beneath its solid crust. Found on Manitoulin Island, several basaltic boulders attracted attention during the fur trade because they produced a bell-like sound when struck.

Bateaux: A French word for light, flat-bottomed boats.

Brigades: A group of men who delivered furs and goods from one location to another, usually via water, but also overland on horseback or with oxcarts.

Canada: The name originated with the Iroquoian term *Kanata*, meaning home territory or homeland. As early as 1610, it was being used to describe all the territory then known to the French, the land along the St. Lawrence River. Gradually it was extended to other areas settled by Europeans, with the French and British settlements being distinguished by the terms "Lower Canada" and "Upper Canada", which described their positions relative to the flow of water from the Great Lakes through the St. Lawrence River.

Canot du maître: Larger than its cousin, the *canoe du maître* literally carried the fur trade. Up to 12 metres long, carrying 2,300 kilograms and paddled at about 45 strokes per minute, these canoes travelled from Montreal to Lake Superior at an average speed of nine kilometres an hour.

Cathay: An old English term meaning China. Also known as "Cathaia".

Coulees: In Western Canada, a deep gulch or ravine, usually dry in the summertime, formed by glacial meltwater or torrential rain. The term originally referred to a stream of molten lava or a sheet of solidified lava (from the French *couler*, "to flow").

Coureur de bois: Originally, anyone who voyaged into the wilderness to trade for furs. Until 1681, French law forbade trading without a license, which gave the term a pejorative sense and those to whom it applied an aura of daring. Later, the term came to mean free trader, a person who traded independently of the Hudson's Bay Company or the large Montreal and Missouri fur companies.

Diabase: A dark gray or black fine-grained igneous rock, often used for monuments.

Engagè: This French term technically means "actively committed", but quickly came to have a specific meaning in the fur trade, where it designated contract employees of Montreal-based companies, particularly the North West Company.

Entrepôt: (pronounced on-tra-poh) A place where goods are stored and from which they are distributed.

Fur Press, Rocky Mountain House, Alberta JERRY KAUTZ

Free traders: See *Coureur de bois.*

Fur Press: A large machine, usually made of wood, used to press the pelts before packing them into bales or packs of 90 pounds or 40 kilograms. Pressing the furs rendered them easier to handle and less likely to spoil. In order to lessen the possibility of loss, packs were often made up of mixed furs, with smaller or more valuable furs inside and larger ones – buffalo robes, deerskins or bearskins – on the outside.

Glaciation: Specifically the formation, movement and recession of ice sheets, but also referring to the geological processes associated with glacial activity, including erosion and deposition, and the resulting effects of such action on Earth's surface.

Habitant: Landowners, below the rank of seigneur, in Canada. The *habitants* were very conscious of their status as free men relative to the indentured state of the peasants of France.

Hanging Valley: A tributary valley that joins a main valley where the latter has been deepened, usually by glacial erosion. There is generally a steep drop from the floor of the tributary valley to that of the main valley.

Hivernants: Fur traders who lived year-round in the wilds of Canada were referred to by the French as "winterers". The term came to mean anyone who spent the winter in the *pays d'en haut*, the upper country, the great northland. To be an *hivernant* was to be strong and self-reliant.

Homeguard Cree: A group of Cree who lived along the west coast of Hudson Bay and soon moved into the role of middlemen in Hudson's Bay Company trade. For decades after the bayside posts were established, the English declined to travel inland and the Homeguard Cree became their eyes and ears over a vast territory. Cree winter villages were established near the bayside forts, which worked for both parties, allowing the Cree access to English goods and the English access to skilled hunters. Well-armed with English weapons, the Cree also established a toll of sorts on trade with the bay, allowing only their allies direct access to HBC posts.

Huron: See Wendat. This was a French term, meaning "prickly boar's head", used to describe the Wendat. It was very likely a reference to the bristly haircut some wore.

Innu: The Algonquian-speaking people who live north of the St. Lawrence River as far east as Labrador.

Iroquoian: A family of languages spoken in eastern North America by such peoples as the Iroquois, Cherokee, Erie, Wendat and Wyandot.

Iroquois: (Pronounced *Ear*-o-kwa). A member of one of six Iroquoian-speaking peoples who inhabited what is now New York State. Five of these groups – the Seneca, Cayuga, Onondaga, Oneida and Mohawk – united in the late 1500s to form the League of Five Nations Iroquois. In 1722, the Tuscaroras joined the federation, which then became the Six Nations.

Isostatic rebound: The rebounding or lifting of Earth's crust once a great weight is removed. Isostatic uplift continues to occur across northern North America (and other northern nations) where great sheets of ice covered the land during the last glaciation.

Jesuit: A member of the Society of Jesus. Jesuit missionaries arrived in North America on the heels of the fur traders in mid-17th century and sought to Christianize many of the North American tribes. Especially influential on the Wendat of Huronia, the Jesuits often lived among North American nations and spoke their languages.

Livre: (Pronounced leeve). The main unit in the monetary system of New France. At the time it varied to equal between one British shilling and one and sixpence.

Kanata: See Canada.

Lake Agassiz: 10,000 years ago, this glacial lake was the largest in

Wendat Longhouse, Michigan COURTESY MARQUETTE MISSION PARK AND MUSEUM OF OJIBWA CULTURE

The Thompson River, British Columbia PETER ST. JOHN

North America, covering most of Manitoba and parts of North Dakota, Minnesota and Ontario. It was named for the Swiss-born naturalist and scientist Jean Louis Rodolphe Agassiz, who was first to recognize the geological signs of the glaciation of North America.

Longhouse: Communal lodges that were central to Iroquoian culture. These houses sheltered several families related through the female line. Generally about 8 metres wide, they were of variable length; one in southern Ontario was 94 metres long. The Onondaga, who lived in such dwellings, were the "keepers of the fire" for the Five Nations Iroquois, responsible for holding meetings of the confederacy.

Manitoulin: The world's largest freshwater island that sits on the Ontario-Michigan border. Manitoulin is named for Manitou, the great spirit.

Metis: (Pronounced *May*-tee). Originally referring to the offspring of French traders and their native North American wives, the term is widely used to refer to anyone who has a mix of European and North American parentage.

Mi'kmaq: (Pronounced *Mig*-maw). An Algonquian-speaking people who inhabited the Gaspé Peninsula, and the three Maritime provinces at the time of European contact. From the early 17th century, they were allied with the French against the English, which caused conflict with the Iroquois and in turn created the need for extensive Algonquian alliances. Today's Mi'kmaq live in many of their traditional lands, as well as in southern Newfoundland.

Mohawk: A large Iroquoian nation that became one of the Five Nations Iroquois in the 1500s. Living in what is now upper New York state, the Mohawk were early allies of the New England colonies.

Montagnais: See Innu. This was a French term, meaning "mountain dwellers" for an Algonquian people who inhabited the uplands of the Canadian Shield north of the St. Lawrence.

New France: Used almost interchangably with "Canada" in the early 1600s, it eventually comprised a much larger area. By 1700, New France included Canada, Acadia, Louisiana and the western posts.

Obsidian: Volcanic glass, usually black or banded, that fractures into shiny, curved planes, with edges that are sharper than surgical steel. Obsidian was widely prized for making spear and arrow-points, and was traded over great distances.

Ochre: An earthy clay colored by iron oxide, usually yellow or reddish brown, used as paint by peoples around the world. Ochre pictographs can be seen along many rivers of the fur trade as well as at Agawa Rock (and other sites) on Lake Superior.

285

Osprey: A fish-eating hawk of cosmopolitan distribution with a white underside and head, a brown body and long pointed wings. Sometimes called a fish eagle or a fish hawk, the osprey feeds by swooping down on fish and snatching them up in their talons.

Oxcart: Also called Red River carts, these large two-wheeled carts drawn by oxen or horses were invented along the Red River by French-Canadians and were a mainstay of plains transportation for more than 75 years. They squeaked loudly.

Papal bull: A directive to the faithful pertaining to or issued by the pope.

Pays d'en haut: Literally "up country", this term was given to the territory north and west of Quebec.

Pisew Falls, Manitoba MIKE GRANDMAISON

Pemmican: Dried meat, normally bison, pounded and compressed, mixed with rendered fat and sometimes with dried berries. This near-perfect travelling food was invented on the western plains thousands of years ago and used to fuel the fur trade. Bridgades relied almost wholly on pemmican, which allowed them to concentrate on travelling without the need to stop and hunt for food.

Petun: See Tionontati. This French term, which describes the tobacco they grew, was used for an Iroquoian people who were closely related to the Wendat.

Pirogue: A canoe made from a hollowed tree trunk.

Portage: The carrying of canoes or goods by land from one river to another, often around falls or rapids. The longest portage west of Montreal is the 20-kilometre Methye Portage, a long but ultimately beautiful trail between the Hudson Bay and Arctic watersheds. Another route of note for its portages was the Hayes River route from the Hudson's Bay to Lake Winnipeg, which had more than 30 "carrying places", as the English often called them.

Potties: A corruption of *les petites*, as employees of Alexander Mackenzie's XY Company were sometimes called by their NWC rivals.

Precambrian Shield: A huge expanse of ancient rock that spans much of northern North America. Created during the oldest and longest division of geologic time, prior to 540 million years ago, the Precambrian or Canadian Shield stretches from Labrador to Yukon.

Régale: A treat of liquor, often accompanied by tobacco, butter and flour – all rare commodities – that accompanied the departure or arrival of a fur brigade.

Sedimentary mesas: A flat-topped elevation with one or more cliff-like sides. Common in the southwestern United States, mesas are also found in other places where water or ice has weathered away the surrounding landscape.

Seigneury: The estate of an appointed lord or landowner formerly found in Canada (Quebec).

Serpent River, Ontario PETER ST. JOHN

Siksika: The main tribe of the Blackfoot Confederacy, which controlled most of Alberta south of the North Saskatchewan River during the contact period (c. 1750). The other groups were the Pikuni (or Piegan) and the Kainai (or Blood).

Stromatolites: A laminated sedimentary rock structure formed primarily during the Proterozoic eon in shallow pools by mats of blue-green algae. The algae trapped layers of silt, especially calcium carbonate. These wavy or round formations provide evidence for dating the first life forms on Earth.

Tionontati: Meaning "People of the Hills", this Iroquoian people lived just southwest of their allies, the Wendat and shared their agrarian lifestyle.

Trading *en dérouine:* Begun by French *coureurs de bois*, this involved travelling to the camps and villages of the trappers to collect furs, rather than waiting at the fur posts for them to be brought in. Though independent traders found it maximized profits, the practice was difficult to control and early English trading companies tried to forbid their men from "wintering over". Later, however, the ends were found to justify the means and even the Hudson's Bay Company often sent its employees into the field for furs.

Tundra: An area between the perpetual snow and ice of Arctic regions and the tree line, having a permanently frozen subsoil and supporting low-growing vegetation such as lichens, mosses, dwarf shrubs and stunted trees.

Voyageur: Essentially a wage-earning canoeman. Though the term was used as early as the first quarter of the 18th century, it came to be particularly applied to the North West Company and the Missouri Fur Company, and the American Fur Company, all both of which relied extensively on French-Canadian labor.

Weir: A row of stakes set in a stream or river to catch fish. Many North American nations used this highly efficient method of fishing for thousands of years.

Wendat: Meaning "Dwellers on a Peninsula", this powerful Iroquoian people lived west

Ground litter, Saskatchewan JERRY KAUTZ

and south of Ontario's Georgian Bay in the 16th and early 17th centuries. They were closely allied to the French, who dubbed them *Huron*, and were largely destroyed during the Iroquois Wars in the mid-17th century.

Windlass: A hauling or lifting machine consisting essentially of a drum or cylinder wound with rope and turned by a crank.

Errata

Page 190, cutline should read: "A plaque on the west side .... recalls the first Jasper House, which was across the lake from the highway."
Page 237, map: Bismark should reach Bismarck; Washbarn should read Washburn
Page 242, cutline should read: "This statue of a radiant mother and son was sculpted by Agnes Vincen Talbot for the Lemhi Shoshoni ..."
Page 275, credit line for painting should read William Henry Jackson
Page 279, col. 2, line 7 should read " ...Fort Hall to the east, ..."

Alphabetical List of Sites

The Missouri River, Montana JERRY KAUTZ

Alphabetical List of Sites

The Clearwater River, Saskatchewan   ROBIN KARPAN